Trevor Griffiths

THEATER: Theory/Text/Performance

Enoch Brater, Series Editor

Trevor Griffiths

Politics, Drama, History

Stanton B. Garner Jr.

ANN ARBOR

THE UNIVERSITY OF MICHIGAN PRESS

Copyright © by the University of Michigan 1999
All rights reserved
Published in the United States of America by
The University of Michigan Press
Manufactured in the United States of America
⊗ Printed on acid-free paper

2002   2001   2000   1999   4   3   2   1

A CIP catalog record for this book is available from the British Library.

Library of Congress Cataloging-in-Publication Data

Garner, Stanton B., 1955–
    Trevor Griffiths : politics, drama, history / Stanton B. Garner
Jr.
        p.   cm. — (Theater : Theory/Text/Performance)
    Includes bibliographical references (p.   ) and index.
    ISBN 0-472-11065-9 (acid-free paper)
    1. Griffiths, Trevor—Criticism and interpretation.   2. Politics
and literature—Great Britain—History—20th century.   3. Literature
and history—Great Britain—History—20th century.   4. Historical
drama, English—History and criticism.   5. Television plays,
English—History and criticism.   6. Political plays,
English—History and criticism.   I. Title.
PR6057.R52 Z75   1999
822'.914—dc21   99-6153
                                                                     CIP

Acknowledgments

Every book arrives bearing specific debts and gratitudes, and this one is no exception. Among those who read parts of the manuscript or helped with its research, I thank the following: Janelle Reinelt, Edward Braun, Enoch Brater, Mary Papke, Norman Sanders, Robert Smallwood, Finlay Donesky, and Nicki Stoddart. As editor of *British Playwrights, 1956–1995: A Research and Production Sourcebook*, William W. Demastes offered an early outlet for my work on Griffiths, while Ann Wilson and Ruby Cohn gave shrewd and helpful readings to the manuscript as a whole.

The book's footnotes will make clear how much I owe to the staff at a number of libraries and research collections: the British Film Institute National Library (particularly Special Collections librarians Janet Moat and Saffron Parker), the British Library, the British Library Newspaper Library, the Westminster Reference Library, the Shakespeare Centre Library, the Bobst Library of New York University (including the librarians in the Tamiment Collection), and the New York Public Library. I am grateful to the staff of the John C. Hodges Library at the University of Tennessee—particularly those in the Interlibrary Loan office, whose labor and resourcefulness were essential to my research. I was aided in writing this book by a Professional Development Grant from the University of Tennessee Graduate School and by leave and summer release time funded by the Hodges Better English Fund of the Tennessee English Department. Among the many colleagues who expressed interest in this project, no one was more solicitous than department head D. Allen Carroll.

I also thank LeAnn Fields of the University of Michigan Press, who supported this book on Griffiths from the start, and her many colleagues at the Press who have had a hand in the publication process. Among these I would single out Laurie Clark Klavins, Shelly Emmett, Mary Meade, Alja Kooistra, Elizabeth Gratch, and Michael Kehoe.

My remaining debts are certainly my biggest ones. I am grateful to

Trevor and Gill Griffiths for their hospitality, help, and good humor throughout the researching and writing of this book; spending time with them in July 1993, July 1995, and November 1997 was one of the real pleasures of this project. I am grateful, too, to my family—Stanton and Lydia Garner, Katherine and the late Philip Young, George Garner, Rosalie Dwyer, and Edward Garner—for their support in this, as in all of my work. I owe an exceptional debt, of course, to Deborah R. Geis, who helped me with every aspect of this project and who brightened it considerably with her enthusiasm, patience, and love.

Portions of chapter 8 previously appeared in "Politics over the Gulf: Trevor Griffiths in the Nineties," *Modern Drama* 39 (1996): 381–91. I am grateful to the editors for permission to use this material in its revised form. An earlier version of the second section of chapter 9 appeared in "History in the Year Two: Trevor Griffiths's Danton," *New Theatre Quarterly* 44 (1995): 333–41. Copyright © 1995 Cambridge University Press, reprinted with the permission of Cambridge University Press. I thank Val Bainbridge of Prime Cut (formerly Mad Cow) Productions for her help securing photographs of the Mad Cow production of *Who Shall Be Happy . . . ?* and Jill Jennings of Chris Hill Photographic for permission to reproduce one of these photographs on the book's jacket.

Contents

Introduction

Strategic Penetration

In the published introduction to his 1981 television adaptation of D. H. Lawrence's *Sons and Lovers* Trevor Griffiths describes a particularly bleak moment in the filming of the six-episode series. Standing in the cold and the rain on the project's location in Nottinghamshire, Griffiths contemplates the difficulty involved in "reconstitut[ing] a past social reality out of the present's scarce and resistant materials."[1] As he describes the scene:

> Ahead, down the blackbrick 19th century street of working-class houses, the unit chippies continue their patient attempts to disguise or dismantle the present tense (aerials, antennae, plastic piping . . .), Cnuts to a man. Costumed extras, miners' families for the day, stand role-less, out of their time, on the narrow pavements. History squirms and twists, glints and is gone. It's now, we're here, that's that. (7)

At the same time, if historical reconstruction presents logistical difficulties, particularly in a bone-chilling Nottinghamshire rain, its attainment is fraught with even greater risks. At a moment in British political and cultural life when history is increasingly subsumed under the rubric of "heritage" and even industrial locales have been transformed by the preservation industry into tourist sites, historical representation risks sacrificing meaning to "period" verisimilitude. This danger is framed for Griffiths when he encounters a visiting American journalist, who praises the British for setting aside and maintaining settings such as the street in front of them for this kind of historical film work. In the United

States, the journalist suggests, a locale like this would have to be built out of plywood and plastic.

Griffiths, of course, is astonished by the suggestion that these surroundings have been maintained for the sake of heritage preservation. Lawrence's distant relatives still reside in these houses, and the lives lived behind these walls are marked by the realities of exploitation. Seventy years earlier Lawrence himself had railed against the dirtiness and ugliness of this cramped urban environment "and the economic system that made them possible" (8). Much of Lawrence's best writing "had been informed by this sense that the real face of capitalism was ugly and inhuman and that the world it reproduced in its image denied the potentiality for human growth in most of its inhabitants." Ugliness and exploitation, Griffiths notes, persist in the lives of the working people who live and die in these houses in contemporary Britain, a stratum of society for whom historical reconstruction and present reality lie depressingly close. In view of these historical continuities, "We *would* finish. It *would* be as good as we could make it. It would, with whatever imperfections, speak of these things" (9).

Griffiths's reflections here suggest much of what has made him such a powerful and unique presence in British theater, television, and film over the past thirty years: an intense awareness of class and its material underpinnings; a concern with realism, its power as tool of counterdescription and its representational instabilities; a commitment to history as a field of political and cultural intervention; and a willingness to examine the terms of this intervention through one of postwar Britain's most politically literate dramatic practices. In its attention to the relationship between the televisual medium (and its production apparatus) and the materially specific life-world of social subjects, Griffiths's account reveals the playwright's preoccupation with the politics of medium and representation and his willingness to adapt the practice of what he calls "strategic penetration" to specific cultural opportunities.[2] "Strategic penetration," for Griffiths, entails challenging ruling accounts of social reality by writing within and against the cultural institutions that serve to reproduce these myths. Opportunistic in terms of subject and cultural location, it is a search for openings, interventions, counter-meanings. In the case of *Sons and Lovers* Griffiths's strategic penetration involves a dual recovery: reclaiming Lawrence's world in its social stresses and historical contradictions and—against Margaret Thatcher's effort to rewrite contemporary Britain's relationship to its nineteenth-century history—illuminating the present's lived historicity in the density of its continuity with this past. *Sons and Lovers* may not loom as prominently in Griffiths's public reputation as *Occupations, The Party, Comedians,* or *Reds,* but, in its effort to claim a space for radical social possibilities within the conventions and institutions of contemporary Britain, Griffiths's Lawrence adaptation is every bit as engaged.

Griffiths's plays of the early 1970s established him as one of the leading voices in the political theater movement(s) that transformed the landscape of postwar British theater, and his plays and films since then have consolidated this place. At the same time, he has always been a complex figure in this tradition, falling, to a remarkable extent, outside the categories that apply to the careers of many of his contemporaries. Griffiths has characterized his life as one of "borders,"[3] and his career reflects the tension and creativity generated by the multiple positions he has inhabited and continues to inhabit. There are, of course, the related issues of geography and class. Like Lawrence, Griffiths is a product of the northern working class. He was born and raised in Manchester and continues to live in the north of England, and his politics have always drawn upon a northern radicalism with roots in a regional tradition of labor activism. Although Griffiths participated to a limited extent in the London Fringe of the early 1970s, from the start of his career he has been largely an outsider—a "stranger," in his words—to the metropolitan alternative theater culture that produced David Hare, Howard Brenton, Snoo Wilson, and others. "It's as if that belt from Liverpool to Hull and upwards were pulling in a different direction and insisting on different verities," he has said.[4]

Griffiths's background in the working class is a decisive influence on the shape and content of his work as a writer: the choice of realism as a dominant aesthetic; the interest in television as a cultural medium; an awareness of class more pervasive, nuanced, and personally grounded than that of many of his contemporaries (David Mercer is a notable exception). A concern with the working class as subject and audience makes itself felt throughout Griffiths's work—from Sam One in Griffiths's autobiographical play *Sam, Sam* and the aspiring performers of *Comedians* through the wall builders of *The Gulf between Us* and Danton's guard Henry in *Hope in the Year Two.* Where his plays and films center on more educated characters, these intellectuals are often drawn against a working-class environment, from which (with a Gramscian logic) they often come and against which their own intellectual, cultural, and political forms of labor are always measured. Griffiths's career reflects the contradictions inherent in his position as a writer of working-class origins. Born in 1935, Griffiths was a member of the first generation of working-class youth to benefit from the 1944 Education Act. Like that of Richard Hoggart's prototypical "scholarship boy," Griffiths's sense of social identity was conditioned by a radical dislocation from the class formation of his childhood and by the social mobility made available to those fortunate enough to take advantage of its postwar trajectories. The contradictions attendant upon social translation of this sort are literalized in the schizophrenic structure of *Sam, Sam,* but they appear everywhere in Griffiths's work. They are foregrounded with particular urgency in his plays of the 1970s, when Griffiths's public success as a writer established him more firmly in the world of social and economic privilege.

In the "border country" of Griffiths's life and career there is also the question of age and generational positioning. While Griffiths is usually grouped with Hare, Brenton, David Edgar, and other dramatists of the post-1968 theatrical Left, he is actually closer in age to John Osborne, John Arden, Arnold Wesker, and Edward Bond, dramatists who constituted the "first wave" of British political theater in the late 1950s and 1960s. This difference in age, Catherine Itzin suggests, helped establish Griffiths as a "Marxist mentor" to his younger contemporaries during the 1970s.[5] But it also led, inevitably, to a certain generational distance from the student radicalism of the late 1960s, even as he found himself caught up in the sense of social upheaval that animated the "second wave" of British political theater of the 1970s and returned the issue of revolution to the Left's agenda. The revolutionary moment of May 1968 has preoccupied Griffiths throughout his career, but when he has returned to this event (in *The Party* and *Real Dreams,* for instance) its energies are contained, distanced, contextualized, within a historically broader dialectic of revolutionary struggle and transformative possibility.

While Griffiths was profoundly influenced by certain currents of 1960s and early 1970s radicalism—he was temperamentally drawn to anarchism and, at the same time, fascinated with the powerful but dangerous "hardness" of revolutionary Leninism—the formative historical juncture in Griffiths's life and career lies a decade earlier, in the New Left of the late 1950s and the early 1960s. Griffiths's political education took place during the heyday of this movement, and he participated actively in its emerging structures and culture: the Campaign for Nuclear Disarmament (CND), the New Left clubs (Griffiths was president of the Manchester New Left Club), educational initiatives (inspired by the Workers' Educational Association), and a progressive Labourism that seemed poised, until Harold Wilson's first government proved otherwise, to transform Britain's principal leftist party. Griffiths's political identity has always resisted categorization, manifesting itself less in preexisting theoretical stances than in the confrontation of often divergent positions and imperatives. But, to the extent that we can speak of a core configuration of commitments and interests, the legacy of the New Left is everywhere in evidence. It is evident in the socialist humanism that forms the cornerstone of Griffiths's Marxism, a commitment to such political categories as agency and subjectivity that defines itself against Stalinism as well as capitalism. It is evident in a concern with education that extends from Griffiths's own work in the classroom to his understanding of the media as a whole. And, finally, it is evident in Griffiths's interest in culture, its institutions and practices, an interest that would lead Griffiths through his work as Further Education Officer for the British Broadcasting Corporation (BBC) and into his own interventionist cultural practice.

Drama and the Real

Griffiths's singularity among his dramatic contemporaries is also reflected in his choices of medium and aesthetic practice. In *Powerplays: Trevor Griffiths in Television*, their 1984 study of Griffiths's television drama, Mike Poole and John Wyver state: "Much of [Griffiths's] career would be shaped . . . by attempts to occupy spaces—intellectual, theatrical and televisual—traditionally viewed as ideological no-go areas for the Left."[6] Whereas much British political drama of the late 1960s and 1970s set itself against the popular media, Griffiths has written with equal facility for theater, television, radio, and film. Following Raymond Williams, he displaces the category of drama from its elitist positioning and broadens its channels of address: "*Theatre*," he commented in 1974, "is one specialized form of drama among several; the television play and the film are others, in my view preeminent in terms of creative challenge and social impact."[7] Like Mercer, Griffiths has demonstrated a particular commitment to television as the vehicle for "strategic penetration." Griffiths's earliest plays were written for television, and at the height of his theatrical celebrity, in the 1970s, he stated a number of times that he considered himself primarily a writer for that medium. Given Griffiths's determination to establish oppositional spaces within dominant cultural institutions (a determination that would result in his theater plays being produced by the National Theatre, the Royal Shakespeare Company (RSC), and on the West End and Broadway and that would see a version of his screenplay *Comrades* produced by Hollywood), the choice of television is strategically significant. "I knew from very early on that I wanted to work on television, do television pieces," Griffiths said in the early 1980s. "Television seemed then and still seems a massively powerful intervention, a means of intervening in society's life."[8] The production and reception history of Griffiths's plays for television bears out this faith in the medium's interventionist reach.

The versatility evident in Griffiths's practice as a writer—his disregard for the distinctions governing such cultural categories as "serious" and "popular," "mainstream" and "avant-garde"—has posed a challenge to his academic critics, most of whom remain bound by traditional categorizings of cultural work. Faber and Faber have reinforced this compartmentalization by publishing Griffiths's collected plays for television and theater in separate volumes. Studies have been written of his television plays, and others have been devoted to those for theater, but few have considered the full range of Griffiths's cultural intervention—his sensitivity to the politics of medium, his understanding of the institutional apparatus that surrounds and differentiates the various media, and the guiding strategies and aesthetic principles that bridge and unite such wide-ranging work.[9]

For, while the dramaturgical strategies governing individual texts reveal an acute awareness of the conventions particular to specific media, Griffiths's plays and films are characterized by a powerful singularity of aim and commitment. One of Griffiths's longtime reviewers has said of the playwright and his work: "No dramatist of the Left better combines incisiveness and heart, none has written about the urgency of political change with greater sophistication of mind or generosity of spirit."[10] Few, it might be added, have so successfully explored the theatrical possibilities inherent in the politically articulate life. All of Griffiths's writing is characterized by a fierce intellectuality, an engagement with issues of politics and culture both current and historical, and a concern with ideas as a field of articulation and interaction. Griffiths's characters claim attention through the impassioned articulation of political stances, holding the stage (or screen) with a virtuosity both verbal and intellectual and establishing dialectical points of confrontation. Whether in theater, television, or film, Griffiths has embraced the perspectival, dialogic space that drama makes available: "it is the sheer multivalency of drama which is exciting, the fact that you have to fully occupy so many spaces. It seems to me the best way afforded to us to explore contradictions and dialectic."[11] When Tom Stoppard (of all people) was asked what contemporary dramatist he most admired, he named Griffiths—"Not for what he writes but for the forms he uses."[12]

Drama, then, allows Griffiths to cultivate a multivocal dramaturgy, grounded in ideological counterpoint: Gramsci and Kabak, Lenin and Trotsky, Waters and Price. This dramaturgical disposition has gotten Griffiths in trouble with more doctrinaire Marxists, who have often accused him of a lack of commitment (it is one of the paradoxes of Griffiths's career that a dramatist who writes within the analytic framework of a Marxist critical tradition, and who has made the history of the Left one of his principal subjects, has received some of his strongest criticism from the radical Left). But Griffiths, deeply suspicious of the dogmatic and the univocal, is committed to a dialectical view of social and individual reality, in which truth is forged through the negotiation of contradiction and diametrically opposed positions can claim equal authority. As Bill Brand, one of Griffiths's most autobiographical creations, says to a radical friend: "What you and the Fourth International will *never* forgive me for, Martin, is not having all the answers."[13] Rejecting the simplistic outlines of partisan advocacy, Griffiths defends the dramatic sensibility that allows him to inhabit the space of all his characters: "If we're going to have a post-revolutionary society where people really are to become agents of their own destiny, if people are going to make themselves and not be made by others, then we have to come to terms with this complexity. And the sooner we start that, by art and culture generally, the better."[14]

Drama is crucial to Griffiths's commitments as a writer for another reason as well. Griffiths has said: "Ideas are to me something enormously concrete: they are things that you can hold in your hands and feel the texture of and reweigh every so often and give to somebody else to feel and to get a feeling from."[15] Ideas, for Griffiths, are grounded in the material world of social reality; they emerge from this world and, in turn, seek to account for it. As Albert Hunt has suggested, one of Griffiths's central themes is "the connection—and sometimes collision—between political ideas and the texture of lived experience."[16] Eddie Waters's humanistic view of laughter's collective role in *Comedians* is inseparable from his visceral experience of Buchenwald, while the confrontational violence underlying his student Gethin Price's routine is the function of particularly observed personal, generational, and economic differences. The debate is conducted in a Manchester classroom whose dilapidated furnishings establish the class parameters of the play's issues. In Griffiths's words: "I try to occupy the space provided by characters and terrain . . . and to get inside that sociologically, psychologically and politically—and *historically.* . . . I think drama is a perfect space to find ways of understanding and reperceiving the world."[17] Such understanding, for Griffiths, derives from the material world of individual and collective experience, in which political ideas and social issues lie close to the longings and limits of people's lives.

The term *reperception* is key to Griffiths's sense of himself as a writer. Metaphors of sight abound in his descriptions of his work, and they are intimately related to his fascination with the "Real." "It is a revolutionary duty to tell the truth," Gramsci has said, in a phrase that Griffiths has adopted as a kind of first principle.[18] To the extent that the material and emotional reality of people's lives is eclipsed and falsified by reigning political and cultural descriptions, Griffiths's plays and films are attempts to challenge official versions of the world with counterdescriptions of his own, grounded in the material world of actual conditions and relationships. This concern with perception and representation has powerful implications for Griffiths's choice of realism as a dramatic and political aesthetic. While dramatists such as Arden, Bond, Brenton, and Caryl Churchill chose to work with a Brechtian drama of alienation, Griffiths found his initial inspiration in the classic realism of Ibsen, Chekhov, and Lawrence. In part this choice reflected his commitment to working with a popular imagination that has been conditioned by naturalistic forms of representation. But it also reflected the powerful influence of Georg Lukács on his view of socialist art. Like Lukács, Griffiths embraced a "critical realism" capable of disclosing the world in its material historicity, a style in which the individual is conceived within the parameters and limitations of social being. In contrast to those of his political contemporaries who view realism as a bourgeois, even reactionary, mode, Griffiths considers it a powerful means of intervention in a society whose collective and individual life has been co-opted by hegemonic representations. Against these ruling representations realism offers "demystifying, undistorted, more accurate, counter descriptions of political processes and social reality."[19] Description is a powerfully subversive gesture precisely because the Real itself is deeply ideological.

Realism, in other words, allows Griffiths access both to the material "texture of lived experience" and to the political/cultural sphere in which representations of this experience are generated and contested. Television and film are important to Griffiths because these media play such a crucial role in the creation and reinforcement of official descriptions (whether they have to do with politics, class, or history). At the same time, although Griffiths is rightly labeled a "realist" within the contemporary field of British political drama, it is important to expand the term beyond its largely clichéd critical construction and to rescue it from the condescension Brechtian-influenced theoretical models have frequently bestowed upon it. As Griffiths himself suggests, realism after Brecht is inescapably "mediated" and "inflected" by Brecht's critique of it.[20] Seen in this post-Brechtian light, realism is a deliberate—and limited—set of aesthetic strategies; it is characterized by contradictions and underpinned by often divergent ideological assumptions. Griffiths, who has spoken of "challenging realism from within,"[21] is aware of the essential paradoxes of realist artifacts, and his plays often transgress and seek to problematize the invisible boundaries upon which realism depends. Griffiths's is a critical realism; from his earliest plays to the present he has been concerned with the border regions between realism and counter- and postrealistic modes. Both early in his career (when Griffiths makes explicit use of vaudeville and agitprop devices) and later (as his work with film makes itself felt in his plays for theater and television), realism exists in an increasingly dialogic relationship with other representational options. Realism, one might say, is the subject of Griffiths's dramatic practice as well as its vehicle—especially in the theater, where the status of the Real is particularly at issue.

Staging History

In the end it is history—and the particular modes of perception, analysis, and action that historical awareness makes possible—that unifies the representational and political dimensions of Griffiths's work. From Noble's recollection of the Spanish Civil War in *The Love Maniac*, Griffiths's early unproduced television play, through the metahistorical meditations of Danton on the eve of his execution in *Hope in the Year Two*, history is Griffiths's principal analytic and dramaturgical lens. Deeply influenced by a Communist and New Left tradition of socialist counter-history, Griffiths understands history as a field of ideological contest, in which a politics of counternarrative and redescription must contend with official, class-bound representations of the past. Whether his subject is industrial activism in Edwardian England, Scott's expedition to the South Pole, or the American Revolution, Griffiths challenges the ruling accounts of history by reclaiming what has been co-opted and disowned, marking the structures of class, power, materiality, and ideology that make history politically readable. Even when Griffiths's plays and films are set in the present, history stands as a point of reference, the necessary other term in the dialectic of political understanding. In keeping with Griffiths's profound interest in the politics of culture and representation, this historical practice is also concerned with the ideological transmission of history, its erasure and construction, and the institutional modes of textuality that constitute the historical in hegemonic terms.

While Griffiths's recent work has expanded to include the Enlightenment revolutions in the American colonies and France, the majority of his plays and films focus on the historical terrain of the past hundred years. A time line of the historical settings of Griffiths's work and a listing of its subjects would reveal Griffiths's particular preoccupation with the period between the late nineteenth century and the immediate aftermath of World War I, the age that saw the decline of the dynastic order in Europe and the convulsive birth of twentieth-century modernity. It was the age of Robert Falcon Scott and the Edwardian social order, but it was also the age of Tom Mann, Irish nationalism, the Russian Revolution, Antonio Gramsci, and the "grail of a social utopia" that animated figures as different as D. H. Lawrence and Lenin.[22] Griffiths's fascination with Chekhov is pertinent here, since of all the late-nineteenth/early-twentieth-century realists, none more fully explored the dialectical tension between the residual and the emergent that characterized this historical threshold.

Although Griffiths has followed a dramaturgical path different from that of his neo-Brechtian contemporaries, it is also true that the intentions and effects of his historicized realism are similar to those of Brecht's strategies of theatrical alienation. History enables Griffiths to occupy a space of distance in relation to the social and political phenomena being observed, to present these phenomena in dialectical relationship to each other and to their structuring political and social contexts (to this end Griffiths often deploys a kind of localized Brechtianism—background projections, historical montage, audience address—in order to force strategic disruptions of the realist scene; these devices can give a play like *Occupations* a surprisingly agitprop feel). If realism allows Griffiths to ground representation in the sociohistorical materiality of people's lives, the profoundly historicized nature of this realism serves the Brechtian end of freeing the representation of historical moments from the fixity and inevitability that characterize traditional historical presentation. It is telling, in this respect, that Griffiths so often dramatizes or alludes to moments of historical crisis in his plays and films: the French Revolution, the 1911 Liverpool Transport Workers' Strike, the Russian Revolution, the 1920 Turin uprisings, the late 1960s. Such moments represent openings in the narrative of history, junctures in which the future lies open as a field of contending possibilities and the present offers itself as a site of action, will, vision, choice. This "present" may be that of the Labour electoral victory in 1945, but the final referent in Griffiths's historical dramaturgy is Griffiths's—and his audience's—actual present. With a logic that is deeply Brechtian, Griffiths takes on history in order to historicize the present—to demonstrate that the contemporary moment is the result of past choices, that it could be different, and that it offers choices out of which the future will be born. When a woman prostitute explains her victimization in *These Are the Times* (a 1989 unproduced screenplay) by observing, "That's the world," Griffiths's Tom Paine replies: "No, no. That's just the world we have."[23]

Griffiths has said: "I think the future has to be made. It has to be made by people who understand the past. That is why history is so important."[24] History, for Griffiths, is the foundation of the revolutionary imagination, and it is in order to provide this imagination with its heritage that Griffiths's work deals so extensively with the history of the Left: its visions, accomplishments, failures, and animating contradictions. More than any of his contemporaries, Griffiths makes the intellectual, political, and psychological life of the Left his dramatic subject, and this preoccupation is rooted in a sense of history and its inheritance. As in Thompson's *The Making of the English Working Class* or Christopher Hill's studies of the English Civil War, this emphasis reflects the desire to challenge official history with a tradition of radical dissent: to recover, in the midst of what we might call the "prevailing past," the voices of social visionaries like Danton, Paine, Mann, Gramsci, and Nye Bevan. At times, as with the recurrent allusions to the Spanish Civil War, this reclamation skirts a kind of romance; as Robert Hewison reminds us in *The Heritage Industry*, the Left is not without its nostalgic mythologies.[25] But Griffiths's dramatization of a leftist historical tradition is unrivaled and uncompromising in its investigation of the specific contradictions and challenges facing socialism on its twentieth-century stages: the conflict between social democratic and revolutionary political strategies; the nature of political commitment; cultural intervention; the politics of sexuality; "the gap between wanting a revolution and making one"; the role of history in political practice.[26]

One of the sources of fascination in Griffiths's now considerable body of work is its recognition that "history" is neither a monolithic nor a singular category. There are histories within histories, moments of recollection and anticipation within Griffiths's historicized moments. Characters in the past look back to earlier pasts and ahead to futures realized and unrealized. Because the plays themselves often evoke the past in specific contemporary contexts (*Such Impossibilities* offers its portrayal of Tom Mann's radical syndicalism against the labor militancy of the early 1970s, while *The Last Place on Earth* reframes the Falklands crisis with its narrative of imperialist adventurism), history stands as a field of shifting temporal referents, and its meanings emerge in intricate patterns of cross-temporal dialogue. This dialogue becomes literalized in Griffiths's most recent work: *Who Shall Be Happy . . . ? / Hope in the Year Two* (1994), *Food for Ravens* (1997), and the unproduced *Willie and Maud* (written in 1997). As Griffiths explores the boundary regions of realist representation, history becomes a spectral site in which the ghosts of past and future confront each other across the space of shared imperatives. These works are among Griffiths's finest, and they represent powerful and haunting responses to the changing stages of history in this century's closing decades.

Spectropoetics

To use the word *spectral* is, of course, to evoke Jacques Derrida, whose 1993 book *Specters of Marx* addresses the ghostly persistence of a Marxism that continues to haunt a world that has lived through the reports of its death. Speaking of Marxism's legacy, Derrida writes: "Inheritance is never a *given,* it is always a task. It remains before us just as unquestionably as we are heirs of Marxism, even before wanting or refusing to be, and, like all inheritors, we are in mourning. In mourning in particular for what is called Marxism."[27] Operating within this space of mourning, Derrida's book is an act of revisiting, though the legacy it revisits is itself revenant, that which returns, a specter that has haunted Europe with its apparitional presence since the opening line of Marx's *Communist Manifesto.*

Griffiths's post-1989 plays and films are also products of mourning: not for the European Communist governments—which, Griffiths strongly believed, had long betrayed the vision of social justice they paid lip service to—but for the vision itself, the future of transformed social relations it proposed, and the political culture it nurtured and sustained. There is a powerful gap between *Occupations* and Griffiths's recent films and plays; the attenuated sense of revolutionary possibility that characterizes these later works measures how much the political, social, and institutional contexts of British political theater have changed since its heyday in the 1970s, when a revolutionary culture was alive and the BBC would commission and broadcast *Absolute Beginners*, a play about Lenin, Trotsky, and the London Second International Congress. The crisis of this political tradition is everywhere in evidence: in addition to the rollback of organized socialism in the Soviet Union and Eastern Europe, the British Labour Party has responded to sixteen years of Conservative government by further marginalizing the trade unions and its other traditionally left-wing constituency, and the United States continues to witness the rapid dismantling of its New Deal and Great Society social order. As recently as 1983, with four years of Thatcherism already behind him, Raymond Williams could still see the chances of an alternative, socialist future as fifty/fifty.[28] Fifteen years later the revised odds aren't finding many takers.

A book about Trevor Griffiths may seem a kind of afterthought at such a time, when politicians and intellectuals alike have proclaimed the end of the political, economic, and ideological order that sustained the leftist tradition in which Griffiths has established his place as a writer. Although Griffiths was surprisingly prolific during the 1980s and remains one of the more active members of the post-1968 generation of political dramatists, his work during these years has been marked by a sense of disenfranchisement that can also be felt in the drama of his contemporaries. The playwrights of this generation have been attacked in recent years by those who find its forms of political theater shrill and outmoded and others, among an emerging generation of dramatists, who bristle against the "official orthodoxies" of its ideological and dramaturgical conventions[29]—this, oddly, even as many of its leading writers (David Hare, Caryl Churchill, and David Edgar come most readily to mind) have acquired unprecedented institutional status in the mainstream theater.

Yet it is, arguably, now—in the midst of the changes, the uncertainties, the recurrent question "What's left of the Left?"—that such a study is most warranted. It is warranted, in part, to help document and assess what has been produced in a movement of political drama that will,

when all is said and done, be recognized as one of Britain's greatest contributions to twentieth-century theater. As one of the most intelligent
and versatile writers within this tradition (and as one who has yet to
receive the sustained critical attention given Bond, Churchill, and Hare),
Trevor Griffiths is a particularly important figure in this regard. Griffiths's career as a writer is intricately involved with the history of the
postwar British Left—both in the sense that his plays and films take this
tradition as one of their principal subjects and in the sense that his life
and work engage the politics of culture and the challenges of a radical
cultural practice with such complexity and force. At a time when cultural studies has assumed a prominent place in the academy, the career
of Trevor Griffiths provides a fascinating opportunity to consider some
of its issues in practice. Indeed, Griffiths's career is uncanny in the
extent to which it takes up, and in some cases anticipates, major concerns of postwar British cultural theory: working-class culture; the politics of medium, particularly television; cultural institutions and the politics of "national spaces"; reception and consumption; youth culture;
Thatcherism and nation; heritage culture; race and the politics of identity; postmodernism and technology; the politics of New Times.

Inevitably, then, an account of Griffiths's life and work is an act of
historical examination in its own right. In order to historicize this
dramatist of history, the following chapters are structured through a
kind of flexible chronology, with roughly contiguous plays and films
grouped according to shared preoccupations. A certain degree of
chronology is essential to understanding the arc of Griffiths's career, but
it is also inescapable, since Griffiths's work is so engaged with its own
changing historical context. As John Bull has noted, a dialectical structure is evident not only within but between Griffiths's plays;[30] the more
one studies these plays and films, the more one is impressed by the
internal dialogue in which they are engaged. That other arrangements
suggest themselves attests both to the complex patterns of recurrence
and reworking that characterize Griffiths's work and to the opportunistic nature of Griffiths's dramatic practice, which embraces a radically
divergent range of subjects and shifts media with tactical mobility (witness the number of times that Griffiths has adapted plays across media:
television to stage, stage to television, radio to stage. A play like *Oi for
England*—which was produced for television and stage within a space of
only two months—exists, simultaneously and undecidably, in two
media). To an unusual extent among his contemporaries, Griffiths operates across multiple sites and through diverse channels; the challenge in

narrating his career is to find its overall shape while allowing rival connections and lines of development to make themselves felt.

This book explores the early stages of Griffiths's life and career, in order to set his career within the sociohistorical conditions out of which it emerged, and it traces the playwright's work during the years of its most concentrated visibility, 1971 to 1976. But, if there is a center to this book, it lies in its consideration of Griffiths's work after *Comedians*, in the plays and films of the 1980s and 1990s. Such an emphasis is called for, in part, because of the comparative neglect of this part of his career in existing studies of Griffiths's work: Poole and Wyver's *Powerplays* covers Griffiths's television plays only through 1982, and the remainder of Griffiths scholarship is overwhelmingly directed to the plays of the 1970s (the chapters on *The Last Place on Earth* and *Fatherland* in John Tulloch's *Television Drama: Agency, Audience and Myth* are a significant exception). Griffiths, of course, is not alone in receiving less attention for his work during the Thatcher years, but his ambidexterity in terms of medium has left him particularly vulnerable to selective critical vision. This selectivity was evident in the critical heralding of *The Gulf between Us* in 1992 as Griffiths's first original theater play since *Comedians*. While such a claim may technically have been correct, its implication is that Griffiths spent the intervening years in an extended sabbatical from the work that mattered. On the contrary, Griffiths was active during this period (and after) on a variety of cultural fronts, and these plays and films represent an important extension of his earlier work in the 1970s. According this work its proper weight redresses an important imbalance in the critical account of Griffiths's career.

Given the impasse that has characterized British political theater over the past fifteen years, there is another, more urgent reason for devoting attention to Griffiths's work since the late 1970s. For Griffiths has been at the forefront of those writers working to rethink the aesthetic and representational assumptions of political theater and to evolve a dramatic practice for the changing political and cultural world of this century's end. In a 1992 interview Griffiths observed that it was impossible to "construct a political play in the Nineties in the same way as in the Seventies."[31] In part as a consequence of Griffiths's work with film (his work on the *Reds* project was followed by a number other screenplays during the 1980s and 1990s, two of which have been produced), Griffiths has relinquished the dialectical realism of his earlier plays and explored a more fluid representational territory, in which the cinematic and the theatrical achieve their own dialectical forms of relationship and realism opens to accommodate the expressionistic and the reflexive. Some of Griffiths's recent plays have met with mixed responses on the part of theater reviewers, most of whom have longed for the particular structuring of issues and ideas in *Occupations*, *The Party*, and *Comedians*. But the seeds of *Real Dreams*, *Fatherland*, and the plays of the 1990s are evident in the earlier work, and their emergence in different dramatic configurations reflects the altered landscape of late- and post–Cold War discourse and practice. Like Caryl Churchill's *Mad Forest* and David Edgar's *Pentecost*, Griffiths's recent plays and films represent an effort to reimagine the possibilities of political theater in the collapse of the Left's guiding narratives and the emergence of an increasingly postmodern—and post-Marxist—political and cultural field.

Much is transformed in this recent work, and much has moved to the foreground as a result of the changing optics of Griffiths's practice: the micropolitics of identity, cultural border zones, the status of the Real in the context of postmodern virtuality. Yet by the late 1990s it is the stage of history that has changed most intricately. In the twilight of organized Marxism history in Griffiths's dramatic and filmic practice becomes the site of retrospect, both interiorized and public, and the boundaries of past, present, and future are troubled by the spectrality that Derrida identifies as the signature of a post-Marxist historical juncture. It may be tempting to contrast the tone of these plays and films with the seeming assurance of Griffiths's earlier work, when the transition to socialism seemed likely—to a Marxist, perhaps even inevitable. But, if Griffiths's work of the 1990s is important as a reflection of our own political impasses, it also offers a lens through which we can begin to reexamine the tradition that stands behind it.

While Griffiths may have claimed in 1976 that socialism had "decisively won" its battle with capitalism,[32] his plays were already characterized by an awareness of socialist transformation as a dream deferred. When William Waite looks with his aging father at photographs of the latter's labor activist past in *All Good Men*—"A man could die of memories like that"[33]—the moment underscores the place of mourning and a certain hauntedness in all of Griffiths's work. As Griffiths traces the legacy of socialist activism in the past in a search for origins, the moment of revolutionary opportunity is always already past, and even in the heyday of early 1970s radicalism Griffiths's plays and films derive much of their power, and their poignancy, from their awareness of loss and dispossession. In this sense an appreciation of Griffiths's recent work can help us rebalance our understanding not only of this play-wright's career but of the tradition of political theater in which he has been such an important figure. To the extent that this tradition achieved its flourishing in the years after 1968, after all, its generating moment was one of disillusionment and the betrayal of revolutionary promise. If, as Derrida suggests, a certain spectrality—not yet, no longer, not here, not now—has been constitutive of Marxism's claim on the present since its earliest emergence, then the spectropoetics of Griffiths's most recent work can help rethink the workings of mourning and hope, nostalgia and utopia, in even the most overtly revolutionary phase of post-war British political theater.

Yet mourning, of course, is never the whole story. Even as Griffiths's latest work explores the social and individual memoryscape of ghosts and all-but-forgotten promises, it continues to affirm the irreducible imperatives that a socialist history has placed on the human agenda—"a new concept of the human, of society, economy, nation," as Derrida writes.[34] "Who shall be happy, if not everyone?" Danton asks as he approaches his death, and his recovery of the question, in the face of the Revolution's failure, is his (and the play's) moment of achievement.[35] Visions of social justice grow increasingly utopian in Griffiths's work as their remoteness from the present deepens, but such commitments, for Griffiths, are "real dreams" nonetheless, grounded in the realities of individual and collective life. Like it or not, Derrida writes, we are all heirs of the Marxist project as an opening to the possible in human history, and this inheritance must be reaffirmed by "transforming it as radically as will be necessary."[36] Griffiths may no longer know what this transformation will look like, if he ever did; Nye Bevan his most recent protagonist, dies still seeking "not just the cause but the cure."[37] But it is a measure of Griffiths's resilience, the singleness of his political longings, and the ineradicable optimism of his will that this agenda has always remained at the center of his cultural and dramatic project.

1

Educations

Manchester and the New Left

Griffiths, we have seen, has characterized his life as one of borders—"of history, of cultures, of languages, borders of class."[1] In light of this, his decision to adapt *Sons and Lovers* is a resonant one, for Lawrence's life, too, according to Griffiths, was one of borders: "It was a life filled with complex stresses, contradictions, tensions, frustrations; its terrain an endless borderland of frontiers, some geographical, others social, cultural, all of them fortified, all of them beckoning."[2] If Lawrence's novel is deeply autobiographical, then Griffiths's act of adapting it was itself autobiographical, a way of exploring both the world of working-class deprivation and the border crossings attendant upon his own emergence from it.

Trevor Griffiths was born in Manchester, the city that would serve as backdrop for many of his plays, on 4 April 1935. His mother (the former Ann Connor) came from Irish stock, while his father (Ernest Griffiths), the son of a Welsh miner, worked as a chemical process worker, shoveling sulphur into hoppers and cleaning out vats in an acid factory until he died of cancer, in 1954. Griffiths describes his father through Bill Brand, one of his many fictional surrogates:

> There's barely an inch of his body hasn't been burnt at some time or other.
> [. . .] A very honest man. Tool-made for exploitation. A fair day's work.
> . . . "Proud" of his lad who was "given the chance" to go to the university.
> (*Pause*) He never talked politics. "Never you mind, I vote the way I vote
> and that's that. . . ." He probably votes Conservative. Out of respect.[3]

Griffiths was born at the height of the Great Depression, and, when he was two, his father became unemployed. Without a home the family was temporarily split up and dispersed among Manchester relatives. Griffiths was sent to live with his grandmother, a Catholic woman who had come to Manchester from County Clare in the 1890s. "A wholly unschooled woman, the daughter of tinkers," she introduced him to "poetry and the dangers of language."[4] She also taught him to read. When he was five, the family was reunited, and they lived in a neighborhood with other family close by. Griffiths was evacuated to the country for a time during the bombing raids on Manchester in World War II.

Griffiths was a precocious child, reading by the age of three; by three and a half he was admitted to a Catholic elementary school and was eventually singled out for his academic promise. One of the initial generation of working-class children to benefit from the 1944 Education Act, which extended the opportunity for secondary education beyond the classes to which it had previously been restricted, Griffiths passed the eleven-plus exam when he was nine and was admitted to St. Bede's College, a Catholic grammar school in Manchester. There Griffiths was exposed to the dynamic precision of Jesuit dialectics and, after an early adolescence of timidity and isolation, acquired around the age of fourteen a passion for "independent academic work."[5] Finding it difficult to work at home, he would often do his work at the Manchester Central Reference Library. During this time Griffiths also played soccer and was good enough at the game to represent England in schoolboy competition and to attract the notice of scouts from several professional teams, including Manchester United.

Griffiths was awarded a state scholarship to attend Manchester University, and in 1952 (at the age of seventeen) he enrolled as part of the "first wave" of Education Act beneficiaries "to wash up on the shores of the university."[6] It was a conflicted period for him: a time of "deeply interior experiences to do with sensitivity, tenderness, caring, belief" but also one of heavy drinking and physical violence (wrecking cafeterias, getting into fights). "This was my street proletarian sense still working its way through, still insisting on being reckoned with."[7] The years were those of the early and mid-1950s, of the Cold War and the Macmillan government, with few of the political outlets that would characterize university life at the end of the decade. At the age of twenty Griffiths graduated with a B.A. degree in English and subsequently enlisted for two years' service as an infantryman in the Manchester Regiment—"again it was a very Northern working-class thing."[8]

After his discharge from the army Griffiths took a post teaching English and games (or sports) at Birch Hall, a private school in Oldham. Within two years he was the senior master of the school. It was here that Griffiths's introduction to politics began. Through other members of the staff—particularly an anarchist/atheist/pacifist named Albert Smith, the model for Waters in *Comedians*—Griffiths "began to read and think and meditate the world in which [he] was living in a much more politically conscious way."[9] The school functioned as a hub of social, political, and intellectual activity. Griffiths became involved in the peace movement and the Campaign for Nuclear Disarmament (CND), participating in his first Aldermaston march around 1959–60. In 1959 he met Janice Stansfield, a sociology student from a militant working-class Labour family who, in 1960, would become his first wife; through her he was introduced to a wider social and academic network of individuals involved in such areas as community medicine, sociology, and anthropology.[10]

As a result of these expanding interests and connections, Griffiths became involved in the emerging New Left movement, which was revitalizing British socialism through a culture of intellectual, political, and cultural debate.[11] The *New Reasoner (NR)*, published by former communists who had left the British Communist Party as a result of the crisis over Stalinism, first appeared during the summer of 1957 (as a sequel to the earlier *Reasoner*), while the *Universities and Left Review (ULR)*, published by a younger generation of independent socialists, had first appeared that spring. The New Left movement represented by these two journals (they would merge as the *New Left Review [NLR]* in January 1960) was thus a joining of the tradition of communist dissidents with a postwar university Left concerned, among other things, with cultural questions. Its founding purpose was to liberate the tradition of socialist debate from communist orthodoxies and from the poverty of ideas in Labourism. The opening editorial of *ULR* offered a statement of these aims:

> What is needed . . . is the regeneration of the whole tradition of free, open, critical debate. The socialist tradition ought to be the most fruitful and the most stringent of the intellectual traditions: a tradition of thought and action, alive to the realities of our contemporary world and sensitive to the pressures of the ideals of equality and social justice which have distinguished it in the past.[12]

Central to this emerging political culture of ideas and debate was a growing network of regional discussion groups, or Left Clubs, which

were sponsored by *NR* and *ULR* (and later by *NLR*). As an editorial in
the inaugural *New Left Review* described them, these clubs would be
"not only discussion groups, but *centers of socialist work and activity*—ral-
lying points of disturbance and discontent within the local community,
the nerve centers of a genuinely popular and informed socialist movement." The Left Clubs operated outside though parallel to the existing
organizations of the Labour and trade union movements and were envisioned as maintaining links with similar "movements and tendencies"
in other countries. "The Left Clubs and New Left centers—the New Left
in general—must pioneer a way forward by working for socialism as the
old missionaries worked: as if consumed by a fire that is capable of
lighting the darker places in our society."[13]

The Left Clubs may have fallen considerably short of this evangeli-
cal vision; indeed, the New Left as a whole never succeeded in generating the organizational structures that might have enabled it to challenge
the established political structure. But in the late 1950s and early 1960s
the Left Clubs provided an energetic and popular left-wing intellectual
circuit. Ten Left Clubs were in existence by the end of 1959, with a particular concentration in Scotland and the north of England; by 1962 the
NLR directory listed forty such groups. Manchester was one of the first
cities to organize a Left Club, forming one in April 1959. Several months
later a left-wing coffeehouse was opened independently in the center of
the city, and it soon provided a site for Left Club meetings, which were
held twice a week.

Griffiths participated actively in the Manchester Left Club, eventually becoming one of the group's chairs in 1960. The Left Club allowed
him to hear and interact with Britain's leading left-wing intellectuals;
Raymond Williams, E. P. Thompson, John Saville, Stuart Hall, Perry
Anderson, Christopher Hill, John Rex, Peter Worsley, and Ken Coates
were among the speakers who visited Manchester (Griffiths also
attended a New Left summer school in Yorkshire, where many of these
speakers also appeared). With discussions and often fierce debates
before and after these talks, the Left Club meetings served as a labora-
tory of New Left ideas. Griffiths has described the intellectual feel of
these meetings and the cultural/political horizons they opened up: "It
was like the Left Bank in Paris. . . . You were in your own city, but you
were completely outside your own culture."[14]

The early New Left registered its mark on Griffiths's life and work
in a number of ways: through its opening of socialism to the unfettered
debate of ideas, its historical and sociological emphases, its emphasis on

education, its focus on culture as lived experience, and its expanded articulation of the political roles of intellectual and cultural worker. One of the most significant of its intellectual legacies was its "socialist humanist" orientation. Both the *New Reasoner* and the *Universities and Left Review* considered themselves journals of socialist humanism, and indeed no phrase more fully captures the terms by which the New Left defined itself as a movement against the anti-intellectualism, elitism, economic determinism, and antihumanism of Stalinism and other versions of communist orthodoxy. Thompson defined this new approach in an essay in the *New Reasoner:*

> In both senses [the present revolt against Stalinism] represents a *return to man:* from abstraction and scholastic formulations to real men: from deceptions and myths to honest history: and so the positive content of this revolt may be described as "socialist humanism." It is *humanist* because it places once again real men and women at the center of socialist theory and aspiration, instead of the resounding abstractions—the Party, Marxism-Leninism-Stalinism, the Two Camps, the Vanguard of the Working-Class—so dear to Stalinism. It is *socialist* because it re-affirms the revolutionary perspectives of Communism, faith in the revolutionary potentialities not only of the Human Race or of the Dictatorship of the Proletariat but of real men and women.[15]

Against "the blind clashing of interests and the arid abstractions which steal us from ourselves"—the twin legacies of capitalism and Stalinism—Thompson counterposed the creativity of people whose initiatives are "freed from slavery to profit or to bureaucracy."[16]

Griffiths, who responded in 1990 to a questionnaire asking, "What living person do you most admire?" with the answer, "E. P. Thompson, who has taught me so much,"[17] has himself used the phrase *socialist humanism* on occasion. But mere usage fails to reflect the profound debt that Griffiths's writing owes to the intersecting commitments animating this term. The drama of socialist theory and aspiration, in Griffiths's plays, is played out in the lives of "real men and women," and the experience of these people reaffirms "revolutionary potentialities." Given its emphasis on socialism as something done by people for people and its reclamation of human agency and moral choice, it is no accident that the New Left would generate some of its richest and most prolific work in the fields of history and drama. It is also no accident that Griffiths, who came of political maturity in the vigorous air of New Left thinking, would choose these fields as his principal artistic territory.

Griffiths's political activities in the early 1960s extended beyond the Manchester Left Club and into a broader field of left-wing activism. It is here that his abilities as a writer (and researcher) were first called upon and developed. In 1962 Griffiths joined the editorial board of *Labour's Northern Voice*, published by the Workers Northern Publishing Society (based in Gorton), and over the next three years served as coeditor for the paper, which was retitled *Labour's Voice*. Not formally connected with the Labour Party, *Labour's Voice*—and its many offshoot editions, with titles like *Stockport Voice* and *Industrial Voice*—were nonetheless sold in Party constituencies across the country and in trade union settings. Appearing monthly, it contained articles and editorials on a range of issues, and, in addition to his editorial supervision, Griffiths researched and wrote articles on subjects as diverse as Indonesia, the sale of arms to South Africa, and comprehensive education. He also contributed film reviews.

In 1961 Griffiths quit his teaching job in Oldham. He briefly considered pursuing an M.A. degree at Manchester University and actually proposed a thesis on the concept of "culture" in D. H. Lawrence, F. R. Leavis, T. S. Eliot, and Raymond Williams. But, instead of pursuing this option, and because he needed the money, he took a part-time job teaching night classes at Stockport Technical College, a further education school in Cheshire (like Oldham, Stockport is in the Greater Manchester area). He was eventually hired as a full-time member of the rapidly expanding Liberal Studies Department. This department included a core of radical educationists; Griffiths and these colleagues developed a curriculum of courses dealing with such issues as class, nation, race, and trade unionism. Their students were mostly workers (nurses, glass workers, electricians); in teaching them, the Liberal Studies faculty rejected the hierarchical conventions that positioned these and other students as passive recipients of learning. Griffiths was nearly fired for teaching *Lady Chatterley's Lover* to a class of second-year nursing students; he was teaching the novel because his students had named it when asked what they wanted to read.

After being passed over for the headship when it became available, Griffiths resigned from Stockport Technical College in 1965, and his formal career as a teacher came to an end. A couple of options presented themselves to him. The Labour Party group in Stockport was highly left-wing in orientation, and its members had considered Griffiths (who worked closely with them) a potential candidate for one of the local parliamentary seats. Griffiths officially joined the Labour Party in 1964 and learned a considerable amount about its internal operations (knowledge and experience that he would draw upon eleven years later in *Bill Brand*). But politics was not the path he would choose. Disillusioned, like others on the Left, with the Wilson government's policies after the Labour victories of 1964 and 1966, Griffiths did not renew his membership when it expired in 1965. Instead, he chose a career in the British cultural establishment, preferring a line of political activity that would combine the fields of education and media. In the fall of 1965 he was hired as further education officer for the BBC.

Further education production departments were established by the regional BBC offices in response to the growth of the British university system during the 1960s. These departments employed twenty-two further education officers, regionally distributed, who were to serve as liaisons between the institutions of education and educational production. Their functions included introducing these educators to the range of broadcasting materials available to them; representing educators to the BBC, so that the corporation's productions in the area of further education could more fully reflect specific needs in the classroom; and conducting research in the general area of educational interests and needs. Griffiths, who worked for the BBC office in Leeds, researched and wrote reports on trade union education, the WEA (Workers' Educational Association), and education in prisons. He traveled extensively over his territory (which included northern England, Scotland, and Northern Ireland), logging 40,000–50,000 miles a year. He describes one such trip:

> I can remember driving up to Sutherland, at the top of Scotland, leaving my car—this was mid-December—in an open airfield, getting on to a nine-seater plane, flying to Shetland and spending a day . . . meeting with further education teachers and education officers, dipping back into Orkney and having the same kind of meeting there, coming back to the car—the car had one turn of juice in it and was covered in ice, it was an old Volvo. I squeezed the bugger alive and got home about four o'clock in the morning. And then I had to write my reports up. . . . That gave me an extraordinary overview of British society and British culture.[18]

Working for the BBC also gave Griffiths a deeper understanding of the broadcast media as cultural institution. He was exposed to the structures of power and interest that characterized the television establishment in Britain, even as he investigated the educational contributions of broadcast technology on people's lives (as part of his job, Griffiths would watch BBC programs with their target audiences: trade union-

ists, pensioners, owners of small businesses).[19] He also received valuable production experience: in 1968, for instance, he directed a discussion series called *Something to Say*, in which guests such as Richard Hoggart and E. P. Thompson discussed extracts from literary texts with a
studio audience of teachers in adult education.

"These were heady times," Griffiths recalls. "I would never have
got a job in the BBC except between 1965 and 1974. That was a period
when everything that was solid seemed to be melting. All the old
rigidities were disappearing with the Labour government."[20] Griffiths
stayed with the BBC until 1972, when he resigned his position to
assume his career as a writer. He had taken on Clive Godwin as literary
agent in 1968, and *Occupations* had been produced by the Royal Shakespeare Company the previous October. Kenneth Tynan had already
approached Griffiths to write a play for the National Theatre, an invitation he would respond to with *The Party*. But by 1972 Griffiths (then
thirty-seven) had been writing plays (and one screenplay) for ten years,
some of them produced, most not. These plays are essential to any
understanding of the issues, preoccupations, and contradictions of his
early career.

Love and Anarchism: *The Love Maniac* and *Dropping Out*

Griffiths's emergence as a professional writer, and the beginnings of his
career as a playwright, coincided with his political awakening. He had
written as a teenager—journals, diaries, novellas, poems, and two west-
erns (the result of extensive reading in the genre). He remembers writing an essay in French in the sixth form, using a stream-of-conscious-
ness style influenced by Joyce's *Ulysses*. In college he published poems
in a magazine called *Manchester University Poetry*. Although these early
efforts were, on the whole, products of the private side at a time when
Griffiths was trying to reconcile his private and social beings, they were
characterized (Griffiths now suggests) by an acute consciousness of the
act of writing: "I had always thought of myself as the one who writes.
Not as a writer, that is a social ascription to do with earning a living, status, but as someone creating texts."[21] Griffiths continued to write poetry
throughout the 1960s, and he wrote a number of short stories, two of
which—a story on the dying stages of a relationship between a man and
a woman and a moving piece based on his father's final illness and
death—were published in 1966.[22]

Though he had always been drawn to drama as a form, Griffiths's working-class upbringing meant that he had little exposure to the theater. He listened to radio drama as a child: the first performance of a play he ever encountered was a broadcast of Strindberg's *Easter* in the late 1940s. Such plays "nourished me. . . . I liked the sense of voices in conflict, of argument, of narrative through argument."[23] And from his childhood on he was deeply impressed by film (at Manchester University he saw *On the Waterfront* six times in seven days and knew every line and camera angle by heart).[24] But even by the time of his first produced play (*The Wages of Thin* in 1969) he had seen comparably few theatrical productions. "The theater was completely outside my social frame of reference. Nobody I knew went to the theater."[25] He saw a student production of *Macbeth* and did a taped version of Eugene O'Neill's *The Emperor Jones* at the university, where he also studied drama. He remembers seeing Claire Bloom and Richard Burton in *Hamlet* at the Manchester Opera House, Osborne's *Plays for England* at the Royal Court, and plays by Harold Pinter, Henry Livings, and Alun Owen. He was particular impressed by the 1959 Royal Court production of Arnold Wesker's play *The Kitchen*, directed by John Dexter: "[It was] just amazing. It was a play about work, it was a play about people I knew."[26] When *Look Back in Anger* revolutionized the British theater, Griffiths was in the army, and he was aware of this seismic shift largely as a sense of expanding possibilities on the horizons of his other activities (he credits Kenneth Tynan with "mediating" the play's influence long before he had read or seen it).[27]

It was television that seized Griffiths's attention and determined him to become a dramatist. In 1958 Sydney Newman took over *Armchair Theatre* on Independent Television (ITV), commissioning plays on contemporary issues; as he told John Wyver, these plays "were going to be about the very people who owned TV sets—which is the working class."[28] In 1964, as head of drama at the BBC, Newman established the "Wednesday Play" slot, which showcased the work of such writers and directors as John McGrath, Dennis Potter, Jim Allen, and Ken Loach. Influenced by this work, by such shows as *Z Cars* and *Cathy Come Home*, and by the early plays of David Mercer, Griffiths started writing television plays himself. In the late 1950s or early 1960s he wrote two plays, *The Mob at the Door* (about the persecution of a homosexual college student) and *The Bastard Childe* (about army conscripts). In 1966 Griffiths wrote a play called *The Daft 'Un*. The story of two brothers out on the town in Manchester, it is the first of Griffiths's plays to explore the personal and sociological implications of his own relationship with his brother. Griffiths sent the play to Granada TV (based in Manchester) and then to the BBC, but neither inquiry was successful, and this play, too, went unproduced.[29]

Griffiths, who was himself working for the BBC by this time, contacted Tony Garnett, one of the producers of "The Wednesday Play," in 1967 with a proposal for a television play based on a strike that he had covered several years earlier for *Labour's Voice*. Garnett met with him and suggested instead that Griffiths write about something closer to his own experience. The result was *The Love Maniac*, a play about teaching that allowed Griffiths to rework his years as a radical educationist at Oldham and Stockport.

That Griffiths would turn to the classroom in this, one of his earliest works, underscores the centrality of teaching and education to his work: while *Comedians* is the most famous example, classroom settings and allusions to education will recur throughout Griffiths's plays and films. There are personal reasons for this, of course: education had been a decisive factor in Griffiths's economic mobility and his awakening to a world of ideas and analytical frameworks that articulated his experience in sociopolitical terms, and his work as a teacher (and later as further education officer) represented his earliest efforts at an interventionist social and cultural practice. There are clear continuities between Griffiths's career as a teacher and his later career as a writer; both activities, he would assert in a 1982 interview, share the goal of "demystifying the world in which we live—actually enabling perception to occur rather than promoting the various deceptions and mystifications that surround reality for all of us."[30] Here, as often in Griffiths's career, the personal has historical contexts as well. Education had been an important arena for the postwar Left. Many figures of the New Left (Hoggart, Williams, and Thompson, for instance) had taught in the workers' education movement and in university extramural departments, and their understanding of their intellectual work was closely tied to this experience (Williams's book *Culture and Society* originated in an adult education class on the idea of culture).[31] The issue of education and educational reform was also on the Labour Party political agenda through the comprehensive education movement. This movement was an attempt to render the educational system more egalitarian by replacing grammar and secondary modern schools, the students of which were usually distinguished by class background and educational opportunities, with schools catering to students of different backgrounds and aptitudes.

Although comprehensive education was never fully institutionalized, it received considerable impetus from the Wilson Government's 1965 circular calling upon local education authorities to submit plans for establishing comprehensive schools. Griffiths himself had contributed to a widely read issue of *Labour's Voice* devoted to comprehensive education.

Inspired by this movement and its vision of educational democracy, *The Love Maniac* opens in a newly built comprehensive school called Murliton with the arrival of Jake Mortimer, a recently hired English teacher who shows up at the school on a white Arabian horse, extravagantly dressed in a Mexican poncho, silk denim trousers, and calf-high boots, his long blond hair streaming behind him. Jake immediately establishes himself as a rebel teacher, rejecting (as Griffiths himself did) the institutional protocols and educational practices that constitute the outmoded tradition of British education. He takes students outside to learn, asks them not to call him "sir," and (in contrast with the rest of the school's faculty) involves students in forms of collaborative teaching. He works to subvert the class hierarchy that continues to structure the community of education inside and outside Murliton; while other teachers consult with parents of the well-to-do students, Jake welcomes working-class parents to his parent-teacher conferences. Education, for Jake, is an act of love. He recites Blake's poem "The Garden of Love," and he has this exchange with his ex-wife, Su, on teaching:

> JAKE: It's the greatest, the best, the worthiest thing a man can do.
> SU: What about loving a woman?
> JAKE: Teaching *is* love.[32]

This belief gets Jake in trouble with an administration already suspicious of his unorthodox teaching practice when he involves himself in the personal lives of his students, kissing one girl because she is insecure about her appearance and helping another to acquire contraception. Only through the intervention of George Noble—a butcher who was forced to leave school at the age of thirteen, fought for twenty years to bring comprehensive education to Murliton, and is now chairman of the Education Committee—does he avoid dismissal.

Anticipating later debates in Griffiths's plays and films, Jake and Noble confront each other near the end of the play over the former's actions. Jake reminds the older man that he was an old labor organizer who spent two years fighting with Tito's partisans in Yugoslavia and who organized the Northern Brigade in the Spanish Civil War. In answer to Noble's claim that Murliton as presently administered is a "sort of bomb" in English society, Jake counters: "It's all the old toffee served up in different wrappers: class, privilege, segregation, deference, repression. It'll train human beings to be fodder as effectively as any grammar or secondary modern school I know" (104). Referring to Noble's past, Jake proposes: "Teaching's my Civil War. I want to organize a second Northern Brigade for you" (108). Noble accepts Jake's offer, and the play ends with the latter appearing in an assembly before the students. Recruits to Jake's "brigade" are dressed as outlandishly as he, and "Guantanamera" plays on the loudspeaker. Jake proposes a new institutional order—no prefects, uniforms, or canes—and announces that a representative student council will be established to determine the future shape of education at Murliton. "Tomorrow, all being well," Jake announces, "we become a democracy" (110).

The Love Maniac is very much an early work, dated in its references and behavioral style and yielding (like its protagonist) to a certain idealizing imagination. Its issues are clear-cut, its oppositions often schematic. In its recourse to earlier revolutionary struggle—chiefly, the Loyalist brigades of the Spanish Civil War—it basks in the romance of such resistance. Jake and Noble both quote from George Orwell's *Homage to Catalonia* ("the deep, deep sleep of England, from which I sometimes fear that we shall never wake till we are jerked out of it by the roar of bombs" [104]), and Jake's democratic classroom owes much to Orwell's description of the worker's collective at Barcelona. But such is history without contradiction or difficulty, history as wish fulfillment, lacking the complexities that later Griffiths plays will acknowledge and explore. The "politics of love" in this play, in other words, operates without the tough-minded dialectical counterpoint that Griffiths will introduce when he returns to this theme in *Occupations*.

Yet, despite its uncritical exuberance, *The Love Maniac* contains, in early form, many of the issues and preoccupations that will recur throughout Griffiths's later work: education and class, institutional conservatism and the challenges of "strategic penetration," history as a resource for the radical imagination. Jake's relationship with his ex-wife anticipates the troubled field of relationship elsewhere in Griffiths's work, in which committed revolutionary love and the love for a specific other usually stand at an impasse. "You love everyone," Su tells Jake. "That's the problem" (99). In a pattern that will recur throughout Griffiths's plays and films, the most deeply felt interpersonal dynamic in this play is that between father (or father figure) and son, between an older figure who has bequeathed the legacy of revolutionary struggle and a younger radical who holds that mentor to his original vision. In Jake and Noble we see the first in a line of pairs that will include Waters and Price (in *Comedians*), Edward and William (in *All Good Men*), and Bill Brand and his many "fathers" inside and outside the Labour Party. And in Noble we see an early attempt to grapple with compromise, one of the central issues in Griffiths's work, and the related question of capitulation. When Jake asks Noble what happened to his earlier activism, the older man responds with a disarming voice that we will hear again: "Nothing happened. I grew old. (*Pause.*) Tell me, revolutionary, is Murliton so bad? If a man is weak enough to need a monument, is Murliton such a bad one?" (104).

Tony Garnett, who had left the BBC to set up Kestrel Productions, bought *The Love Maniac* from Griffiths, who completed a revised version of the play in May 1968 (when student brigades from the universities and *lycées* were bringing Paris and the whole of France to a standstill). But since a ninety-minute slot could not be found for it the play was never produced. Griffiths eventually adapted the play for radio, retitling it *Jake's Brigade*, and this version was broadcast on 11 December 1971 as part of the "Afternoon Theatre" program on BBC Radio 4. *Jake's Brigade* is an abridged version of *The Love Maniac*, and its action is rather severely condensed: the play is set during the hearing into Jake's conduct, with earlier events presented through flashback. Griffiths added passages to the important encounter between Jake and Noble, but on the whole the revised version lacks the exuberance of the original play.

In the years 1967–68 Griffiths also wrote a screenplay (his first) entitled *Dropping Out*. Garnett and Ken Loach had formed Kestrel Productions, and the two were approached by Vanessa Redgrave with an idea for a project on "life in the margins."[33] After meeting with Redgrave (on Garnett's suggestion), Griffiths wrote a screenplay, which he didn't like and eventually abandoned.

Different in subject, tone, and structure from *The Love Maniac, Dropping Out* is the story of a group of individuals, all of whom have dropped out of society for various reasons. Its members vary by age, gender, race, and sexual orientation; prominent among these are Blackie, a thirty-four-year-old Liverpool brickie; Arthur, a fifty-year-old "digger manqué"; and Tinker, a seventeen-year-old of Manchester working-class background who walked out of a pre-diploma course and has joined the group seeking relevance. They are joined by Emma, an upper-class married woman who has left home and attempted suicide. The screenplay follows her movement into life and her search for meaning.

At one point Emma asks about the group: "Some sort of . . . group, is it? Like a . . . religious community of some sort?" Blackie replies: "Sort of. Not religious though. Just drop-outs. We've all dropped out. One reason or another. Kissed the treadmill goodbye."[34] Griffiths explores the existence of these dropouts as they wander about, living from day to day in squatters' quarters and make-shift camps and trying to survive in a society that looks upon them with undisguised antagonism (their camp is attacked by thugs on motorcycles and by neighbors attempting to drive them away). With radical political activity going on around them, their decision to turn their backs on society is confronted with the challenge of political involvement. Two members of the group end up joining a Vietnam Solidarity Committee (VSC) demonstration, and the group is later joined by Elio, a fugitive Italian radical who speaks of being in Paris during the May demonstrations and who asks for their assistance in setting up a revolutionary underground. Emma joins Elio and learns from him a connection between love and politics. He tells her, in a rare moment of nonalienated sexual love in Griffiths's early writing: "We must learn how to make the I into the We. Then, what I am feeling for you now, tenderness, joy, I will feel for all people. That is love. It is also community" (128). Elio is eventually caught, and the remaining members of the group reassemble at the screenplay's end.

Like *The Love Maniac, Dropping Out* is a portrait of its decade, and, in addition to its often gritty portrayal of those members of its generation who chose to drop out of society, it includes glimpses into the now-dated world of the 1960s counterculture (one scene includes a "happening" at a party, with a nun and priest reciting Blake after an erotic dance of self-discovery). It is an awkward work, with an attempt at effects that Griffiths's later work with film would teach him how to produce more subtly and economically. Griffiths seems uncertain, for instance, about how to handle the political dimensions of the screenplay's narrative of social withdrawal—how to "read" its apathy in political terms. In an obvious attempt to contextualize the action of *Dropping Out,* Griffiths includes references to political texts as well as actual passages (from journals such as the *New Left Review* and *Black Dwarf*) delivered on screen by their authors: Tariq Ali, Stokley Carmichael, Michael Foot, R. D. Laing, David Mercer, Jean-Paul Sartre, Gerry Healey. This device is obviously intended to have a somewhat Brechtian, agitprop effect. But, though Griffiths's reading will continue to inform his plays and films, here the effect seems jarring, a bookish intrusion into a story that could, in fact, stand on its own.

Perhaps sensing these problems, Griffiths abandoned the project after finishing a first draft (sometime in mid-late 1968). But even in its unrevised state *Dropping Out* is interesting for what it reveals about Griffiths's political preoccupations at this time. For one thing its interpolated political texts suggest the continued voraciousness of Griffiths's political reading and the extent of his engagement, at this time, with the more radical wave of New Left thinking that characterized the late 1960s. Of particular interest in terms of Griffiths's later career is Laing, quoted here on madness in its relation to the norms of society. Along with Wilhelm Reich and Herbert Marcuse, both of whom Griffiths has acknowledged as influences, Laing explored the psychosexual components of social repression and helped establish a link between sexual and other forms of oppression that helped shape the politics of sexuality in the 1960s. This perspective will characterize the field of sexuality and relationship throughout Griffiths's plays and films, and it stands as one of the ways in which the political manifests itself in the lived experience of his characters. In *Dropping Out* a concern with the politics of sexual expression manifests itself in Emma's repressed life in an upper-class marriage, her attempt at suicide, and her subsequent journey (with Blackie and Elio) toward sexual awakening.

Like *The Love Maniac, Dropping Out* also underscores an attraction on Griffiths's part to 1960s anarchism, which found its political voice in an unprogrammatic opposition to existing forms of social and political organization and a commitment to spontaneous structures of relationship. Colin Ward describes the flowering of anarchist tendencies in 1968: "All of a sudden people were talking about the need for the kind of politics in which ordinary men, women and children decide their own fate and make their own future, about the need for social and political decentralization, about workers' control of industry, about pupil power in school, about community control of the social services."[35] *The Love Maniac* demonstrates this impulse at its most utopian, as the community of Murliton students embarks on the process of inventing its own forms of organization. Both Jake's description of teaching and Elio's speech to Emma in *Dropping Out* reflect the emphasis on love as a generating principle of social relationship (and social structure) that was very much at the heart of 1960s anarchism.

A commitment to individual rebellion, grounded in love and other natural instincts, would always form part of Griffiths's political sensibility; in the late 1980s and 1990s he would actually label himself an anarchist. But, while the year 1968 witnessed a flowering of anarchism as a political stance—with slogans such as "L'anarchie, c'est je" and "Créativité. Spontanéité. Vie." scrawled on Paris walls[36]—in the wake of the failure of the Paris rebellion and the restoration of law and order, the year also saw the beginnings of a turn away from anarchism toward a more revolutionary politics grounded in the writings of Lenin, Mao, and other revolutionaries.[37] What makes *Dropping Out* such a revealing prelude to *Occupations* and Griffiths's other plays of revolution in the 1970s is the extent to which it dramatizes the mental conflict of these divergent political stances and engages in a debate over their relative merits. While Griffiths's interests are clearly drawn to the search for alternative forms of social relationship, the play is also marked by the awareness of a more activist politics, most clearly in the voices of Tariq Ali and Stokley Carmichael and in the street activism of the VSC. And, while the relationships within this group of social dropouts represent the reaching toward new possibilities of interaction, the play reveals a certain impatience with their inertia and their lack of coordination and political will. When Arthur responds to Elio's request by pointing out that he left home to set up "something outside the mainstream, some-thing better, something more human, more honest, more . . . beautiful" (99), Blackie responds: "Dreams aren't programs. When you've under-stood that, you'll have grown up politically" (102).

Embryonic and unpolished, then, *Dropping Out* considers the con-flicting ways that the social and political discontent in the 1960s chose to establish itself as a "*counter*culture"—alternative or oppositional—and the impasse that results from these different aims and strategies. Not surprisingly, perhaps, it was written during the very period when Grif-fiths himself was confronting the possibility of a career as an interven-tionist writer.

Plays for Voices: *The Wages of Thin* and *The Big House*

In 1969 Clive Godwin approached the Stables Theatre Club, a recently founded avant-garde Manchester theater company in search of new scripts, with a stage play that Griffiths had written in 1968–69. This play, Griffiths's first for the theatrical medium, was punningly titled *The Wages of Thin*. The Stables Theatre accepted the play and produced it in three late-night performances from 13 to 15 November 1969; on 14

December 1970 a lunchtime production of the play opened at London's Basement Theatre.

Griffiths wrote *The Wages of Thin* in two weeks as a kind of exercise play about "three blokes in a lavatory."[38] The play concerns the interrogation in a public lavatory of an unassuming businessman named Arthur Rimbaud Thin by two plainclothes policemen (identified simply as One and Two), who beat him up and accuse him of murdering someone whose body lies in an adjoining cubicle. They accuse him of pornographic interests and homosexual practices and force a confession from him concerning his underground sexual activities at home and abroad. After breaking him down in this way, the two men let him go and subsequently undergo a transformation of their own. They shed their trench coats, revealing evening dress underneath; having spoken in working-class accents up to this point, they assume "normal establishment voices" now that Thin has left. Placing a phone call as the play comes to an end, one of the men says mysteriously: "I think we might have found something. Perhaps we could use him abroad."[39]

The Wages of Thin displays an intense language consciousness, as the two interrogators engineer the breakdown of Thin through an intensive and self-consciously patterned linguistic barrage. Marked by class and education, language is very much a tool of power in the play. But, as its reviewers pointed out, Griffiths's exercise play is finally derivative of other drama (Pinter's *The Birthday Party* is an obvious prototype of its mysterious linguistic interrogation), and its meaning and sympathies are, in the end, unclear. Forced to acknowledge his hidden life, Thin delivers an impassioned plea for homosexual freedom, but Griffith undercuts this potentially moving speech by referring to it (in a stage direction) as "pukingly embarrassing." Griffiths has himself criticized this early play for its lack of meaning and direction: "It had been so much of an exercise that I hadn't really worked out what it was about or for. In a sense it wasn't about or for anything except somebody trying to write."[40]

He has also called *The Wages of Thin* "a play for voices, much more a radio thing."[41] The experience of having a play produced in the theater taught Griffiths a lot about the very different demands and possibilities of the medium of live performance. But at least one reviewer found its use of the stage strikingly innovative, and his tongue-in-cheek praise allows us to glimpse the play with "real space" in this, Griffiths's first foray into the theater. Irving Wardle, who otherwise disliked *The Wages of Thin* when he saw the Basement Theatre production, noted how unusual it was to see actors making use of the lavatory in the course of the dialogue: "if it catches on it should prove a godsend to actors who don't know what to do with their hands."[42]

Griffiths, it turned out, never abandoned the idea he brought to Tony Garnett when the latter suggested he write *The Love Maniac,* nor did he forget the incident upon which it was based. While writing for *Labour's Northern Voice,* Griffiths had covered a strike that took place at Amalgamated Engineering Industry (AEI), located in south Manchester. One of the shop stewards there had been fired for negligence after failing to repair a lathe he had signed a clearance check on, and the lathe broke the next day. It came to light that he had failed to do so because he had called the hospital where his wife had gone in for a cancer checkup and learned that she had to have her stomach removed. Too proud to admit that anxiety had caused his lapse, the steward felt that his punishment was justified. But the men struck.[43] When Griffiths returned to this incident in 1968–69, it formed the basis for his radio play *The Big House* (the title is taken from the nickname for the AEI factory building). Directed by Alan Ayckbourn, *The Big House* was broadcast on the BBC's Radio 4 *Afternoon Theatre* program on 10 December 1969; along with *The Wages of Thin,* performed a month earlier, this play signals Griffiths's emergence as a public playwright.

 The Big House is set in and around the factory of Lazarus Ltd., where preparations are being made for the retirement of Commander Percy, the company's personnel manager. A young woman, Victoria Hayes, arrives as his replacement, just in time to hear the news of George Potts's suspension for negligence (the facts surrounding this negligence are modeled on the incident mentioned earlier). His cause is championed by Tom Yates, the head shop steward, who attempts to have the matter investigated by Percy and by Bill Walmsley, branch secretary of the major union at Lazarus. Walmsley, who collaborates so closely with management that he seems almost an arm of the company, is eager to have Potts dismissed, since the latter (like Yates and the other shop stewards) is a militant threat to the union-management entente he enjoys. Yates succeeds in forcing a meeting on Potts's case then engineers a walkout during the lunchtime ceremony staged in honor of Percy's retirement. Through Victoria's intervention Potts's dismissal is revoked, and the play ends with a conversation between Victoria and Yates, suggesting the possibility of a new relationship between the personnel office and the men who actually work the factory floor.

As this brief synopsis suggests, the political and institutional land-scape of *The Big House* is easily the most complex in Griffiths's early work; at moments the number of characters and their relationships tests the limits of radio's ability to convey and structure information.[44] Griffiths shows considerable skill in delineating the play's political field: its institutional structures of consent and collaboration, its points and tensions, and its precarious forms of equilibrium. Addressing the conflict in the union community between the radical and the moderate/rightist Left, he focuses on the militant wing within a movement that has legit-imized itself and found reliable channels of influence by adapting itself to the capitalist system. Walmsley, who is so crucial a part of the com-pany's operations that he is given his own office and secretary, speaks about "bringing these bloody shop stewards into line" and wishes that the Union would pass "a no-reds clause," while Yates accuses him of "collaborating with the capitalist and selling your men down the river."[45] This particular conflict was very much a part of its historical moment and would remain so: earlier in 1969 the Wilson government had proposed curbing unofficial, "wildcat" strikes, and the power of shop stewards—elected locally, from the floor—to initiate independent industrial activity would continue to be a target of government (espe-cially Conservative) attempts to regulate the trade unions. But the prob-lem within the trade union movement was only one manifestation of the broader fissure at the heart of Britain's postwar Left. This confrontation between the militant Left and an often accommodationist Center/Right will reappear in Griffiths's plays of the 1970s, achieving its richest artic-ulation in *Bill Brand*, the playwright's exploration of a Labour Party riven by this political/ideological conflict. That the conservative wing of such oppositions in Griffiths often consists of former militants gives this conflict further complexity and poignancy.

The dialectical confrontation of positions animates and structures *The Big House,* and its participants are boldly and economically drawn. At the same time, the most tantalizing characters in Griffiths's play are those whose politics and intentions elude explicit confrontation. Ray Frost, works manager at Lazarus, participates in institutional moves and countermoves as cynically as anyone else, yet it was he who hired Victoria as personnel manager: "Thanks to Percy, for two years or more I've had the growing feeling that we're all perched on the lip of a vol-canic crater, scared to breathe or look down. Well, sooner or later we've got to do both. That's *your* job" (97). Victoria herself also plays her cards close, deflecting the sexism of both management and workers with a sardonic smile, dropping indications of her family's working-class background and her own radically different sense of labor relations almost casually. "You were magnificent," she tells Yates after his staged walkout: "Best performance I've seen in years" (131). As with all her words and actions, the precise balance of conviction and irony here is indeterminable, and she is left at the end of the play (like Richard Massingham in *All Good Men* and Philip Carlion in *Country*) an intriguing, mysteriously liminal figure within the institutions of power. When Yates is asked whom he spoke to outside the pub, he says, both bewildered and intrigued: "No-one you'd know. No'one I'd know, come to that" (133).

The Big House closes with Yates and his coworkers watching a reporter's interview with Percy on the pub television; "Bit on t'box about t'Big House," Jack calls over (133). The reflexivity of this moment—television evoked through radio, with its program on the Big House in a play by the same name—is something that will characterize Griffiths's work throughout his career. As Percy speaks about the transformation of management into "a more rigorous science," the media collaborates in erasing the truth of management exploitation and militant resistance. Yates orders the set to be turned off and offers a promise, one that will serve as a manifesto for Griffiths's own interventionist use of the television medium: "One day somebody's gonna say it the way it really is, Jack. And all the sets in England'll explode with the impact." Orwell's "roar of bombs" has been reconceived within the field of a revolutionary cultural practice.

Where the Difference Begins: *Sam, Sam*

Sam, Sam, Griffiths's earliest-written full-length play to be produced, is in many ways the culmination of Griffiths's dramatic writing before *Occupations*. A play about two brothers, one working-class and the other upper-middle-class, *Sam, Sam* was written in two parts, the first in 1968 and the second in 1969 (it would not be performed until 9 February 1972, when it was produced at Charles Marowitz's Open Space Theatre in London). *Sam, Sam* is an attempt, both autobiographical and sociological, to come to terms with the playwright's own experience of "class translation" (the phrase is Poole and Wyver's),[46] and it effects this through a theatrical revisiting of Griffiths's past, with its radically divergent social worlds. That *Sam, Sam* remains an uneven play attests to the profound contradictions it seeks to negotiate and the conflicts of immersion and distance that make this kind of negotiation so difficult.

As a play (in part) about the working class, *Sam, Sam* draws upon a broader literary and sociological interest in working-class experience and culture that began in the late 1950s and extended into the 1960s.[47] This movement (we might call it) was reflected in Richard Hoggart's influential work *The Uses of Literacy* (1957) and E. P. Thompson's *Making of the English Working Class* (1963); the fiction of Alan Sillitoe and the plays of Arnold Wesker, Shelagh Delaney, and Edward Bond; the gritty films of British New Wave cinema; and television and radio programs like *Crossroads*, *The Archers*, and the highly popular *Coronation Street.* Like David Mercer's Generations trilogy or Raymond Williams's novel *Border Country*, *Sam, Sam* addresses working-class life in the context of recent experiences in class mobility. The play, Griffiths has stated, is an autobiography of "the post-1944 Education Act people" who have moved from the working class to the professional middle class.[48] With the Welfare State largely established, some commentators argued that the working class as it had always been known had ceased to exist. The "discovery" of working-class culture, Chas Critcher suggests, was a response to such claims, and it was implemented by "a whole generation of scholarship boys and girls whose relationship to the working class and the Labour Party was crucial to their own identity."[49] In a famous chapter of *The Uses of Literacy* Hoggart described the uprootedness and anxiety of the "scholarship boy," caught "at the friction-point of two cultures."[50]

Such portraits of "declassed" working-class intellectuals suggest the particular patterns of need and conflict that Griffiths dramatizes in *Sam, Sam.* The act of being educated beyond his family and class created a profound sense of alienation from his background and (inevitably) from the new world he was invited to join. Griffiths has described how, as a member of the initial influx of post-1944 working-class students in secondary grammar schools, he had felt marked by speech, dress, and manner. He has also described the exhilarating access to new cultural and intellectual spheres and the profound conflicts that this posed:

> Then began for me a very long struggle to hold on to where I had come from and also to get hold of this new thing which, outside of its class aspects, dealt with intellect, with feeling, objectivity to some extent, standing outside one's own being and seeing things from another position. So I was living a massive contradiction which I couldn't, unaided anyway,

resolve. And indeed it was not until many years later . . . that I began,
through reading sociology, to see what that contradiction had been made
of, and incidentally, to see how badly I had responded to it by becoming
very elitist, very avant-garde, very detached from my own class.[51]

Griffiths, we have seen, felt himself a "stranger" in the differently
classed world of the London cultural scene. What this quotation makes
clear is the extent to which the experience of class translation entails a
double displacement and alienation. Griffiths's remarks on northern
writers applies as well to the writer of working-class origins: "you are
not only a stranger in the centre of the society, but you also become a
stranger in the place where you come from. You are a person arrested in
movement. Neither going nor coming but both at the same time."[52]

On one level *Sam, Sam* is a dramatic exploration of Griffiths's relation with his own brother, who, born two years before Griffiths and
(according to the playwright) the smarter of the two, had left school at
fifteen and ended up working (among other jobs) as a shirt cutter and
bricklayer. In this sense the play interrogates family history in order to
consider the issue of class and the vexed question of "where the difference begins" (to borrow the title of Mercer's early television work, also
a "brother" play). On another level it dramatizes and explores the split
self that constitutes the legacy of class translation. From this perspective
both brothers are aspects of Griffiths himself, components of a double
estrangement that results from feeling a stranger in two worlds.

In the play's central device the two brothers at the center of *Sam,
Sam*, one year apart in age, are each named Sam Shatlock; in order to
demonstrate what Griffiths calls "the Pyrrhic victory of environment
over genes,"[53] both are played by the same actor. Act 1 belongs to the
elder Sam, an unemployed worker who lives in the cramped family
home with his wife, Sandra, and his mother. Conceived as a kind of
stand-up working-class comedian, Sam One narrates and performs the
first act as a kind of music-hall routine: he opens the play, as he ladles
cake icing in a bowl, by asking the audience, "How do you like me up to
now?" (65), and, when his mother comes in asking for the icing, he
hands the bowl to a member of the audience ("Help yourself"). He
engages with his wife and mother in rude combat over the limited space
in their home and acts out earlier scenes (an interview with a labor
exchange clerk, his father's death) in the mode of flashback. Throughout
these scenes his address to audience and characters alike is charged
with savage, confrontational humor.

The main subject of Sam's routine—its comic theme, as it were—is the life of the working class. To this end Sam One adopts a sharply parodic tone toward prevailing modes of representing that class. Sam directly challenges the audience's responses to his stories and actions, quoting dismissively the discourse of middle-class social compassion and its easy determinism: "I bet you're saying 'Christ, the poor benaighted blaighter, livin' in all that lot. What chance has he ever had!' Well, actually, it's got nowt to do wi' chance. Nothing whatsoever" (68). The set, too, is used to spotlight clichés in a kind of visual quotation. Much of the early action in the Shatlock house, for instance, centers on the bathroom and the competition for its use: Sam wants to take his bath; Sandra is in no hurry to finish hers (she leaves the tub filthy when she gets out); Mrs. Shatlock uses the toilet and smells the room up. In its preoccupation with bathroom fixtures and the Swiftian exaggeration of its focus on the body, this scene establishes a hypernaturalistic parody of the kitchen-sink realism that had, by 1968, become an outworn convention of novels, plays, and films about the working class (*Sam, Sam*, we might say, deploys "bathroom-tub realism"). Sam One replays a scene with his parents in dialogue taken from D. H. Lawrence's *Sons and Lovers*. At the end of this scene he taunts the audience with its conditioned expectations:

> How's that then? A bit better? That a bit closer to your authentic working class drudgery, is it? 'Course it is. Come on, own up, that's the real thing, innit? Eh? Who was it said Lawrence was more authentic than life itself? (69)[54]

By playing against convention and genre (a strategy that Griffiths will return to throughout his career), the first act of *Sam, Sam* inhabits a reflexive space in which the audience's attempts to "read" its representation of the working class are exposed and unsettled. At the same time, parody and burlesque are counterpointed in this play by an insistent undertone of genuine deprivation and loss, the realities of working-class lives that conventional representations seek to frame and usually misrepresent. Beneath the comic banter runs a current of condemnation that cuts through any illusions of lightheartedness. Sam One speaks of his father, a figure of Griffiths's own, as "the perfect mechanical man, the human workslave. [. . .] Trot trot click he went all his bloody miserable exploited life and I fillup with snot and tears and shame and anger whenever I remember the way he was" (71). As the act ends, he comments on his brother's ("our kid's") socialist beliefs in a better future:

"It's all gonna be all right. So there we are. (*Thinks*) I don't honestly know what all right'd be, really. What it'd be like, if it *was* all right" (71).

The often unsettling mixture of theatricality and realism that characterizes the play's first act, then, underscores the constructedness of much of what is considered "class" and "class culture" while insisting on the economic conditions that enforce genuine differences of opportunity and experience. The performative aspects of this difference are heightened by the transition between acts. Sam One ends the first act by putting on a dress suit that his brother keeps in the family home. The moment is startling in a Brechtian way: like *A Man's a Man*, this scene offers a glimpse of a character being "remade" through a change of props and circumstance. As Sam One stands dressed like this, listening to the "Ode to Joy" from Beethoven's Ninth Symphony (intensifying the moment's Brechtian effect, a hanging flat drops down with the words printed on it), he could be the younger brother whose life he earlier described: "Nowt like me. We still have a pint now and then, but, well, he's living a DIFFERENT SORT OF LIFE now, isn't he?" (68).

Acts 2 and 3 introduce the younger Sam, a Stockport teacher lined up for a nomination for one of the local parliamentary seats. In the second act, a brief interlude, Sam rehearses his address to the Labour Party National Executive (more precisely, the scene fades between rehearsal and actual delivery, with the conference hall indicated as a "thinly realized reality"). True to the preoccupation we have observed elsewhere in Griffiths's early work, Sam's speech is on education, and he offers a radical proposal for reforming the school system and the capitalist system it reinforces: "*Education* is at the base of this capitalist society of ours, and if you want to change the one you'll bloody well *have* to change the other." Somewhat too obviously, the act stands in an explanatory relationship to the acts that surround it, asserting the educational and capitalist causes of the social inequities we see elsewhere in the play. At the same time, the radical edge of Sam's speech is subtly undermined, or rather "framed." The voice of Patricia, Sam's wife, interrupts his speech, and the sound of a baby crying can be heard. When the conference hall setting disappears at the end, it is replaced by the living room of an early Victorian house, expensively furnished, with portraits of Marx, Lenin, and other revolutionaries on the walls in "a sort of design motif" (72). The effect is one of revolutionary ardor rendered domestic, comfortable, in a setting radically opposed to that of act 1.

The play's style undergoes a dramatic shift as well. It took Griffiths a year to write the second half; when he did, he wrote the majority of it (act 3) in the style of realism. Gone are the theatrical tricks and the volatile staginess of act 1; in their place is the static living room of conventional bourgeois theater. This setting embodies the world that Sam Two's education has given access to, and it suggests the alienation that he experiences in relation to this world. Naturalism is an important component of this effect, for it sets into place the sense of entrapment and alienation that has marked the realist mise-en-scène since the claustrophobic rooms of Ibsen's trapped idealists. Sam Two is alienated from the world of impassioned political theory by the domestic interior that calls him back with its things and relationship; as William J. Free suggests, he is further alienated from the audience by the formal code of the fourth wall.[55]

Class, of course, is the principal source of Sam's alienation. His wife (with whom he has an "agreement" that allows each to take on other sexual partners) is from upper-class stock, and the two engage in tense joking about his "proletarian" origins. If *Sons and Lovers, Coronation Street,* and films like *Saturday Night and Sunday Morning* are background texts of act 1, *Look Back in Anger* is clearly a shaping text of act 2. While Sam Two occupies a higher station in life than Osborne's protagonist, he shares Jimmy Porter's class resentment. He directs this at his wife—or, rather, at her lovers, who seem to give her even more power over him—and at her affluent parents. They, it turns out, feel a similar antagonism toward one they consider "a squalid proletarian romantic" (75). Sam's simmering hostility comes out in the middle of the act. Patricia hurries out Sam's mother, who has visited just before her own parents are expected, and Sam lashes out at her parents, spitting his drink in her father's face. When her parents have gone, Patricia, humiliated, presses Sam to the floor, mounts him in an act of "hyenal" sex, and taunts him in what seems to be a ritual of sexual and class degradation (a far cry from the little squirrels of Jimmy Porter and Alison):

> PATRICIA: And where do you come from, Shatlock?
> SAM: Water Lane, Madam. Number Three, Water Lane, East Stockport.
> PATRICIA: And what kind of district is that, Shatlock?
> SAM: Poor, Ma'am. Very poor.
> PATRICIA: And dirty.
> SAM: And dirty, ma'am.
>
> (77)

When their sadomasochistic confrontation, with its eroticizing of class power, is over, they return to the accommodation that constitutes their marriage. Sam pleads with Patricia not to go to her lover, but she leaves anyway, and the play ends with Sam listening to a recording of a brass band.

Sam, Sam, according to Griffiths, explores "that which is changeable in the individual psyche, which is not to do with genes, but with environment, background, the shaping and molding which goes on inside a society."[56] The decision to have the two brothers played by the same actor reinforces this emphasis, for the difference between the two characters becomes a matter of performance: a change of clothes and manner, the alteration of dialect. From this perspective, the differences of class behavior are largely acquired, or imposed. Each envisions the other living a different life, but what is striking about the two Sams is how similar they are, particularly in their relationships with their wives. Despite Sam One's claims to the contrary, neither is happy in his life, whether that life offers the cramped closeness of an emasculating poverty or the ostensibly open marriage and the domestication (likewise emasculating) brought by affluence. Each Sam carries traces of the other within, like a disowned or unrealized set of social possibilities. Sam One quotes F. R. Leavis and listens to Beethoven; Sam Two's standard pronunciation retains traces of his northern working-class beginnings, and he listens to that signature of northern working-class culture, brass bands. But of the two it is the younger brother who is most conflicted, perhaps because of the political education that renders the contradictions in his life so much more apparent.

Sam, Sam is not without its flaws. The structure is theatrically unbalanced, with the domestic realism of the second half rendered somewhat flat by the performative energy of act 1. The attitude of its protagonists toward women is troubling, and the marital resentment that both brothers feel edges, in spots, into overt misogyny. Finally, its balance between the personal and the political—between involvement and the detachment necessary to understanding and political vision—is uncertain, vulnerable. Politics remains caught in entanglements and animosities. When Patricia has left, Sam Two quotes Trotsky: "'We shall not enter into the kingdom of socialism in white gloves on a polished floor.' [. . .] Put that in your calendars sometimes" (78). But the anger that fuels this quotation, like that of Jimmy Porter, is the anger of a personal disappointment grounded in class—and sexual—resentment. Griffiths has suggested that his difficulty in writing the play's second half resulted from a difficulty in writing directly about himself,[57] and, despite its fictionalizing touches, the second half never overcomes this problem.

Throughout his career, of course, Griffiths has been a deeply autobiographical writer: he once observed that personal experiences litter his plays "like tombstones," and no other British dramatist, political or otherwise, has so deeply mined the resources of personal experience in his or her writing.[58] The self, for Griffiths, is an intensely political field, a site where contradictions and imperatives contend, a repository of social and historical traces: "My plays are about the contradictions in my life," he has stated.[59] Autobiography, however, is not without its risks: the very closeness of its material can mitigate against the distance essential to sociopolitical understanding. Although autobiography will continue to inform—even haunt—Griffiths's work, later plays will adjust the balance between the personal and the political, positioning the former within the guiding orbit of the latter. And, as Griffiths turns to the field of history, he will discover a more creative matrix for combining politics and lived experience. In 1973 Griffiths said of *The Party*, which reexamines the 1960s through the lens of history: "Nearly every major character in the play is me or is the scintilla of me. But in fact it's walking round in extraordinary frames that aren't mine."[60] Historical consciousness will allow Griffiths's writing the objectivity—"standing outside one's own being and seeing from another position"—that both his life and education taught him to prize.

Still, *Sam, Sam* is a fascinating play, bold in the directness of its sociological investigation and not without its own historical awareness. With the exception of Mercer's early drama, no play explores so fully the psychological and social contradictions of postwar working-class mobility. Its stylistic unevenness is a direct result of the daring of its theatrical imagination: *Sam, Sam* is clearly a breakthrough play in Griffiths's experimentation with theatrical styles and the different possibilities inherent in the audience-stage relationship. Griffiths notes: "*Sam, Sam* was the first [play] where I really thought in terms of a space, and of people being co-present with the work."[61] Its stylistic legacies (both realist and antirealist) are evident throughout his later plays and films, as are its central figures and preoccupations. Sam Two will reappear as Joe Shawcross, Sam One as Gethin Price, and fraternal "doubles" will continue to constitute one of the central dialectical oppositions in Griffiths's work. Griffiths's plays will remain consumed with the issues that *Sam, Sam* raises so directly: the experience and dilemmas of class entryism, the nature of difference, the relationship of identity to its origins.

2

Occupying History

1968: May Days

After directing *The Wages of Thin,* Gordon McDougall asked Griffiths if he wanted to write a full-length play for the Stables Theatre Club. Griffiths responded by proposing a play about the Turin factory occupations of 1920. The result, which premiered on 28 October 1970, was *Occupations,* one of Griffiths's finest plays and the one that identified him as an emerging voice on the British stage. Responding to the acclaim that greeted the play, the Royal Shakespeare Company offered to produce it in London, and on 13 October 1971 *Occupations* opened at its Fringe venue, The Place, with Buzz Goodbody as director and Patrick Stewart and Ben Kingsley in the roles of Kabak and Gramsci. A revised version of the play was mounted as part of a touring production by John McGrath's 7:84 Theatre Company in May 1972, and major productions have taken place in Amsterdam, New York, Cologne, Toronto, Australia, France, and Italy. A television adaptation of the play, directed by Michael Lindsay-Hogg and starring Donald Pleasence and Jack Shepherd, was broadcast by Granada TV on 1 September 1974.

Researched and written during the early months of a new decade—a decade that would shortly see the election of a new Conservative Government—*Occupations* is the first of Griffiths's plays to offer a retrospective look at the late 1960s, years of radical aspiration and popular revolt. The year 1968, of course, was critical in this period of upheavals, when capitalist society seemed driven to the brink, with demonstrations, occupations, and other political disturbances throughout the Western

47

countries. Catherine Itzin writes, "Rarely can one year be singled out as an isolated turning point, but in the case of 1968 so many events coincided on a global scale that it clearly marked the end of an era and the beginning of a period of equally unprecedented political consciousness and activism."[1] In January the Tet Offensive presented a major setback for the United States military campaign in Vietnam, while Western demonstrations against the war escalated in numbers and militancy. And in May students, joined by workers throughout France, brought Paris and France as a whole to a standstill. The activities in France were matched by similar uprisings elsewhere, but none more radically suggested the possibility of revolutionary change. The suddenness and scale of the events in Paris caught many on the Left off guard. As the editors of the *New Left Review* noted in the immediate aftermath of these events, socialist strategists had assumed that no such cataclysm would occur in Europe: "For years the Left in Europe has been writing 'Letters from Afar,' attempting analysis, expressing solidarity, discussing strategy. Now the struggle has suddenly arrived at home."[2] In the heady early weeks of the May uprisings, as students battled police on the streets of Paris and nine million workers went on strike, it seemed to many on the Left that the formidable structures of Western capitalism—in Germany, Italy, Japan, the United States, but most immediately and dramatically in France—were suddenly at risk.

And yet the ultimate legacies of 1968 were failure and disappointment. The students of Paris found themselves unable to parlay anarchistic revolution into any kind of lasting political transformation, and the government of Charles de Gaulle succeeded in neutralizing the civil insurrection through the time-honored moves of announcing a referendum, speaking of workers' "participation," and thereby outflanking extra-electoral protest. The established organs of industrial and political resistance—organized labor and the French Communist Party—greeted this spontaneous, nonorganized militancy with mistrust, even opposition, thereby establishing their own stake in the status quo. Even as the events of 1968 seemed to put revolution back on the socialist table, then, they raised a set of difficult questions concerning the nature and implementation of revolutionary change. As suggested in the previous chapter, the years following 1968 saw a deepening conflict between anarchistic currents of social protest and a more radical militancy, evident in Britain in the turn to Leninism, Maoism, and other revolutionary models; the expansion and intensification of labor militancy throughout the Heath administration; and (particularly germane to the study of British political drama) the emergence of a cultural fringe committed to socialist opposition and the question of revolution. But this turn to militancy was accompanied by anger and disillusionment and by an awareness of the many ways by which the revolutionary impulse is blocked, coopted, dissipated, lost.

"I was deeply involved with and deeply affected by the student unrest of the 60s," Griffiths said in a 1979 interview. "The detonations set off then put revolutionary transformation back on the agenda of the society. But by 1970, one could see it was all a failure, it was gone, and I was trying to account for my feelings. I felt anger, and I felt pain, and I wanted to make a play that said something about it."[3] Much of Griffiths's career can be seen as an attempt to come to terms with the particular gap between possibility and realization dramatized so starkly during the Paris May. But it was not, for Griffiths, an easy time to understand or write about. *Dropping Out,* written during the months preceding and following the Paris May, may have convinced Griffiths of the difficulties involved in approaching this period directly; the screenplay's awkward interpolation of left-wing writings may reflect a failed attempt to establish an analytical stance in relation to these contemporary events. When he came to write *Occupations,* Griffiths turned to the past as a vantage point from which the present (and the recent present) could be subject to examination. Speaking of the play's composition, Griffiths noted: "I wanted to draw some lessons and conclusions about this latest defeat and emptiness of the socialist struggle. But I couldn't do it directly and write what was going on in France and Britain in 1968 and '69. I felt I needed some distance, an historical correlative, some way of perceiving what had happened."[4]

The turn to history represented a decisive shift in Griffiths's development as a playwright; although he occasionally returned to the contemporary moment as the setting for individual plays, the field of history became his principal dramatic and filmic "scene." History allowed Griffiths to overcome the problem of distance that characterized *Dropping Out* and *Sam, Sam,* and the discovery of "historical correlatives" enabled him to establish the dynamics that characterize his mature work: the dialectical tension between past and present, the dramaturgical play of objectivity and engagement. History provided Griffiths with a space of observation and analysis; drama allowed him to people this space with human subjects who sought to remake history in the image of their aspirations.

Griffiths's work, we have noted, stands in sharp contrast to the

Brechtian aesthetic that characterizes the work of Bond, Churchill, Brenton, and others on the theatrical Left, and he himself has underscored his disagreements with many of Brecht's theories and assumptions.[5] At the same time, Griffiths shares Brecht's commitment to historicizing dramatic strategies. In his "Short Organum for the Theater" Brecht speaks of the field of human relationships that forms the subject of drama:

> The field has to be defined in historically relative terms. In other words we must drop our habit of taking the different social structures of past periods, then stripping them of everything that makes them different. . . . Instead we must leave them their distinguishing marks and keep their impermanence always before our eyes, so that our own period can be seen to be impermanent too.[6]

Because of its theoretical rejection of realism and verisimilitude, Brecht's theater precludes the texturality of historical detail. History, when it is deployed in a play like *Galileo* or *Mother Courage and Her Children*, is evoked in a kind of gestic shorthand, and its localizing details are conveyed—often parodically—through the mode of quotation. Griffiths, on the other hand, is concerned with history as a field of political, institutional, economic, and sociological forces; a site of agency; and a specific configuration of lived possibilities and constraints. To delineate the contours of this field, he engages in extensive research, archival and otherwise, and his plays and films assert a verisimilitude absent in the plays of Churchill, Bond, and Brenton. At the same time, as his published exchange with Tom Nairn about *Occupations* demonstrated, Griffiths's use of history is subordinated to dramatic ends. Griffiths has said: "I do very painstaking, steady, attritional work on the background, and make mounds of notes. I'm keen to get things right, but not so keen that I'll cut out an important creative notion because somehow it doesn't fit historically. I usually think that the play is the whole and history the part."[7]

Although *Occupations* concerns itself with a set of issues that were foregrounded in the 1960s, the roots of its concern with history lie very much in the New Left of the late 1950s and early 1960s and the tradition of historiography that the movement inherited from the Communist Party Historians' Group and earlier Marxist historians. "For reasons which are even now difficult to understand," Eric Hobsbawm has noted, "the bulk of British Marxist theoretical effort was directed into historical work."[8] The Communist Party Historians' Group was formed after World War II, and its members (figures like Hobsbawm, Thompson, and Christopher Hill) were concerned to bring about, as Bill Schwarz of the History Workshop describes it, "the anglicization of the marxist tradition."[9] This project entailed (among other things) reclaiming (and often discovering) a native tradition of popular radicalism. Not surprisingly, given the issues of history and its falsification, communist historians were among the most vocal in response to Khrushchev's speech denouncing Stalin: the Historians' Group passed resolutions expressing dissatisfaction with the British Communist Party for its failure to discuss the political implications of Khrushchev's disclosures. Dissident communist historians founded the *Reasoner*, the forerunner of the New Left publications, and history remained very much at the heart of the movement that followed. The first issue of the *New Reasoner* opened, for example, with an act of historical positioning: "We have no desire to break impetuously with the Marxist and Communist tradition in Britain. On the contrary, we believe that this tradition, which stems from such men as William Morris and Tom Mann . . . is in need of discovery and re-affirmation."[10]

Griffiths's plays and films owe specific debts to British Marxist and New Left historiography: a focus on figures in the British radical tradition (Mann, Tom Paine) that forms a significant strand of his broader interest in the international Left, a concern with labor history, and a general awareness of the working class and working-class culture as historical formations. Indeed, there is a sense in which the contours of Griffiths's career owe as much (or more) to such writers as Edward Thompson, Eric Hobsbawm, and Angus Calder as they do to figures within the theater. But the influence of this historiographic tradition on Griffiths's work goes much deeper than specific debts suggest. Marxist historiography provided Griffiths with a radical conception of history as counter-description, mounted against the hegemonic "past" constructed and recirculated within capitalist memory. For Griffiths, as for the historians who influenced him, the making of history is an interventionist act, ideological in strategy and impact. As Schwarz expresses it, "the *active* construction of conceptions of the past [is] a continual and defining moment in political practice, engaging with and deconstructing reactionary 'memories' and histories."[11]

"Most of the history that is taught is ruling class history," Griffiths has stated.[12] To the extent that the past serves a legitimating function in terms of the present and its structures of relationship, history becomes—like the Fiat factories of Turin—a site for potential occupation. Radical or interventionist history, for Griffiths, operates to "set straight the record," to tell the truth obscured within hegemonic historical accounts and delegitimate the interests served by these accounts. It also works to reclaim aspects of the past erased by ruling-class history. Griffiths speaks of the need to enlarge the "usable past" in contemporary consciousness (the phrase is Gwyn Williams's) "by bringing our attention to those men and women, those organizers and agents of social change, those movements which have never been put on the record. Now that's most people, of course, but it's also most opposition leaders, particularly socialists."[13] From this point of view the making of history is an act of re-legitimation, empowering radical action in the present through the recovery of a socialist culture and tradition. For Griffiths a contemporary politics of social change can only come to know itself through an awareness of this culture and tradition, and the intellectual and political challenges facing a revolutionary politics can only be met through an engagement with history. As Jake suggests to Noble with his passionate evocation of the Spanish Civil War in *The Love Maniac,* the past is a place where the present discovers itself as history, where socialism comes to know its own revolutionary dilemmas and possibilities, and where the Left affirms its own tradition of radical achievement and heroic failure.

Revolutionary Dialectics: *Occupations*

The Turin factory occupations of 1920 were the most dramatic episode in the turbulent period of political and industrial disturbance that followed the Russian Revolution and the end of World War I. The occupations had their origins in the development of Factory Councils in the Turin industrial plants. These councils, controlled democratically by workers, had been advocated in the pages of Antonio Gramsci's *L'Ordine Nuovo* as organs of workers' power and precursors of a society-wide proletariat rule. In an attempt to destroy these councils, Italian employers, supported by government troops, proclaimed a lockout in April 1920, to which the workers responded by declaring a general strike that involved 500,000 industrial and agricultural laborers throughout Piedmont. But the national Italian Socialist Party and Confederation of Labour refused to give assistance to the strike, and it ended with the Factory Councils intact.

In the late summer and early autumn of 1920 industrial action erupted again, this time on a much larger scale. In response to a lockout at the Milanese Alfa Romeo plant, factories were occupied throughout Milan. On 1 September the metallurgical workers in Turin followed suit, and the occupations spread through Turin industry. As Perry Anderson writes:

> Turin rapidly became the vortex of the movement, which assumed the character of a general challenge to capitalist society as a whole. The Factory Councils controlled production within the factories, while protecting the plant from counter-attack by organizing Red Guards. Great efforts were made to maintain output. Armed workers in Turin clashed with the city's security forces. The question of power had clearly been posed on a national scale.[14]

Faced with workers' militancy outside its organized structures and anxious to secure a compromise position, the Confederation of Labour (with the support of the Socialist Party) organized a referendum on negotiations, and it was approved by a narrow majority. An economic settlement was reached with the employers, and by the end of September the occupations were over. With the cessation of industrial militancy the revolutionary period of postwar Italy came to an end, and the resulting social backlash led to the emergence of fascism (fascist squads began carrying out raids in the autumn of 1920, and a number of prominent industrialists began contributing money to Mussolini's organization). For the workers who had envisioned—and within the walls of the factory momentarily realized—a revolutionary form of social organization, the legacy of the occupations was betrayal and bitter defeat. Acknowledging (when it was too late for the Turin insurrection) the critical absence of a vanguard party that might have channeled the spontaneous insurrection into actual social revolution, Gramsci joined others on the Italian Socialist Left in forming the Italian Communist Party at the Livorno Congress in January 1921.

With their pattern of spontaneous uprising and counterrevolution, the Turin insurrections were a natural "historical correlative" for the uprisings of 1968, as many commentators on the Left were quick to realize. In the fall of 1968 the *New Left Review* published selections from Gramsci's *L'Ordine Nuovo* texts on the occupations, drawing an explicit connection to the events of the previous spring: "The parallel between the fate of the great wave of occupations in Italy and that of the recent occupations in France needs no emphasis: it is cruelly evident."[15] This sense of historical recurrence was intensified in the "hot autumn" of 1969, when Italian workers, led by Fiat assembly line workers in Turin and supported by students, mounted a strike that was exceeded in size only by the strikes of the French May and the British General Strike of 1926. The upheavals of 1920 raised questions relevant to the aftermath of 1968–69: to what extent did the factory uprisings constitute a revolutionary situation? How did the established interests of both Right and Left succeed in neutralizing popular revolutionary energies? And (most crucially) what is required in order to translate these energies into systemic revolutionary change? As the *New Left Review* article demonstrates, one of the results of these questions was a renewed interest in Gramsci's writings both before and after the events of 1920, many of which were translated for the first time. So pronounced was this "discovery" of Gramsci by the Left in the late 1960s and early 1970s that one writer could speak in 1970 (the year of *Occupations*) of a "cult" or "legend" of the political theorist.[16] The issues raised by the events in Turin would deepen in relevance during the Heath administration, as the strategy of "occupation" became increasingly adopted by trade union militants. In September 1970 workers at the Upper Clyde Shipbuilders occupied the shipyards and began to run them under the control of shop stewards; a wave of other occupations soon followed.[17]

Griffiths approached the subject of the Turin occupations with the kind of extensive research that would characterize all of his later historical projects. He read widely in published primary and secondary historical material, including published Fiat historical notes, and in the winter of 1970 he traveled to Italy to conduct further research. There he visited the sites of the occupations and consulted photographic and other documentary material at the Gobetti Center in Turin, the Gramsci Institute in Rome, and the Feltrinelli Institute in Milan. Identifying himself as a journalist writing an article on the historical Fiat, he was taken around the factory at the Fiat Center in Turin and shown the company files. He also secured an interview with Umberto Terracini, one of the cofounders (with Gramsci) of *L'Ordine Nuovo,* a key figure in the factory occupations, and one of the founding members of the Italian Communist Party. In Griffiths's notes on this interview, in which he asked about such matters as how Gramsci dressed and whether he laughed a lot, we get a clear sense of Griffiths the dramatist seeking the individuating strokes of personality in the materials of history.[18]

Historical research shapes *Occupations* in different, often divergent, ways. On the one hand, Griffiths uses factual and documentary material to provide an explicit historical frame for the play's onstage action. *Occupations* opens with a multimedia sequence featuring projected images of a 1920 Soviet propaganda poster and El Lissitsky's abstract painting *With the Red Wedge Divide the White,* a sung version of the Internationale, and a recorded (fictional) voice delivering a speech to the Second Congress of the Third International: "Comrade delegates, Europe is little more than dry couch-grass and kindling, waiting for a spark."[19] Later scenes include projected pictures of the actual occupations and the events surrounding and following it. Factual details from Griffiths's research are also woven into the fabric of the play's action and dialogue: a Turin official lists over fifty towns and cities affected by the occupations, and some of Gramsci's lines are taken or modified from the historical figure's published speeches. At the same time, the play is very much "the whole" and history "the part." Griffiths has shaped his exploration of the Turin factory occupations around the dialectical opposition of characters and personalities in an action almost severe in its constraint. History provides the localizing frame, but personality— the domain of moral, political, and personal choice—becomes a field for the playing out of revolutionary conflicts and contradictions.

Occupations opens on the eve of the factory occupations in the hotel room of Christo Kabak, a Bulgarian communist in Turin as a representative of the Third International (Kabak is loosely based on the historical figure Khristo Kabakchiev, a Bulgarian communist who was the Comintern's official representative to the Livorno Congress, which took place five months after the end of the uprisings). Kabak has arrived in Turin on an undisclosed mission, and he spends much of the play trying to ascertain the nature and direction of political currents in the dramatically unfolding events. Among the visitors he entertains in his hotel room (most of the play takes place in this single room) is Gramsci, one of the uprisings' agitational leaders. After an initial guardedness, as Gramsci determines the legitimacy of the bearded stranger, the two discuss the situation in Turin and debate the strategies for exploiting its revolutionary potentials.

Mussolini referred to the historical Gramsci as "a Sardinian hunchback . . . with a brain of undeniable power."[20] Griffiths's Gramsci combines an awkward, dwarflike stature with a grace of movement and a keenness of eye and intellect. Outside the glare of public events he analyzes the imminent occupations with a sense of their revolutionary import but also with an awareness (born of the failed strikes in April) of the forces of reaction in the capitalist state and in the ranks of socialist and labor leaders. "There are only two possible outcomes to the present situation," he tells Kabak. "Revolution. Or the most horrendous reaction. No other possibility exists. If we fail, perhaps we fail utterly" (30). At the play's structural center is Gramsci's act 1, scene 3, speech to representatives of the factory councils on Red Sunday of the first week of occupations. Griffiths stages the speech in a way that breaks the realism of the scenes in Kabak's hotel room and exploits the "real space" of the theater's own auditorium. Projected on the back wall is a photograph of Red Guards on the factory roof, while the side walls are lit to reveal blowup photographs of the actual factory meeting. Gramsci speaks from a lectern at the front of the stage, addressing the audience as if it were the factory workers. His speech is an inspirational but measured delineation of the opportunities facing the workers, the obstacles they will confront, and the need for individual choice based on deliberate consideration of options. Gramsci's own advice is that they prepare to wage war on the state as well as the employers and to arm themselves for a long offensive. At the same time, he reminds them, they will not be accused of cowardice if they choose not to fight at this particular moment, nor will they be seen as heroic if they choose to take on the state and are destroyed by their enemies while their party and unions stand by. "Find your courage where it is. Beware rhetoric! Even mine!" (42).

The dialectical confrontation underlying the play is made explicit in the discussion between Gramsci and Kabak that follows this speech. While the leaders of the General Confederation of Labour have asked the Turin section if they are prepared to lead an insurrection, they have failed to commit the national organization to supporting an insurrection. Kabak, arguing that without an insurrection there is no revolution, states that the Turin workers must commit themselves to such an act, no matter what the consequences. Gramsci, however, is unwilling to risk the Turin working class in an operation undertaken without national support: "I will not allow that class to be wiped out. I could not survive it" (45). What emerges as the argument continues is a fundamental disagreement about the attitude required for revolutionary leadership. To Gramsci's acknowledgment that his position toward the workers is governed by love, Kabak argues that love is incompatible with the making of revolution: "You cannot *love* an army, comrade. An army is a machine. This one makes revolutions. If it breaks down, you get another one. Love has nothing to do with it." Gramsci responds by insisting upon the inseparability of ends and means and by arguing against the dehumanizing reduction of individuals to "mass":

You would be wrong to see this . . . love . . . as the product of petit-bour-
geois idealism. It is the correct, the only true dialectical relationship
between leaders and led, vanguard and masses, that can ensure the political health of the new order the revolution seeks to create. Treat masses as
expendable, as fodder, *during* the revolution, you will always treat them
thus. (*Pause*) I'll tell you this, Comrade Kabak, if you see masses this way,
there can be no revolution worth the blood it spills. (46)

This debate is framed, of course, by the facts of history and their
harsh lesson: that the revolutionary opportunities of the 1920 uprisings
were lost because of the timidity of the institutional representatives of
the working class and the absence of an organization that might fan the
spark of revolution and direct its flames to the capitalist state itself.
When Gramsci next appears before the factory workers to announce the
result of the referendum that will end the occupations, he does so with
a deepening understanding of this absence. In his earlier speech, delivered in the optimistic early days of upheaval, he had quoted Lenin:
"What is to be done?" (41). Now, however, he quotes Trotsky, offering
the same line that Sam II speaks so ineffectually in Griffiths's *Sam, Sam:*
"We shall not enter into the kingdom of socialism with white gloves on
a polished floor" (60). And, although he encourages the workers not to
use the outcome of the occupations as an opportunity for despair, he
also urges upon them the need for a new politics of discipline. In words
drawn from one of the historical Gramsci's articles of late September
1920, he says, his voice "*hardening*":

A revolutionary movement can only be led by a revolutionary vanguard,
with no commitment to prior consultation, with no apparatus of representative assemblies. (*Pause. Then very big.*) Revolution is like war; it must be
scrupulously prepared by a working-class general staff, as a national war
is prepared by the army's general staff. (59–60)

The military analogy, of course, is Kabak's, but the wider historical reference is to Lenin's revolutionary theory. This Leninist shift in Gramsci's thought in *Occupations* can be traced in his changing use of the
word *vanguard*. In Gramsci's first speech the word refers to the Turin
workers, courageously organizing their occupation of the factories
through democratically controlled soviets, or factory councils. By the
final speech *vanguard* has come to signify a tightly knit, disciplined body
of militants who direct the revolution without democratic constraints.
The questions of love, loyalty, and revolutionary leadership are

extended and complicated through the character of Kabak, the bearded, dark-haired Bulgarian whose personal and "occupational" contradictions are at the play's center. Kabak counterpoints Gramsci's politics of love with a ruthless pragmatism and expediency, refusing emotion as sentimentality and putting situational needs ahead of the individual. As elsewhere in his play, Griffiths takes pains to establish the personal register of moral and political contradiction. By setting most of the play in Kabak's hotel room, a space simultaneously public and private, he focuses on the overlaps of the two realms and the conflicts between them. Sharing the room with Kabak is his mistress, Angelica, a Russian countess who left revolutionary Russia with him after her husband ran off and who is now dying of uterine cancer. Kabak's treatment of her demonstrates, in intimate terms, the conflict of love and revolutionary expediency and the costs of repressing the former to meet the requirements of the latter. He makes arrangements for her, even plays along with her cocaine-induced illusions that she is back in revolutionary Russia, but his relationship with her is characterized by detachment and an unsentimental calculation of personal and political need. He asks Polya, the maid, for sex as Angelica lies apparently asleep and, forced out of Turin by the authorities, leaves his mistress to her death—even telling her, before he leaves, that she's dying. Her dignified request, "I don't want to die on my own," is the play's most painful moment (71).

Earlier in the play, as Gramsci watches from across the room, Angelica comes out of her sleep and asks Kabak to tell her he loves her. He does, and she asks, "Why is it always so hard?" "It isn't," he replies. "It's just . . . so pointless" (48). Coming immediately after the discussion of love and revolution, in which Gramsci asked, "How can a man love a collectivity, when he has not profoundly loved single human creatures?" (46), the moment underscores the different outlooks of the two men. But it is a mistake to see Kabak as a character who has successfully banished attachment, who comfortably lives the disengaged emotional life he advocates to Gramsci. Angelica, whose bed remains onstage throughout the play, is a reminder of the claims that Kabak's occupation as an agent of the revolution requires him to disown. The costs of this self-suppression are evident throughout this play, especially in those moments when Kabak is alone, or with Polya, and allows himself moments of the emotion he must otherwise deny. Giving these moments their proper weight allows us to appreciate the self-protecting nihilism in Kabak's character, and it suggests a certain longing beneath his cynical dismissal of Gramsci's commitment to love. When Gramsci leaves Kabak's room for the last time to visit his dying sister in Sardinia, the Bulgarian's farewell is not without self-irony: "(*Softly*) You still love them too much, comrade" (68).

These conflicts between loyalty and expediency are equally apparent in Kabak's relationship to the political activity in Turin. From the moment of his arrival in the city he works to "read" the situation and its participants, soliciting information and opinions and calibrating the revolutionary possibilities of the unfolding events. As a representative of the Comintern who arrives on the eve of the occupations, his own intentions and loyalties are objects of scrutiny and interpretation on the part of the numerous visitors who visit him in his hotel room. Like his vodka, he is "deceptive" (33). What distinguishes Kabak in these interactions is his skill as an actor and his willingness to suit his performance to specific visitors. As Richard Allen Cave notes, Kabak dresses to suit each role he assumes—suave dressing gown for bribing the official D'Avanzo, Bulgarian national costume for meeting Gramsci, business suit for the final meeting with Fiat representative Valletta—and even arranges the angle and quality of lighting for each encounter. "With Kabak," Cave writes, "what obtains is an exemplary technique . . . an intense self-consciousness calculating the success of every effect."[21] Griffiths's stage directions introducing Kabak stress the artifice of the character's public appearance: "Dressed as he is in impeccable bourgeois style, there is something not quite right about him, as though the form were somehow at war with the content." Entering the room with his traveling bags, Kabak picks up a used ampule, but his face, Griffiths specifies, "gives no sort of clue to state of mind or to any discovery he may have made" (18).

This last direction suggests the extent to which the motives and intentions governing Kabak's performance remain undecidable for the audience as well. Once his identity is confirmed, Gramsci greets him enthusiastically—"The factories will welcome your arrival with open arms" (26)—but this representative of the Third International never visits the workers who have organized factory "soviets," speaking instead of a "delicate" and "secret" mission (26). It turns out, in the play's final scene, that Kabak has been sent to negotiate with Fiat concerning concessions in the young Soviet Union, but this mission is kept secret up to this point from characters and spectators alike. Kabak speaks passionately to Gramsci of the need to seize the revolutionary opportunity, but, when he speaks of the failure of the occupations to Valletta later in the play, he says: "The outcome never really seemed in much doubt, I regret to say" (65). Clearly, from the moment of his arrival Kabak is hedging his bets on the revolution, and, if his revolutionary sentiments are genuine, they are counterbalanced by a willingness to exploit the situation however it turns out. If the occupations are defeated, as they eventually are, Kabak can conduct negotiations with the capitalists who regain control as efficiently as he might have with the victors in a revolutionary workers' cooperative. The cynicism of this final maneuver is underscored in the scene with Valletta, when Kabak hands out cigars and brandy, offers the Fiat representative his credentials and a portfolio, and speaks of capital investments and rates of return. Valletta responds with a mixture of irony and admiration: "You'll make a good capitalist, Mr. Kabak" (63). When the two toast "to business" (62), the moment has a sardonic—almost Brechtian—gestic resonance.

At the same time, it is important to Griffiths's investigation of the compromises involved in revolutionary politics that the reasons for Kabak's attempts to secure investments for a Soviet Union in need of capitalist development be kept in mind. Griffiths has himself stated that he considers the Soviet Union's policy in this regard to be "correct."[22] As Albert Hunt points out, Kabak's actions represent two contradictory strands in Lenin's 1920 policy: the imperative to encourage worldwide revolutions and the effort to secure the revolution already achieved in Russia.[23] As such, his seemingly divergent attitudes to the revolutionary opportunities in Italy reflect not cynical opportunism but, rather, an attempt to negotiate the impossible contradictions posed by revolutionary solidarity and the pragmatics of survival. From this perspective Kabak's political sangfroid forms part of Griffith's broader concern with the repressions and contradictions, the necessary but tragic hardening, that are required to move the revolutionary impulse (in Gramsci's words) "between *here* and *there*" (41).

Kabak's pragmatism, then, is a necessary counterpoint to Gramsci's politics of love, and the unanswerability of his view of revolution is evidenced by the former's adoption of its terminology of war and discipline. In the failure of the uprisings of 1968 Griffiths returns to the politics of *The Love Maniac* with a tougher understanding of spontaneous organization and the revolutionary power of love. He also returns to the socialist humanism through which the New Left sought to repudiate the dehumanizing politics of Stalinism and asks whether its "warm, personal, and humane socialist morality" is enough to break the hold of capitalism.[24] But Gramsci is also an essential counterpoint to Kabak, measuring what is lost in the compromises and repressions of revolutionary leadership. Griffiths writes:

> Occupations was written as a sort of Jacobinical response to the failure of the '68 revolution in France. What it asserts is that courage and optimism do not, of themselves, ensure the success of revolutions, unless they are harnessed, disciplined, tightly organized; in a word, led. And what it asks—because it's a play that, characteristically, asks rather than asserts—is whether the courage and optimism aren't in some way necessarily damaged, distorted, in that disciplining process.[25]

In its double focus on the socialist humanist and the Leninist/Stalinist, Occupations isolates a fundamental duality in the revolutionary consciousness, that split between the idealism essential to the socialist vision and the discipline necessary to its realization. As Griffiths commented in 1983: "Psychologically, the authoritarian and the libertarian live very close in my Left sensibility and in most Left sensibilities that I've encountered."[26]

Occupations closes with Angelica alone onstage. Her presence has been a disquieting one since she was first revealed in the play's opening moments. There, as the slides establish the context of the Russian revolution and a voice from the Second Congress of the Third International celebrates the consolidation of Bolshevik power, Polya injects Angelica with cocaine as she writhes in convulsions. In a startlingly emblematic way her body has served as the symbol of aristocratic Russia convulsed by the eruption of revolutionary forces: "It's here," she says in a later delirium. "Underneath. Under the skin. It's not a part of me. It's foreign. I can feel it moving. Underneath. In the hands. In the legs" (47). The play ends with Angelica, again under the influence of cocaine, surrendering to "voluptuous spasms" and the return of her revolutionary nightmare: "All things will bend all things the iron brain of Lenin hammering the future will will will what will stop them stop them who . . ." (72).[27] This time slide projections detail the future: the triumph of fascism, foretold by Gramsci in his closing words to Kabak, and the Stalin-Hitler nonaggression pact, a grotesque culmination of East-West realpolitik. It is a bleak ending, dark in its vision of revolutionary failure and even darker in its understanding of the consequences of such failure. As Kenn Stitt wrote in an early review of the play, "Both Kabak's mechanical dicta-

torship, Gramsci's democratic submission and love—both Russia and
Italy fail. It is a heavily, even terribly pessimistic vision that is saved
only by the want to know, to do better."[28]

Postscript: The Nairn Debate
As the first of Griffiths's plays to earn extensive critical notice, *Occupations* was, on the whole, well received by the mainstream press, though
it had its detractors, and even those who liked it pointed to what they
considered structural and other weaknesses.[29] Perhaps not surprisingly,
given its engagement with issues of deep importance and sensitivity
among socialist intellectuals, the play's sharpest criticism came from the
Left. A review of the television adaptation of *Occupations* in the *Workers
Press* called it "a polished and obscene slander against Gramsci and
against Lenin's Third International" that "falsif[ies] the problems of revolutionary leadership."[30] The most detailed criticism of the play
appeared in a two-page article by Tom Nairn, entitled "Mucking About
with Love and Revolution," in the 10 November 1971 issue of *7 Days;*
Griffiths responded to this article with an essay of his own ("In Defense
of *Occupations*"), also published in *7 Days* and subsequently printed as a
foreword to the 1980 edition of the play. The debate between these writers offers an insight into how politicized the field of radical history, and
how urgently contested the historical reputation of a figure like Gramsci, could be. It also provides an important clarification of the assumptions shaping Griffiths's emerging practice as a historical dramatist.

Nairn, whose translation of Giuseppe Fiori's *Antonio Gramsci: Life of
a Revolutionary* had been published in 1970, challenges the accuracy of
Occupations' historical account, particularly its characterization of
Gramsci, which Nairn sees as romantic and sentimental. The historical
Gramsci, Nairn contends, was characterized by a "sinewy intolerance";
he was "a hard, even a harsh, figure in most public situations." He was
also no orator. The portrait of Kabak is similarly inaccurate because
ahistorical: Griffiths, Nairn claims, has conflated later moments of
Soviet foreign policy with the period in question, drawing an inaccurate
portrait of Comintern policy in the postrevolutionary period. More generally, the play's meditation on revolution is remote and humanist in
outlook, and its central antithesis is a false one: "To say that social revolutions are necessarily divisive whirlwinds, partly inhuman tragedies
where 'love' is swept aside, is not to justify the kind of ruthlessness and
authoritarianism [Kabak] stands for here." In the inevitable defeat of
Gramsci's romantic utopianism, Nairn sees an unrevolutionary pes-

simism: "The 'revolutionary play' imposes, finally, a sense of fatality which is the opposite of revolutionary."[31]

Griffiths responds to Nairn's historical claims with a detailed historical counterargument, based on the presentation of counterevidence and a critique of Nairn's use of sources. He challenges Nairn's view of Gramsci's hardness as partial, based on descriptions of Gramsci in earlier years and later, during his years in prison in the 1930s. Drawing upon his own historical reading, he offers the testimony of Terracini on the affection the Turin workers felt for Gramsci and cites the latter's writings to argue for the centrality of love in Gramsci's thought. In response to Nairn's critique of Kabak, Griffiths discusses Soviet foreign policy before and after the events of 1920 and suggests that the decree that formed the basis of Kabak's negotiation with Valletta, though passed five weeks after the scene took place, was consistent with Soviet policy since 1918. Griffiths concedes that the compression of meanings on Kabak in this final scene is excessive and that the character's need to play a role in his interaction with Valletta "obscures the representative values of his actions by inviting a cynical and pessimistic response."[32]

Although Griffiths offers this pointed counterstatement to Nairn's historical critique, the most important section of his essay is its claim for the different historicity governing a work of art. "It's important to respond to historical plays as art-works, not as selected documentary accumulations containing historico-political speculations evaluable largely in terms of a 'known,' historical and political reality." Against this latter view Griffiths proposes a Lukácsian conception of historical art, in which (Griffiths quotes Lukács on Shakespeare's histories) conflicts are stated in terms of "typical-human opposites" and characters represent "the most characteristic and central features of a social crisis" (7). By defining historical drama in these terms, Griffiths defends a literary and political practice in which the details of history become representative of social forces and character, the conventional province of humanist art, becomes the site of representative sociohistorical contradictions. In an implicit comment on Nairn's use of the word *remoteness* Griffiths accuses him of neglecting the "muscle, skin and sinew" of *Occupations,* that embodied, peopled dimension of complexity, contradiction, and paradox in which a work of historical drama *asks* rather than *asserts* (9).

In response to Nairn's critique of the play's pessimism—"One can certainly doubt whether any revolution will ever be regulated by love, without falling straight into the arms of Kabak"[33]—Griffiths is uncompromising in his refusal of easy or false answers. "As to whether the play is pessimistic and whether, if it is, it is therefore necessarily non-revolutionary, I would support Gramsci's assertion that 'It is a revolutionary duty to tell the truth,' even when there is little comfort to be had from it" (8).

Building the Party: *Absolute Beginners*

Occupations is the first of Griffiths's plays to explore the irreconcilable conflict between what he calls the "hard" and the "soft" dimensions of revolutionary struggle. This opposition—between the exercise of ruthless discipline and will and more humanistic concerns—exists, for Griffiths, within any revolutionary movement and within the individual revolutionary psyche. "If you look at your own history," he commented in a 1976 interview, "you see at certain points you're more convinced of the right of the 'hards'—Lenin, democratic centralism, the cell—at other points in your history, you're much more convinced about the rightness of the early Gramsci, or whoever. That is to say, that only human beings can create revolution, not machines."[34] Elsewhere he has contrasted "the toughness, the hardness, the honing down of personality until it becomes an instrument of your will" with that part of one's political sensibility "that actually grows alive when you're with people, and when you're interacting, recharging sensitivities through relationships."[35] The latter is the domain of Marx's early writings, in which he speaks of becoming more fully human; the former, as Gramsci comes to see in the failure of the workers' occupations, is the necessary domain of effective revolutionary struggle. If there's going to be revolutionary change in Britain, Griffiths suggested in 1973, "it's going to be led by people like Lenin, people prepared to sacrifice their private lives to public needs."[36]

This last remark was printed in a *Sunday Times* interview when Griffiths's play *The Party* was entering its final rehearsals at the National Theatre. But while *The Party* (considered in the next chapter) is organized around many of the same concerns as *Occupations* and continues Griffiths's struggle with the legacy of 1968, there is a sense in which the real sequel to Griffiths's breakthrough play—the fullest response to Gramsci's own migration between the poles of "soft" and "hard"—is *Absolute Beginners,* a television play broadcast in the spring of 1974. If one of the outcomes of the failed Turin uprisings was the creation of the Italian Communist Party as a party capable of directing future revolutionary energies, then Griffiths's later play about Lenin and the establishment of a centralized, disciplined revolutionary vanguard within the Russian Socialist Democratic Labor Party represents a natural continuation of *Occupations*.

Absolute Beginners (Griffiths appropriated the title of Colin MacInnes's 1959 novel) was written for the BBC's *Fall of Eagles* series. Composed of thirteen plays by different authors, *Fall of Eagles* traced the collapse of the Romanov, Hohenzollern, and Hapsburg dynasties, and it covered the period from the end of the nineteenth century until the final years of World War I and the dawn of revolution. Stuart Burge, who was brought in to produce the series after a number of its plays had already been commissioned, wanted to counterpoint the tendency toward romantic nostalgia in its presentation of dynastic history: "I needed a demonstration somewhere in the series of what was happening in the undergrowth, in the revolutionary world."[37] Griffiths jumped at the opportunity and produced a play that he has termed "as dense and as difficult as anything I've written."[38] The play (number 6 in the series) was broadcast on BBC1 on 19 April 1974 and was rebroadcast twice. As Edward Braun points out, *Fall of Eagles* was sold to fifty-four countries, making it one of the half-dozen most popular series ever made by the BBC and *Absolute Beginners* one of the most widely seen of Griffiths's plays.[39]

Commenting on the series and the place of his play in it, Griffiths has made clear the interventionist opportunity that this project provided and the chance that it offered for the deployment of a strategic counter-history:

> Here was the opportunity to write a play about a very serious event in socialist and revolutionary history pretty well unimpeded, with a fair amount of resource, and—most important—lodged in a series which was going to be contemptibly popular. . . . This was a series with one sugar-coating after another, and I sensed that to put a bitter pill inside that sugar-coating would actually get it swallowed, and tasted and used quite extensively.[40]

Against the sense of dynastic nostalgia and twilight grandeur evoked by the series title, *Absolute Beginners* dramatizes (with a decided lack of sentimentality) the events leading up to and including the Second Congress of the Russian Social Democratic Labor Party (RSDLP) in Brussels and London in 1903. It was at this congress that Lenin sought to act on his conviction, argued the previous year in *What Is to Be Done?* that the conditions of backwardness and repression in Russia mandated an elite, centralized party of professional revolutionaries who would wage revolution on behalf of the Russian workers. The Congress became deeply divided over Lenin's proposals concerning Party membership and the degree of autonomy allowed local organizations within the RSDLP (such as the Jewish Bund), and a split developed between Lenin and Julius Martov, one of the cofounders (with Lenin) of the revolutionary newspaper *Iskra*. After the departure of the Bund delegates and a group of others who had sided with Martov (and despite the opposition of others, such as the long-standing revolutionary Vera Zasulich), Lenin's motions prevailed, and he used the opportunity to elect his supporters to the Central Committee and the stripped-down editorial board of *Iskra*. Centralism and vanguard leadership would become guiding principles of the RSDLP and the later Communist Party of the Soviet Union, while the 1903 split in the émigré revolutionary community between the Bolsheviks and Mensheviks (as Lenin termed them) would have its own consequences for the success and shape of the revolution to come.

Refusing to oversimplify these remarkably complex historical issues and events, Griffiths dramatizes the pivotal encounters of the Second Congress with a careful delineation of factions, strategies, and counterstrategies. He shows the uneasy alliance between Lenin and Georges Plekhanov, one of the founders of the Russian Marxist movement; the maneuvering by which the Bund is eventually expelled from the Party; and the even greater maneuvering to isolate Martov and deny his supporters their voting majority. At the same time, much of the play takes place not in the Brussels and London meeting rooms but in more informal, domestic spaces: the study, bedroom, and kitchen of the London flat that Lenin shares with his wife, Nadezhda Krupskaya; Plekhanov's more elaborately furnished Geneva study. Like *Occupations*, with its hotel room setting, *Absolute Beginners* explores the connection between the public and private worlds and the nature of agency and choice. Recorded history stands behind Griffiths's play as a narrative of outcomes (and as the source of multiple levels of irony), but Griffiths's dramatic focus remains on the process by which this history is forged within the parameters of a present moment when its outcomes remain in doubt. If Lenin and the other delegates to the Second Congress are "absolute beginners," they are so in view of a history whose meanings and outcomes they seek to direct. From this perspective the private is an important dramatic territory, the arena in which political will is formed, tested against, and often challenged by the flesh-and-blood realities of everyday pleasures and relationships.

As one might expect, *Absolute Beginners* is dominated by the figure of Lenin (played by Patrick Stewart, a choice that underscored the play's link with *Occupations*). Lenin, the most formidable of Griffiths's "hards," is driven by ideas of discipline, will, organization, the ruthless suppression of softness, whatever forms it takes. Delivering a speech to the other members of the *Iskra* editorial board, he asserts: "It's we who are weak. We're . . . émigrés. Dilettante, intellectual. Unreliable. We must change that. We must begin with ourselves, if we are to create an organization of professional revolutionaries whose duty is to devote not only their free evenings but their whole lives to working for the Revolution."[41] What is so striking about Griffiths's Lenin is how much the discipline of this public persona carries over to the private self and how deliberately the effort to "begin with ourselves" entails an effort of self-hardening. Lenin is first shown in his study/bedroom doing push-ups, while his wife prepares a frugal breakfast in the next room. Although his relationship with Krupskaya is not without affection (he brushes wisps of hair off her forehead in a repeated gesture of tenderness and lies in bed with his head in her arms), it is characterized by restraint in its expression of feeling: he declines when she offers herself in bed ("Do you want me?" [91]) and forces himself to ask her to stop after she sings him a Russian song: "No more music. It's too . . . moving. (*Pause.*) It softens" (98). The contrast with Lenin's fellow revolutionaries is explicit. When Martov greets Lenin outside the British Museum with papers and pamphlets bulging from his pockets, his "untidy" appearance suggests a looseness of discipline. And the florid rhetoric of Trotsky's writing ("that radiant future in which man, strong and beautiful, will become master of the drifting stream of his history" [95]) is contrasted with the streamlined urgency of Lenin's letters. He tells Trotsky: "It's not the style that bothers me. I think it's too . . . soft" (96). For Lenin himself style is the man, the reflection of a necessary struggle for self-mastery.

As his speech to the *Iskra* board indicates, Lenin's vision of Party organization is dictated by the same commitment to discipline and single-minded commitment. The confrontation between this and its rival position, represented by Martov, comes to a head in several crucial public encounters. In a later meeting with the *Iskra* group Martov and Zasulich seek to introduce a petition for justice on behalf of a man who seeks to bring charges against an *Iskra* agent, N. E. Bauman. According to the charge, Bauman seduced the man's wife, got her pregnant, then slandered her after abandoning her. Seeking to reclaim her honor, she killed herself, and her husband has brought her suicide note. Lenin, noting that Bauman is one of the Party's most important agents, rules an inquiry detrimental to the Party's interests. Enraged, Martov argues for an ethics of revolutionary behavior that maintains a link between the private and the public: "Party morality is more than just loyalty to the party . . . it's the highest level of ethical consideration yet afforded the human species" (102). But Lenin dismisses this argument as a metaphysical irrelevancy and asserts the pragmatics of the revolutionary mission: "Another time, perhaps, we may speculate. Just now we're trying to make the revolution *possible*" (103).

This conflict—between human concerns and revolutionary expediency, between democracy and centralized authority—is played out in an even more crucial arena during the Second Congress itself. In the confrontation over Party membership between Martov and Lenin lie fundamentally different notions of revolutionary organization and authority. Martov argues for inclusiveness: "the more widespread the title of Party membership the better" (110). Lenin, advancing a view of the party as army and vanguard, demands "coherence, organization, discipline, above all, power, at the *centre* . . . Vote for Martov's proposal, and you create a tea party, not a party of revolutionaries ready to lead a class into battle" (111–12). The principles governing this new revolutionary ethos are demonstrated in the ruthlessness by which Lenin outmaneuvers Martov and centralizes the Party in terms of his single-minded revolutionary idea. Lenin locks Martov out of the caucus he holds with his supporters and forces him to collaborate in the expulsion of the Bund and other groups that resist the centralizing of Party control. Once his ascendancy is assured, he proposes to change the membership of the *Iskra* board in a way that eliminates Zasulich and others resistant to the Leninist line. As each of the purged delegates leaves (and others walk out in protest), Lenin's supporters hurl insults and derision. Having himself declared opposition to Lenin's image of the party, Trotsky is greeted by the same jeers. "Comrades," he announces before leaving, "we are privileged to be listening to the sound of Party debate— new style" (119).

Ethical and political choices are starkly delineated in *Absolute Beginners,* as they were in the 1903 Congress that proved so significant for Russian revolutionary history. But, if the choices are boldly drawn, their contexts and implications are explored by Griffiths with an aware-ness of complexity, paradox, and the genuinely conflicting claims of revolutionary and human need. Griffiths, for instance, underscores the realities of state power that mandate revolutionary discipline and con-trol. The play opens with a meeting in Tsarskoe Selo between Nicholas and Von Plehve, his minister of the interior known for the ruthlessness and cruelty of his antiterrorist tactics. Von Plehve speaks of all agita-tors—Jews, anarchists, revolutionaries—as "being the same size in a gun-sight" and assures the feckless Nicholas that his secret police are monitoring the activities of dissidents abroad. In his concern "to pro-mote discipline and the rule of law" and his warning to Nicholas that they will win the war against terrorism only if they "have the will to" and are willing to be coherent, ruthless, and intelligent, he stands as a clear counterpoint to Lenin in terms of tactics and style (84–85). The power, danger, and reach of the czarist state are evident in the elaborate security measures that Lenin and the other émigré revolutionaries must undertake when meeting. Griffiths offers a metaphor for this anti-dissi-dent terrorism: the final scene of the London Congress ends with Nicholas shooting crows, missing, and reloading.

Nevertheless, inevitable as a politics of ruthlessness and discipline may be, Griffiths maintains an awareness of the human sacrifices atten-dant upon the revolutionary tactics that Lenin has chosen. The purging of Zasulich from the new Party leadership represents the loss not only of an indomitable spirit but of the movement's very history (Krupskaya assures her earlier in the play that the revolution will "honor her" [92]). And the expulsion of the Jewish Bund (which bears an uncomfortable echo of Nicholas's anti-Semitism) marks the loss of a group that shares the same revolutionary dreams. Zasulich calls Lenin "Comrade Robes-pierre" (91), Martov calls him "Dictator of the Party" (115), and Lieber (head of the Bund delegation) calls him a "Napoleon who craves after personal power" (117). The accusations are delivered in bitterness, but they speak to disturbing features of Lenin's centralizing ruthlessness. Throughout the play Lenin's stance on party organization and revolu-tionary discipline carry with them a single-mindedness and disregard for opposition that look ahead uneasily to the dangers attendant upon governmental centralism and the problems of Leninism (and Stalinism) in postrevolutionary Russia. Plekhanov tells him: "I've always been fas-cinated by your hardness. It always seems so . . . unrelative" (107). Though Griffiths's Lenin argues persuasively for the importance of discipline, the history of twentieth-century totalitarianism yields disturbing echoes when he states to Krupskaya: "I say the Party must be built like a fist" (104).

At one point early in the play Lenin lies in bed consumed with fever, his body suffering from nerve inflammation. Delirious, he bucks and screams, and his speech is a disjointed expression of the turmoil inside:

> It's simple. See. I am the party. Right. Party organ . . . unh? (*He indicates his head.*) . . . Unh? Central Organ, Central Committee . . . (*He indicates a clenched fist.*) Right? Central Organ, Central Committee. (103)

The moment, which recalls the staging of Angelica's convulsive body in *Occupations*, is a metaphor both of the imminent convulsions within the RSDLP and of the struggle for self-control essential to Leninist discipline. But it also indicates an identification with the revolutionary Party that has disturbing implications for the future. Like the revolutionary Marat in Peter Weiss's *Marat/Sade*, who cries out in a similar moment of delirium, "Simonne / I am the revolution,"[42] Lenin demonstrates a muddying, on the borders of consciousness, of the lines between ego and idea. Despite Lenin's warning to Trotsky to "avoid personalities" (110), the scene establishes a disturbingly personal underside to Lenin's program of Party centralism, and it suggests further connections between this centralism and the autocracy of the czarist state. Zasulich seizes this analogy: "You're a dictator. . . . You're a bloody *Tsar*" (118). Against these rival portraits of absolutism, the play of meanings in Griffiths's title—*Absolute Beginners*—become particularly resonant.

In the moral "yes, but" of Griffiths's dramaturgy, of course, even this way of reading Lenin is not allowed to solidify into easy judgment. As the participants of the Second Congress prepare to disperse, they meet at Marx's grave in Highgate cemetery. Split into two groups, the delegates listen to Plekhanov dedicate "this great . . . unifying Congress" to Marx's memory. The irony of this dedication is not lost on Trotsky, who accuses Lenin of having destroyed the Party at the previous day's meeting. Lenin's response underscores the realities against which the Party must contend: "Yesterday the Party was *made,* not destroyed. What is more, history will prove it to be the only party—the only sort of party—capable of capturing state power" (120). Lenin points out that the czarist state is organizing its defense and that only a movement that considers the success of the revolution its supreme law is capable of defeating it: "Until you can say that, comrade, and mean it, history will have no use for you." Trotsky replies, "I suppose it will depend on who writes the history" (121). But, as Nicholas prepares to shoot crows (and as the Russian Revolution lies on the horizon), it is hard to escape the implacable logic of Lenin's analysis. As with *Occupations*, what makes *Absolute Beginners* such a complex exploration of revolutionary leadership is its awareness of all that is lost in this act of sacrifice, its understanding of the human price of victory. Gramsci/Kabak, Lenin/Martov—the competing voices of this paradox mark the dilemma at the heart of Griffiths's plays of revolution. In Trotsky's pamphlet, which he reads to Lenin earlier in the play, he alludes to "the new century, this gigantic newcomer" (95). *Absolute Beginners* dramatizes a pivotal moment in one of this century's most cataclysmic victories and the seeds of what will turn out to be one of its greatest human failures.

3

Politics and Sexuality

In the year between the Stables and RSC productions of *Occupations* Griffiths wrote or contributed to several plays for Fringe theater venues. One of these, *Lay By*, was a collaborative project with Howard Brenton, Brian Clark, David Hare, Stephen Poliakoff, Hugh Stoddart, and Snoo Wilson. As Griffiths recounts the project's origins, he joined these other writers for the Sunday afternoon of a weekend Royal Court writers' meeting that had begun the previous morning. "The dominant mood was that this was the worst weekend any of them had ever spent—the pubs aren't open, let's for Christ sake do something!"[1] The group trudged off into the closed Royal Court bar, and Hare expressed an interest in group writing. Griffiths had been reading an article in the *Sunday Times* about a controversial case involving a hitchhiker and charges of rape and indecent assault, and the others were interested. Brenton describes the process of composition: "The Court rented us a rehearsal room, and we had great rolls of wallpaper, and big children's crayons and the seven of us crawled around on the floor, scribbling a continuous text, and you looked down and saw the latest line, and there'd be an argument about the next line."[2]

After initially being turned down by the Royal Court, *Lay By* opened on 24 August 1971 at the Traverse Theatre Club during that summer's Edinburgh Festival, in a production mounted by Hare, Brenton, and Wilson's Portable Theatre Company. It subsequently played at the Royal Court (in a Sundays-only production) and at Marowitz's Open Space Theatre. But although, according to Hare, Griffiths's voice had been the loudest during the play's group composition,[3] the subordination of this voice in the process of collaboration keeps *Lay By* (like *Deeds*, Griffiths's 1978 collaboration with Brenton, Hare, and Ken Campbell) on the margins of his career.[4] Much more indicative of Griffiths's dramatic preoccupations at this time are *Apricots* and *Thermidor*, two short plays "written for particular spaces" within the flourishing culture of the Fringe.[5] *Apricots* received its first production on 28 June 1971 at the Basement Theatre in London, and the two plays were produced together at the Edinburgh Festival that August by John McGrath's newly formed 7:84 Theatre Company (opening at the converted Cranston Street Church Hall the night after *Lay By*, the two plays were mounted as a late-night show following 7:84's inaugural production, McGrath's *Trees in the Wind*).[6] Although *Apricots* and *Thermidor* are often overlooked in discussions of Griffiths's career, they are powerfully distilled dramatic explorations; together they clarify a tension between the sexual and the political that recurs in *The Party* and elsewhere in Griffiths's plays and films.

Scenes from a Marriage: *Apricots*

Called "a tiny sensation" by its first (and probably only) theater critic,[7] *Apricots* is a stripped-down portrait of a marriage in its terminal stage. The play (only eight pages in its printed version) falls into three scenes that feature the ritualistic gestures and countergestures—the endgame moves—of Sam and Anna as they seek to negotiate what little territory remains in their relationship. *Apricots* opens with the couple in their garden in late evening, after Anna has put the baby to sleep. The two begin talking about their sexual relationships with others in what seems to be the aftermath of a party earlier that evening. Sam asks Anna, "Did you see them?"

> ANNA: I saw you.
> SAM: Big.
> ANNA: All right.
> SAM: I never saw areolae that brown.
> ANNA: All right.[8]

Like the play itself, this exchange is elliptical and disarming. The attention is on looking—Anna watching Sam watching the unnamed woman—and its attendant voyeurism and detachment. As the scene continues, this precise geometry of watching is expanded to include a "he" (Anna's lover and possibly the husband of the woman in question).

To the suggestion that "he" must mind Sam's visual scrutiny of the breasts, Anna states: "He loves watching you watching her. He likes your eyes on her breasts. It saves him having you" (2). As in the plays of Harold Pinter, whose influences are marked throughout *Apricots* (among other things, in the skillful patterning of pauses and silences that shape the play's dialogue),[9] the act of looking in this play is a source of both power and vulnerability, an engulfing of the other in a sexualizing gaze and a surrender of self under the gaze of another.

Power may reside in the look, but, as Sam's opening lines make clear, the more immediate source of power in this exchange is language and its ability to displace sexuality and restage eroticism within a surrogate realm. Sam asks Anna "What's he like?" and, when Anna expresses bewilderment, protests: "You *know* what I mean. Every sodding time we have to go through this boring ritual of rendering down the euphemism. (*Pause; very deliberate.*) Does. He. Fuck. Well?" Anna replies "Yes. Very." Unable to rattle her, and clearly stung by her cool answer, Sam pursues a different verbal tack, reminiscing about her body when she (and their relationship) were younger: "I remember you when you had clean, firm, unpracticed breasts. So new. [. . .] Fucking you then was like running a finger over a green apple. I remember you when your cunt smelt of apricots" (2). Intense and evocative (extravagantly so), the imagery signals the first move in a struggle to assert verbal control over the past, to use memory as a tool for controlling relationships in the present.[10] It is important to recognize the aggression in such a move— Sam seeks to mark Anna's body as old and used by contrasting it to an almost hyperrealistically pristine recollected body—but it is also important to hear the loss and yearning in the very intensity of its verbal excess. Like Ruth in Pinter's play *The Homecoming*, Anna challenges this attempt at verbal control by asserting her body's disquieting actuality: Ruth silences the room by speaking of her underwear "moving," while Anna orders Sam in front of her. He kneels and pushes his head up her skirt "until his lips meet her crotch." "I like you best of all on your knees," she taunts him, underscoring the helplessness and momentary silence to which she has reduced him (3).

The second scene, which takes place later in the evening, extends the play's exploration of the vicariousness and displacement that governs their relationship. The scene opens with Sam mounting Anna from behind on the garden patio; both are fully dressed, and their sex is simulated, though it "feels real" (3). This act of simulation is compounded by displacement, for Anna takes Sam through an act of imagined sex with "Margaret." Sam is aroused by this fantasy, and even Anna seems to respond to the imagined scenario. But the nonactuality of their lovemaking remains obvious beneath the intensifying language of pleasure, and the two disengage. When Anna leaves to get tea for the two of them, Sam takes out a tape recorder and replays the exchange while masturbating. Masturbating to a tape of a pretend role-play: sexual climax is possible only through a triple displacement, and its intensity only underscores the profound estrangement that this sexual ritual is designed to negotiate. Anna enters and watches him ejaculate, and when he is done the two stand and look at each other in silence. "That was nice," Anna states in a parody of postcoital intimacy (5).

The final scene of *Apricots* represents a moment of retrospect—or, as Anna's phrase bleakly suggests, "Extreme Unction," the sacrament of the dead—over this marriage that has, like the evening setting, descended into cold and darkness. Sam speaks of their earlier relationship as something "holy" or "sacramental" (6). Anna rejects this characterization, and in the play's longest speech offers her own countermemory of their early lovemaking. She remembers her underwear, appropriating in her description the fruit imagery that Sam had previously evoked ("I remember choosing my underwear. Apricot knickers; apple green slip and bra" [7]). Her memory dramatically reverses the linguistic voyeurism governing Sam's earlier recollections. Here it is she who looks and Sam who becomes the object of sexual curiosity: "I remember thinking I wonder what his . . . thing's like. I wonder if it's big, fat, small, thin, light, dark, sallow, hot, cool, red, white." But her curiosity remained unsatisfied, because he undressed in the dark, kept his penis in a condom, and showed no willingness to explore her body with the sensuousness she demonstrated in preparing it for him. "I was, to you, a face and a hole. That's all. I don't think I've ever known such absolute fear in anyone. And now you have the . . . nerve to call it holy."

Having accused him of a fear of sexuality and having deconstructed the surrogate verbal world in which he has sublimated the arena of actual human contact, Anna asks Sam to fuck her. To his reply that he can't, she elaborates:

> Yes. You can. You will. I want you to fuck me hard and strong and long. I want you to make my cunt sing with it. Scream with it. I want you to get in there, all of you, I want the whole of you in there, prick and balls and body and mind and senses and conscience and remorse and hope. Everything. I want it *all in there.* (7)

Her lines are poignant in their eruption of repressed longing but also exultant in their celebration of the female body's power (a power that is as much maternal here as sexual). They express the desire for intimacy and the ecstasy of union, even as their dream of incorporating another is tinged with masochism and the fantasy of devouring. For Sam, who has indulged the fantasy of engulfment in the Margaret dialogue (and who has already experienced a version of capitulation under Anna's skirt), the prospect of actual sexuality is fraught with insupportable risk. He declines her request: "I can't. I can't." "You won't. You mean," she insists (7). Apricots, apples—in this failed Garden of Eden Anna's body stands as the ultimate forbidden fruit.

In the end the ease with which the two lapse into the mundane rituals of clearing the table suggests the stasis at the heart of their relationship, the gulf that they can't—or won't—manage to bridge. Anna, at least, senses the depth of this gulf. Sam bends to kiss her good night, but she doesn't respond. When her husband has left, she puts her hand between her legs, rubs it there, then smells her fingers. *Apricots* ends with the sense of loss and regret that has characterized it throughout, as its possibility of "communion" (a word that resonates in the play's final scene) fades like the evening light.

Apricots is uncompromising in its exploration of frustrated, even broken, sexuality but also suffused with a deep sense of longing and regret. As a portrait of voyeurism and displacement, it tracks the channels by which sexual desire gradually surrenders its primary object. The play's language—aching in its sensory evocation of sight, touch, taste, and smell—is among the most lyrical Griffiths has written, though its very evocativeness is evidence of how successfully the verbal realm has taken the place of actual human contact. Language offers a vision of intensity and aliveness, of bodies singing in contact, but the play itself dramatizes the ritualized dance of estrangement and mutual aloneness.

The Grammar of Subjectivity: *Thermidor*

If *Apricots* uses the cooling of evening into night as a metaphor for the terminal coldness that has overcome the marriage at its center, *Thermidor* takes its title from the eleventh month of the French Revolutionary calendar. Literally "having to do with heat," Thermidor extended from mid-July to mid-August, the hottest time of the summer. The connotations are fitting, for Griffiths's play is set in a time of heat, the period of

Stalinist purges in the 1930s. Like Arthur Miller's *The Crucible, Thermidor* is a study of institutional persecution and what is learned about the individual under the pressure of political interrogation and the dehumanizing demands of political orthodoxy.

In its treatment of the purges *Thermidor* exemplifies the stand against Stalinism that has always formed an essential part of Griffiths's oppositional politics. "The real enemy of socialism," he has commented, "is Stalinism, and it has to be seen as that."[11] And elsewhere: "A lot of my work is about Stalinism because I think that is a major responsibility for the Left. It has to answer the questions raised by its own history."[12] Griffiths's concern with Stalinism links a play like *Thermidor* with the New Left of the late 1950s, which constituted itself through the repudiation of Stalinism and its legacy of dehumanization. But the disavowal of Stalinism remained one of the constituting acts of the noncommunist Left well into the 1970s. As a play like *Thermidor* reminds us, the revolutionary movements of Western Europe and the United States in 1968 were matched by the Prague Spring in Czechoslovakia, where the popular attempt to liberalize a repressive system was crushed (in a reenactment of Hungary in 1956) by Soviet tanks. Griffiths's challenge, in view of the continuing Stalinist problem, is to condemn Stalinism without discrediting socialism—to criticize the excesses to which the Left is vulnerable without allying himself with reactionary critiques of the socialist project (to this end it is significant that Anya, the persecuted protagonist of *Thermidor*, maintains her faith in the Party whatever excesses it has fallen prey to).

The importance of this critique in Griffiths's political thinking in the early 1970s is indicated by a project that the playwright undertook at this time. In the year before *Occupations* was moved to London, Griffiths had begun research on a play about the March 1921 Kronstadt mutiny, the most significant of a number of internal uprisings against Soviet rule in Russia after the Civil War. Sailors at the Kronstadt naval base, whose support had been crucial to the success of the Bolshevik Revolution, formed a Revolutionary Committee in support of worker strikes and demonstrations. They demanded economic reforms, the end of Communist Party dictatorship, and the establishment of political freedoms and civil rights. Trotsky, who had called the sailors "the flowers of the revolution," led a force that crushed the rebellion. Despite its brutal suppression, the uprising (and others like it) led the Communist Party to adopt a program of economic liberalism (the New Economic Policy). "They were marvelous, heroic figures," Griffiths commented in 1979, when he was still hoping to return to the project.[13] In 1972 he had compiled fourteen months' research on the uprising, and the project was aborted only when the Soviet embassy refused him a visa that would have enabled him to complete his research. Over the years Griffiths has contemplated a number of projects that he ended up not pursuing. But Kronstadt is clearly one of Griffiths's great unwritten projects, as his numerous references to it in later years suggests. Taking place only six months after the Turin occupations, whose events it echoes in significant ways, the Kronstadt mutiny would have made a powerful companion play to *Occupations,* and it would have underscored—like *Thermidor*—the intimate connection in Griffiths's political thinking between a critique of capitalist and Stalinist forms of oppression.

Thermidor takes place in an office in the People's Commissariat of Internal Affairs (NKVD) Headquarters in Moscow in late summer 1937; its set includes a cluttered desk, a few tables and chairs, and a cheap carpet on the floor, and a large photograph of Stalin and a map of the USSR are displayed prominently on the wall. The play's action involves the preliminary questioning of Anya Pakhanova, a former history teacher who now cleans offices, by Gennadi Yukhov, an NKVD investigator. Anya has recently been expelled from the Communist Party for "insufficient vigilance" in relation to an individual accused of being in the pay of an imperialist agent, and she is now being questioned (among other things) about her connections with an alleged Trotskyist named Volsky. As Yukhov asks about her past and her former political associations, Anya calmly insists upon the integrity of her actions at the time, refusing to acknowledge (in an act of "disarming," as the party calls it)[14] the retroactive discrediting of her actions and their contexts. Clearly more in command of theoretical arguments than her questioner (she even corrects him at one point), Anya defends, for instance, the change in her opinions concerning rapid industrialization between 1923 and 1928, refusing the implication that she allowed herself to fall into historical contradiction. To Yukhov's accusation that she associated with "the Trotskyist Volsky," she insists that, despite the party's retroactive charges against him, she never knew him as a Trotskyist (18).

On the public stage of history Stalin's purges were presented to the East and West alike as an elaborate form of theater, with kangaroo trials their most public manifestation. *Thermidor,* by contrast, is an intimate piece, conducted within the interrelational space between two people. Paraphrasing Griffiths in interview, Catherine Itzin writes: "Writing the play was like going inside Ginsberg's 'whirlwind' and discovering an anti-dramatic moment that would illustrate the terrible, inexcusable 'mistakes' that were being made. Hence the quiet, 'human' tone of the interrogation, the concern with old friendships and the welfare of children."[15] In the play's momentary but sharp peripeteia Anya reminds Yukhov that, as a boy of thirteen, he had chaired a session at the All-Moscow League of Youth Conference that she also attended and that they had tea afterward and talked. For a moment, at least, this disclosure shifts their interrogation into a personal realm, in which Yukhov shares an embarrassed relationship with the woman across from him: "You've changed." "So have you. You wear long trousers now." "Your hair's . . . darker." "Yes. It was summer. It bleaches on top, that's all" (18).

In the French Revolution the Thermidorean Reaction (1794–95) was the period following the execution of Robespierre and his followers, when the Convention sought to regain popularity by abolishing the Terror. Suspects were released from prison, the Revolutionary Tribunal was dissolved, and a constitution was drawn up protecting individuals against political retaliation. Griffiths's *Thermidor* has its own thawing in the moment of humanity shared by its two characters, though this opening—like that of the Prague Spring—proves evanescent. The personal, intensely and poignantly realized in the exchange between Yukhov and Anna, is elevated to a political and ethical imperative in the play's central confrontation, an exchange that lays out exactly what is at stake in the play's struggle over the past and how it is understood. In response to Yukhov's repeated insistence that, since Volsky is a convicted Trotskyist, "objectively, you knew the Trotskyist Volsky," Anna asserts:

> There is no power in the world that can give you the right to *tell me what I know*. The I is *me*, comrade. Me. *I know* means all those things I have seen and smelt and tasted and touched and held, all those people I've talked to and waited for, married, slept with, given birth to; all those ideals I have fought for and believed in. (*Pause. Strong now.*) And *I* am the *only* subject of *know*. (20)

Faced with the unexpected information that charges have been filed against her and that she faces an uncertain fate ("What will happen to my children?" [19]), Anya asserts the inviolability of individual experience and the personalized grammar of subjectivity. She claims the truth of the *I* and its experiential world as something radically incommensurate with the communal abstraction of official "truth." Noting his lack of interest in "philosophical speculation" (and dismissing the personal intimacy that the two of them had momentarily shared), Yukhov denies the distinction on which she has insisted: "No matter. In time you will come to realize that for most purposes there is very little difference between 'subjective' and 'objective.'" Anya protests: "You cannot treat people this way in a soviet institution." With more than a touch of menace, he makes explicit the objectification that represents the corollary of Stalinist objectivity: "Enemies . . . are no longer people" (20).

As companion pieces, *Apricots* and *Thermidor* exist in a relationship of counterpoint, dialogue, and mutual reflection. Juxtaposed as they were meant to be (in the 7:84 productions they were performed by the same actors and shared the same director), the two plays demonstrate a number of shared preoccupations: the conflict of subjective experience and objectification, whether in the sexual or the political realm; the integrity of memory; and the importance of language as a tool for constructing (or eclipsing) the real. Both plays explore the breakdown of relationship, and each is haunted by a vision of spontaneous relationship and lost vitality. In the closing moments of *Thermidor* Anya asks Yukhov: "What has happened to you? You used not to be so . . . inert. I can remember you, you know, that July day. You were so alive. [. . .] What has happened? What has happened to us?" (2). These questions, rooted in the anguish of lost relationship, could be asked by Anna, her double with a similar name in the earlier play. In both plays the rituals of power and the game of missed connection serve to measure the distance from a natural mutuality, in which the gulf between *I* and *we* would no longer loom so wide.

Finally, *Apricots* and *Thermidor* establish a connection between the sexual and the political essential to Griffiths's writing, especially in the 1970s. In their counterpoint the plays suggest the interpenetration, or cross-marking, of these two realms. Anya's speech on subjectivity in *Thermidor* illuminates the politics of sexual objectification in *Apricots*, while Sam's simulated act of fucking his wife from the rear contributes a disturbingly sexual dimension to Yukhov's interrogation of Anya. The politics of sexuality, the sexuality of politics—as we shall see, these two areas of experience exist throughout Griffiths's plays and films in uneasy, even problematic, relation to each other.

National Spaces: *The Party*

Griffiths wrote a number of other short plays and sketches during the years 1969–72 that were clearly intended for the "particular spaces" of the London Fringe; one of these, a play called *Poems*, was produced in a lunchtime double bill with a Tennessee Williams play about D. H. Lawrence at the Basement Theatre in March 1971. In spring 1973 Griffiths directed *Gun*, a dramatic fragment, at the Pool Theatre, Edinburgh.[16] But, like the culture of the early 1970s Fringe itself, Griffiths's experience of writing for such venues was, it turned out, short-lived. "It had never been my desire to work in a cellar talking to twenty seven people about things you believed in. I'd always thought in terms of broad communication across the classes."[17] The very notion of a "Fringe," with its elitist tendencies and its self-marginalization, proved problematic to a writer whose work as BBC education officer (and whose own emerging practice) had led to a broader understanding of cultural relations and opportunities. Griffiths would continue to make use of nonmainstream theatrical venues to broaden and often redirect the exposure of his plays: the 7:84 production of *Occupations* and the touring productions that took *Oi for England* to nontheatrical community venues in London and northern England reflect this process of strategic repositioning. But more characteristic of Griffiths's interventionist practice, from his earliest attempts to write for television through his work for the BBC and Hollywood, is the "strategic penetration" of existing cultural institutions.

The possibility of more explicitly interventionist work in the theater offered itself to Griffiths in the aftermath of *Occupations'* success at the Stables Theatre. Although the RSC ended up acquiring the play, Griffiths was initially contacted concerning *Occupations* by Kenneth Tynan, literary manager for the National Theatre. Tynan was unsuccessful in persuading the National Theatre to do the play but expressed interest in commissioning a different play. The play Griffiths sent him was *The Party*, which he wrote in the summer of 1972 and revised six months later. Tynan telegrammed Griffiths from Ceylon with the news that the National planned to do the play, and Griffiths was contacted by its director Sir Laurence Olivier.[18] *The Party* opened at the National (then housed at the Old Vic) on 20 December 1973, with Olivier himself playing the Glaswegian Trotskyite John Tagg in what was billed as his final performance on the National stage and would turn out to be his last performance on any stage. In the fall of 1974 a revised version of the play was taken on a tour of universities in a production directed by David Hare.

Griffiths was aware of the opportunities presented by the National Theatre as venue: "I was developing a political notion of appropriating these so-called national spaces for a viewpoint and a politics quite different from the ones that habitually get expressed there."[19] As its name suggested, the National Theatre was a particularly resonant site for such intervention; since its founding—and particularly now, as it prepared to move to its present South Bank home (this complex would open in 1976)—the National had been the focus of intense debates on the nature and purpose of a "national" theater.[20] In the months after *The Party*'s run at the National, Griffiths elaborated his views on the theater (and national institutions as a whole) in an exchange with Peter Hall, who had replaced Olivier as director of the National Theatre. Hall invited Griffiths to submit another play to the National; when Griffiths asserted that his next play would be "unmountable" there, Hall responded that the National Theatre was open to all opinions, whether controversial or otherwise: "If you say I won't do it, you are turning me into the sort of theatre that you want to turn me into and you're not giving me the chance to be anything else."[21] In a letter to *Plays and Players* Griffiths clarified his argument, which had to do with "the nature of *national institutions*, as far as I understand them. Peter talks as though there is *no* remit whatsoever, as though it is possible to create a theatre *outside* the traditional structures of power and value of the society that brought it into being in the first place."[22] As a national institution, the National cannot escape its positioning within such structures, nor can it deny the hegemonic pressures with which the ruling echelon seeks to control its channels of cultural power, particularly during times (like the present) of social crisis. The National, Griffiths maintained, can either help or hinder the forces that seek to transform Britain's capitalist system; the position it occupies in relation to these conflicts can never be one of political disinterestedness.

It is this hegemonic role within a network of national cultural institutions that makes the National Theatre (and other cultural institutions like the Royal Shakespeare Company and the BBC) such attractive targets for Griffiths's "strategic penetration." "Talking to a National Theatre audience about things that interested me seemed to me quite a good ruse."[23] But Griffiths also understood the dilemmas posed by such appropriation, the contradictions inherent in the mainstreaming of a socialist cultural practice. In addition to the other questions it sets into play, *The Party* addresses the issue of radical art in a capitalist system and the phenomenon of Herbert Marcuse's "repressive tolerance,"[24] by which this system appropriates its counterforces within strictly limited bounds. On a more personal level *The Party* explores the psychological and political conflicts facing the socialist artist within this system, the paradoxical position of a cultural revolutionary making a living in a capitalist world. In early 1972 Griffiths had quit his job with the BBC to pursue a career as a writer, and by late 1973—with *Occupations* behind him and *The Party, All Good Men,* and *Absolute Beginners* on the horizon—he was establishing himself as a public figure on the British cultural landscape. The contradictions facing the socialist artist, which would concern Griffiths throughout his career, asserted themselves at this point with particular immediacy.

The Party, another of Griffiths's plays about 1968 and its failures, is set in London during the evening of 10–11 May, the night of student clashes with police outside the Sorbonne. At the same time, while the urgency and violence of the Paris disturbances is evoked onstage, Griffiths subjects these events to a series of distancing strategies that keep them curiously remote, technologically mediated. The play's prologue—which opens with projected pictures of Marx, Lenin, and Trotsky and features a stand-up Groucho Marx who reads and jokes about passages written by the pictured theorists—concludes with the projection of revolutionary slogans ("*Je Suis Marxiste, Tendance Groucho*"), photographs, and film of the student demonstrations.[25] As the play shifts to living room naturalism, such projections continue to punctuate the action, silhouetting the action of the present against an almost surreal backdrop of cinematic and televisual images.[26] Within the action itself characters follow the events in France on television, as the story jockeys with other items on the nine o'clock news ("The new 50 penny piece was announced today" [19]) and the events themselves are narrated in breathless newscaster tones. Griffiths's mediated evocation of the events of the Paris May call attention to contemporary history as something processed and received through the framing devices of information technology; as elsewhere in Griffiths's work, such evocations constitute a reflexive meditation on representational media and their multiple, often conflicting, channels of address. By presenting the French insurrection in this way, Griffiths shifts attention from the historical events to the process of watching that constitutes both an inescapable component of the historical act (the audience watches characters watching events at a five and a half year remove from the events in question) and a particular condition of British response to the revolutionary eruption across the Channel. In the words of one of the play's reviewers Griffiths's British are the world's "political voyeurs."[27]

As this remark suggests, Griffiths's interests in *The Party* are less with the revolutionary situation in France than with the disorganized and ultimately ineffectual response of the British Left to this situation. In a real sense Britain never had its May 1968. Pete Gowan, a Trotskyite student leader at Birmingham University, remembers: "As we listened to the news from Paris, we were aware that what was going on there was worlds away from the everyday realities of the British student movement."[28] Student activism at British universities began in 1967 and reached a peak in the spring and summer of 1968. But, while sit-ins and even more militant occupations at schools like the London School of Economics (LSE) brought about liberal reforms at many British universities, this activism never evolved into a more revolutionary challenge to the British establishment. As one writer put it, "There were results, to be sure, but in a bitter, classical, British pattern they tended to strengthen the system rather than assist its destruction."[29] Nor did the British working class show much willingness to participate within a revolutionary alliance: only days before the events of the French May erupted in Paris, London dock workers, traditionally among the most militant members of the British working class, marched with meat porters in support of Enoch Powell's speech against black immigration.[30]

Griffiths has described the genesis of *The Party* in terms that suggest his awareness of political ineffectuality on the part of the British Left: "[The play] started with the experience of the Friday night meetings at Tony Garnett's where sixty or seventy people would cram into a room, and the whole sense, the aching need . . . to do more, to get it right, to be correct, to read the situation as a first step toward changing it utterly. . . . And with it all, the faint sense of, not silliness exactly, but lack of candor that people proffered."[31] *The Party* is set in the London living room of Joe Shawcross, a television producer of working-class background. This setting embodies the tensions and conflicts that characterize Shawcross as a radical figure within the media establishment. Wall pictures of Lenin and Trotsky and a racy pop print (all of which are lit up in the stage darkness before revealing their place in the living room) are hung in the midst of expensive, though tentative, furnishings. Griffiths specifies "purpose narrowly triumphing over comfort; of rich ease scored by persisting puritan principle" (18). As in the second act of *Sam, Sam,* the setting reflects a personality profoundly at war with its own bourgeois identity. Explaining the boorish behavior of the writer Malcolm Sloman, who has promised to write a television play for his "Play of the Month" program, Shawcross described himself as well: "He . . . can't bear the

thought of himself as . . . successful . . . in a society he longs to destroy"
(15). The keynote of his character is self-contempt, a disgust directed at
his own complicity with a bourgeois political order. Sam II's antagonism was directed at a social class he would never really belong to;
Shawcross's antipathy is toward the markings of that class within himself. "We've got upper second souls," he tells his ex-wife, Kara Massingham (46). As part of his cycle of contempt, his very opposition to this
class-based capitalist system causes boredom and disgust, as if this, too,
were a kind of fashionable class-bound game. Sick of opinions and
debates, he longs for revolutionary affirmation: as he tells Sloman, "I
just once . . . want to say yes to . . . something" (68).

In ways that clearly echo *Sam, Sam* Shawcross's conflict over his
own "embourgeoisement" (57) extends into his relationships with his
brother. Eddie Shawcross, down from Manchester, has asked him for a
loan to establish his own shirt-making business, and Shawcross must
confront the dilemma of whether he should support his brother in setting up a capitalist enterprise (he eventually does). Shawcross's relationship with his wife, Angie (and, we infer, with Kara when he was
married to her), is even more deeply conditioned by the producer's self-
loathing and sense of political impotency. As elsewhere in Griffiths's
plays, problems of political efficacy are mirrored in the sexual realm,
and Shawcross's sexual interactions with Angie are as inhibited and dissatisfying as those in *Sam, Sam* and *Apricots*. The two engage in "a sort
of abstracted fuck ballet" of failed sex (12), and after Angie leaves (to
spend the night with a lover, it turns out), Joe tries masturbating. As
film of the Paris barricades and photos of the French student leaders are
projected on the set, the counterpoint between saying yes in the arena of
political action and political/sexual ineffectuality is brutally (even
somewhat blatantly) underscored.

The Party—one of Griffiths's compressed, multiply referential titles
that bear within themselves clusters of issues and contradictions—captures the disjunction between the political organization necessary for
coordinated revolutionary action and a Left whose theoretical debates
take place in upper-class living rooms complete with drinks and food
cart. "We do this like we do everything else," Shawcross tells Kara: "It's
a game. It's an intellectual pursuit" (45–46). On the urging of John Tagg,
a Glaswegian Trotskyite from the Revolutionary Socialist Party, Shawcross has called a meeting to open a dialogue on the Left; the need, he
tells the gathering, is for theory, a socialist analysis of the situation that
would provide the British Left with "a united and coherent focus for its

efforts" (33). In addition to Shawcross and Sloman, the group's composition reflects the Left's fragmented composition: several students from
the London School of Economics; "Grease" Ball, a north London anarchist doing work in street theater; Louis Preece, an American black
activist; Jeremy Hayes, a literary agent who is starting a left-wing journal; and Kara, who helps run it. Invited to address the group are
Andrew Ford, from the LSE and the *New Left Review*, and Tagg, who
arrives late. Even before the speeches begin, however, the group is
divided on procedure, and, after Ford has given his speech on terminology and the history of Marxism, those listening reveal the micropolitical
disagreements that have always plagued the Left and kept it internally
divided. Hayes wants to know why Ford excluded students as a sub-
class, while Louis stresses the importance of blacks to the contemporary
struggle. Kara asks about women, and Grease dismisses the need for
theory altogether: "What are we going to *do?*" (40). As Griffiths notes
parenthetically, "The lack of direction is showing" (41).

The intellectual and theatrical center of *The Party* lies in the two
speeches delivered at the end of the play's first act. Holding the stage for
ten to fifteen minutes apiece, these speeches represent a daring appropriation of the "national" theater for dialectical debate. With Olivier
particularly, Griffiths's writing provided the opportunity for a commanding verbal and intellectual performance, and it is clear that Griffiths shaped Tagg's extended verbal excursions to demonstrate the
powerful seductions of theoretical argument. Olivier, for his part, was
attracted to the role largely because of the virtuoso possibilities in this
rhetorical performance: "I am grateful to Trevor Griffiths for giving me
such an *animal* to fight with night after night."[32] The dissolving of stage
space into a less naturalistically situated rhetorical space is intensified in
Tagg's speech, which is staged with the speaker on a stool in the center
of the room, lit more brightly than the surrounding room. Throughout
his speech the red alarm signal that Shawcross has left in the back yard
flashes across the set. When the speech is over the film screen / rear wall
"bursts into life" with the scene of confrontation around the Sorbonne
(153), as if Tagg/Olivier's speech has momentarily elided the distance
between Paris and London.

The two speakers deliver antithetical analyses of contemporary
political configurations and the potential for revolutionary action.
Arguing that twentieth-century transformations in capitalism leave
Marx's nineteenth-century analysis behind, Ford argues that the European proletariat no longer constitutes the leading subversive force

within capitalism that Marx posited. Ford suggests that the center of revolutionary struggle has shifted to the Third World, with its national liberation movements in colonial enclaves: "The 'weak link' in the capitalist chain is now at the periphery, and it is there, if anywhere, that the chain will be induced to snap" (39). The obligation now facing the Left in the former metropolitan centers is to assist these revolutionaries in causing the chain to snap.

Tagg responds to this speech by attacking its intellectuality, a recourse to theory (he claims) grounded in the intellectual's ineffectuality and distance from the actual experience of working-class life: "You see the difficulties and you see the complexities and contradictions, and you settle for those as a sort of game you can play with each other. Finally, you learn to enjoy your pain; to need it, so that you have nothing to offer your bourgeois peers but a sort of moral exhaustion." No revolutionary movement, he claims, that does not establish itself in the working class is worth serious attention. For theory to be useful to such a struggle, it must relinquish its arbitrariness and abstraction: "Theory is felt, in the veins, in the muscles, in the sweat on your forehead. In that sense, it's moral . . . and binding" (49). The failure of the working class, Tagg argues, derives from the failure of its leadership, which has sought to dampen genuine revolutionary potential. Tagg, another of Griffiths's "hards," urges the formation of a genuinely revolutionary leadership based on discipline and organization. If intellectuals are to play any role in this historic revolutionary opportunity, they must surrender their position of comfort and prestige within the system of capitalist relations: "The intellectual's problem is not vision, it's commitment. You enjoy biting the hand that feeds you, but you'll never bite it off" (53). Those "brave and foolish youths" in Paris will offer their heads to the baton, but this will not stop them from graduating and assuming places in the centers of ruling-class power and privilege.

In its vision of commitment and involvement and its grounding in Tagg's own working-class background, Tagg's speech asserts a powerful moral authority in *The Party*. But no position is allowed to dominate this play of voices, and no position escapes Griffiths's dialectical qualifications. Rejecting his "working-class crap" as sentimental, Kara refers to him as "a brutal shite underneath with a fist where his mind used to be" (46). And when we next see Tagg (after the meeting has broken up) he is on the phone trying to secure news from Paris. To Joe's surprise Tagg's section there has refused to fight in support of the students, who lack revolutionary perspective (Tagg asserts) and whose undirected revolt will lead to "a massive defeat for the revolutionary spirit" (60). A revolutionary faction cannot afford to be sentimental, he tells Joe; those who promote the uprising are, in the objective sense, "enemies of the working-class revolution in France" (59). Paradoxically, Tagg's revolutionary commitment leads him to the sidelines when the form of political contestation does not fit his objective blueprint. His prediction concerning de Gaulle's successful countermove may turn out to be accurate, but, when support like his is withheld, such predictions risk a certain self-fulfillment. As with Kabak, pragmatism and hardness act upon the revolutionary consciousness in sometimes problematic ways, and there is a decided irony in his quotation from Trotsky: "We only die when we fail to take root in others" (61).

Griffiths (we have seen) has suggested that nearly every character in *The Party* represents some facet of himself, but this only underscores the play's own dramaturgy, through which each voice is allowed authority in its dialectical confrontations with other voices. Of all the characters in *The Party*, the most discordant is Sloman, the drunken writer whose act of hurling a bottle through the window is only one of a number of attempts to deflate the revolutionary pretensions of those around him. Sloman is driven by anger and by an intensified version of the self-loathing that animates Shawcross, but his defiant refusal of sociability cannot completely hide his disappointed revolutionary vision. Stumbling, drunk, "in pain," it is Sloman who most powerfully articulates the "real dream" that guides these and all of Griffiths's flawed revolutionaries, that lyrical voice of socialist aspiration that always (in Griffiths's plays) has a certain elegiac melancholy to it. Quoting Trotsky's *Optimism and Pessimism*, he says: "As long as I breathe I shall fight for the future, that . . . radiant future, in which man, strong and beautiful, will become master of the drifting stream of his own history" (43). And it is Sloman who, the next morning, offers the most sustained critique of Tagg's speech. With an anarchist's faith in the spontaneous emergence of revolutionary will, Sloman suggests to Shawcross that the germ for revolutionary action lies within people and that when masses of such people decide to take on the state they will do so without the voice of Trotsky or anyone else: "They'll be too busy 'practicing the revolution.' And the class will throw up its own leaders and its own structures of leadership and responsibility" (71).

Finally, it is Sloman who serves as the focal point for the play's meditation on its own interventionist strategy, the dilemma it faces as a socialist artifact within a capitalist system. In one of the play's pointedly self-referential moments Ford alludes to "the machinery of what Marcuse calls the 'repressive tolerance' of neocapitalist societies, of which, if I may say so, we are all living, breathing examples" (39). His reference to the centers and peripheries of revolutionary struggle has clear implications for the cultural sphere as well. But Sloman is the one who most directly confronts the implications of systemic tolerance for his work as writer and Shawcross's as producer. Calling the phrase *socialist producer* a contradiction and an irrelevancy, he confronts Joe with the willingness of capitalism to assimilate and absorb dissent: "Joe, this is a system that has 'matured' on descriptions of its inequity and injustice. Poverty is one of its best favoured *spectacles*" (67). To Shawcross's request for a play that isn't a fake, Sloman responds: "Wednesday Plays? It's the Liberal heartland, Joe. [. . .] It's the consensus. It's the condition of our times." Coming as it does during the National Theatre's appropriation of *The Party* as "spectacle," this exchange suggests Griffiths's intense concern with the problems attendant upon an entryist cultural strategy. As someone who had already embarked on the "strategic penetration" of mainstream cultural institutions, Griffiths thematizes within his play the contradictions involved in mounting a socialist critique from within national cultural institutions.

   The Party, it turned out, was widely criticized by the mainstream critical press, taken to task for everything from "self-indulgence" to its "intellectual tirades" and "directionless, inconclusive ironies."[33] The *Guardian's* Michael Billington, who called *The Party* "one of the most mind-stretching and politically sophisticated works" he had seen on the modern stage, was one of the few dissenting voices.[34] This is not the only time in Griffiths's career that theater critics would show themselves less willing to accept a dramaturgy of openness and inconclusiveness than the more tightly organized dialectical structure of *Occupations* (or *Comedians*). *The Party* is, as Griffiths himself notes, an "atmospheric" play, one of the first of his works to attempt a Chekhovian decentering of voices and positions.[35] If *Occupations* and *Absolute Beginners* achieve their intellectual confrontation through the sharp demarcation of dialectical polarities, *The Party* works by expanding dialectic into a more loosely structured field of counterpoint and qualification, in which meaning occurs at the juncture of multiply competing moral and political claims. As a writer, Griffiths has alternated between these two uses of dialectic, and we might think of his plays as deploying "hard" and "soft" principles of organization—keeping in mind, of course, that the playwright's more Chekhovian plays are usually characterized by a tautness of conception and execution and that Griffiths's most tightly dialectical plays are complicated by the play of local antitheses.

But the critical reaction to *The Party* may reflect something else as well. Billington suggested that the play's National Theatre venue had something to do with the widespread negative response, since the National is not a place where critics are used to seeing radical social critique.[36] John Elsom (of the *Listener*) pointed to some of the ironies attendant upon this production: "While it's nice to know that our Establishment takes the cause of the workers so much to heart, there's something definitely knotty about sitting in an audience of bourgeois intellectuals watching a play about anguished bourgeois intellectuals who are perplexed about the methods of persuading the People to destroy them."[37] The fact that this pronouncement echoes the play's own ruminations on "repressive tolerance" and the bourgeois intellectual's dilemma suggests the connection between Griffiths's exploration of socialist art in a capitalist context and the play's own contradictory positioning. From this point of view the negative reaction that greeted *The Party*—this play of living room revolutionaries, with Olivier in the role of its most radical figure—may reflect the tension in the play's conscious use of this particular cultural platform. Critical discomfort, in other words, may be symptomatic of a certain dissonance in *The Party* itself, a play that foregrounds (and obviously transgresses) the unstated boundaries of hegemonic institutions. That Griffiths's interventionist strategy found critics on the Left as well suggests that the distinction between center and periphery may serve more than one set of ideological interests.[38]

Postscript: Commemorations
The layering of historical awareness that forms such an important part of *The Party*'s dramaturgical strategy would intensify throughout the play's subsequent performance history, as May 1968 and the play itself increasingly became the subject of anniversaries and commemorations. *The Party* was revived by the RSC in August 1984 at the Other Place in Stratford-upon-Avon (in a production codirected by Howard Davies and David Edgar) and was moved the following April to the Barbican Centre's Pit stage. When Griffiths attended the Stratford revival with a group of "six or eight old comrades," the experience was a difficult one: a play that was once a "kind of radical triumph against the establishment" was now being revived as a classic,[39] and the sense of anniversary only underscored the loss of the political culture that the play por-

trayed. *The Party* was subsequently adapted for television and broadcast by BBC1 on 9 March 1988, two months shy of the twentieth anniversary of the Paris May.

By this time, in an odd twist to the story of "repressive tolerance" and "national spaces," the 1973 National production had itself become a historical event. In June 1982 the Royal Court gave a public reading of *Building the Party*, a log kept by Clive Morrison during John Dexter's original production. Simon Callow played Dexter, Ian McKellan played Olivier, Richard Eyre played Kenneth Tynan, and Paul Moriarty played Griffiths.[40] Postcards of Olivier as Tagg can still be purchased at the National bookstore among other "highlights" of the theater company's history. In a real sense its own performance history is now an object of the play's cultural and historical awareness.

Gendering the Revolution

The Party ends with Joe and Angie, now alone in their house after the others have left and Angie has returned from her night out. Angie asks Joe to come to bed with her, but he declines her offer. In response to his question "How's David?" Angie notes, briefly: "David's fine. He sends his regards." When she has left the room, Joe stands by himself— "dead," in Griffiths's direction—then puts on a contemporary recording of the spiritual "Balm in Gilead": "There is a balm in Gilead / To make the wounded whole" (75).

Echoing the conclusion of *Sam, Sam*, this sequence returns the play to the domestic arena in which it opened, thereby shifting the anxiety over political involvement back to the sphere of relationship and sexuality. As we have seen, the juxtaposition of the political and the relational is a familiar one for Griffiths, whose interest in troubled periods always extends into the domestic as well as the public. Griffiths has acknowledged the origins of this preoccupation in the difficulties he was experiencing in his marriage (and other relationships) during this period. Edged with autobiography in this way, the recurrent concern with marital difficulty—with love frozen and relationship at an impasse—constitutes a decidedly Strindbergian side of Griffiths's dramatic practice. Griffiths has acknowledged the Swedish dramatist as one of his principal dramatic influences, and he has demonstrated the self-consciousness of this influence in striking ways. He agreed to allow *Sam, Sam* to be produced at the Open Space Theatre when Charles Marowitz mentioned Strindberg in connection with the play's fractured relationships.[41] And shortly after this production Griffiths was convinced by the film director Wolfgang Reinhardt (son of Max Reinhardt) to undertake a screenplay on the three marriages of Strindberg. Griffiths worked on this project between 1972 and 1975, eventually producing several versions of a screenplay entitled *Marriages* (intriguingly, his working title for the project was *Comrades*, which would later serve as his title for the screenplay that would become *Reds*). Although Griffiths's Strindberg screenplay was never produced, it stands as another of those shadow projects that can sharpen our understanding of the playwright's dramatic concerns. The fact that Griffiths began *The Party* while on a Continental trip researching Strindberg's life (he was accompanied on this trip by Gill Cliff, a teacher whom he had met in 1969 and who would become his second wife) casts the play's interest in marital complications in a markedly different light.

Strindberg's writings provided Griffiths with a vehicle for exploring the possibilities of autobiography in art—particularly those aspects of one's life dealing with troubled relationships—while Strindberg himself joined Lawrence and Chekhov as a figure for Griffiths of the writer's relationship to his social and interpersonal worlds. Where Griffiths departs from Strindberg is in his attempt to politicize the field of sexuality and human relationship. In a 1980 interview he noted: "I've always been interested in sexuality as an aspect of human freedom. I see sexual repression as a form of social and political repression, as, in a way, a necessary precondition of it."[42] Griffiths, we have seen, was strongly influenced by the writings of Wilhelm Reich, who saw sexual inhibition as the function of a broader deformation of human relationships under capitalism, and he goes to considerable pains in his work to explore the connection between the political and the sexual. Shawcross's sexual impasse with Angie forms part of his broader political impotence, a connection underscored (somewhat awkwardly) by the juxtaposition of their frustrated sexual encounter with political quotations and slides of the Paris activism.

Griffiths's interest in the politics of sexuality is illuminated by yet another project that he participated in around this time. Shortly after *The Party* completed its run at the National, Tynan approached Griffiths to see if he was interested in collaborating on a sequel to *Oh! Calcutta!* Tynan's controversial but successful 1969 erotic revue. Tynan, who was writing a book on the life of Reich, felt that such shows attempted the revolutionary aim of breaking through people's psyches at the level of sexuality by confronting them, even seducing them. He proposed a sequel that would explore a range of questions associated with human sexuality and with its staging in the theater. Griffiths agreed to participate in this project, and in July 1974 the two men traveled to France and Germany to observe Continental sex shows. Based on these experiences and on his own extensive reading, Griffiths wrote part of a script that he titled *Come,* in which (following Tynan's original conception) four spectators watch an erotic show and act out their own private fantasies. Tynan found the piece excessively earnest, and it became clear that Griffiths was interested in positioning human sexuality within a wider set of political, sociological, and historical contexts. In November 1974 Griffiths gave up on the project.[43]

　·　By insisting on the relationships between the intimate and the public, Griffiths raises questions concerning both the politics of sexuality and (it often turns out) the sexuality of politics. But it is also true, as Colin Chambers and Mike Prior suggest about *Apricots,* that the correlation between the political and the sexual in Griffiths's actual work is often unsteady or unclear.[44] Particularly in the early plays, gender and sexuality often exist in uncomfortable relationship to the political structures that seek to contain them, and Griffiths's dramatization of relationships—specifically those between the sexes—has struck more than one observer as conditioned by unexamined and sometimes troubling attitudes and emotions. "There is something a little frightening about Griffiths's writing on sexuality and personal relationships," Chambers and Prior write, "though it is veiled behind a strong intellectual vigor."[45] Griffiths is by no means alone in this regard; the question of gender was an uneasy, usually invisible one for the New Left and the 1960s counterculture, and the staging of gender and sexuality is certainly problematic in the drama of Osborne and the male leftist tradition that succeeded it. But, if it is true that the politics of relationship in Griffiths's work is an essential corollary to the more public sphere of political action, then it is important to consider the dynamics governing the politics of sexuality and the gendering of politics. Consideration of Griffiths's early plays is incomplete without at least some attempt to confront the unexamined ways in which sexuality and gender function within the playwright's political/theatrical project. When it comes to gender, Strindberg (like Lawrence) is a problematic mentor.

    One of the most pronounced manifestations of the gendering of Griffiths's dramatic world is the intersection of sexuality and class. As Chambers and Prior suggest in their discussion of working-class representation in post-1956 British drama, the 1960s saw a Lawrentian tendency to view working-class men as the bearers of a natural virility denied more middle- and upper-class males.[46] From a cultural standpoint the controversies over *Lady Chatterley's Lover* (and the popularity of such cultural figures as the Beatles and the Rolling Stones) reflect the broader anxieties and fascinations bred by postwar class mobility. Griffiths, almost fired from his Stockport teaching position in the early 1960s for teaching Lawrence's novel, replicates the sexualizing of class difference with striking intensity. Sexuality becomes a site of class conflict, a battlefield in which class power is exerted and countered. The second act of *Sam, Sam* dramatizes this contest with particular nakedness. Following the precedent of Jimmy Porter, Sam II asserts antagonism toward his wife and her family through gestures of verbal disruption. When her parents are gone, Patricia strikes back with an act of sexual aggression that neatly combines sexual and class domination.

The upwardly mobile protagonists of Griffiths's early plays (Sam II, Shawcross, Bill Brand) are particularly disadvantaged by this sexual dynamic: never fully a part of the upper-class world they now inhabit, they are nonetheless (Griffiths seems to suggest) cut off from the natural virility of their working-class origins. The sexualizing of class antagonism operates more starkly when class difference is more clearly defined. Since none of Griffiths's published plays dramatizes the sexual encounter of an upper-class man with a lower-class woman (*Country*, with its marriage of convenience between Philip Carlion and Faith, is scant exception), such conflict usually follows the Lawrentian model, with social privilege coded female and working-class power coded male. *Occupations* is a prime example of this—with Kabak, the proletarian revolutionary, and Angelica, the dying aristocrat—though this particular struggle of class and sexuality bears the touch of Strindberg rather than Lawrence (such a connection would have been underscored for the play's 1971 audience by the fact that the RSC staged *Occupations* in repertory with *Miss Julie*).

As *Occupations* demonstrates, Griffiths's preoccupation with issues of masculinity infiltrates, and to an extent conditions, his presentation of revolutionary politics. Griffiths's revolutionary world has been, until recently in his career, a strikingly male one, and its most passionate intellectual confrontations take place between men.[47] In part this gendering of political activity is a product of the socialist history that Griffiths dramatizes, but the marginalizing or neglect of female political voices makes itself felt even in his more contemporary historical settings. Shawcross's meeting in *The Party* includes a number of women, but none participate in the play's central theoretical debate. Indeed, through the character of Sloman, the play bears witness to a considerable degree of antagonism directed at its female presence. Sloman (who refers to his own wife as "the thin bitch in Salford" and his mistress as "Sally Svelte from SW7 with the manicured mind and a We Never Closed sign in neon at the top of her legs" [63]) behaves in a predatory or hostile way to all of the play's women. Of these, none comes in for greater antagonism than Kara, Shawcross's ex-wife and the most politically active woman in attendance at the meeting. Shawcross's deprecating description of her suggests that her political literacy and activism encroaches on an essentially male prerogative: "Kara's not a woman, she's a political position. [. . .] It's a cunt, innit!" (27). The echoes of Strindberg's hated "man-woman" here gives a problematic coloring to Griffiths's own description of Kate as "attractively mannish" (30).

Kara, Angie, and the other women in *The Party* hold their own against Sloman's misogynistic assaults, and his woman hating is only one of a number of voices in the play's dialectical polyphony. But his gestures toward exclusion—like Kabak's abandonment of Angelica and Lenin's coldblooded dismissal of Zasulich—are only crude versions of a process at work in this and Griffiths's other early plays of political confrontation. *Absolute Beginners,* with its focus on revolutionary discipline and repression, suggests that this exclusion of the female may be rooted in the psychology of the revolutionary will. Lenin's campaign against softness involves a turning away from female sexuality and tenderness: he refuses his wife when she offers herself to him and fears the softening effects of her singing. The psychology of hardness, here and elsewhere in Griffiths's early plays, genders power as male and conceives the female in terms of a weakness that must be repressed. The dilemma that has concerned Griffiths since *The Love Maniac*—the incompatibility of committed love and the political life, the difficulty of reconciling love for one with the more abstract love of many—often plays itself out as a marginalizing of the female with its seductive emotional claims.

In *Look Back in Gender: Sexuality and the Family in Post-War British Drama* Michelene Wandor considers the issues of sexuality and gender in *Occupations.* Her reading focuses on Kabak's, and the play's, symbolic appropriation of the dying Angelica. Angelica, according to Wandor, represents not only Kabak's conflicted links to a bourgeois past but also the personal life that he cannot cope with emotionally; since the emotional is represented by a woman, she must be destroyed. "The threat here is not to male sexuality, but to man as a political animal, and this makes the personal the enemy of the political, setting up an unresolvable contradiction for Kabak and his socialist politics."[48] In terms of the play's broader symbolic economy Griffiths appropriates Angelica's very body as a symbol of a dying order. Significantly, for Wandor this appropriation involves the simultaneous appropriation and damaging of her capacity for motherhood: although she has cancer of the womb, her dying screams enable socialism to give birth to a new age. Underlying this symbolic use of Angelica is a repudiation of her sexuality and a misogynistic revulsion at the female body not unlike that of Jimmy Porter toward the pregnant Allison: "Equating the reactionary bourgeoisie with a diseased womb can only work by evoking fear and disgust at . . . the private parts of women and their reproductive capacity." Although Angelica remains onstage in this capacity throughout the play, women are excluded from the play's political debate. Woman, Wandor claims, has no part in generating the play's animating political metaphor; she is "the passive representative of it."[49]

This description may not be entirely fair as a portrait of Griffiths's attitude toward gender and sexuality here and elsewhere in his early plays. He often demonstrates an awareness of female experience and its independent claims and authority: *Absolute Beginners* includes several scenes in which Zasulich and Krupskaya occupy a female space independent of male-directed political maneuverings, and *Through the Night* stands as one of the decade's most powerful defenses of female bodily experience against the objectifications of a predominantly male medical establishment. Griffiths is more aware than Wandor acknowledges of the repudiation involved in his characters' rejection of the female and its costs. The psychosexual pathology evident in a play like *Apricots* or *The Party* is there, to a significant extent, in order to be critiqued (in both plays the male protagonists actively resist invitations to mutuality; as Angie tells Shawcross: "I want *you*, Joe" [16]).

But Wandor's reading of *Occupations* isolates a set of gender problems that Griffiths's plays and films will never entirely escape: a privileging of the male as a site of political vision and agency, a fear of the female that (in the early work, at least) borders on the antagonistic, and a difficulty in imagining the terms by which a cross-gendered mutuality might be achieved and sustained. Particularly in the early plays, the conflicted attitude toward women makes itself felt in disturbing moments and currents: the terror and fantasy of female engulfment in *Apricots*, with its conflation of the sexual and the maternal; misogynistic attacks on the female body that run from Sam I's tirade on his wife's bathing habits ("the dirty bugger") to Gethin Price's physical attack on his female dummy ("I wonder what happened. P'raps it pierced a vein"). Most pervasive of all is the relative invisibility of women on Griffiths's political landscape and the frequent sense one gets that they serve as backdrops for the more centrally realized struggles of men.

Griffiths has not been unaware of the problems with the staging of gender and sexuality in his early plays. Of his portrayal of women in these plays he has since noted: "I was struggling with stuff that I knew wasn't right, but I didn't know why it was wrong."[50] While Griffiths was working on *The Party* (and, later, the *After Calcutta* project), he began reading anything he could find on the conjunction of politics and sexuality: "By that time I suspect I was feeling that I really did need to get a politics of the sexuality in my experience and . . . to embody that experience in the pieces I was writing."[51] By the late 1970s, when Griffiths started writing *Reds*, he approached the question of "sexuality as an aspect of human freedom" with a less exclusively masculinist set of assumptions, and his later plays explore the political sphere with less exclusive gender roles: *Oi for England* ends with a man and woman joining forces to combat racism, and one of the most passionate political speeches in Griffiths's most recent plays is delivered, in *The Gulf between Us*, by the woman doctor Aziz. *Heartlands*, Griffiths's unproduced 1987 play about the 1984–85 Miners' Strike, includes a focus on women's participation in the strike, and *March Time*, an unproduced screenplay from around the same time, also challenges the notion of activism as an exclusively male sphere: "If I can't keep up, sack me," the character Ellen tells the leader of the march to London, "But don't tell me this is men's work. Men've said it all my life and look where it's got us."[52] In Griffiths's most recent screenplay it is a woman, Maud Gonne, who carries the torch of revolutionary aspiration.

To acknowledge that gender is a frequent blind spot in Griffiths's drama is not to deny the energy with which he sets its issues in play. Nor is it to deny the efforts that Griffiths has made to see through and beyond the sexual roles embedded in the worlds that produced him. As Wandor's study demonstrates, Griffiths's male contemporaries have not fared much better in this area. Griffiths's plays and films may fail to achieve a vision of mutuality and unalienated love, but his work remains haunted by the claims of "a cleared or free space in which men and women could engage on relatively equal terms."[53]

4

Medium, Reflexivity, Counternarrative: Griffiths in Television

Television against Itself

Between 1971 and 1975 (when *Comedians* had its widely acclaimed London premiere) Trevor Griffiths established himself as one of the most important voices in the British theater. Yet the playwright's feelings about the theatrical institution in which he had earned this reception remained, throughout this time, ambivalent. Looking back on his early career from the vantage point of 1985, Griffiths pointed out: "In a sense theatre work was always an accident for me. I stumbled into theatre. I had always imagined my writing being television writing."[1] Even as he was exploring the opportunities for a radical artistic practice within its boundaries, Griffiths's comments on the theater reveal his belief that the medium had been superseded as an interventionist forum. In a 1972 interview he was even more direct: "I'm very pessimistic about theatre. I don't see it as in any way a major form of communicating descriptions or analyses or modifying attitudes. . . . It's in television that I think, as a political writer, I want to be, because very large numbers of people, who are not accessible any other way, *are* accessible in television."[2]

Even if we take into account a certain provocativeness in these remarks designed to counter the cultural priority traditionally accorded the theater over more "popular" representational media, there is no denying the importance that television has retained as a medium of cultural communication throughout Griffiths's career. Griffiths's earliest dramatic writing was for television, and his initial attempts to secure production were directed toward this medium. Of the playwright's produced plays nearly half were written for television, and an additional four were adapted to television from the stage. This commitment to television should come as no surprise, given the playwright's own background and early career. The product of a northern working-class upbringing, Griffiths understood a culture into which the theater, a bourgeois institution, had made comparatively few inroads. History reinforced this emphasis: as television ownership increased during the 1950s and 1960s (75 percent of British families owned a set in 1961, 91 percent in 1971),[3] the televisual medium established itself, in contrast to theater, as a truly popular representational medium, perhaps the only genuinely "national" theater that Britain has ever achieved.

For a dramatist concerned with extending the reach of his writing beyond the upper- and middle-class audiences of the traditional theater, the appeal of television was inescapable. "I simply cannot understand socialist playwrights who do not devote most of their time to television. That they can write for the Royal Court and the National Theatre, and only that, seems to me a wilful self-delusion about the nature of theatre in a bourgeois culture now."[4] Television promised a much wider social accessibility, the opportunity to reach audiences across the boundaries of region and class. For Griffiths the televisual medium enabled a writer to contact his or her audience where they conducted their lives, to address these lives, and to intervene in the process by which social, economic, and political forces made themselves felt in the everyday. Because of the increasing importance of television in the British cultural landscape, the medium offered "a massively powerful . . . means of intervening in society's life."[5]

Griffiths's faith in the communicative potential of television, formed through observation and experience in the 1950s, was intensified during the 1960s. Not only did this decade see the medium exploited by a number of leftist writers and producers (David Mercer, John McGrath, Tony Garnett) eager to take advantage of its opportunities for single-play and serial programming, but leftist cultural theorists had begun to analyze the medium as a cultural tool. Of these Griffiths was most influenced by the work of Raymond Williams. From *The Long Revolution* (1961), which Griffiths has acknowledged as a pivotal book in his thinking about politics and culture, through *Communications* (1962), *Television: Technology and Cultural Form* (1974), and other later books and articles, Williams explored television as a form of cultural technology within a broader field of social communication. On the relations between communication, social perception, and community Williams wrote: "Since our way of seeing things is literally our way of living, the process of communication is in fact the process of community: the sharing of common meanings, and thence common activities and purposes; the offering, reception and comparison of new meanings, leading to the tensions and achievements of growth and change."[6] Television was an instrument of increasing importance within this process of cultural negotiation, and it offered the potential of a truly democratic medium.

Griffiths's personal understanding of both the communicative potentials inherent in television and of the institutional contexts by which this potential is constrained was deepened, of course, by his work in the late 1960s and early 1970s as further education officer with the BBC. Working for the BBC gave Griffiths the opportunity to learn about the educational uses of broadcast material and to observe, firsthand, the situations and audiences in which such materials would be used. It also gave him valuable exposure to the BBC as institution and organizational structure, at a particular historical juncture when progressive uses of the broadcast media were tolerated and even encouraged. Despite these opportunities, of course, Griffiths had no illusions about television's institutional function within capitalist society. His 1969 radio play *The Big House* ends, we recall, with a scene in which Yates and his fellow agitators watch a television broadcast whitewashing the management-labor conflicts at Lazarus Ltd. Throughout his career as a television writer Griffiths confronted television not only as a medium but as an establishment, one dependent on an extensive and essentially conservative institutional apparatus.

The extent of the institutional control involved in production and broadcast decisions was sharply underscored for Griffiths during his first actual project for the medium. In 1971, after earning a name for himself with *Occupations*, Griffiths was offered work scripting episodes for a Granada TV series entitled *Adam Smith*. This series, which centered on a Church of Scotland minister who deals with the relational and social issues facing his parishioners in Scotland and (later) South Africa, was conceived by Granada's Denis Forman and presented to Griffiths for dramatic development. Under the pseudonym Ben Rae (as an employee of the BBC, Griffiths was not allowed to write for an independent television company under his own name), Griffiths wrote nine of twelve episodes in the show's first series (broadcast 23 January–10 April

1972) and two episodes of the second series (broadcast 17 September 1972–25 March 1973).[7] Although it was not a project he would have chosen for himself, Griffiths managed to use the series' narrative situation to address issues of economic and social justice, sexuality and social mores, and racial inequality. At the same time, the experience of working on the *Adam Smith* project was a sobering one, in large part because of the interference he encountered with the scripts he produced. Others in the collaborative process (from the producer to the designers) changed or eliminated parts of Griffiths's text, often in a kind of specific ideological screening; one of the cuts, for example, involved a passage on capitalist exploitation from a sermon delivered by Smith to an affluent Edinburgh congregation. Enraged by these changes, Griffiths resigned from the project in protest. He later recalled the experience:

> I had no automatic right of entry into the production process and I found that many ideological insertions were being made from producers, directors and actors. . . . It taught me a very important lesson, which is that television is very powerful, not just as a medium of communication but as an institution, an establishment, a set of practices and relationships. I learnt that that power had to be tackled if a writer was going to do anything.[8]

Determined to tackle this power, Griffiths's subsequent work in television has involved him in a recurrent battle over textual revision, production and transmission. The struggle for textual control has often assumed quite particular form: whether a lovemaking scene would be included in an episode of *Bill Brand*, for instance, or whether the serial as a whole would be broadcast at 9:00 or 10:30 P.M. As Griffiths has insisted, issues like these have consequences, both ideological and logistical: sexuality (for Griffiths) is an inseparable aspect of social and political relationship, and an audience that gets up early in the morning to go to work will not be able to watch a play that starts at 10:30. (Griffiths lost the first of these battles but won the second, after seventy people showed up for a meeting on the subject with the Thames TV program controller.)

As his problems with censorship and other manifestations of institutional control indicate, Griffiths's practice as a television dramatist has always sought to counter the medium's ideological functions. In his 1977 preface to *Through the Night* and *Such Impossibilities* Griffiths cites Hans Enzensberger's argument that the "consciousness industry" (of which television was rapidly becoming the key sector) now functioned as the principal industry in the management of modern society. "In a society predicated on the exploitation of the many by the few," Griffiths writes, paraphrasing Enzensberger, "the shaping of consciousness, the erection of the superstructure of consent, will become the major cultural concern of the state and the dominant class or classes it represents."9 The challenge facing a radical artistic practice is to disrupt, or counter, the superstructure of consent constructed through the dominant practices of institution and medium. In response to those on the Left who dismiss television as monolithic in its institutional/ideological controls, Griffiths evokes Enzensberger's notion that communications systems (like television) beyond a certain size are characterized by a certain "leakiness," the escape of meanings from the system's efforts of control. "To work in television as a playwright will be to seek to exploit the system's basic 'leakiness,' so as to speak intimately and openly, with whatever seriousness and relevance one can generate."10

Even while Griffiths exploits television as a medium, then, embracing its radically democratic opportunities for communications, he does so with a Gramscian awareness of television's dominant role in the production and management of consent. "If a dramatist is interested in influence and persuasion," Griffiths insists, "he has to understand the structures through which persuasion and influence work."11 Griffiths's practice as a television writer remains consistent with the interventionist, counterhegemonic strategies that have characterized his work in other media. Just as Griffiths exploits the institutional authority of national theater spaces for subversive ends, so his plays for television challenge the medium's normative (and normalizing) function. Strategic penetration in this case involves setting television against itself in a gesture that is both stridently rhetorical (aware of audience, message, and situation) and metadiscursive.

Griffiths's television plays address a range of dramatic subjects, and they do so with an awareness of video and filmic techniques particular to the televisual medium (techniques of editing, frame composition, camera angle, and points of view). This chapter will suggest some of these techniques as they are employed in Griffiths's television plays of the mid 1970s; in these (and in the television plays discussed in later chapters) one can see the playwright's increasing control of the medium's formal possibilities. But the main purpose of this chapter will be to outline the central strategies governing Griffiths's use of television as a mode of cultural communication. Among these I will consider Griffiths's use of counternarrative, a strategy similar to—and at times identical with—the impulses evident in the playwright's staging of history.

Deeply implicated in this is Griffiths's awareness of the generic boundaries governing televisual representation and his attempt to both evoke
and subvert such categories. Finally, I will consider one of the most
striking features of Griffiths's television drama: the deployment of
reflexive strategies in order to expose both the structures of relationship,
normally effaced, that govern televisual production and the technological apparatuses by which television conducts its ideologically conditioned mode of seeing.

Roughing Up the Edwardians: *Such Impossibilities*

One of the earliest and most intriguing of Griffiths's attempts to take on
the representational constraints of the television medium was a play
that, in the end, was never produced. In 1971 Griffiths was commissioned by the BBC to write a play for *The Edwardians*, a series devoted to
the lives of prominent figures from prewar Britain. Griffiths proposed a
script on Tom Mann, the labor and socialist activist who helped organize the London Dock Strike of 1889 and led the Liverpool Transport
Workers' Strike of 1911. In a letter to the BBC's Margaret Hare in July
1971 Griffiths called Mann "the most important and able working class
leader this society has thrown up," and he argued the relevance of the
1911 strike (sixty years earlier) to the contemporary moment, which saw
widening industrial unrest and antilabor legislation once again on the
agenda of British politics. Under the Heath administration's Industrial
Relations Bill, scheduled to become law in January 1972, Griffiths wrote,
"workers will lose important, hard-won rights. 'Militants' will risk
imprisonment for 'incitement to unauthorized industrial action.' It
remains to be seen what the precise response of organized labor will be,
but it is not impossible to see ourselves on the threshold of a new era of
grassroots agitation and action. Men will go to jail. Police will be once
again squarely in the middle of industrial activity."[12] Griffiths's prediction concerning the escalation of labor militarism turned out to be accurate: in January and February 1972 Britain's 280,000 coal miners went on
strike and, with the support of railway workers, won pay concessions
from the Coal Board. While similar activism on the part of the miners
would lead to the defeat of the Heath Administration in the February
1974 general election, the antilabor antagonism reflected in the Industrial Relations Bill would prove to be even longer lasting, with a later,
more radically Conservative government resuming the battle against
industrial militancy.

Like the playwright's other explorations of history, Griffiths's proposal (and the script that he completed over the ensuing months) reflected his determination to underscore the correlations between past and present—"to restore, however tinily, an important but suppressed area of our collective history; to enlarge our 'usable past' and connect it with a lived present; and to celebrate a victory."[13] Such Impossibilities was also written to intervene in the specific constructions of the past represented by a series like the proposed Edwardians. Just as Absolute Beginners would counter and disrupt the historical nostalgia of the Fall of Eagles series, with its elegiac reconstructions of imperial twilight, Such Impossibilities targeted a nostalgic evocation of prewar Britain that had become one of the staples of television history. As Poole and Wyver note, the late Victorian and Edwardian years had become (along with Tudor England) a favorite setting for historical or costume drama; a twenty-six-part adaptation of Galsworthy's Edwardian novel The Forsyte Saga was broadcast by the BBC in 1967 (and again in 1968, 1970, and 1974), and London Weekend TV first broadcast the Edwardian serial Upstairs, Downstairs in 1971.[14] This historical nostalgia, Colin McArthur suggests in his book Television and History, is not without sociohistorical motivation: "For post-war Britain, faced as it is with adjustment to being a post-colonial power, a mediocre economic performer, a multi-racial society and a society in which the consensus of acceptable social and political behavior is fragmenting . . . what better ideological choice, in its art, than to return to the period of the zenith of bourgeois and imperial power or to immediately succeeding periods in which the façade of that power appeared convincing."[15] Although its focus on historical figures established it as something different than the novelistically based series mentioned earlier, The Edwardians was clearly designed to appeal to this interest in a turn-of-the-century world conceived and represented in a certain way. If the Edwardian world constructed by and for television was an ordered and securely structured one, the figures chosen as the center of each episode were pillars of that world: David Lloyd George, Marie Lloyd, Sir Arthur Conan Doyle, Baden-Powell, Horatio Bottomley, Rolls and Royce.

Griffiths's contribution to the series was a deliberate act of counter-history, a challenge from within this representational project directed toward the picture of the Edwardian world offered up by the series and the historical complacency that sought to see imperial British society in such a light. Addressing the fact that Such Impossibilities was never made, Griffiths underscored the corrective function that his play was written to provide: "Tom Mann might have roughed the series up a bit, but it's arguable he might also have done something toward redressing its 'balance' too."[16]

As Griffiths's remark suggests, the play's combative stance is embodied in the figure of Mann, whose short, powerful frame suggests an aggressive energy directed toward Edwardian society and its fiercely protected class interests. The representatives of this society—the General Manager of the Shipping Federation, the Police Superintendent, and the Lord Mayor of Liverpool—are presented as figures of almost decadent privilege (Cuthbert Laws, the Shipping Federation leader, lounges in his hotel suite with the remains of a room service dinner still on the table, while the Superintendent trims his moustache in narcissistic self-absorption). Beneath this affluence and protocol lies a smug contempt toward those determined to change the structures of status and power. Faced with the initial actions of the striking transport workers, Laws is quoted in a newspaper article as saying: "Even if the men win better wages now, it will not do them much good. We shall be here day after day, every time a crew signs on, whittling away the increase until it disappears. We are always here. The men's union is here only once and again."[17] Behind this arrogance is the threat of physical force, a threat made real when a demonstration of unarmed workers is brutally attacked by policemen wielding staves (the events of Bloody Sunday, as it was quickly named, led to an escalation of the labor unrest into a Liverpool general strike).

When asked by Laws (whose father fought him in the 1889 strike) why he goes on doing what he does, Mann replies, "To rid the world of people like you, Mr. Laws" (211). From the play's opening moments, when he arrives at the Liverpool train station, until the closing moments, when, with the strikers largely victorious, he finds himself jailed for the publication of an incendiary tract addressed at military conscripts, Mann must work his way through the logistical, strategic, and philosophical terrain that confronts other Griffiths activists who seek to renegotiate or overthrow industrial and state power. Like Kabak, Lenin, and other "hards" from Griffiths's plays of the early 1970s, he advocates the discipline, organization, unity, and solidarity sufficient to combat a capitalist state firmly in possession of these qualities. Of particular concern to Mann and others in the Strike Committee room that serves as the play's central setting are "the evils of sectionalism" (208) and the risk that independent unions will reject the policy of collective gains and seek to negotiate their own settlements with employers. In one of the strike's crucial moments the dockers break rank with the Strike Committee strategy, and Mann must deal with the potential splintering of his united workers' front (this outflanking of an organized left-wing organization by a radical wing recalls the shop steward activism of *The Big House*). Mann responds to this breakdown of organizational unity by harnessing rather than suppressing the breakaway radical energies: he admits that the Strike Committee has lost control over its workers, names the leader of the dockers to the Strike Committee, and convinces the committee to embrace their demands.

Mainstream telehistory is governed, McArthur argues, not by the needs of historical knowledge but by the categories of television itself, which are designed "to facilitate a particular construction of the social world, a construction which is uncongenial to radical change." One of the ways in which this social construction is legitimated is through the use—McArthur calls it the "fetishization"—of actuality film: location filming, detailed reconstruction/dramatizations, documentary footage, nonfilmic documents, and other resources that confer upon the represented world the authority of the Real.[18] Like Griffiths's other historical plays and films, the script of *Such Impossibilities* is constituted through an extensive recourse to historical materials: dialogue drawn from historical sources, the filming of actual sites in Liverpool, and the inclusion of filmic and nonfilmic documentary material (in one scene Mann's speech to the Strike Committee is counterpointed by an "actuality sequence" designed to convey the broader field of events unfolding across the city). Griffiths includes such material, as he has throughout his career, to assert a rival claim upon the Real, one grounded in a different, and often suppressed, field of historical evidence from that made available in mainstream historical reconstructions of the period. Actuality material functions also to establish the past's *material* historicity; resisting the individualist account of traditional biohistory, it connects the specific and often intimate relationships between the play's central characters to the play's wider historical moment.

Griffiths's use of actuality devices represents a refusal of the social reality offered by traditional television representation. At the same time, as Griffiths recognizes, the Real often functions, in mainstream television, to efface issues of ideology and to deny the "constructedness" of historical accounts. While he insists on the material reality of the past he seeks to reclaim (with its class divisions and its hard-edged working-class militancy), Griffiths also establishes the fact that the representation of the past is never disinterested and that the historical evidence upon which this representation is based is itself conditioned by class interest. Griffiths writes into his play one of the most striking side notes of the Liverpool disturbances: the fact that the events of Bloody Sunday were in fact filmed and that, after being confiscated by the police, this film was subsequently lost.[19] Mann warns the Superintendent in advance of the demonstration: "You might be interested to know, we've arranged for two cinemaphotographers to take a film of the proceedings. It'll make a useful . . . record" (225). That this "record" of police brutality is lost leaves the play's actuality/documentary stratum decisively rent: the establishment of documentary authority is marked by what is *not* available, the result of official suppression. History, this moment suggests, is constructed out of evidence the existence and survival of which is dependent on a network of competing interests. To the extent that this moment is also designed to call attention to the play's own filming camera, it also underscores the "interestedness" of the act of filming, whether it is exercised in the violence-disrupted streets of 1911 Liverpool or as part of a radical attempt, sixty years later, to reconstruct this historical moment.

Alone with his wife in his jail cell in the play's final scene, Mann addresses her bewilderment at the life he has chosen: "The working class don't cry, lass. We've nothing to cry for. We're winning" (232). In a kind of counterpoint to *Occupations* what Griffiths is concerned with here is less the inevitable failures of revolutionary activism than a moment of victory within this historical struggle. Although the optimism of this ending is muted by an understanding of personal sacrifices and the awareness of subsequent history (with its rollbacks and defeats) that always tends to qualify such affirmations in Griffiths's plays, the attention here is on the vision of something better that powers this struggle and its sacrifices. In the words of Thomas Carlyle that give the play its title:

> There is not a horse in England willing and able to work but has due food and lodgings. . . . And you say it is impossible. Brothers, I answer, if for you it be impossible, what is to become of you? It is impossible for us to believe it to be impossible. The human brain, looking at these sleek English horses, refuses to believe in such impossibilities for Englishmen.

After Mann reads these lines in his make-shift bedroom at night, Griffiths instructs the camera to pan to the headline of a Red handbill at the side of his bed: "It May Be Tomorrow" (200).

After failing to get Griffiths to agree to changes in the script, the

BBC offered as its reason for rejecting *Such Impossibilities* that it was too expensive to produce. Poole and Wyver's account of the decision not to air the play suggests that there was some truth to this claim, but Griffiths himself maintained that the reason had more to do with the play's challenge to the series' governing historical tone: "it's at least as likely that the play offered too brutal and too overtly political a contrast with the remainder of the series."[20] Certainly, Griffiths's metahistorical investigation of telehistory and historical reconstruction stands as a direct attack on the privileged class of Edwardian society and the world it has created. And it stands as a counterstatement to television's ruling—and nostalgic—image of the Edwardian social order. Whatever the causes of its rejection by the BBC, the play's own fate confirms one of its insights: that history is never disinterested and that its documentation is a function of society and its structures of institutional control.

Documenting Labour: *All Good Men*

Griffiths's first single television play to be produced was a piece called *The Silver Mask*, an adaptation of Hugh Walpole's short story by the same name. It was broadcast by London Weekend Television on 15 June 1973 as part of a series entitled *Between the Wars*. As his notes on this project indicate, Griffiths worked to accentuate the sociological aspects of Walpole's nightmare of class infiltration, but the adaptation seemed to offer him little challenge to deepen his explorations of history and the politics of medium.[21] His next play for television would provide myriad opportunities on both counts. Invited that summer to submit a play for the BBC's *Play for Today* series, Griffiths wrote *All Good Men*, the first of his works to investigate the politics of Labourism, its historical record, and the viability of parliamentary socialism as vehicle for social change. Broadcast on 31 January 1974 (two and a half months before *Absolute Beginners*), *All Good Men* also continues Griffiths's reflexive meditation on the politics of televisual production and the inescapably ideological nature of its representations.

The play takes place in a Surrey country house belonging to Edward Waite, a seventy-year-old Labour politician whose life was spent in trade union and labor activism. Born a member of the Manchester working class, Waite has risen beyond this upbringing: his two children (Maria, presently a teacher in a London comprehensive school, and William, a researcher in history and sociology at Manchester University) were born and raised in more affluent surroundings, and he now faces the prospects of elevation to the peerage in a setting that embodies upper-class privilege. Griffiths underscores the ironies and contradictions of Waite's life through an intricate register of class and regional markings. Waite, who "in the old days" once loved a glass of stout, now displays a drinks table with brandy and liqueurs given to him by friends in the City. Yet the process of class translation that Waite has undergone is by no means easy or complete, and his Manchester origins reassert themselves. Branded on the tongue (like other Griffiths protagonists), Waite speaks with "the jagged Manchester consonants still glinting in the oily wash of his received standard English."[22] Working-class Manchester and the home counties, seat of English Conservatism, exist in uneasy relation to each other. Richard Massingham, a television producer there to produce a documentary on Waite's life for a series entitled *Living History*, notes the contradiction: "I wouldn't have thought Surrey . . . right, somehow, given your life" (40).

The title *All Good Men* is taken from a standard typing exercise: "Now is the time for all good men to come to the aid of the party."[23] Through the figure of Waite, Griffiths explores the roots of the Labour Party, its relationship to the working class it ostensibly champions, and (most crucially of all) its relationship while in power to the capitalist system its rhetoric has historically challenged. In keeping with Griffiths's original title for the play, *History*, the historical background of Waite and the Labour movement as a whole is evoked in a number of ways: auditory flashbacks to speeches by Ramsy MacDonald, Clement Attlee, Nye Bevan, and Hugh Gaitskell; a photograph on the wall of Labour's 1945 government, with Waite seated (symbolically?) to the right of Attlee; an album of photographs from Waite's past, including one of him marching at the head of a miners' picket in Manchester during the 1926 General Strike. Looking over his father's shoulder at these photographs, William tells the elder Waite, "A man could die of memories like that" (63).[24]

The political legacy of this personal and collective past is the subject of the play's central confrontation, an argument between William and his father over the latter's record while in power. William, whose doctoral thesis concerns the relationship between leadership and the grassroots in working-class political organizations, accuses his father of having betrayed the spirit of revolutionary activism, a claim he supports by referring to Waite's voting record as District Association executive of the miners' union during the strike that preceded the General Strike. Despite his public pronouncements on the strike, Waite voted against it and, when it failed, served on a committee with the owners to agree upon pay reductions and layoffs. William, who earlier compared his father to the Kiowan Indian chief who had worked to make his people follow the white man's will, sees in his father's actions the accommodationist history of a Labour Party that has lost experiential connection with the people it has claimed to lead. Echoing the critique of the Labour Party that had characterized the British radical Left since the Wilson administration of the 1960s (Waite's pipe is an allusion to Wilson's famous prop), William accuses postwar Labourism of resisting real social revolution and settling for minimal social adjustment in its place. "You didn't create a new social order, you merely humanized the old one" (68).

Waite, who defends the achievements of the Attlee government, counters with the political exigencies of the world as it exists and as Labour has been forced to deal with it. Against academic blueprints of theoretical revolution, Waite asserts the challenges of actual leadership: "Taking people with you. Arguing with people who disagree, passionately. [. . .] Reality is priorities" (69). As a master of the strategic retreat since his earliest childhood encounters with authority, a shrewd analyst of the possible, Waite defends his actions in 1926 by arguing that the miners' position was essentially hopeless and that the General Strike as a whole was (in Beatrice Webb's phrase) "a proletarian distemper that had to run its course" (72).

The confrontation is a familiar one in Griffiths's plays: between the radical and centrist/rightist Left, between the imperative of revolutionary vision and the compromises and failures attendant upon its implementation, between the almost inhuman rigors of an oppositional stance and the temptations of accommodation. Yet, more fundamentally, what is contested between father and son is the nature of the Real itself. For Waite reality is an essentially empirical, pragmatic concept; it belongs to the world, which "doesn't change because we shut our eyes and dream." For William, on the other hand, reality lies in desire and what it envisions: "It doesn't change *unless* we shut our eyes and dream. 'I take my desires for reality, because I believe in the reality of my desires'" (69). William's position has the authority—and even the poetry—of longing, which links him with Griffiths's other dreamers of a better world. And Waite himself is clearly troubled by the compromises he has made (and is about to make by accepting elevation to the peerage): the mild coronary seizure that he suffers while listening to his memory of early Labour leaders suggests his inner strain.[25] But Waite's position has the authority of experience, and his understanding of the possible reflects a sense of complexity absent from his son's single-mindedness. There is something unpracticed, even academic, about William's attack on his father's life and an unpleasantness to his unbridled animosity toward him (Maria's attitude toward her father, while rooted in the same political leanings as her brother, is far more compassionate). Only when he faces the enigmatic Massingham and questions the purpose of his documentary does he acknowledge his father as "a man who's spent the best part of his life working and slaving, however benightedly, to make things just a little bit better for people" (74). Even this, however, doesn't keep him from handing Massingham the incriminating documents concerning Waite's betrayal of the 1926 Miners' Strike.

Throughout the confrontation between Waite and his son, Massingham sits apart, observing the exchange (during Michael Lindsay-Hogg's BBC production the camera catches him looking). *All Good Men* is filled with looks both literal and metaphorical—at photographs, at the signs of class translation, at Labour history, at the complexities of a life lived in the political realm. With the presence of Massingham as television documentarist this structure of observation widens to include the institution of television itself. The play opens with Waite facing a tripod camera, with light battens, wiring, and other film production paraphernalia on the floor around it. In the play's middle scenes Massingham makes preparations for the filmed interview, speaks to production assistants over the phone, and even proposes a trial run-through, which leads to the unplanned, heated exchange. By the end of *All Good Men* Waite's Surrey conservatory has been transformed into a studio—with a cameraman, assistants, and more equipment. Massingham's closing interview begins with the filming camera in full view.

The visible presence of this film equipment is a powerfully reflexive disclosure, on Griffiths's part, of television's technological machinery. This gesture is all the more striking for the usual invisibility of this machinery in television programming. As Stuart Hall points out, standard television production generally effaces the technical activities responsible for the finished product:

> Despite recent innovations, it is still the case that, by and large, in "good" professional television, the technical nature of the medium is thoroughly suppressed: any reminders that there are cameras, cameramen, sound booms, interviewers, commentators, technicians, secretaries, script-girls,

location or studio-managers, producers, directors, telecine recordists and so on, invisibly intervening as a collective production unit between "reality" and the viewer, destroys the illusion of immediacy and transparency.[26]

By foregrounding the means of production with such Brechtian straightforwardness, Griffiths highlights the producedness of his own television play (the fact that Massingham's interview is filmed in a makeshift conservatory studio calls attention to *All Good Men* as a studio product). But camera, sound board, and their like are only the means of representation, and Griffiths's larger concern is with the ideological uses to which they are put. To this end he uses televisual reflexivity to challenge the notion of objectivity deployed in mainstream documentary programming. The question of objectivity is explicitly raised in connection with Massingham, the observer whose documentary project provides the pretext for the play's interactions. Massingham goes through the requisite steps of assembling his documentary on Waite's life—tracking down photographs, filming relevant locales—and he presents himself as a disinterested presenter of this evidence. To Maria's question "What would *you* say?" he answers: "That's not my brief. I present; others judge" (49). When William later asks him what his guiding point of view toward his subject is, Massingham reiterates this position: that he will observe the conventional rules of biography and historiography without imposing an agenda. "I'm simply the film camera, the tape-recorder, the lighting man" (54). William rejects such a stance: "you're too intelligent, too clever, really to believe that you can talk as it were neutrally about the past" (53). As William insists, the presentation of a phenomenon such as Labourism necessarily involves accounting for it as a social process and evaluating it in the context of specific values. Even the choice *not* to ask certain questions or engage in explicit judgment, he implies, constitutes an ideological act.

Radical workers in the arts and other fields must reveal the theoretical underpinnings and normative implications of dominant practices, Colin McArthur argues, because these practices (particularly in Britain) "have traditionally denied that they had theoretical bases or normative implications."[27] In *All Good Men* Griffiths critiques the aesthetic/historiographic notion of objectivity to suggest that the television lens is always interested, whether or not this is acknowledged, and that the telling of history is inevitably an ideological gesture. Massingham himself never discloses his real intentions in pursuing the documentary of

Waite's life and career, but there are indications throughout the play that his disinterestedness is indeed a front. Maria, who (like her brother) develops an immediate dislike of him, reads his origin and upbringing in his public school manner, and both she and William react with profound suspicion to someone they perceive as a class enemy. When William confronts him with the report of a mutual acquaintance in the television industry—that no such series as *Living History* seems to be in the works, that Massingham has a reputation for setting up fake projects with other ends in mind—he neither confirms nor denies this. Yet he does accept William's file of incriminating information on his father— "Maybe that way, *your* class loyalty and his . . . objective treachery . . . will stand out more clearly," William tells him (74). And, when Massingham opens the actual interview by jumping right on the events of 1926, it becomes clear that, whatever his ultimate agenda, "objectivity" has served as little more than a strategic tool, implicated in the realities of class difference and class antagonism.

In the play's closing moments Massingham's voice fades out, and the light blazes up to wash out the contours of Waite's face. Gradually moving back, the camera reveals Waite alone in his chair in an empty room, "his baronet's robes draping his still form" (78). In the television version "There'll Always Be an England" is played in the background. Braun sees this closing tableau as "an image of the shabby pragmatism of Labour in office."[28] But this closing portrait of Waite as a mannequin, wearing clothes that ill fit him, has a more personal register as well. The stillness and isolation reflect a life, the roots of which have been repudiated, a life that has seen its past leveled like the pre-1914 Manchester neighborhood that Waite grew up in ("We saw it off, rooted it up and thousands like it. [*Pause.*] Part of our history" [45]). Waite has made the journey between classes so problematic to Griffiths's translated protagonists, and he has found himself a part of neither. Earlier in the play William refers to the squirrels killing a yew outside; Maria explains: "They eat the bark. When the stripped parts meet in a circle, the tree dies" (60). Waite is not dead by the end of the play (though the flaring light and sudden silence have an eerily strokelike feel), but clearly the squirrels have been at work, stripping the old man from both Right and Left and bringing to light a past filled with contradictions and compromise.[29] Perhaps the best pronouncement on his life and works is his own, offered to Maria when they are playing cards: "When I know I'm licked, there's nobody gives up faster" (56).[30]

The Politics of Care: *Through the Night*

Television, Hall writes, revolutionizes the boundaries between art and everyday life; in so doing, it "raises everyday life into a sort of artistic communication" and "continuously transforms the 'real world' into a powerful image of itself."[31] *Through the Night*, one of Griffiths's most widely watched plays, is also his boldest foray into the terrain of everyday experience and its (mis)handling by public institutions. Griffiths had originally been commissioned by Granada TV to write a play about a Sheffield prison, but he abandoned the project when his wife, Jan, was admitted to the hospital for a biopsy on a lump in her breast; when she recovered from the anesthesia she discovered that her breast had been removed. She kept a journal of her experience there, and when Griffiths read this journal he quickly composed a play based on her experiences. Written in "anger and fear," the result is a critique of the medical establishment that draws to an unprecedented—and even harrowing—extent on the lived experience of physical disability and medical dehumanization.

Through the Night (Griffiths's working title for the play was *Maiming of Parts*) follows the working-class Christine Potts from her initial visit to the hospital for an examination through her subsequent stay for a biopsy and (as it turns out) the removal of her left breast. Deliberately challenging the genre of contemporary hospital drama, with its cleaned-up hospital wards and heroic community of doctors, nurses, and other staff, Griffiths's play employs a gritty realism to illustrate the actual conditions of hospital work and treatment. In addition to the grim details of physical suffering and medical treatment, which Griffiths presents with unsparing directness, *Through the Night* also demonstrates the institutional structure of the British medical establishment and the limitations of the National Health Service: a hierarchy of hospitals; within each hospital a clearly delineated professional hierarchy, with its rituals and structures of deference; an underpaid staff responsible for virtually all hands-on care; a shortage of facilities and the resulting delays in consultation and treatment (Christine waits three weeks for each, a time lag that may have allowed her cancer to spread to her lymph nodes).

From the play's opening shot—a close-up of Christine's face, with the voices in the consulting room next to hers barely audible—Griffiths examines medical treatment from the patient's point of view. *Through the Night* offers almost visceral evocations of the fear, helplessness, and disorientation of hospital experience: being wheeled down a hall to the operating "theater" (this journey is filmed entirely from Christine's point of view), unexplained sounds coming from elsewhere in the room at night (when much of the play takes place), having to go to the bathroom, the difficulty of walking. In part the contours of this experience result from the experience of illness and disability, the reversion of the body from a vehicle for encountering the world to what medical phenomenologists call the "thing body," suffering and in need of care.[32] Part of the discomfort evoked by Griffiths's play derives from its portrayal of the body's vulnerable physicality: its weight (resting, being lifted), its composition (tissue, glands, skin), its needs. Beyond the fear connected with something as serious as cancer, illness is a rupture in normalcy, and this is perhaps best captured in the scenes between Christine and her husband, Joe, who is in some ways more frightened than she by the loss of the everyday and its reassurances. In view of such realities there is a certain compassion in the play's presentation of the hospital staff (particularly some of the lower-level workers, like the apprentice nurse Chatterjee), doing what they can to alleviate the facts of mortality.

At the same time, Griffiths's institutional critique suggests, fear and alienation are exacerbated by the dehumanizing practices of the medical establishment itself, which approaches its patients as objects of medical intervention rather than dignified individuals and independent agents. Doctors speak about Christine without addressing her directly and speculate about her condition in technical language to which she has no access. She is asked to sign consent forms she has difficulty reading without having them explained to her (when she signs the second one, the camera catches the word *mastectomy*). If one of Griffiths's principal concerns has always been the interface between subjective and objective reality, television allows him an unprecedented technical opportunity for such dialectical exploration. Exploiting the resources of camera point of view, Griffiths establishes telling counterpoints between events and their experiential register. In her early consultation Christine is completely out of the shot as the doctors discuss her condition. Later, during routine medical rounds following her operation, the camera follows Christine's point of view on the proceedings. When the doctors reach her bed, the head doctor Staunton faces away from her, and the dialogue concerning her condition is "indistinct, barely audible, the odd word floating down the bed to CHRISTINE."[33] Staunton never faces, addresses, or otherwise acknowledges her; as she later describes it: "Nobody says anything. They treat you as if you were already dead. The specialist, he never even looked at me, let alone spoke" (172). *Through the Night* explores the difference between looking and seeing. To most of the senior staff Christine is an object of medical intervention; the callousness underlying this dehumanization is underscored when one of the first scenes after her operation involves a segment of her cancerous tissue being sent to the lab for testing on mice.

When she awakes from her operation to discover that she has lost the breast, Christine is plunged into postoperative trauma and depression, her grief and fear now compounded by uncertainty concerning her prognosis ("I don't know why they did it. Nobody's said" [156]). Her husband's assurances that the doctors know what they're doing ring noticeably hollow. In the middle of the night a day or two later Christine gets up by herself and makes her way to the bathroom; there she locks herself in one of the cubicles. It is a gesture of reclamation, as she seeks a personal space not subject to intrusion, a womblike protective enclosure. But it also becomes a gesture of resistance, her first, when she refuses to open the door when she's discovered there. Only when the junior doctor Pearce arrives, doing a Humphrey Bogart imitation over the top of the cubicle door, does she consent to leave. Pearce, whose unshaven, jacket-and-T-shirt appearance is scruffy and undoctorlike (like O'Toole in Griffith's later play *The Gulf between Us*, he is a gadfly of sorts), has stood throughout the play in counterpoint to the hospital's conventions of institutional behavior and patient address. In contrast to Staunton (who handles her impersonally and speaks in a "patient-excluding voice" [136]), Pearce examines Christine's breast in the play's opening scene after smiling at her, calling her by name, and asking her permission. Resisting the compromises of the institution he has chosen to join, he jokes and flirts with the ward's women patients yet also addresses them with directness and concern.

Pearce brings Christine to his office—messy, human, it is the first hospital room to feel lived in—for hot cocoa. There he responds to her questions forthrightly, explaining her condition to her and discussing her symptoms and prognosis. In a speech that even Griffiths has acknowledged is overly rhetorical and explicit, Pearce broadens his discussion to include the failures and limitations of the medical system as a whole.[34] Christine was never told about her symptoms, he tells her, because the system as a whole has lost sight of her as "a whole, human being, with a past, a personality, dependants, needs, hopes, wishes." He explains:

> Our power is strongest when you are dependent upon it. We invite you to behave as the sum of your *symptoms*. And on the whole you are pleased to oblige. (*Long pause*.) Mr. Staunton's a good man. He's just . . . not used, not equipped . . . to deal with you as a person. The gap is too great. (173)

Pearce quotes Hippocrates on the need to bridge this gap: "Whoever treats of this art should treat of things which are familiar to the common people. [. . .] For whoever does not reach the capacity of the common people and fails to make them listen to him, misses his mark." At the end of this speech, after Christine has thanked him, he urges her to a further stage of self-repossession: "Don't thank. Demand" (174).

Pearce's final words to Christine are a charge to live every day for keeps: "The rest of us may continue to cherish the illusion that we're immortal. You know you're not" (173). Although she can be given no greater assurance than Pearce's assessment that her chances are good, Christine has clearly begun to come to terms with her now-changed body. For one thing she can now look at the scar on her chest. The gulf that she crosses by doing so is considerable. Like Louise Page's 1978 play *Tissue*, which also explores the trauma of mastectomy, *Through the Night* deliberately sets itself against the cultural eroticizing of the female breast. Shortly after her operation Christine opens a copy of the *Sun* only to come upon the page-three pinup, "both stunning breasts on display" (165). When Christine's own breasts are revealed (for medical and television audience alike), the context of their visibility has already been shifted from the erotic to the medical (one shot of her breast also reveals the biopsy mark). At the end of the play the camera will be directed to the scar that remains and the beginnings, for Christine, of a difficult process of re-aestheticizing. "It's a *beautiful* scar," Chatterjee exclaims. "What did he do it with," Christine grins—"a bottle?" (175).

In the play's final scene Christine joins other women in the ward for surreptitious drinks behind the bed curtains of Mrs. Scully, a woman who has had most of her stomach removed and is one of the most irreverent and least passive of the ward's patients. Like Christine's solo trip to the bathroom, this action is transgressive beyond its flouting of nighttime ward regulations. In an institution that operates through the enforced isolation of its patients, the makeshift party represents a coming together and the assertion of solidarity. To the extent that the exercise of institutional authority has also involved subtle and not-so-subtle gender hierarchies, the surreptitious gathering is also the achievement of a specifically female community. If the institutions of capitalist society work to "split us up, set us against each other and against ourselves, in classes, in thought, in lifestyles, in aspirations and all the rest of it" (the words are from *Bill Brand*),[35] we are reminded here of the vision that has always stood at the center of Griffiths's socialist ideal: the sense of spontaneous community, grounded in shared experience and mutual support. Edward Waite's description in *All Good Men* of his boyhood in Manchester applies equally to the defiant yet life-affirming end of Griffiths's most painful play: "We were *alive*, for one thing. That was something. (*Pause.*) And . . . we had each other. [. . .] *Bound* to each other, you might say."[36]

Postscript: Reception
More than any other of Griffiths's plays for television, *Through the Night* bore out the playwright's faith in television as a powerful, wide-reaching tool for social engagement. When the play was aired by the BBC on 2 December 1975 (a year after Griffiths wrote it; claiming that the play was too harsh and that it would cost too much to produce, Granada had turned down the project), it was watched by an estimated eleven million viewers. The BBC switchboard was jammed with nearly a hundred calls immediately after the program, and the BBC Audience Research Bulletin reported that the play's reaction index of 76 and audience figure of 23 percent were outstandingly high for the *Play for Today* series.[37] Features sparked by the series appeared in the popular press. A woman columnist for the *Sunday Mirror* invited women to write in with their experience of mastectomy and received over eighteen hundred letters in ten days, while a columnist for the *Somerset County Gazette* was moved by the play to go to a woman's transportable screening unit for gynecological and breast exams (her article describes the exam and tells women how to make appointments).[38] Several weeks later a consultant hematologist at St. George's Hospital, London, published an article in *World Medicine* in which he commended Griffiths's play: "I have no comments or criticism on Griffiths's play—he said it all and I for one just watched, stunned by the shame of it all and just a little encouraged by the possibility of a new start."[39]

Griffiths himself received some 180 letters from viewers responding to the play's power and accuracy. Some of these letters were written by medical personnel; others came from women who saw their own experience reflected in the play. A London woman wrote: "Your Chris-

tine's ordeal was like a picnic compared to the treatment I received. . . .
How I loved your scruffy Doctor because he cared and spoke to Christine as if she mattered," while a woman from Hertfordshire commented,
"So many small incidents were exact recreations of my experience."
Writing of her four-month wait before being admitted to the hospital for
breast cancer, a Dundee woman wrote: "If your play had been on TV
last year I am sure I would have done more by kicking up a fuss to get
into hospital sooner." A woman from New Zealand said that the play
reduced her to tears; clearly, she was not alone.[40]

One of Griffiths's correspondents wrote that for the first time she
was "sufficiently moved by the quality of a television [program] to be
compelled to write to its author"; another noted that the play was disturbing but added: "far better to be disturbed by a good play that rings
true than put to sleep by a fairy tale."[41] As these articles and letters testify, Griffiths's refusal to minimize the difficulty of the play's medical,
political, and emotional issues found an audience far more sophisticated than the mass audience generally posited by practitioners of the
medium. In *Culture and Society* Raymond Williams challenged the
notion of the "masses" implicit in elite culture's denigration of mass
communication: "The conception of persons as masses springs, not from
an inability to know them, but from an interpretation of them according
to a formula. . . . If our purpose is art, education, the giving of information or opinion, our interpretation will be in terms of the rational and
interested being."[42] From this point of view *Through the Night*'s exploration of institutional communication mirrors Griffiths's similar challenging of television and its portrayal of social and individual experience. His determination not to condescend to his audience and his
willingness to challenge his viewers with a portrayal dramatically outside the conventions of hospital drama were met by an audience eager
enough for such communication that it took the opportunity to speak
back.

Toward the Recent Future: *Bill Brand*

On the night of the February 1974 general election Griffiths met with
Stella Richardson, an independent producer who had seen *The Party*
and was interested in talking with him. They met at a restaurant-club on
the Thames where (in Griffiths's words) a number of "rich showbiz
types" were awaiting the election results, having laid out money on a

Tory victory.[43] As the results came in and it became clear that Harold Wilson's Labour Party would return to power, Griffiths watched as the buoyant mood yielded to shock and dismay. Against this backdrop Richardson and Griffiths discussed the possibility of a series on a Labour MP in Parliament, and before the evening was over they had begun sketching out a preliminary outline for the series. The result was *Bill Brand*, and, after Stuart Burge was brought in as producer, the project was eventually sold to Thames TV. Griffiths has described the production process as one of the most satisfying he has been involved in, with all members of the production team committed and democratically involved in decisions concerning the project. Faced with a decision by the Thames program controller to televise the series at 10:30 P.M. during the summer, as we have seen, approximately seventy people showed up in protest; though the summer scheduling was retained, the series was placed in the more widely exposed 9:00 P.M. slot. After budgetary limitations forced Griffiths to reduce the script from thirteen to eleven episodes, *Bill Brand* was broadcast on Monday nights from 7 June to 16 August 1976. Widely viewed and extensively discussed in the popular press and in political publications, the series was clearly (in Braun's words) "an unequalled example of television drama as a form of extended political dialogue."[44]

Coming on the heels of *All Good Men*, Griffiths's decision to continue his exploration of the Labour Party represented his intensifying interest in the politics and possibilities of parliamentary socialism. Griffiths's own relationship with the Labour Party had always, we have seen, been deeply conflicted. Griffiths's brief membership in the party lasted little more than a year, and his decision to leave it reflected a wider disillusionment on the Left with the policies pursued by the Wilson administration. But the Labour Party overlapped with a broader Left culture in important ways, and Griffiths's participation in both Manchester and Stockport Left circles involved him with radical groupings both within and outside Labour's more formal organizational structures (the fact that Griffiths was himself considered as a candidate for a Labour seat clearly planted the seed for *Bill Brand*). It also exposed him to the constituency level of party politics and allowed him to observe the complicated interface of party machinery and local experience. Griffiths's description of the project shows his almost pedagogical concern with conveying the particularity of this and other aspects of a leftist MP's experience:

It seemed an important thing to do, if you're talking about politics in Britain now, to examine and to explore social democracy as well as revolutionism. What I've tried to do, is present as full a picture as I can of a Member's life in all its complexity and its density. So I spend quite a lot of time in the constituency, quite a lot of time in Parliament, in committee, in the desk room, the bar, wherever. We're investigating the stuff, the actual tissue and texture, of the social democratic process within a major party.[45]

The preoccupation with Labourism in both *All Good Men* and *Bill Brand* also has more contemporary motivations and ramifications. By the early-middle 1970s the Labour Party found itself increasingly divided between a moderate-Right revisionist wing and an increasingly radical left-wing membership (with links to Trotskyite and trade union radicalism). *Labour's Program 1973*, with its call for the nationalization of twenty-five of Britain's largest manufacturers, sweeping extensions of welfare services, and a shift of wealth toward the working class, was one of the party's most radical manifestos since 1945. Wilson's rejection of the nationalization provision underscored ideological and policy divisions that would plague Labour as it prepared for its return to office (a division that would eventually lead, after Thatcher's election, to the Labour Party's leftward tracking and the splintering off, in 1981, of the centrist-Right Social Democratic Party). As it assumed office for the third time since 1964—against a backdrop of economic difficulty, industrial unrest, and perceived national decline—the Labour Party contained sharply divergent opinions about its role in a capitalist society in crisis. By March 1976, when Wilson made the surprise announcement that he would retire and the Party was forced to negotiate his succession, the differences between Left and Center-Right were cast in even greater relief.

Although the episodes of *Bill Brand* were written before the leadership crisis and vote, Griffiths's play anticipated these events and their eventual outcome (support from the Center-Right gave James Callaghan victory over the leftist Michael Foot) with uncanny prescience. Much of the discussion of the series within the British press involved speculations on the "identities" of Griffiths's fictional politicians, and, though resemblances are undeniable between characters in the series and leading Labor politicians, Griffiths has been at pains to insist that his characters occupy "a fictional metaworld," in which they represent political stances more than individuals.[46] Griffiths's alternate title for the series, "Toward the Recent Future," suggests that its temporal reference goes beyond the merely topical.

The protagonist of the series is Brand, a former liberal studies teacher at a local technical school and former member of the International Socialists, who narrowly wins a parliamentary by-election in Leighley, a fictional suburb of Manchester. Conceived with the autobiographical touches familiar among Griffiths's characters, he interacts throughout the series with his chemical worker father (who dies before the series is over); his shirt cutter brother, Eddie; his estranged wife, Miriam; and his mistress, Alex Ferguson, a community activist and feminist. Brand's victory is a cause for excitement among Al Jowett, his agent, and other supporters within the constituency. But Brand himself seems uneasy at the prospect of the political career he is embarking upon and at the inevitable conflict between his socialist beliefs and the compromises of institutional politics. Over the course of the play he runs into situations that dramatize this conflict, and, though he takes stands on principles that set him against his constituency, the party machinery, and even the left-wing Journal Group (a fictional version of the Labour Party's Tribune Group), he acknowledges that the conflicts he faces are internal ones as well. Speaking to Alex in bed after an awkward session of lovemaking, he confesses to her that he's "stopped feeling real." He says: "I have these two voices, in here. (*Hand on head*) I say two, it's never less than two, sometimes it's in the upper thirties. . . . They say: might, right; power, principle; pragmatism, precept; slow, quick; one day, now." Alex adds: "Parliament, people; consensus, struggle?"[47]

The terms of these contradictions are explored in Brand's interactions with the play's other characters, many of whom are themselves drawn in terms of contradiction. These characters, individuals who have given their lives to politics, confront Brand with the often conflicting demands of principle and pragmatism. In episode 7 Brand argues passionately against a government-sponsored antiterrorism motion, maintaining that the bill would erode democratic freedoms, that the problem of violence in Northern Ireland is a function of Britain's imperialist intervention, and that the violence of terrorists is nothing compared to the violence intrinsic to capitalist exploitation. In episode 8 he must deal with anger in his constituency at his stance (his wife's house is attacked). Brand argues with Frank Hilton, a regional party official, that he cannot do his job "with one eye over my shoulder to see what the *people* are gonna say." Hilton responds with a reminder that the people are his ultimate responsibility and that there is no greater error than for the leader to lose touch with the led: "I know that, Bill. But you can't do that despising them, either. . . . Do you know what Gorki said when he arrived at some godforsaken spot in outer Russia somewhere to lecture the peasants on socialism? He said: 'Is this the rabble on which we are to build the revolution?' Well, the answer's yes, Mr. Gorki, yes, Mr. Brand. Because without them there *is* no revolution. We're all you've got, comrade" (8:17–18). Aware himself of the importance of this connection, Brand has taken a house in a working-class neighborhood.

Earlier, in episode 4, Brand has a long conversation with David Last, the leftist minister of employment who invites Brand to join his party leadership campaign as parliamentary party secretary. Echoing Jake's earlier conversation with the former labor organizer Noble in *The Love Maniac,* Brand accuses Last of abandoning his earlier radical integrity: "I read your book on Morris when I was seventeen, your book on Tom Mann a bit later. (*Pause*) I've always seen you as in the tradition, a fixity, part of an earlier Great Refusal. [. . .] Now . . . there's nobody where you were . . . and there's nobody where you are" (4:43–44). Responding that he's sixty suddenly and that rhetoric for him is no longer enough, Last counters that socialist transformation "has to be made, and it has to be led." He acknowledges that the greatest challenge is to combat the inertia of government itself: "If parliament *is* the seat of real political power in this society, why, when we're in office, do we slide and squelch about like shysters and milksops when it comes to translating our programs into realities?" (4:45). Brand decides to accept his invitation, and the two end the scene by jointly quoting from T. S. Eliot's "Little Gidding": "But this is the nearest in place and time,/ Now and in England" (4:50).

Exercising the power and the prerogatives of political power, Brand is able to take effective action and to find a platform for advocating his socialist beliefs. He fights to prevent closures in the textile industry, speaking during a factory occupation and pursuing a motion for restructuring the industry. He obtains an abortion for a woman who has been denied one, risking the wrath of his predominantly Catholic constituency. But his recurrent feeling is one of ineffectuality. As he tells Alex: "A year ago I thought this was the place to push. I think I was wrong. If I'm gonna be a social worker, I might as well do social work. I just . . . can't find the politics. They aren't there. Maybe they never were" (8:37). This impotence is reflected, as is so often in Griffiths's plays, in sexual ineffectuality. His marriage with Miriam has failed, and his relationship with Alex is characterized by awkwardness and failure. Alex leaves Brand and the series after episode 8 (she acknowledges sleeping with other men and tells him that she's moved on), and the connection is left without further development or resolution.

Griffiths has stated that one of his intentions in writing *Bill Brand* was to play off the formal conventions of the popular TV series.[48] Related to this goal is the series' critique of television and its presentation of politics, both electoral and otherwise. In *Bill Brand* the presence of television in the individual and public realm has broadened and intensified to the point where politics itself is seen as deeply implicated in media culture and televisual modes of apprehension. Television sets are everywhere in the play—in Brand's living room, in the chief whip's office—and they are often tuned to political programming. In episode 8 Brand meets Last in a Granada TV studio dressing room, where the latter is preparing to be interviewed for a program entitled "A Year from Now"; later, after meeting his brother in a local Conservative Club, Brand watches Last's appearance on TV. Episode 11 has a scene at Lime Grove studio, with a television on in the corner (broadcasting the *Play for Today*); later in the episode Brand watches John Venables's ministerial speech on television after the Center-Right candidate has won the leadership battle.

By giving the media (and television in particular) such prominence in the series, Griffiths calls attention once again to the politics of the medium that his interventionist strategy has led him to exploit. The reflexive presence of camera and screen serves to underscore the mystifications and misrepresentations of television coverage. The process by which television constructs its subject and thereby frames the Real as media artifact is the metatextual superstructure of episode 6. This episode, which centers on the Labour Party's Blackpool Conference, opens in the office of the director responsible for filming the conference. He goes through a rehearsal of the planned shots (we see a bank of four television monitors), runs the opening sequence (with music and titles), then prepares for the real thing: "Right. All we need now is a few bodies and we're away" (6:1). As the conference gets under way, Griffiths cuts between the actual conference and those responsible for presenting it (technicians in the van, commentators). The discrepancy between reality and presentation could not be more pronounced, especially when the behind-the-scene maneuvering that we see is counterpointed by commentators discussing the Labour Party as a democratic party whose decisions are made on the floor. In the episode's closing sequences Griffiths shows Last, Jowett, and Brand watching scenes from the confer-

ence on television; in the scene's sharpest irony (given the profound
divisions that exist within the party), the episode ends with the televisual spectacle of delegates holding hands and singing the "Red Flag."

Despite the series's obvious fascination with organized politics and
its contradictory imperatives, its view of the Labour Party in office is a
critical one. "What I was trying to say throughout the series," Griffiths
observes, "was that the traditions of the Labour movement were inade-
quate to take the struggle further, and that we had to discover new traditions, or revive even older ones. And that we had to seek connective
tissue between electoral party politics, which still has a mystifying mass
appeal, and extra-parliamentary socialist activity."[49] The view of the
Labour Party offered by *Bill Brand* is one in which truly meaningful
change is always sacrificed to a pragmatic defense of the capitalist system. In the final episode (entitled "It Is the People Who Create") Brand
himself seems to reaffirm the roots of political struggle in the people and
their aspirations. After watching Venables's speech, he goes to see a
touring Fringe political theater group headed by an old university
friend. The evening includes a collection of performance pieces on the
politics of sexuality, and, while the quality of what he sees is decidedly
uneven, Brand loves it.[50] He stays around as the group discusses
whether their piece is elitist and wonders how they might make it relevant to working-class audiences, and he later houses the young performers. After an exchange with a Chilean woman who says she will
return to her country "when we have won" (11:63), Brand receives a
parcel of letters from people signing up for the Fight for Work campaign. He watches from his doorway as the group sings "Venceremos"
(a song from the Cuban Revolution) and a woman neighbor encourages
them to "Keep it up won't you" (11:64).

In the previous scene Jowett affirmed to Brand that capitalism
"*breeds* resistance, in every worker who goes down the road, in every
tenant evicted, in every man and woman denied the chance to be
human" (11:56). Like other moments of spontaneous activism and revolutionary sentiment in Griffiths's plays, the image of people singing
while a popular campaign to combat unemployment gathers support is
intended as an image of the solidarity that Jowett's words imply. But the
focus of this scene is on Brand, who watches the scene "half moved, half
critically separate from the experience" (11:66). The balance is important, for he remains a troubled observer, still struggling over the terms
of his participation, no more able to resolve the contradictions of socialist vision and its implementation than he was ten episodes earlier.[51]

5

Class Comedy, Classic Texts

Laughter, Complicity, Performance: *Comedians*

Midway through *Reds*, the 1981 film based on Griffiths's screenplay collaboration with Warren Beatty, John Reed and Louise Bryant journey by train to St. Petersburg to witness the early stages of the Russian Revolution. At one point on the journey Reed tells a joke about a diminutive logger who boasts of having cleared "the Sahara Forest." Although Joe Volski, the Russian émigré who is accompanying them on the journey, has had Louise in stitches with his own patter of jokes, the two of them stare blankly at Reed when he completes his own bid for attention. Politeness might have dictated otherwise, but it's hard to blame them: the delivery is off, the timing all wrong, and the joke (as it turns out) is a pretty feeble one.

While the scene offers little to the film's historical or psychological development beyond the demonstration of a social awkwardness on Reed's part and the chilliness of his relationship with Louise at this point, it resonates in interesting ways with Griffiths's work as a whole. Griffiths himself may not be able to tell a joke for the life of him (so he claims), but humor and comic performance occupy an important place in his plays and films. The first act of *Sam, Sam* is written in the mode of stand-up comedy, while the opening sequence of *The Party* filters Karl through Groucho in Griffiths's own agitprop Marx Brothers routine. Pearce jokes with his patients in *Through the Night*, and even Bill Brand (not one of Griffiths's most light-spirited characters) tries his hand at a couple. As these plays demonstrate, Griffiths's work can be surprisingly funny, opening to moments of humor out of the most serious circumstances and playing even the most difficult issues and experiences through a comic register ("A man walks into surgery," one of Brand's jokes begins, echoing and reframing Griffiths's almost unbearably intimate earlier play).[1] For all the earnestness that often characterizes his work, politics and laughter have always been deeply intertwined in Griffiths's political and dramatic imagination.

The scene in *Reds* is also, of course, an allusion to what had become, for many, Griffiths's signature play. More than any other play he has written, *Comedians* has identified Griffiths in the popular, theatrical, and academic imagination. From its opening at the Nottingham Playhouse on 20 February 1975 (under the direction of Richard Eyre) to its subsequent opening in London at the Old Vic (24 September) and on the West End (Wyndham's Theatre, 27 January 1976), *Comedians* was widely acclaimed in the popular press. It soon became the work by which most North Americans were introduced to Griffiths as a writer. A production directed by Mike Nichols opened on Broadway at the Music Box Theater on 28 November 1976, and, although this particular production received mixed reviews, it was widely considered one of the season's most significant plays. Jonathan Pryce, a previously unknown actor who had originated the role of Gethin Price in Nottingham, earned a Tony Award for his performance, and a film version of the play was briefly considered (Griffiths's television adaptation of the play was broadcast as part of the BBC's *Play for Today* series on 25 October 1979). The play has been revived a number of times—a highly acclaimed 1993 revival of the play by the West Yorkshire Playhouse moved that summer to the Lyric Theatre, Hammersmith—and it has been performed in translation around the world: *L'école des comiques* was performed by Le Théâtre National de Belgique in May 1976, *Komiker* was produced in Hamburg in January 1978, and the play has subsequently been staged as far away as Shanghai.[2] In March 1987 *Comedians* was presented by an all-woman cast at the Everyman Theatre in Liverpool; in April 1992 it was performed at the Court Theater in Chicago by an all-black and Hispanic cast in a production directed by Barney Simon of the Johannesburg Market Theatre. Griffiths adapted the play for both productions (Chicago comedian Aaron Freeman helped him with the latter adaptation). The play's influence has extended beyond the theater: until it was withdrawn in 1993, *Comedians* was on the Associated Examining Board A-level exam list, and Griffiths accepted a dozen or so invitations a year to discuss the play with students and teachers.[3]

It is easy to see why *Comedians* received such widespread popular interest. "I wanted it to be like some of my television plays," Griffiths has commented, "more immediately accessible to people who haven't had a background in revolutionary theory or revolutionary history or whatever."[4] Shifting terrain from the history of socialist struggle and the Left's internal debates, Griffiths chose a topic more fully grounded in interpersonal interactions and hence (as the play's amenability to cultural translation suggests) more generalizable. At the same time, while *Comedians* may not be "overtly" marked by revolutionary theory (given the scarcity of socialist writings on the topic of humor, this isn't surprising), its concerns and techniques draw upon the central preoccupations of Griffiths's work as a whole. Indeed, part of the play's achievement is its demonstration that comedy and laughter constitute sites of often intricate political and ethical negotiation. Laughter, for Griffiths, is a social act that is caught up in questions of inclusion and exclusion, liberation and entrapment, involvement and distance. Griffiths explores the politics of this ostensibly apolitical field while using the device of comedic performance to engage his audience with unusual directness. Through a series of reflexive gestures *Comedians* asks us to think about its own dramaturgical foundations, raising questions about performativity (comic and otherwise) while exploring the instabilities and interfaces of realism as a political aesthetic.

The idea for *Comedians* came to Griffiths in a Manchester bar, where he fell into conversation with a couple of stand-up comedians who had been taping sessions for a Granada TV series entitled *The Comedians* (this popular show, which ran between 1971 and 1985, featured stand-up comics delivering jokes from the workingmen's club circuit to a studio audience).[5] These comedians mentioned an older comedian, veteran of the local club circuit, who ran a class for local comics upstairs in a pub. Griffiths, who had been fascinated by stand-up comics since he first encountered them in local halls during the late 1940s and early 1950s, was drawn to this anecdote. In addition to the question of what it took to be a stand-up comic (and how someone would go about teaching a skill that seems so instinctual), the anecdote underscored a contradiction within the profession as a whole. While the comedians spoke of this teacher as someone whose practice was grounded in principle, their own careers were based on jokes that pandered to the audience's basest prejudices. Griffiths found himself reflecting upon the tradition of stand-up comedy and the contrasts between the antagonistic stance of much contemporary comedy and the tradition's earlier roots in a music-hall, working-class culture, in which comedy (in the hands of comedians like Frank Randall) was used to confront and come to terms with shared concerns. These reflections were also personal, for the issue of comedy foregrounded for Griffiths his own involvement in the contradictions he encountered: "What none of us really explores inside the liberal cultural tradition is contradiction. And the contradiction that increasingly preoccupied me was: 'Why do I laugh until my frame shakes at something as ugly as this joke?'"[6]

Griffiths's decision to write a play about the politics of stand-up comedy reflects his interest in popular culture and its modes of political negotiation; this interest, already evident in *Sam, Sam,* would deepen in his plays and films of the 1980s. But Griffiths's focus on the political psychology of laughter reveals a more specific concern with pleasure and complicity, with the modes by which culture—popular and otherwise—compels assent to its ideological content. In so doing, Griffiths anticipates an issue that would increasingly concern the field of cultural studies in the 1980s and 1990s. In his 1986 article "Complicit Pleasures" Colin Mercer discusses the "problem of pleasure" as it has emerged within cultural analysis. As Mercer suggests, Brecht, Bakhtin, and Barthes are among the few theorists who have addressed "the nature of our *contract*—the complex nature of our complicity—with cultural forms."[7] Drawing upon Gramsci's notion of consent (with a nod to Barthes's term *jouissance*), Mercer describes the analysis of this pleasure as, in part, an "interrogation of the 'fact' of ideology . . . a rejection of the ascribed unity and omniscience, of its depth and homogeneity, of its stasis within a given cultural form." Mercer continues: "It may now be important to look over our shoulders and try to explain a certain 'guilt' of enjoyment of such and such *in spite of* its known ideological and political provenance." In words that underscore the link between *Comedians* and Griffiths's broader project of cultural penetration, such an analysis recognizes both "the complexity of our relationship to cultural forms and . . . the recognition of fissures, points of 'non-communication' and of resistance in what is sometimes called the area of 'mass communications.'"[8]

The opening and closing acts of *Comedians* take place in a Manchester secondary school classroom, now open as an evening center for adult education courses. The school was built in 1947, three years after the Education Act that sought to free education from its class hierarchy, but its present condition attests to the decayed state of this originating vision. The desks are worn and chipped, the charts and maps on the walls frayed and torn. The building is marked by neglect, and, when adults return to the school to take courses in a variety of subjects, the school can muster only "its sullen best" to accommodate them.[9] Like the Eton backdrop that opens Griffiths's 1981 play *Country*, the setting of *Comedians* constitutes a "classroom" in all the word's socioeconomic and ideological meanings. The school offers its services to the nonprivileged, and the grudging opportunities for further education it provides must be understood in the context of an urgent desire for economic advancement. The students who make up Eddie Waters's class in stand-up comedy represent a mixture of the (male) working class: Gethin Price, who drives a van for British Rail; George McBrain, a Northern Irish docker; Phil Murray, an insurance salesman; Ged Murray, a milkman; Sammy Samuels, a Jewish small-club owner; and Mick Connor, an Irish builder. Some arrive directly from work, and the pressures and privations that constitute their lives are revealed in a number of ways (Price, who arrives early, has to shave in the classroom). They dream of "making it" and thereby rescuing their lives from social anonymity. When Samuels is asked why he doesn't just perform in his own club, he responds in anger: "I wouldn't be seen dead working in a club like mine, I want the tops, I want TV, I want the Palladium" (24).

The play's setting, like most of Griffiths's others, is drawn with a realist's attention to particularizing detail, and this specificity locates the play's field of action in historically and geographically definable terms: Manchester, mid-1970s. But Griffiths's stage directions also play with the parameters of realism, exploiting its contradictions and confronting it with rival manipulations of the Real. Griffith specifies that the clock above the blackboard registers real time throughout the scene, marking 7:27 before the performance begins and continuing thereafter to indicate the audience's time. By doing so, Griffiths exposes the sleight-of-hand that underlines realism's pretense to authenticity. As the term *verisimilitude* indicates, realism hinges on the principle of illusionism, whereby a world seemingly contiguous with the audience's own world acquires this "true-seeming" effect by effacing the actuality of its own theatrical moment. Dramatic time, one crucial aspect of realism's represented world, is constituted through an erasure of theatrical time—the time of performance, the time of the audience's own lives. Breaking the parameters of realist illusionism, Griffiths subverts its claims to representational adequacy, confronting time and place with a radical historicity and offering his spectators a world that both refers to and *includes* their own. Griffiths's onstage clock complicates the notion of realism by counterpointing illusionism with actuality, the dramatically "real" with the actual-real of the theatrical present. In so doing, it opens the play to audience-stage interactions normally precluded by the realist aesthetic. Griffiths's later acts will further exploit these opportunities.[10]

In order to explore the complex, often divergent ways in which humor implicates its participants in the world it takes as its subject, Griffiths sets up a confrontation in the play's first act between contrasting views of the comedian's art. The most urgent of these is presented by Waters, the seventy-year-old former comedian who teaches the course for aspiring comics. Played in the original production by Jimmy Jewel, a veteran of the music-hall comedy circuit himself, Waters seeks to impress upon his apprentices the comedian's higher social calling. True comedy, for Waters, is more than just a form of entertainment; it is a tool for confronting the often painful truths of people's lives. "A comedian draws pictures of the world," he is fond of telling them. "The closer you look, the better you'll draw" (20). In an exercise designed to develop verbal suppleness, Waters rehearses his students in a tongue-twister: "The traitor distrusts the truth" (18).

But comedy's truth-telling mission, for Waters, involves more than merely evoking the uncomfortable or the taboo. While ordinary comedians draw upon the socially unsayable for the sake of merely discharging it, the true comedian strives for the truth as an act of individual and social empowerment:

> A real comedian—that's a daring man. He *dares* to see what his listeners shy away from, fear to express. And what he sees is a sort of truth about people, about their situation, about what hurts or terrifies them, about what's hard, above all, about what they *want*. A joke releases the tension, says the unsayable, any joke pretty well. But a true joke, a comedian's joke, has to do more than release tension. It has to *liberate* the will and the desire, it has to *change* the situation. (20)

Comedy, for Waters, is both educative and transformative; it makes people confront "their prejudices and fear and blinkered vision" so that they can "find their pain and their beauty." By defamiliarizing the everyday and performing its contradictions, the best comics illuminate the troubling aspects of social experience, "make them clearer to see, easier to deal with" (23). In Waters's view comedy is a kind of medicine, and its healing function derives from the honesty and transformative vision that underlie it. The revolutionary overtones of Waters's language here underscore his faith that the truth-telling essential to true comedy is a radical mode of social communication.

If one of the functions of humor is to establish a space of community through the release of laughter and the achievement of shared recognition, then the terms by which this community is constituted become a central political issue. Community can form through an acknowledgment of shared experience, but it can also be asserted through the scapegoating of others. Waters contrasts his view of comedy as remedy with humor predicated on stereotype as a mode of exclusion. When Price recites a dirty limerick that he has made up (about a woman who masturbates with her teeth while hanging from a light), Waters responds by calmly delivering a list of stereotypes directed at the Irish, Jews, blacks, women, cripples, the working class. Having established the degradation implicit in such stereotypes (all of the members of the class find themselves the targets of one or more of these), he analyzes the misogyny animating Price's limerick. "It's a joke that hates women *and* sex," he tells Price, pointing out the dynamic by which the woman is blamed for the fear her sexuality occasions (22). When McBrain asks if the joke doesn't succeed in liberating the fear, Waters insists that it merely traps fear—leaves it exactly where it is without doing anything to change it—thereby feeding on ignorance and starving its audience.

In keeping with Griffiths's dialectical strategy, Waters's conception of comedy as a redemptive social calling is contrasted with the view of Bert Challenor, a talent spotter for the Comedy Artists and Managers Federation who will evaluate the aspiring comedians during their scheduled public performances. Waters has known Challenor for years and despises everything he stands for; when Challenor speaks to the class (in Waters's absence), the reason becomes clear. Challenor presents comedy as entertainment, and he urges the aspiring comics to play to whatever desires their audience brings with them: "It's the people who pay the bills, remember, yours and mine . . . Mr. Waters's. We're servants, that's all. They demand, we supply. Any good comedian can lead an audience by the nose. But only in the direction they're going. And that direction is, quite simply . . . escape. We're not missionaries, we're suppliers of laughter" (33). Waters's language of interventionism and social transformation has been replaced here by a mercantilist discourse of supply and demand. Challenor rejects any possibility that comedy might act upon the world it describes and addresses; indeed, he proposes comedy as a way out of the world. Although his portrait of the audience may seem to elevate it to a position of power within the comedic interaction (demand dictating supply), his language reflects a contempt for those who pay the comedian's bills. Challenor's conception of comedy diminishes the audience by identifying it with its crudest, most unexamined desires and by denying it a vision of anything better. Escape, in the end, is the ultimate form of disempowerment.

"Shuffling towards Bethlehem"

Because Challenor represents access to the professional world they so desperately want to join, the dilemma with which the aspiring comics are faced is an acute one: maintaining a principled stance at the price of continued professional exclusion or pursuing institutional acceptance by compromising their ethical stance. The response of each to such antithetical imperatives forms the subject of the play's second act, the moment when the comedians deliver their own routines in their first public forum.

Act 2 of *Comedians* is set in a workingmen's club during a break in the bingo games that provide the evening's main activity. In keeping with his dramaturgical critique of realism and its illusionistic parameters, Griffiths's staging of this act directly implicates the audience in the play's analysis of comic performance and response. The actors perform their routines on a small club stage positioned on the play's stage, and their acts are addressed to an invisible club audience positioned where the actual audience sits. Further complicating the line between fictional time and the real time of performance, the effect of this doubled staging is to make Griffiths's audience both actual and surrogate addressees of the stand-up routines. As in *Sam, Sam* and *The Party*, stand-up comedy enables Griffiths to open up the audience-stage relationship to more direct forms of address.[11] Encouraged by the play's earlier debate to remain critically self-conscious, Griffiths's spectators find themselves both recipients of the act's stand-up jokes and analysts of their own laughter, forced to acknowledge the political stance implicit in their response. Griffiths, who believes that humor has a place in public self-examination, underscores the importance of audience self-critique to *Comedians'* reflexive laughter: "The characteristic of the play is to set up something as funny and then take a look at it and say, 'Well, that's not really so funny' and this could become increasingly disturbing for audiences. If the play works at all, by the end the audience should be making some very conscious evaluations about what they laugh at."[12]

Throughout act 2 Waters and Challenor sit at tables on either side of the club stage, underscoring through their positions the moral choices facing both performers and audience. The comics respond to these choices in different ways. Connor, who goes first, follows Waters's ethical prescriptions. His jokes poke fun at his own Irishness, but they do so in the context of what it means to be a foreigner and encounter a wall of stereotypes. He ends by encouraging them to "speak well of the living. Especially within earshot" (40). Samuels starts off in a similar vein, exploiting the rich tradition of Jewish humor with its warm self-mocking and its delight in cleverness and resilience. But midway through the routine Samuels looks at Challenor, who sits unresponsively, and he decides to shift ground. The remainder of his routine is a brutal medley of jokes directed at the Irish, women, blacks, and gays.

Phil and Ged Murray, who ended the previous act in violent disagreement about what to do with the joint routine they had so carefully rehearsed, run into immediate conflict during their onstage performance. The two have worked out a vaudeville routine in which Ged is placed as a ventriloquist's dummy on his brother's leg. In the middle of their performance, however, Phil changes the routine and asks his brother to tell a Pakistani joke. Refusing to play along, Ged leaves his brother to stammer through the joke on his own. Although the two manage to exit the stage with a song, their routine is a fiasco, torn apart by the conflicting pressures that Ged (at least) is unwilling to paper over.

When asked by Samuels what he is going to do in response to Challenor's instructions, McBrain responds: "I'll think of something. Well known you know for my flexibility" (34). He has clearly arrived at his decision before taking the stage, for he delivers a routine that is in every way the antithesis of Connor's. His jokes are directed at the Irish, though, with a self-hating logic, they rely on stereotypes and insult. They also target his wife with a misogyny ("God, what a slut" [47]) that echoes the working-class Sam One's stand-up derision of his wife's sexuality and physical habits in the earlier *Sam, Sam*. As a measure of the compromise implicit in these jokes, we will later learn that McBrain's wife has been ill.

It would have been easy for Griffiths to end *Comedians* at this point: with the comic performances and their varied negotiations of the dialectical structure that has guided the play up to this point. Indeed, such was Griffiths's original intention for the play. "I carried the idea for the play around for over two years, and for a long time it was only two acts. And then I started to write it, and after ten pages I discovered this curious thing growing up, this strange beast shuffling towards Bethlehem to be born—Gethin Price."[13] The result of this emergence was an eclipsing of his familiar thesis-antithesis structure by a more complex field of political alternatives. When Price takes the stage to begin his act 2 performance—a performance outside the parameters of either Waters or Challenor—he establishes a third possibility for comic art. Breaking through these theories as ruthlessly as he does any vestiges of audience-stage protocol, Price's performance erupts within the play's structure not as a synthesis of what has gone before but as something dramatically, dangerously new.

Even before his appearance onstage at the conclusion of act 2, Price has occupied an uneasy presence in the play's dialectical presentation. His shaved-head appearance at the opening of the first act startles even Waters. When he makes jokes, he does so with switchblade technical virtuosity, and his humor is unsettling in the anger and volatility it expresses. His stance toward Waters is complicated, ambivalent: he is acknowledged by the others to be the older comedian's pet student, but he bristles at the teacher's moral prescriptions. When Waters is forced to leave the room after criticizing his limerick, Price jumps on the table and does a flawless, devastating parody of the lecture he has just received, using a joke that McBrain has just told (about a poacher carrying a deer) in order to deconstruct Waters's authoritative tone and the moral distinctions he insists on ("It's a joke that hates *deer*, George" [25]).

Price's uneasy relationship with Waters emerges with increasing clarity as the play's first act develops. In the minutes before Challenor's arrival Waters proposes a final exercise to underscore his view that true comedy seeks to root itself in pain and beauty. He asks them to think of an incident that means something to them—"maybe something that embarrasses you or haunts you or still makes you frightened, something you can't deal with maybe"—then challenges them to tell it in their own way: "But make it funny" (28). Volunteering, Ged Murray recounts the birth of his first child, the fear he felt that it would inherit his own father's mental instability, and his joy when he saw it in his wife's arms: "He were bloody perfect." The story leaves most who hear it riveted, profoundly moved. The only one willing to follow this performance is Price, who tells a story of the time he hit a woman teacher at the age of thirteen for calling him a "guttersnipe" and was forced to see a psychologist. When the psychologist suggested that all he wanted was to be loved, Price insulted him with a wisecrack about his hairpiece. "That's when I decided I'd be a comedian" (29).

As his anecdote reveals, comedy, for Price, is an act of aggression, a verbal punch. Hard-edged and dangerous, it is also a gesture of assertion, in this case against a pat psychologizing that Price finds just as condescending as his teacher's class-based slur. Price's often brutal use of humor refuses sentimentality as it does anything else that might blunt the directness of its statement. That Price tells his story at this particular moment is itself a challenge: to the uncomplicated emotion of Ged's tender recollection, free of the leaven of irony, and to the sanitized truth telling of Waters's comedy, which asks for the truth of people's lives while excluding anger and alienation from its emotional field. As Price makes clear in act 3, his view of comedy is deeply indebted to Waters's teaching, but the image of him "thumping" a teacher is a disturbing one. The story of his behavior in an earlier classroom underscores his problematic place in this one.

As he tells Waters early in act 1, Gethin has changed his act from the one he had been rehearsing. What he produces when he takes the stage after the other comics in act 2 is something startlingly original, a pastiche of mime and clown theater closer to performance art than conventional stand-up comedy. Price appears in half-mast trousers, boots, studded denim jacket with a Manchester United scarf tied to his arm, his face "deadened" with white. The effect, Griffiths specifies, is "half clown, half this year's version of bovver boy . . . calculatedly eerie, funny, and chill" (48). Price's opening routine evokes the uncanny menace of things: he takes out a toy violin, sets fire to a loose thread, watches in horror as the violin starts to play on its own, then stamps out the smoldering bow and violin with his boot. Muttering to himself that he wishes he had a train to smash up, he proceeds to engage in kung fu and other Asian martial exercises. As he does so, club hands carry on larger-than-life-size dummies of a young man and woman dressed for the evening. Sensing himself being ignored by the couple, Price begins to address them in steadily more menacing ways. At first he attempts to befriend the man; when this fails he speaks increasingly aggressively about the woman's sexual appetites, the man's masculinity, and the possibility of violence. "I suppose I could just give you a clout," he tells the man, "just to let you know I exist" (49). He tells them jokes then compels their laughter by shaking them up and down. In the routine's most horrifying gesture he pins a flower between the girl's breasts then watches (with shrieks changing to laughter) as a red stain appears and widens on her dress. "P'raps it pierced a vein."[14] Price turns to the audience, shouts a soccer chant ("U-n-i-ted. Uni-ted"), and calls back to the departed couple: "National Unity? Up yours, sunshine." In his closing gesture he plays "The Red Flag" on his violin then exits with the sardonic observation, "Still, I made the buggers laugh" (51).

With a brilliance that even Waters will subsequently acknowledge, the act is mordant and volatile, pushing beyond humor into something surreal, dangerous, cruel. As Albert Wertheim memorably describes it, Price's routine is "a stunning display of black comedy, a chillingly comic *danse macabre*, a controlled venture into the area in which comical satire borders on tragical satire and in which the strong medicines of the satirist very nearly become the corrosives of the sadist."[15] The act involves considerable athleticism, though the body Price foregrounds is threatening, explosive. A self-acknowledged student of comedic history, Price draws upon its darker traditions: its often savage powers of satire, its ventures into the noncomic, that edge of negativity that makes the clown a figure of nihilism as well as mirth. Price will later credit the Swiss clown Grock, who fascinated pre–World War I European society with his often aggressively unfunny comic persona, as a major influence on his act.[16]

By introducing a polished animosity unprepared for by the more benign discussions that preceded it, Gethin's performance hijacks Griffiths's play, stripping away the protective disclaimer that allows the comic to pretend: this is only a joke. Price's comic performance bares its antagonism, denying any rationalization that might blunt its impact or disguise its target. In an observation that is both a warning to the onstage dummies and an aside to the audience, Price remarks: "There's people'd call this envy, you know, it's not, it's hate" (50). That Jonathan Pryce's performance occasioned strong audience reactions—spectators heckled him, he had pocketbooks thrown at him, and he was forced to complete his routine while a man had what seemed to be a nervous breakdown in the middle of the orchestra—only underscores the extent to which his act directly targets the play's audience.[17] In a much more daring breach of the barrier separating stage from spectator than anything attempted by his fellow comics, Price addresses his audience (actual as well as fictional) in fiercely delineated class terms. He marks himself with the emblems of class hatred, crafting himself into a classed society's nightmare of working-class violence. His self-presentation as a train-smashing soccer hooligan, for instance, evoked a social fear that was escalating to near-hysterical proportions in the mid-1970s: the wrecking of trains by traveling soccer fans had become a recurrent problem, "bovver alerts" were commonplace in the papers, and by 1974 the

Daily Mirror had placed Manchester United's "Red Army" at the top of its "League of Violence."[18] When Price chants, "U-n-i-ted. Uni-ted. You won't keep us down there for long, don't worry. We're coming up *there where* we can gerrat yer," he calls up both a style of male working-class self-assertion and a public image of class-directed violence from below (51). The Soviet allusion inherent in the Manchester hooligans' well-known nickname (and the radical echoes of "Man United") only intensify this sense of class threat.

Price, of course, makes his target explicit by bringing his audience—or their surrogates—onstage. Bypassing his fictional audience of working-class bingo players, Price devises caricatured versions of a conventional theater audience (Griffiths specifies that they stand as if waiting for a cab after the theater). The choice to make them dummies is a revealing one, for their silence and immobility literalize Price's invisibility to them. The second half of Gethin's routine (in which they appear) is a series of attempts to be noticed by them, and the lack of acknowledgment, as much as anything else, is what spurs his animosity and escalates his violence. As Cave notes, Gethin "knows in himself the humiliations that bring a 'bovver boy' into being; his artistic purpose is to bring that mental condition and *conditioning* to an audience's understanding."[19] But the plain fact of being *noticed*, of being heard, is what counts most. In his own words (looking back on the routine), "It was all ice out there tonight. I loved it. I felt . . . expressed" (65–66). Like the act of punching his teacher, Gethin's gesture of drawing blood with his flower pin represents, in a ghastly and misogynistic fashion, his insistence on leaving a mark, on reversing the roles of actor and acted-upon as constructed within a class-based social hierarchy.

As arranged beforehand, the members of Waters's class reconvene in their classroom to hear Challenor's verdict on their stand-up performances. With the exception of Gethin, who enters singing, the mood is somber. Challenor arrives and gives the predictable verdicts: although he sees a great deal of promise in the group, the only comics he is presently interested in signing are McBrain and Samuels, the two whose acts pandered to his cynical view of comedy. He dismisses Price's act as "repulsive." The contempt in which he holds the audience is evident in the closing advice he gives: "All audiences are thick, collectively, but it's a bad comedian who lets 'em know it" (58). The atmosphere as the comedians leave for the last time is one of defeat. Those who take the next step into the field of professional comedy do so branded with what they have sacrificed in order to be accepted: though Samuels tries to hide his guilt, McBrain leaves "kiln-fired, hard inside the compromise" (59). Those who failed to make it must return to the lives they had worked so urgently to advance. Their collective failure underscores the extent to which *Comedians*, for Griffiths, is a play about the waste of working-class resources and about "the suppression of talent for success."[20]

Inevitably, Waters and Price are left alone, the former reluctant and the latter determined to address the gulf in sensibility that Gethin's act has exposed between them. When pressed about his opinion of the performance, Waters conceded "You were *brilliant!*" yet he also accuses the act of "drowning in hate" and neglecting truth (62–63). Price insists that his performance was faithful to the truth as he sees it, that the realities of a class-ridden world are not beautiful, and that Waters himself understood this when he started off playing the halls as the Lancashire Lad: "Nobody hit harder than Eddie Waters, that's what they say. Because you were still in touch with what made you . . . hunger, diphtheria, filth, unemployment, penny clubs, means tests, bed bugs, head lice. . . . Was all *that* truth beautiful? [. . .] Truth was a fist you hit with." For all Waters's attempts to redefine the truth into something less harsh, the fundamental realities of social exclusion and institutional suppression have not changed:

> When I stand upright—like tonight at that club—I bang my head on the ceiling. Just like you fifty years ago. We're still caged, exploited, prodded and pulled at, milked, fattened, slaughtered, cut up, fed out. We still don't belong to ourselves. Nothing's changed. You've just forgotten, that's all.

Price points out something that the play's audience may also have observed: that this teacher of comedy has not laughed during the entire play and that he himself has said little that is funny: "Maybe you lost your hate, Mr. Waters" (63).

Stung by Price's accusation, Waters counters with an anecdote that acknowledges its truth and seeks to explain his retreat from laughter. On a trip to Germany immediately after the war he had visited a concentration camp located just four miles from Mozart's house at Weimar. At the camp he saw the showers and cyanide pellets of the extermination and realized that what he was seeing was "the logic of our world . . . extended." That night, during a stand-up routine, a fellow comedian told a joke about a Jew, and Waters found himself unable to laugh: "I discovered . . . that there were no jokes left. Every joke was a little pellet, a . . . final solution" (64). In the shadow of Buchenwald Waters discovers that the cruelty of laughter and that of the Holocaust are different in degree, not kind. Moreover, after realizing his own arousal at the spectacle of extermination (he had an erection at the camp), he must acknowledge within himself the same sadistic impulses. Profoundly shaken by this experience, Waters has dedicated himself to repairing comedy, nurturing its medicinal potential as a way of countering its more dangerous impulses. "We've gotta get deeper than hate," he tells Gethin. "Hate's no help" (65).

Comedians approaches its end, therefore, with a set of dialectical possibilities far more difficult to reconcile than those presented by the Challenor-Waters confrontation. Griffiths, who commented in a 1976 interview that "I inhabit the tension between Eddie Waters and Gethin Price,"[21] presents the positions of these two protagonists with full awareness of their strengths and inadequacies. Waters articulates and professes all that Griffiths considers best in an earlier tradition of working-class comedians: he advocates a comedy that deals with a community's shared concerns as a way of helping that community come to terms with them (Griffiths would later characterize this as "the politics of coping").[22] He battles the ugliness of a comedy that seeks laughter through belittlement. In his belief that a real comedian respects the humanity of his audience he is an heir of Griffiths's Gramsci, who argues that a revolution not based on love is not worth leading. At the same time, Waters remains profoundly blocked by his unwillingness to make any accommodations with humor's destructive energies. He can himself no longer laugh, and the humor he advocates, while morally upright, is increasingly irrelevant to the conditions and experiences of a class-divided society. His is a humor without teeth. That he cannot deliver even a brief warm-up routine to the working-class audience of act 2 suggests, as Price points out, how little he now has to offer them.

Drawing upon an earlier and different tradition (that of Grock and his precursors) to rejuvenate a comedy of aggressive truth telling and disturbing social illumination, Gethin carries Waters's views on comedy and truth to their logical (and electrifying) end. He may lack the "compassion" evident in Waters's comedy of concern, but he would subscribe to Gramsci's pronouncement—"It is a revolutionary duty to tell the truth"—as readily as his teacher. His comedy is confrontational, radically anticonsensual; Price refuses a medicinal politics and opts instead for the politics of refusal. "I stand in no line," he tells Waters. "I refuse my consent" (66). He is, one might say, the "hard" to Waters's "soft," that necessary (and problematic) other term of the dialectic that Griffiths sees at the heart of the radical sensibility.

And yet, despite his antagonism toward the institutions and structures of British society, Gethin is a different figure from the "hards" of Griffiths's earlier plays, and he is difficult to position within the spectrum of left-wing political positions. Unlike the ruthlessness of Kabak or Lenin, Gethin's anger lacks the guidance of revolutionary vision. He appears in the play's opening scene wearing a Lenin-like cloth or denim hat, and before he leaves at the end he tells Waters, somewhat cryptically, that he plans to "wait for it to happen" (66). But, like the chant "U-n-i-ted. Uni-ted" or his violin rendition of the "Red Flag," these gestures and pronouncements are more emblems of resistance than signposts of a revolutionary program. Price evokes the trappings of traditional revolutionary iconography, but these are subsumed by images of a politically unguided social rage: kung fu kicks, the wounding flower pin, the menace of soccer hooliganism. Unlike the aging Waters, he taps a brutal social reality and the anger of those trapped within it, but the performance he devises offers little direction for such disruptive energies. Like his other gestures, his act is expressive rather than transformative, and there is more than an edge of nihilism to Gethin's performativity. He may indeed take "the first steps toward repossessing himself" (as Griffiths suggests),[23] but his anger leads nowhere. In one of his closing lines we learn that his wife and child have recently left him; as he leaves the stage to return to his job driving the British Rail truck, he seems caught in loneliness and ineffectuality.

Comedians ends, fittingly, with a joke. After Gethin has left, Waters is joined by Patel, an Asian man who, while looking for a reading class, has shown up on and off since act 1. Remarking that the "funny men" have all gone home, he offers to tell Waters a joke from his own country. "Try me," Waters says, and Patel does:

> A man has many children, wife, in the South. His crop fail, he have nothing, the skin shrivel on his children's ribs, his wife's milk dries. They lie outside the house starving. All around them, the sacred cows, ten, twenty, more, eating grass. One day he take sharp knife, mm? He creep up on a big white cow, just as he lift knife the cow see him and the cow say, Hey, aren't you knowing you not permitted to kill me? And the man say, What do you know, a talking horse. (67)

Patel laughs in appreciation at his own joke, and for the first time in the play Waters laughs, too. He invites Patel to join his next class, which he's already started to put together.

Coming (as it does) at this point in the play, Patel's joke is rich in meanings and implications. More deftly than theoretical argument, it manages to reconcile elements of Waters's and Price's comic visions, rooting itself in the harsh realities of starvation while affirming the creativity of the human will in subverting the strictures of religious and class oppression. As the last instance of comic performance in a play that has radically questioned comedy's political foundations, it is also a final invitation to the spectators to engage in the process of examining their laughter and its complicities. Comedy, the play has shown, positions those who laugh as firmly as it does its object(s).

In what it achieves and what it does not, the play's closing joke allows us to draw some conclusions about the place that humor occupies in Griffiths's dramatic and political arsenal. Humor, for Griffiths, is a particularly sophisticated mode of apprehension, one capable of capturing human reality in its dialectical complexity with unusual subtlety and directness. To borrow one of Brecht's phrases it is a mode of "complex seeing," defamiliarizing the world upon which it operates and negotiating the space of contradiction. Patel's joke proposes—in the same mental space—contradictory frames of reference, and its humor lies in the way it oscillates between religious proscription and the different moral codes of poverty. Through the resources of both comedy and survival a starving man can be devout and adequately fed. Indeed, the joke makes clear, there is something of the survival instinct in humor itself. As Waters understands (tell something deeply felt and make it funny), humor is a way of attaining distance on a painful reality, of bringing problems to the point where they can be seen and dealt with. Like an "impossible" optical illusion, laughter brings emotion and perception into the same space, and, in so doing, it offers a particularly complex form of social and personal self-possession. Christine's journey to acceptance in *Through the Night* is crowned by her ability to joke about her scar; that laughter also allows this triumph to be shared is confirmed by the defiantly mirthful party at Mrs. Scully's bedside. As Oscar Lee Brownstein observes, "If the real revolution lies in the way we think, the way we 'see' the world, if revolution lies in overturning the frames of reference and therefore the limited options available to us, then there is a way that comedy, art, perception shifts of any kind, can be revolutionary."[24]

In a play still bruised by Gethin's visceral routine, however, the redemptive feel of this closing laughter is noticeably tempered. In the midst of its affirmations Patel's joke is haunted by an awareness that the space within which comedy achieves its empowering vision and balance is only make-believe, that its transgression is circumscribed, and that the distance it achieves on problems may entail the co-opting of its own anger. Patel's joke affirms a coping ingenuity, but the sacrifice of a single "talking horse" leaves the caste system and its religious strictures unchanged. Moreover, the telling of that joke—in this Manchester schoolroom at this moment in history—leaves unchallenged the ceilings enforced by Britain's own caste system and its institutions. Comedy may aspire to "change the situation," but what may be required for anything structural to take place is something much more direct than coping laughter. As Price's own performance has demonstrated, the realities of class inequality compel different, less benign kinds of laughter. And when the truths of this world are brought onstage—exploitation from above, anger from below—the line between the comic and the noncomic can be a fragile one, indeed.

Postscript: The Working Class Revisited
After an impressive series of plays about left-wing activists, politicians, and intellectuals, *Comedians* turns to the working class with a fullness and directness not seen since *Sam, Sam*. Griffiths brings to his portrayal of the working class here a Hoggartian concern with culture and the lived parameters of everyday life: workingmen's clubs with their bingo games and amateur entertainment; sports and its rituals of participation; television habits (Ged's excuse for arriving late is that he was watching *Crossroads*, a long-running soap opera serial set in a Midlands halfway house motel); pubs; work; extramural education. The pleasures of this world and its textures were at one point very much Griffiths's own. "I know that world very well. I know the world of the snooker hall and of working men clubs. . . . I'd actually seen comedians and singers and dancers auditioning at lunch time in the clubs that I used to drink in. I just wrote about those lives as I understood them."[25]

At the same time, *Comedians* is also a transitional play in Griffiths's dramatic portrayal of the working class. Although he would turn again to this class in his writings (most extensively in his dramatization of Lawrence's *Sons and Lovers*), and although class itself would remain a principal variable in his political sensibility, he has referred to *Comedi-*

ans as "the last play where I felt I could honestly occupy [a working-class] space, directly and without going back."[26] This change in attitude no doubt reflected the fact that Griffiths's own life had continued to move beyond its class origins. When Griffiths states, in the same interview, that his later project of adapting *The Cherry Orchard* taught him "a fantastic amount" about class, he acknowledges that these lessons derive from his changed situation: "When I look to my experiences over the last five or ten years for a play, I find that experience is middle class professional experience, it's not proletarian experience."[27] But on the evidence of *Comedians* itself it is clear that something much more fundamental is also coming into play in Griffiths's understanding of class. *Comedians* (and *Bill Brand*, which followed close upon it) dramatize a conflict in Griffiths's sense of the working class that has been evident in his work from the beginning. On the one hand, as the title of *Bill Brand*'s closing episode indicates ("It Is the People Who Create"), Griffiths has always been drawn to an image of the working class as a natural repository of the sense of community and as the site of a nascent political activism. But by the mid-1970s it was also clear that the working class had failed to fulfill its Marxist historical destiny as the vehicle of socialist revolution. In a passage that Griffiths cites in his preface to *Through the Night* Raymond Williams writes: "What the masses, old or new, might do is anybody's guess. But the actual men and women, under permanent kinds of difficulty, will observe and learn, and I do not think in the long run they will be anybody's windfall."[28] While the heightened labor militancy of the 1970s suggested a return of popular left-wing activism, there was more than enough counter-evidence to suggest the truth of Williams's assessment. In the days before the May 1968 Paris uprising, we have seen, London dockers and meat market porters marched on Parliament in support of Enoch Powell's denunciation of black immigration.

An awareness of the gap between Britain's working-class population and the socialist political movements that claim to represent it is largely responsible for the schizophrenic structure of Griffiths's *Sam, Sam*, in which worker and Marxist politician inhabit what appear to be separate plays. By the mid-1970s, as the postwar consensus governing British politics began to unravel, Griffiths's plays reveal a deeper sense that the working class may no longer be the willing seat of left-wing activism and support. A look at the brothers in *Bill Brand* suggests this uneasiness. When Brand meets his brother Eddie in a local Conservative Club, the now-unemployed textile worker warns him:

Well somebody'd better do someat and bloody quick. There's fellers round here bin outa work two years. They won't be voting Labour next time, I can tell you. And neither will I. [. . .] I've voted Labour since I got the vote and every time it's the same bloody story, socialist paradise before, freeze and squeeze after, and the unions sit back and let it happen. At least when the Conservatives are in we can have a bloody go. (8:69)

Two episodes later Brand encounters his brother on a Fight to Work march, and the change from helplessness to activism seems meant to be politically reassuring. But the earlier speech is not so easily countered, and in the light of subsequent British history Eddie's words on behalf of the working class are uncannily prophetic.

Comedians—which, in the words of Chambers and Prior, "brings together the different images of the working class that have held sway since the Second World War and finds them irrevocably in conflict"[29]— offers an even more uneasy sense of the working class and its political allegiances. In the figure of Gethin Price, hardened by hatred, and in the violent currents of working-class culture he performs in his comic routine, Griffiths introduces something new to his political and dramatic landscape: a sense of working-class political alienation so profound that it leaves the realm of politics entirely, directing its rage in purely reactive ways. The distance between (say) Yates in *The Big House* and the persona with which Gethin takes the stage is the distance between a radical political agenda and an apolitical social violence. Although Griffiths somewhat qualifies his presentation of Gethin (his "bovver boy" is a persona, after all, and he derives his performance style from a book), the currents of working-class culture Price draws upon are real, and as a potential political field they stand at a decided remove from the Hoggartian cultural world of Waters.

As the dock workers marching to Powell's racist speech suggest, this current of working-class resentment is vulnerable to the most reactionary exploitation. If the seeds for *Comedians* can be found in the confrontational structure of *Sam, Sam*, then its own offspring is clearly *Oi for England*, a play that delves into working-class anger in some of its most strident physical and cultural manifestations. Gethin's "I refuse my consent" becomes, in this later play, a working-class youth rebellion defiantly adrift from the political self-definitions within which Griffiths's earlier drama positioned it.

Chekhovian Counter-Meanings: *The Cherry Orchard*

Not long after his production of *Comedians* had completed its London run, Richard Eyre commissioned Griffiths to write a version of Anton Chekhov's play *The Cherry Orchard*. "I believe *The Cherry Orchard* is the model play of the twentieth century," Eyre later stated: "It presents an entire spectrum of society, in which every social gradation, every class interest, is represented. . . . The brief . . . was not to 'politicize' the play, but to strip away the varnish; to enable us to see the picture more clearly."[30] Griffiths, who had long admired Chekhov's work, eagerly accepted the project. Working with Helen Rappaport's literal translation of Chekhov's Russian text, Griffiths produced a "version" of *The Cherry Orchard* that sought to redress the apolitical sentimentality that characterized traditional British productions of Chekhov. Such productions have tended to present Chekhov's plays as nostalgic laments for a dying social order, suffused with the melancholy of twilight and "the tragedy of dispossession."[31] In Griffiths's words:

> For half a century now, in England as elsewhere, Chekhov has been the almost exclusive property of theatrical class sectaries for whom the plays have been plangent and sorrowful evocations of an "ordered" past no longer with "us," its passing greatly to be mourned. For theatergoers . . . Chekhov's tough, bright-eyed complexity was dulced into swallowable sacs of sentimental morality.

Through numerous translations and productions *The Cherry Orchard* had been robbed of its "specific historicity and precise sociological imagination" and reduced to the ideologically charged propositions "that the fine will always be undermined by the crude and that the 'human condition' can for all essential purposes be equated with 'the plight of the middle classes.' "[32]

Griffiths refused the conventional portrait of Chekhov as a playwright of universalized pathos and class-bound lament:

> From the age of fifteen, when I had my first exposure to his work via radio, I have always looked *straight through* the productions to the counter-meanings and counter-intentions screaming out to be realized. To come to cases, *The Cherry Orchard* has *always* seemed to me to be dealing not only with the subjective pain of property-loss but also and more importantly with its objective *necessity*. To present it as the first is to celebrate a pessimism; as to see it as both is to redress an important political

balance potent in the text Chekhov wrote but in *practice* almost wholly ignored. [vi]

Chekhov, of course, subtitled *The Cherry Orchard* "A Comedy," and he underscored this intention in his letters, calling it "at times almost a farce" and stating: "The last act will be gay. In fact the whole play is light and gay." Chekhov maintained this position against Stanislavsky, who considered the play "a tragedy, despite the sort of outlet towards a better life you foresee in the last act."[33] As Griffiths's remarks make clear, however, comedy in Chekhov is a matter less of genre and formula than of dialect and distance. In Chekhov's hands comedy and farce are the dramaturgical modes by which discrepancy is illuminated and the competing pulls of empathy and detachment controlled. By decentering subjectivity, Chekhov's comedy juxtaposes the personal with the social and the historical. At the beginning of act 2 of *The Cherry Orchard* Charlotte laments the fact that she doesn't know who she is: "I have no papers. I could be anybody, from anywhere" (18). Yet, as she delivers this speech "to no one, deep in herself," she takes a cucumber from her jacket pocket and begins to eat it. With a subtlety of perceptual negotiation that the author of *Comedians* must surely have appreciated, this unconscious act checks the moment's pathos, allows it a precise weight and no more, and reminds us of the networks of relationship in which Charlotte's "being" participates.

What Griffiths sought to reactivate in Chekhov's dramaturgy was this subtle play of counterpoint and dialectic. Against the pathos that has tended to rule productions of the play, Griffiths championed contradiction, balance, and counter-meanings. In *Modern Tragedy* Raymond Williams distinguishes two extremes of Chekhov production, each of which fails to grasp the "whole structure" of Chekhov's dramatic art: the English, which stresses the "pathetic charm" of a dying world, and the Soviet, which reduces the plays to a "voice simply prophetic of the future."[34] Griffiths's version of *The Cherry Orchard* is designed to open up the distinctly Chekhovian dialectical space in which both apprehensions—the subjective pain of historical change and its objective necessity—exist in a relationship of mutual illumination. To the extent that the "pathetic" Chekhov has emerged from a Stanislavskian focus on emotional depths, Griffiths's version works to reestablish the balance between psychological subtext and the "supratext" of sociohistorical meanings. The result is a bracing version of Chekhov's play that stakes a claim in the English theater for the political power—and relevance—of Chekhov's art.

"I had no feeling that I wanted to impose contemporary meanings on the play," Griffiths commented in a later interview. "It just seemed to me that the spaces were there for contemporary meanings to emerge."[35] This desire to mediate between Chekhov's world and that of Griffiths's audience created challenges of translation/adaptation. On the one hand, Griffiths's was a calculatedly "English version": drawing upon a notion of intercultural translation that owes a debt to Williams, he worked to adapt its idiom to "a different history and a different national, cultural structure of feeling."[36] As one consequence, Chekhov's patronymics are gone, and the characters' names are anglicized. At the same time, Griffiths also included touches that stress the play's sociocultural and historical moment: the faded Russian Orthodox icon of the Virgin Mary on a traveler's shrine in act 2, for instance. Rather than smoothing over these contradictory impulses, Griffiths foregrounds the issue of translation. In a dramaturgical gesture that serves to frame his own dramatic and stylistic interventions, each act opens and closes with a taped recitation of Chekhov's Russian dialogue. As in Caryl Churchill's 1991 play *Mad Forest*, this device calls attention to the act of historical and cultural seeing and to the facts of linguistic difference that an adaptation like this must negotiate.

Although Griffiths made surprisingly few changes to Chekhov's text—as he pointed out (in response to those who accused him of writing the play he wanted to find), he edited out next to nothing, made no effort to transpose lines within the play, and added fewer than fifty words of dialogue to a play of some twenty-one thousand words [vi]— his version is very much a reading of the play's textual possibilities. Much of this reading occurs at the level of style. Working with the material of Rappaport's literal translation, Griffiths produced a stripped-down dialogue that emphasizes simplicity and directness. As he later noted, "I was looking for a certain litheness and leanness of language, that eschewed floweriness or ornateness."[37] Accompanying this stylistic paring down is a pronounced muting of emotionalism. Characters cry less often, succumb to fewer rapturous outbursts. Griffiths has justified his choice of understatement over outburst on the grounds of cultural difference—that English audiences tend to find emotional overstatement "operatic"—and he characterizes one of his aims as rendering the emotional life of his characters "coherent."[38]

By muting the play's emotional register, Griffiths allows issues of class to emerge with greater clarity, and these are reinforced by his scattered modifications to Chekhov's text. Varya, for instance, the adoptive child who does and does not belong to the landed aristocracy, displays a class condescension that serves to shore up her own uncertain standing. After she tells Anya about vagrants staying in the empty servants' quarters, she recounts her confrontation with an older servant who spread the rumor that she was forcing them to eat peas and nothing else: "'So, you silly old man, what's this you've been saying about me . . . *and stand still when I'm . . .*'" (17; emph. added). Griffiths's addition to the end of her sentence here underscores a certain authoritarianism in Varya's character, and it highlights (at the end of a speech that passes without notice in most productions of the play) the impact—on both Varya and the Ranevsky estate as a whole—of poverty and social dislocation. An often bitter awareness of class characterizes Varya throughout. When Lopakhin tells her during their final interview that he is taking on the family servant Epikhodov, she answers him with "disdain beneath the cool neutral tone." Left alone at the end of their encounter, Chekhov's "crybaby" doesn't "sob quietly" as she does in other versions; instead, sitting silently on a bundle in the corner of the room, she stares out into space, "seeing nothing, her hands on her breasts, the fingers almost touching the wooden cross between them" (51).[39] Like so many others in Griffiths's version, the moment draws its meanings together with Brechtian directness. Far from passive in the abortive negotiation with Lopakhin, Griffiths's Varya sits in the midst of her conflicted class allegiances, fumbling for the self-renunciation that represents her usual retreat from such conflicts.

Not surprisingly, given Griffiths's emphasis on the play's sociohistorical contexts, the characters of Lopakhin and Trofimov occupy more central roles in the play's sociological spectrum. In most readings of *The Cherry Orchard*, according to Griffiths, Ranevsky is generally taken to be the center of the play; hers is the field of attraction within which characters move. As he read the play, Griffiths came to feel that this view misrepresented the play's structure: "Trofimov and Lopakhin represent two possibilities for the future: bourgeoisification and commoditization, or revolutionary change. . . . Together, they form an arch over the other characters."[40] Griffiths's version of the play works to heighten these possibilities and their class underpinnings. Lopakhin's business instincts are accentuated—in an addition to Chekhov's original, he calculates that five men could clear the cherry orchard in "less than a week" (9)—as are his wealth and the shift in power relationships it enables. In another of the play's moments of gestic clarification, when Lopakhin knocks over a candelabra in his giddiness after buying the estate, he observes simply, "Leave it! I can pay!" But the poverty and violence of his upbringing are also firmly etched in Griffiths's version, and these give even greater edge to his act 3 celebration: "This is the new master speaking" (43).

Griffiths's Trofimov is similarly foregrounded. Griffiths felt that Chekhov had been limited in his characterization of Trofimov by the censor's watchful eye, and he accordingly tried to reimagine the character in light of the currents of revolutionary theory that were in the air (Lenin's *What Is to Be Done?* was published in 1901 and was circulating in Russia in 1902).[41] Griffiths clarifies what he feels are the implications in Chekhov's text that Trofimov, "the eternal undergraduate," has been forced to leave school because of his revolutionary activities. Trofimov's revolutionary speeches in act 2, already powerful rhetorical evocations of social transformation in Chekhov's original play, are given a more explicitly political point in Griffiths's version. Instead of "work" (as Ronald Hingley's Oxford translation has it), he calls for "unremitting struggle" (26),[42] and to Anna he calls: "Forward, mes amis, meine Kameraden. We're on the march toward the brightest star in all history" (29). In Eyre's production (which opened at the Nottingham Playhouse on 10 March 1977) Trofimov leaped on a bench, his arm raised in a Bolshevik salute—"an embryo Lenin," Benedict Nightingale wrote, "but not without humour, self-mockery and tenderness, the most forceful, persuasive voice on offer."[43] The visionary power of Trofimov's revolutionary stance and the social conditions to which it responds are reinforced by the arrival of the unknown Man, who hails the aristocratic party with the words: "Brothers, starving and suffering comrades, unite now by the river, let them *hear* your misery" (28). As in Trofimov's speeches, the words *comrades* and *unite* are Griffiths's contributions.

In another of Griffiths's additions the clumsy-tongued Epikhodov addresses Lopakhin and Dunyasha as he stumbles offstage during the play's opening sequence: "Beware the clam before the storm. At least in my opinion" (3). This sense of historical juncture, sharpened by intimations of convulsive change, serves as backdrop to the play's drama of relinquishment. An awareness of loss is registered in Griffiths's version—most hauntingly in the funereal "rond" that turns the act 3 ball into an aristocratic danse macabre—but it is counterpointed by the pressures of change and possibility. As Liuba and Gayev say good-bye to their family estate, Trofimov's voice can be heard shouting "Tomorrow . . . ow . . . ow . . . ow" (53). Even after Firs appears onstage, now abandoned by the others, the play refuses to sentimentalize what is being lost. As this representative of feudal Russia rocks in his chair, he is "top-pled" to the ground by the offstage axe (54). The sound of a snapping string, one of Chekhov's most famous stage directions, is heard offstage. In Griffiths's version, however, the sound is sharp, clearly measured—certainly not, as in other versions, "mournfully" or "sadly" dying away.

"*This* Lawrence": *Sons and Lovers*

The politics of adaptation—the liberation of counter-meanings in can-onized, "classic" texts—continued to occupy Griffiths in the late 1970s. In the fall of 1978 (after two years' work on the *Comrades* screenplay) he was contacted by Stella Richardson, who had conceived the idea of a television adaptation of D. H. Lawrence's *Sons and Lovers* for 1980, the fifty-year anniversary of Lawrence's death. This would be the first time one of Lawrence's novels had been adapted for the medium, and Asso-ciated Television (ATV) quickly took on the project (with Stuart Burge as director). Griffiths, excited by the chance to work with a novel that he had been deeply influenced by since first encountering it as a schoolboy, wrote a six-episode script in the winter and early spring of 1978–79. But the project subsequently ran into difficulties. After an industrial dispute held up production for nine months, ATV unexpectedly dropped the project, which was already in rehearsal. Jonathan Powell, the producer responsible for the "classic serial slot" on BBC2, agreed to take it on, and, after some recasting, filming began in the summer of 1980. *Sons and Lovers* was broadcast between 14 January and 25 February 1981.[44]

Griffiths's intentions in adapting Lawrence's novel were several. On the one hand, he was concerned to challenge the received interpre-tation of *Sons and Lovers* as a narrative about artistic vocation and to insist upon the broader contexts of class and material circumstance that frame and ultimately determine the pathways of Paul Morel's (and Lawrence's) escape. For Griffiths *Sons and Lovers* is a novel about "the nature of capitalist society and the damage that it does to the human project."[45] In its intensely realized portrait of the late nineteenth-century East Midlands working class it delineates the social and historical forces that constrain relationships and political opportunities within this envi-ronment. Since the Midlands at this time were relatively untouched by the movements of political activism that arose in the big cities and on the docks, the focus of Lawrence's novel is on coping with a life of bru-tal labor conditions and numbing material restrictions. With a figure like Paul, who lacks the politics that would allow him to conceptualize his condition, escape takes the form not of militant resistance but of "internal migration or flight."[46]

For Griffiths the act of revisioning *Sons and Lovers* entailed a certain writing against Lawrence's text itself. Years earlier Griffiths's response to the novel had been guided by its narrative focus on Paul Morel: "I first read it down the line of Paul Morel's perception—because I was having many of the experiences he had and saw the world as tension between the classes."[47] But when he encountered the novel again in the late 1970s he was able to read beyond Paul's centralizing point of view to the other figures that inhabit and often contest Lawrence's novelistic terrain. The shift to drama was a useful one: in adapting Lawrence's text, Griffiths was able to exploit the differences of voice and presentation that distinguish the realistic novel from realistic plays in order to objectify Paul within his field of social and material relations:

> Realistic drama demands that characters shall be both subjects and objects. Hence, as Paul's subjective view of the social reality is de-centered, so the other characters' perceptions acquire a newly-charged subjective dimension. Revelations ensue, each one a subtle shift in the flow of meaning, a redistribution of effect, a rupture with the prevailing protective empathy that urges the reader to see Paul as the subject and perceive his world—family, work, friends, lovers, problematic—through his eyes and, often unthinkingly, at his valuation.[48]

Within the objectified, relativistic space of drama, in other words, these other voices and points of reference acquire their own autonomy. Griffiths was particularly interested in rescuing the character of Walter Morel from his dismissal by Paul and his mother within the text and by a critical tradition that has replicated this condescension: "The portrait of Morel is important to me. I have tried to integrate him into a community shaped by history, whereas the conventional reading of him is as a primitive force of nature."[49] As Poole and Wyver suggest, Griffiths's Morel becomes "a study in resistance, an assertion of the positive values of the culture Paul rejects . . . the working-class voice suppressed in the text."[50] Griffiths was also concerned to strengthen the presence of the novel's women characters and to allow them being and voice independent of Paul's psychological appropriation of them. Clara's suffragist and socialist backgrounds, for instance, were reinforced.

As Griffiths's discussion of the filming of *Sons and Lovers* (and his encounter with the American journalist) makes clear, the Lawrence project was also driven by an effort to challenge the limitations of the classic "period" serial, with its concern for verisimilitude as an end in its own right and its deployment of the past as undifferentiated background for characters and actions conceived in essentially ahistorical terms. As we shall see in chapter 6, this effort reflects Griffiths's deepening interest in the politics of heritage and the national past as these were being exploited in the Thatcherite early 1980s. It reflects, too, a concern with the conventions of television production by which (in the hands of producers like Powell) the historical serial was conceived and presented. What Griffiths discovered in the filming of *Sons and Lovers* was how difficult these conventions are to subvert:

> I never anticipated just how difficult it would be to break the mould of the classic serial. You are basically working in a factory where these things are being turned out one after another. Methods of working have evolved geared to a certain kind of "period" look and once the logistics of the operation take over a totality of effect is set in motion that becomes almost unstoppable.[51]

Though Griffiths admired the professional expertise and skill that went into the period "look" of the *Sons and Lovers* project, he felt that the attention to verisimilitude misrepresented the lived experience he had attempted to capture. The period wig, for instance, that the actress playing Miriam was made to wear created a hairstyle that, while faithful in period terms, would have been inappropriate for the daughter of a subsistence farmer. "What is right in period terms can often be wrong in class terms, and in the case of *Sons and Lovers*, where I had set out to reproduce the *material* reality of a nineteenth century mining community, this had damaging effects."[52]

Still, by its final episode Griffiths's adaptation of *Sons and Lovers* had built an audience of some seven million people, and during that period Penguin sold roughly a half-million copies of Lawrence's novel.[53] Despite the ways in which the BBC's period production factory had blurred the text's historical awareness, the serial nonetheless provided a richer sense of working-class history than other television offerings.[54] In this sense, even as Griffiths's understanding of the postwar working class was becoming more complicated, *Sons and Lovers* stands, more than any of the playwright's other works, in the tradition of Thompson's *Making of the English Working Class* and other texts of postwar Marxist historiography that sought to reclaim a legacy of working-class culture and resistance. In keeping with this tradition, and with Griffiths's practice as a whole, the target of this historical reclamation is the present, which mirrors its past in many ways. As Griffiths explains in his introduction to the published text:

> I chose to do this work because, under all the incipient mysticism of the perception, under the incipient derogation of women, there is, in *this* Lawrence, and vibrantly so, a powerful and radical celebration of dignity in resistance within working-class culture in industrial class-societies; as well as a dark, tortured cry against the waste of human resources such societies require as part of their logic. It is no bad thing to be saying when unemployment has reached over three million. (12)

6

Thatcherism and the Myth of Nation

1979: Right Turn

In contrast with Griffiths's remarkable output earlier in the decade, the years between 1977 and 1981 were a time of relatively little public activity. During the year after Eyre's production of *The Cherry Orchard* Griffiths tried his hand again at collaborative writing, producing *Deeds* with Howard Brenton, Ken Campbell, and David Hare. This play, a largely uneven treatment of infant formula and its marketing in Britain and abroad, was presented at Nottingham (in a production directed by Eyre) on 9 March 1978.[1] After the production Griffiths would not return to the stage for over four years, and, with the exception of his television adaptation of *Comedians* (broadcast in October 1979), Griffiths had no productions of any kind until his striking reemergence in 1981 with the broadcasts of *Sons and Lovers*, a television version of *The Cherry Orchard*, and *Country*, and the release by Paramount Pictures of *Reds*.

Much of Griffiths's attention during this period was taken up with the *Comrades* and *Sons and Lovers* projects and with dislocation in his own life: having survived breast cancer, his first wife, Jan, was killed in an airplane crash in Cuba in May 1977. But, while Griffiths himself somewhat retreated from the public arena, the political and cultural landscape within which he had articulated his practice as a writer underwent its most radical transformation since the Labour Party victory in 1945. Margaret Thatcher's election in 1979 marked the end not just of Labourism's failed attempts to bring Britain out of its 1970s malaise but of the broader consensus politics that had ruled British governmental policies since the war. Eddie Brand's warning to his parliamentarian brother that he and his unemployed friends "won't be voting Labour next time, I can tell you that" proved prophetic, and Britain now found itself governed by a militant Conservatism committed to privatization, the unleashing of market forces, and radical curtailment of the Welfare State.

The Conservative victory in 1979 was not exactly unexpected. Books on British national decline had grown into a mini-genre in their own right, and the sense of national crisis was acute on both sides of the political spectrum. In a September 1978 article Peter Jenkins, of the *Guardian*, expressed the depth of concern over the economy: "No country has yet made the journey from developed to under-developed. Britain could be the first to embark upon that route."[2] The opinion that Callaghan's Labour government had proven ineffectual in dealing with Britain's social and economic problems was widespread. But the scope of Thatcher's victory (the largest swing to either party in any postwar election up to that point) was nonetheless deeply traumatic to a Left that saw in its results a massive challenge to Labour's postwar legacy. That the Labour Party had squandered its historic opportunity and thereby poised itself for such repudiation was a theme in radical Left political writings even before the Thatcherite revolution. In his 1977 book *The Break-Up of Britain* Tom Nairn charged: "The Labour Party's so-called 'social revolution' of the post-war years led not to national revival but to what Tony Benn now describes as 'de-industrialization': that is, to rapidly accelerating backwardness, economic stagnation, social decay, and cultural despair."[3]

Margaret Thatcher, having moved the Conservative Party to the extreme Right when she replaced Heath as its leader in 1975, took political electoral power on the promise to reverse this economic and social decline through a return to market principles and traditional social values. In her efforts to implement these twin projects over the eleven years of her administration, she would make radical changes in the relationship between government, the business community, and the labor unions; in the jurisdictional balance between national and local government; in the funding of arts and education; and in the social contract that had governed British politics since World War II. But Thatcherism was more than a political, economic, and social program. As its rhetorical evocations of eighteenth-century laissez-faire capitalism and nineteenth-century Victorian social values indicate, Thatcherism sought to legitimize its radically conservative agenda through the mobilization of ideological categories, historical traditions, and cultural references. At the heart of this project were the concepts of "nation" and "Britishness," both of which became, during the Thatcherite 1980s, crucial legitimizing categories. Even before the culminating moment of the 1982 Falklands War, which allowed Thatcher to subsume and thereby neutralize divisions within the country (and within her own party) with the Churchillian rhetoric of "England's final hour," Thatcherism sought to contain difference within a conservative construction of national identity. Stuart Hall, who devoted considerable energy in the late 1970s and 1980s to the analysis of Thatcherism, has described this ideological project:

> Ideologically, Thatcherism is seen as forging new discursive articulations between the liberal discourses of the "free market" and economic man and the organic conservative themes of tradition, family and nation, respectability, patriarchalism and order. Its reworking of these different repertoires of "Englishness" constantly repositions both individual subjects and "the people" as a whole—their needs, experiences, aspirations, pleasures and desires—contesting space in terms of shifting social, sexual and ethnic identities, against the background of a crisis of national identity and culture precipitated by the unresolved psychic trauma of the "end of empire." Culturally, the project of Thatcherism is defined as a form of "regressive modernization"—the attempt to "educate" and discipline the society into a particularly regressive version of modernity by, paradoxically, dragging it backwards through an equally regressive version of the past.[4]

Nationalism, Benedict Anderson points out, entails the construction of "imagined communities,"[5] and it involves notions of belonging that seek to map the social in terms of identity and exclusion. In the ideological economy of the British New Right the categories of "nation" and "people" are evident in such aspects of the Thatcherite program as its attempts to limit immigration, its attacks on working class militancy, and (paradoxically) its assault on the institutions of "society" and the "state."

Hall's reference to "the end of empire" is important, for it reminds us that the preoccupation with national identity and the "state of the nation" that underlay both the crisis rhetoric of decline in the 1970s and the Thatcherite rhetoric of the 1980s had roots in a broader postwar British crisis of identity. This crisis derives from a number of factors: the loss of an imperial role central to Britain's self-conception since the eighteenth century; a consistently lower rate of economic growth than other Western countries (in 1987 Italy would surpass Britain in terms of GNP per capita); pressures toward devolution on the part of England, Scotland, and Wales and the military occupation of Northern Ireland; a crisis of "Englishness" as a consequence of immigration and the emergence of an increasingly multiracial population; instability in the notion of "nation" itself in the context of capitalist globalization. The anxiety generated by these factors manifested itself in a range of ways. Politically, it was apparent in the extremism of Powellism and the National Front. Culturally and socially, it played itself out in cinematic and other evocations of World War II and its myths of national unity; "Raj revival" films and television programs of the early 1980s; the emergence of a heritage industry through which the British could contemplate constructed versions of its past; and moments of intensified royalism, such as those surrounding the coronation of Elizabeth II in 1953 and the Royal Wedding of 1981. Thatcherism exploited these cultural anxieties through a version of nationhood that drew upon selected (and often conflicting) motifs from Britain's imperial and pre-imperial past. The campaign on behalf of this national idea—which occupies "a symbolic rather than a territorial space," in Raphael Samuel's words—involved more than rhetoric.[6] In 1983 Lord Hugh Thomas, historian-advisor to the prime minister, called for a more patriotic orientation to teaching history in the schools; this call was taken up by Sir Keith Thomas, then minister of education.[7] And in April of the previous year British soldiers sailed to the South Atlantic in defense of "the British way of life." Nothing more starkly illustrates the disjunction between the idea of "Britain" and the realities of fragmentation and breakdown against which it was frequently mobilized than the juxtaposition, in July 1981, of rioting in Southall, Toxteth, and Moss Side ("Britain's Days of Rage," as one headline put it) with the Royal Wedding and its ritual of national legitimation.[8]

The Falklands War, of course, was the crowning moment in Thatcher's political deployment of Britishness and the myth of nation. The rhetoric of an "island race" displaying its strength and resolve against an enemy of military dictators enabled Thatcher to draw links with a primordial national essence and, in so doing, magically displace the anxieties of Britain's postimperial decline. The week before the British landing, Thatcher acclaimed "this ancient country rising as one nation. . . . Too long submerged, too often denigrated, too easily forgotten, the springs of pride in Britain flow again."[9] The surge of popularity that followed the British victory enabled Thatcher (temporarily at least) to subsume the ideological divisions within her Conservative Coalition (between old-style Conservatives and monetarist reformers, "wets" and "dries") within the symbology of a Britain now "Great" again. This image of national unity also provided Thatcher with a rhetoric with which she could denigrate dissent by branding it unpatriotic. One of the targets of her famous Cheltenham speech (delivered to a Conservative Rally in the aftermath of the British victory) was a strike by railway workers—"this tiny group"—who refused to participate in the "spirit of the South Atlantic."[10]

The Falklands Crisis was, it turned out, also a galvanizing moment for the Left's critique of Thatcherism and the ideology of nation that the New Right so deliberately exploited. By the end of 1982 Anthony Barnett's *Iron Britannia* was published, and articles addressing the Falklands phenomenon had appeared throughout the leftist press. Articles on the Falklands were published in Stuart Hall and Martin Jaques's 1983 collection *The Politics of Thatcherism* (Hall's own articles on Thatcherism would be gathered in *The Hard Road to Renewal* [1988]). In July 1983 a seminar entitled "National Fictions: Struggles over the Meaning of World War II" was run by the British Film Institute Summer School; in addition to an examination of World War II's role in the construction of "national identity," its participants considered ways in which the myth of Britain's "Finest Hour" was reworked during the Falklands conflict. Throughout the 1980s questions of nation and national identity were central to British cultural studies, and the Falklands War was revisited as a particularly rich nexus of ideological, political, and social issues. In *There Ain't No Black in the Union Jack* Paul Gilroy examined the war as a playing out of racial categories; in this reading the rhetoric of island races evokes the deeper role of racial boundaries in the discourse of British nationhood.[11]

When Griffiths returned to television and the public stage in 1981, two years after Thatcher's election, his interests were inevitably focused on the ascendancy of Conservatism as a political, ideological, and cultural force and on its appropriation of *nation* and the *national past* as legitimizing myths. This interest, on Griffiths's part, is not new. As we have seen, Griffiths's practice of strategic penetration has always been directed at cultural institutions and the production of "national culture." Moreover, Griffiths's historical writing has always been conducted as a kind of counter-memory to official, class-bound accounts. One of the most direct references to the narrative of nation in Griffiths's early work comes in *Don't Make Waves,* a minor television play cowritten with Snoo Wilson and broadcast as part of the BBC series *Eleventh Hour* on 12 July 1975. In this play, which has the disjointedness and surreality of a Fringe piece, a bomb has gone off in a club where several people have congregated for what seems to be a costume ball: one character is dressed as Henry VIII, another as Queen Elizabeth. Near the end of the play, as water rises everywhere, Robert, dressed as the Chief Scout, offers a mock-heroic speech on England's glorious history:

> This is a great country, a great country still. Difficulties there are undoubtedly, but when were there not, down the long arc of our island history. Cometh the hour, cometh the man. Vikings, Normans, Spaniards, Scots, Irish, Germans, Japanese, they've all done their worst and here we are still, a country, a nation, an idea, an ideal, a tiny but indomitable family, fingers on a hand, quick to greet, but ready to curl into a fist the moment danger sounds.[12]

Robert's speech lampoons the rhetoric of British nationalism; as he wades away through the water, the spectacle both underscores and parodies the image of England's "island history." That the bomb damage alludes to recent IRA bombings in mainland Britain only heightens the irony of Robert's pugnacious Little Englandism.

Such concerns move to the forefront in Griffiths's plays of the early 1980s, in large part because the stakes involved in such ideological posturing have themselves so dramatically changed. In *Country* (1981), *Oi for England* (1982), and *Judgment over the Dead / The Last Place on Earth* (1985) Griffiths confronts the ideological and historical underpinnings of Thatcherite Conservatism, and he examines some of the central myths, symbols, and rhetoric out of which a nostalgic/reactionary concept of nationhood has been fashioned. In so doing, he also considers some of the issues attendant upon the politics of Britishness in the 1980s (and 1990s): heritage culture; nationhood, class, and race; and the narrative of empire.

Heritage Culture: *Country*

Country, which was broadcast as a BBC1 "Play for Today" on 20 October 1981, was originally intended as part of a six-part series of plays entitled *Tory Stories*. As Griffiths conceived the project and brought it to the BBC, the series was to offer an overview of postwar British Toryism, with each play centering on a watershed moment in contemporary British political and social history: 1945 (the end of the war and Attlee's electoral landslide), 1957 (the aftermath of Suez and the bank rate leak), 1963 (the Profumo affair), 1968 (student revolution in Paris and the attempt of certain businessmen and retired military leaders to lead a coup in Britain), 1972–74 (the miners' strike and the fall of the Heath administration). The final play, which was to deal with Thatcherism, would be set in the mid-1980s. As it turned out, the first play of *Tory Stories*, titled *The Gang's All Here*, was projected to cost nearly 400,000 pounds, or half the project's entire budget. Griffiths then set about "to settle everything from the whole series in one play" and retitled his revised script *Country: "A Tory Story."*[13] The play was directed by Richard Eyre with an ensemble cast that included Leo McKern, Wendy Hiller, James Fox, Penelope Wilton, and Joan Greenwood.

The play takes place at Seal Park, the country estate of the Carlions, a landed brewing family. Sir Frederic Carlion, now seventy, has convened his immediate and extended family for Carlion Week, an annual celebration that includes a formal ball for selected members of the local population, in order to settle the transfer of power within the family business (Sir Frederic's eldest son was killed in the war). Philip, a tabloid journalist from London, is Frederic's choice, and, although he expresses reluctance early on, by the end of the play he agrees to assume the leadership of company and family. Radio broadcasts throughout the play bring the traumatic news of Labour's electoral victory, but, as Philip stands with his father watching the local population at a celebratory bonfire, it becomes clear that the promise of social transformation is, in all real senses, illusory. "Is it a funeral?" Sir Frederic asks. "I rather think it is, Father," Philip answers. "They have not yet noticed that the grave is empty."[14]

Country, then, addresses the phenomenon of contemporary Toryism in the aftermath of Thatcher's rise to power by revisiting its earliest postwar resurrection. The view that the socialist promise of the Attlee victory was deflected by a Conservatism that managed to keep the myths and institutions of the British class system intact was central to the British Left's analysis of 1945 as a missed revolutionary opportunity. Nairn wrote:

> It is true that the war effort of 1939–45 produced much more social egalitarianism in England than any other event in her recent history, enough to result in the electoral defeat of Churchill in 1945. Yet—paradoxically—it also contained the social upheaval more firmly than ever in a renewed "national" ideology of unity, a sense of patriotic purpose and regeneration. Hence (given the Labour Party's subscription to these myths) it led inevitably to the stifling new conservatism of the 1950s and 1960s.[15]

By focusing on this process, *Country* joins David Hare's *Licking Hitler*, Ian McEwan's *The Imitation Game*, and other plays from the late 1970s and early 1980s that, taking their lead from Angus Calder's 1969 study *The People's War*, reexamined Britain's participation in World War II in the context of competing class interests.[16]

In its genealogical concern with Conservatism's political and ideological formation *Country* fulfills Griffiths's broader exercise of revisionist historical memory, his search—against official historical accounts—for those moments in the past in which the present comes to be chosen out of the alternative futures that crisis offers up. But the play is also deeply rooted in its present historical/cultural moment in ways that represent an intensification of interests that have remained largely in the background of Griffiths's earlier history plays. *Country* reflects a deepening of Griffiths's concern with cultural evocations of the national past by a heritage industry engaged in the task of selective reconstruction and conservation; in so doing, it concerns itself as much with the popularizing manipulations of the past as it does with the political contours of the past itself. "We have a heritage politics as well as a heritage culture," writes Robert Hewison in his study *The Heritage Industry*.[17] Not only, then, is *Country* about the origins of postwar British Conservatism in the past; it is also about the (re)construction of this past within an essentially conservative cultural project.

Hewison, Patrick Wright, and others have studied the proliferation of theme parks, historical enactments, industrial museums, and interactive displays that have characterized the heritage industry before and during the Thatcher years: the Wigan Pier Heritage Centre, Liverpool's Albert Dock, the Camelot Theme Park at Charnock Richard, the Shakespeare Trust in Stratford-upon-Avon.[18] Griffiths, we have seen, was himself forced to come to terms with the question of historical reconstruction and the dangers of heritage periodization during the *Sons and Lovers* project. But, while the British heritage industry, backed by the Heritage Acts of 1980 and 1983, has extended its definitions of *culture* to include industrial sites and regions of working-class culture, the English country house and the social values it embodies remain at the heart of the conservationist project and its marketing of nostalgia. Rich in symbolic political and cultural meanings, the country house enshrines an image of rural serenity, dynastic continuity, and an aristocratic order grounded in landed wealth. The "green and pleasant land" it offers to symbolic contemplation is the England of Tory One Nationhood, its class stratifications naturalized and rendered beneficent through images of agrarian harmony.

Country evokes the symbolic territory of this heritage construction with particular economy. The play's title conflates the idea of nation with the image of a rural social order essential to the traditional conservative construction of nationhood. Griffiths's play addresses this ideological juncture in generic terms by evoking the tradition of the "country-house play," with its nostalgic retrospect and its celebration of aristocratic values. Country is not the first of Griffiths's plays to address this genre. All Good Men—in many ways a companion play to Country, with its seventy-year-old patriarch and its generational confrontation— also evokes the country house and its conservative values. And the adaptation of The Cherry Orchard addressed another watershed class encounter within the dynastic world of the landed estate. As it turned out, the television version of Griffiths's Cherry Orchard (again directed by Richard Eyre) was broadcast by the BBC on 13 October 1981, one week before the broadcast of Country—a juxtaposition that underscored the mutual allusions of these two country house plays. In an even more serendipitous piece of television scheduling, the second episode of John Mortimer's dramatization of Brideshead Revisited was broadcast by Granada TV on the same evening that Country aired (and in overlapping time slots). More than one reviewer noted the powerful juxtaposition of Waugh's "romantic vision of opulence" and Griffiths's "rigorous class analysis."[19]

"The country-house play is a piece of propaganda," Griffiths asserted in a 1981 interview. "It maintains that the aristocratic rich are just the same as us, with the same problems, the same pleasures. Well, they're not."[20] Citing the deference of the working class toward the upper class during the recent Royal Wedding (of Prince Charles and Lady Diana Spencer), Griffiths proposed to offer, in Country, a view of the ruling class at work (his tongue-in-cheek informal subtitle for the play was The Working of the English Making Class). But Griffiths also insisted that this class world be portrayed with a detachment fitting the repression of its interactions and the remoteness of its social codes and way of life. This stylistic distance was achieved, in large part, through the play's filmic atmosphere. Country was the first of Griffiths's television plays to be filmed entirely on location (as opposed to being produced in a studio), and Eyre's production impressively captures the stillness and remoteness aimed for in Griffiths's script. Long shots alternate with stylized close-ups, background with foreground, in a way that serves to frame individuals and groups, while effects of lighting (and a certain muting of sound) add to this effect of detached observation. It is a dark, occasionally dreamlike production, much of it filmed in hallways and studies in a kind of visual eavesdropping. Griffiths has characterized the play's camera as "like a very detached inquiring eye. Part anthropological, part sociological, part political, part psychological, always stranger, always detached."[21] As Edward Braun notes, this stylistic principle is embodied in the figure of Virginia, the estranged daughter, who observes the manor and its residents from a distance before making her appearance toward the play's end; when she photographs the house's occupants the filmic scene is momentarily fixed in black-and-white stills.[22]

    Country opens in one of the institutional sites of class formation, Eton College. In an arresting series of images boy after uniformed boy is forced to conquer his fear and jump from a window onto a stretched canvas below, while a bored monitor controls the waiting queue. Accompanying this fire drill is the sound of a boy's choir singing "Roll Out the Barrel" to the tune of the "Eton Boating Song" and the voice of Churchill denouncing socialism in his first election broadcast. His warnings—"Here, in Great Britain, the cradle of free democracy throughout the world, we do not like to be regimented and ordered about and have every action of our lives prescribed for us" (237)—stand in ironic contrast to this spectacle of class privilege, hierarchical regimentation, and repressed sadism and homoeroticism. The continuity between this world and that of Seal Park is everywhere in evidence. The Carlion world is one of tradition and stasis, but it is also a decadent one: rituals of social interaction and the props of wealth and family history serve as fronts for illicit but oddly joyless sexual encounters, power maneuvers, fascist sympathies, and emotional distance. It is also a world—like that of the grammar school—characterized by male spaces, sanctums of privilege and patriarchal authority that extend beyond the manor to the seats of power themselves (Carlion's son-in-law is a member of the Coalition government and stands to assume a higher post in the expected Conservative administration). The ideology of beneficent rural Toryism underlying the genre of country house drama and country house heritage as a whole is countered here by the fierceness with which this class holds on to its privilege. During the ball held for the neighboring middle class, the Carlions and their relatives barely hide their contempt for their guests. And in the play's second half Carlion must deal with the unexpected occupation of his barns by itinerant hop pickers from the East End, who demand that they be treated as well as the horses they set free to wander about the estate. Like the ballroom scene, this incident plays off of similar scenes in *The Cherry Orchard*, in this case, Varya's reference at the end of act 1 to vagrants sleeping in the empty servants' quarters. The Inspector called in to handle the problem says to Philip, "There's a widespread feeling that people have earned the right to a decent roof over their heads. . . . You know the sort of thing, sir" (270). These are the participants in Calder's "People's War," and their forcible eviction by the play's end unmasks the threat of violence upholding traditional social order.

The family name *Carlion* suggests *Carling*, one of Britain's major beer brands.[23] As Mike Poole suggests, the beer industry was chosen for this sociocultural exploration not only because of the historical importance of beer to working-class culture but also because twentieth-century changes in the brewing industry—"first keg, then lager, then multinational mergers"—could serve as a metaphor for the restructuring of British capital.[24] But in this, one of the most deeply intertextual of Griffiths's plays, the name is also a direct allusion to *Corleone*, the family name of *The Godfather*. By linking *Country* with Mario Puzo's novel (and Francis Ford Coppola's 1972 film), Griffiths underscores the patriarchal, hermetic nature of Sir Frederic's world, its networks of influence, and the unscrupulous exercise of power behind the family's dynastic codes and protocols.

If *Country* is an English *Godfather*, then Philip Carlion is its Michael Corleone, the youngest son drawn back to the world of family and asked to assume its leadership and rejuvenate its fortunes after trying to form a life on the outside (Shakespeare's prodigal Prince Hal is echoed here as well). Philip, who now works as a tabloid journalist in London and lives with a male lover, was once enough of a rebel to have inspired his sister's abandonment of the family for left-wing activism. But Philip's choice of a career collecting gossip on Britain's rich and famous bespeaks a fascination with the world he has left behind, and his intentions as he returns to Seal Park remain an enigma. In what may be the closest he comes to an unguarded moment, he tells Virginia, "In the main I have come to believe that *belief* is not really my bag" (285). "God, but I hate the country," he declares, and while his statement indicates his distance from Seal Park and its rural aristocratic culture, the ambiguity of his phrasing also suggests a class-based contempt for the nation as a whole. By the end of the play Philip has led the assault to evict the laborers occupying the barn, accepted his father's request that he take over as chairman and managing director of Carlion's Brewery, and in a gesture of realpolitik asked the family assistant Faith to join him in a marriage of "respectability." At a family dinner, he toasts "the Family" (291), and at a subsequent meeting of the Carlion men he speaks of the threat posed to their class interests by the Labour Government's evident landslide:

> I don't suppose it's entirely slipped your notice, gentlemen, that today, Thursday, 26th July, the people of this country have declared war on us. [. . .] Before the year's out, we may all be living in the West Indies on such capital as we've been able to muster from the expropriation of our possessions the socialists have been elected to effect. The ship's *sinking*, gentlemen. That's water around your ankles. (294)

With a Thatcherite willingness to adapt tradition to the demands of an entrepreneurial postwar world, he reveals that the Carlion chemists have developed recarbonated beer, which will travel farther, keep longer, and cost half the price to make: "Let me give you: The Future" (295).

Virginia, who refuses to leave the dinner table with the other women and whose plain dress has marked her apartness from family rituals, condemns the world of upper-class privilege and wealth. Having lived the romance of the Left (she abandoned her husband and child to fight in the Spanish Civil War) and now working as a journalist exposing the rural aristocracy (the play suggests), she offers a dream of social revolution that links her with Griffiths's earlier socialist visionaries:

> I've never been able to resist a good funeral. One day—soon, I hope— there'll be a banging at your door. It will be the people. Because they'll be English, they'll probably give you a third-class rail ticket to Dover or Southampton, when they ask you to go. Personally, I would not object if they simply disembowelled you in front of your children and fed your bits to the chickens. Because I feel that, were there a God, he would want you to suffer for the suffering you cause.

She leaves. When Philip catches up with her and asks "You won't be friends," she replies, "Not while there's a war on" (295–96).

As the dinner guests enter their cars to leave, Clement Attlee speaks in voice-over of "freedom, democracy and social justice" (297). The scene changes to a V-J Day bonfire and the local villagers burning an effigy with Eton collar. It is a moment of carnival, celebrating the end of

wartime sacrifice and the symbolic overthrow of class hierarchy and its
attendant injustices. But carnival, as its theorists remind us, is a temporary phenomenon, its license often linked to the maintenance of social
order. While Sir Frederic and Philip watch these festivities from the
shadows, themselves now voyeurs of an alien class, the camera reveals
a Carlion's Brewery barrel being dragged out and tapped. The song
"Roll Out the Barrel"—sung "lusty, vital" (298)—embodies the energies
of a social class with its own culture and rituals. But it also recalls the
choirboys of Eton, secure in a hierarchical educational system that the
1944 Education Act and the subsequent legislation of the Welfare State
would largely preserve. Like these uniformed boys in the play's opening image, the upper class has been forced to jump from a smoke-filled
building, only to land on a safety net of its own devising. One is
reminded of William's charge against his father in *All Good Men:* that the
Attlee revolution amounted to little more than a "minimal social adjustment." While *The Cherry Orchard* concludes with the displacing of a
landed aristocracy, *Country* ends, less sanguinely, with resilience, adaptation, and rebirth. From the twin perspectives of Philip Carlion's and
Margaret Thatcher's resourceful Toryism the grave dug for the upper-
class and its heritage culture turns out, indeed, to be empty.

Fascism and Youth Subculture: *Oi for England*

In early July 1981 two busloads of skinheads arrived in Southall, a predominantly Indian and Pakistani area of London, to hear the 4-Skins,
one of Britain's leading Oi bands, play at the Hamborough Tavern.
After trashing several shops, the band's supporters were confronted by
a group of Asians. The ensuing riot, during which the Hamborough
Tavern was burned to the ground, unleashed a wave of violence that
spread to Liverpool (notably Toxteth), other areas in Greater London
(including Brixton, where the police-rioter confrontations were particularly fierce), Manchester, and more than thirty other cities throughout
Britain. In Toxteth rioters hurled bricks and gasoline bombs at police,
and the police responded with tear gas, the first time this was used in
Britain outside of Northern Ireland. Stores were looted; fires raged. It
was not until the eve of the Royal Wedding—with its pageantry of a sto-
rybook England impossibly remote from the spectacle of violence and
the social conditions of poverty, unemployment, and racial division that
provoked it—that the disturbances, the worst ever on (non-Irish) British
soil, finally subsided.

Griffiths, who had been involved with the Anti-Nazi League, attended a Leeds conference in the spring of 1981 on Race in the Classroom at which he heard numerous stories about fascist recruitment in the schools, playgrounds, and soccer terraces. As a counter-gesture to this infiltration, Griffiths conceived the idea of writing a classroom drama aimed at teenagers. After the summer riots this project assumed an increasing urgency, and Griffiths wrote a television script about skinhead culture, its uneasy relationship with the extreme Right, and the increasing visibility of race within the national political and social consciousness. "After a long involvement with nuanced scripts like *Country* and *The Cherry Orchard*—not to mention the *Reds* saga—I felt the need to write something more urgent and immediate. And there's nothing more urgent than racism."[25] Having negotiated a time slot with Margaret Matheson of Central TV, he wrote a script by Christmas. *Oi for England* was broadcast on 17 April 1982.

Griffiths's decision to write a play about the skinheads enabled him to address a particularly rich nexus of social, political, and cultural issues. For one thing it allowed him to continue to explore the politics of working-class culture, a subject that had concerned him since *Sam, Sam* and *Comedians* and that he had returned to—at historical remove—in his adaptation of *Sons and Lovers*. It also enabled him to confront the increasingly defiant stance of youth subcultural expression within this culture.[26] With their shaved heads, heavy work boots, and links to traditional sites of working-class culture (the term *Oi* is Cockney in origin and evokes the chants of soccer terraces), skinheads transformed the culture handed down to unemployed white working-class youth into a masculinized gesture of violence directed toward "Pakis," gays, and other figures on the margins of society and toward society as a whole. As Dave Laing notes, the skins' music and the group names they chose—Infra-Riot, Exploited, Criminal Class, Vice Squad, Last Resort, Cockney Rejects—reflected "the terms in which mainstream social discourse rejected them."[27] Skinhead culture, according to John Clarke, represented a "magical" attempt to recover a community in cultural terms that was increasingly being lost in real terms, and its currents of racism, homophobia, and sexism are usefully considered in this light.[28]

Because of the racism that marked the defensive alienation of skinhead culture, the skinheads were natural targets for reactionary political appropriation. One of the early Oi compilation albums was titled *Strength through Oi*, a disturbing echo of Hitler's slogan "Strength through Joy," and its cover featured a young skinhead with the insignia of the fascist British Movement on his shoulder. The sudden cultural prominence of the skinheads in the wake of the events that set off the July riots enabled Griffiths, therefore, to confront the issue of working-class racism and its articulation under the banner of particularly extreme constructions of nationhood. From the late 1960s, when members of the working class rallied under Enoch Powell's rhetoric of an England purged of immigration, through the 1970s, when the National Front made highly publicized gains in British polls, the mobilization of working-class disaffection under the banner of reactionary nationalism had been particularly acute. As one National Front member put it in the late 1970s, "If being British means being fascist, thank God I'm a fascist."[29] By confronting the contemporary juncture between working-class politics and the rhetoric of Britishness at its most regressive, Griffiths opened up the even more extreme populist underside of Thatcher's ideological project. Thatcher's own use of Powellite language (in a 1978 interview she spoke of a Britain "swamped" by immigrants) only highlights the continuity between the rhetoric of nationhood in what Stuart Hall calls Thatcherism's "authoritarian populism" and the rhetoric offered the working class (and the nation) by far Right groups.[30] Speaking of the Tottenham riots in the fall of 1985—and the Heysel disaster the previous May, in which Liverpool soccer fans fought with fans of the Italian club Juventus and left thirty-nine dead—Hall argues that "Thatcherism produced the riots; as certainly as it produced the rioting skinheads on the football terraces a few months ago, itching to 'get at the Eyties' just as the fleet was 'itching to get at the Argies'—both swathed to the eyeballs in Union Jacks."[31]

In the March 1981 issue of the National Front journal *Spearhead* an NF activist argued that "punk rock and its attendant new wave style" should be supported because they were "totally white in origin" and "carried a message of the frustration of the masses of White working-class youth."[32] But the Oi musicians themselves frequently denied such political affiliation and often dissociated themselves from the philosophy of the National Front and the British Movement. The producer for one group (named Bad Manners) that had been targeted by fascist groups noted that the musicians (including a black drummer) had been forced to stop playing by extreme right-wing activity, including "Seig Heil!" chants and salutes, at their concerts.[33] It is this space between the right-wing attempts to appropriate skinhead culture and the ambiguously political nature of that culture itself that Griffiths sought to exploit. As in *Comedians*, the culture of working-class youth alienation was a field, Griffiths believed, that was very much open to political contestation. Arguing in a 1982 interview that the skins were not "all fascists," Griffiths recalled working for an Anti-Nazi League carnival in Leeds at which some one hundred of the marshals were skinheads. He characterized the skinheads as occupying "a pre-political phase, strongly aware of Them and Us, but more concerned with their own identity as a group. It's a phase that generates a similar consciousness across the board—and it can develop either way, or not at all. That's why it has to be contested."[34] *Oi for England*, then, is both a portrayal of a cultural field and an intervention in the struggle over that field's appropriation. To the extent that the skinheads had been portrayed throughout the press as fascist in affiliation, Griffiths's play is also a challenge to the terms by which this form of youth aggression was represented in the culture at large.[35]

"Urgency" and "immediacy" are indeed the signatures of this, Griffiths's most driving, rough-edged play. Produced at a fraction of the cost of *Country* (its skinhead actors had never acted before, and it was filmed in the same studio in which the long-running soap opera *Crossroads* was produced), the play's central narrative line has a directness that approaches the structural simplicity of morality drama. *Oi for England* opens with a rapidly edited montage that sets the background of urban violence and the conditions that helped bring it about: actual footage of the riots, flames, groups of youths, a Union Jack, and—amid the grainy, almost surreal colors with which these scenes are presented—newspaper headlines announcing unemployment figures and a billion-pound defense budget. Accompanying this visual mix is the driving beat of an Oi song, the opening lyrics of which (like the Sex Pistols' 1977 "God Save the Queen," which topped the charts during the week of the Silver Jubilee) evoke the iconography of England in order to challenge the consensual myths of Britain and British society:

> In England's green and pleasant land
> There's them as sit and them as stand,
> There's some as eat and some as don't,
> And some who will and a few who won't.
>
> Oi, oi, join the few.
> Oi, oi, it's me and you.
> Oi, oi, what'll we do?
> Oi, oi, turn the screw.[36]

As the song nears its end, three members of the band "Ammunition" are discovered playing their instruments in a rented basement in Moss Side, Manchester, one of the principal sites of the July 1981 riots. The basement is filled with looted goods, and the three musicians—Swells, Landry, and Finn (of Irish descent)—appear agitated, dissatisfied, bored. A sense of directionless energy is pervasive; as Landry later states: "I just wanna *do* someat, get outa the pighole" (325–26). The almost casual racism through which their alienation finds expression makes itself felt when Swells notices Gloria, the daughter of their Jamaican landlord, listening in the doorway: "Piss off, chocolate drop. Black get" (304).

As the sounds of police sirens and street violence begin to be heard outside, the group's fourth member, Napper, enters with the news that he met someone interested in signing up a skinhead group for a paid appearance at a carnival being organized nearby. Upon questioning, he discloses that he met "the Man" (his name is never disclosed) at a skinhead pub with fascist connections and that he has presented the group's name as "White Ammunition." Finn challenges him on his receptivity to this overture, and the argument that follows underscores the issue of capitulation (political and cultural) and the politics of selling out. In one of a number of allusions to *Comedians* (Griffiths has referred to *Oi for England* as "carved out of *Comedians*")[37] Napper defends his desire to escape the bored anonymity of their lives: "I mean, this may be your scene bangin' away in a cellar. I'm after someat better, you know" (307). The performance spheres are different, but with a few adjustments the line could be Sammy Samuels's.

"I'm English," Finn asserts. "I don't wear a swastika for nobody" (310). As Griffiths's title underscores, this "Englishness" is what is at stake in the play. When Swells reminds Finn that he is in fact "fuckin' Irish," he directs attention to Englishness as a "metaphysical order of belonging" (the phrase is Gilroy's),[38] grounded in the dynamics of inclusion and exclusion. In the play's second act Finn demands to know "the politics" behind the event at which they are being asked to perform (319); pretending suspicion that the event is being sponsored by the Anti-Nazi League, he warns that the band is not willing to fire its musical ammunition against "our own" (320). In response the Man (who turns out to be a member of the British Movement) articulates a fascist vision of nationalism, with its anti-immigrant rhetoric and its mythical evocation of a racially pure England. He describes the youth who will attend the Moss Side concert as

> English. Working class. White. [. . .] Sicker bein' kicked around, ignored, shat on, pushed to the bottom of the midden, up to their necks in brown scum, the diarrhoea their rulers have seen fit to flood this England with.

[. . .] Their England. Made on the backs, made by the sweat and bone of the white working class, generation after generation. This England, run *by* foreigners, *for* foreigners. Jews, Arabs, coons, Pakis, wogs from all corners of the earth. Chocolate England.

The specific group he represents is called Movement Music Inc.; in ideological counterpoint to the leftist cultural practice that Griffiths had himself pursued since the 1960s and early 1970s, this group advocates "concerts, music: politics by other means" (321).

By insisting that the politics behind the gig be articulated, Finn redefines the issues of choice and action. As in *Comedians,* each of the band members must choose a stance in full understanding of its political implications. Napper, who discloses the fact that he robbed an Indian earlier and thus sparked off the riots that now rage in full earshot, admits that he subscribes to the Man's racist nationalism. He leaves, followed by Swells, to join the looting outside. Landry, who confesses to having never bothered much about politics, also leaves. Finn stays behind and is soon joined by Gloria, who comes down thinking that all four have left. The two speak with a quiet, tentative intimacy. When Gloria mentions that she plans to go outside, Finn prepares to join her. Gathering an incongruous assortment of boxer training caps, cricket chest protectors, and other sports paraphernalia from the looted boxes, Finn invites her to join him in what Griffiths calls a "gladiatorial transformation": "Be. Prepared. They are" (328). Their movements and gestures as they dress themselves are slow, almost balletic. When Gloria asks him what nationality his name reflects, Finn's answer, "Irish," suggests that he has chosen an identity affiliation in direct refusal of a coercive and exclusionist "England." Gloria goes out, but Finn stays behind. He puts a tape in a radio, and, as he begins cleaning up, an Irish folk ballad joins and gradually subsumes the sounds of offstage violence. Finn listens, absorbed by the sound, then proceeds systematically to smash both the radio and the musical equipment that lies around the room. As Poole suggests, this hand-held camera sequence "concentrates the play's central concern with cultural and political co-option as a struggle over representation—the instruments can't produce any meaning he wants to be associated with."[39] While Finn stares at his hardened face in the mirror, the music takes over the soundtrack.

This sequence is an oddly dissatisfying close to a play that has up to this point been characterized by its hard-edged focus on skinhead subculture and the class positioning it reflects. Griffiths's intention is clearly to ground Finn's solidarity with Gloria in the context of Britain's imperial relationship to Ireland; the song's lyrics imply this: "And I wish the Queen would call home her army / From the West Indies, Americay and Spain" (330). The folk song is clearly also intended to suggest a softer side to Finn's aggressive hardness, a tenderness inexpressible in the context of skinhead subculture. "It's his frustration at having to deny that more tender, lyrical side of himself that, as much as anything, provokes his violent outburst."[40] But the unprepared-for recourse to folk music risks both sentimentality and a nostalgic portrayal of identity not unlike the Right's romanticized Englishness. While Griffiths makes gestures toward complicating this moment—Finn smashes the radio along with the equipment, suggesting that he finds himself caught between incommensurate ways of being, and in the video version the song's lyrical cadences are counterpointed by the image of an open mouth silently shouting, "Oi, oi"—the overall effect of this "sad, very Irish sound" is to supplant clear political choice with the politics of sentiment and nostalgic origin (329). Suggesting that Griffiths has lost the dialectical control of hardness and softness evident in the best of his earlier work, Poole and Wyver consider this ending "dramatically clumsy and politically retrograde"; Stuart Cosgrove characterized it as "trapped in inarticulacy and idealism."[41] While this and other problems that critics noted in the play's initial script may partially result, in this case, from the speed with which the play was written and moved through production, nostalgia and what Alan Sinfield has termed "magical resolution" will recur as issues in Griffiths's work of the 1980s.[42]

Postscript: Audience and Cultural Location

Because of its subsequent production history, *Oi for England* offers a particularly rich opportunity to appreciate the mobility of Griffiths's dramatic practice, its willingness to address audiences across the boundaries of culture, medium, and social grouping. Although the eruption of racism and working-class youth aggression on the national level led Griffiths to write *Oi for England* for a television audience, the playwright never abandoned his original vision of the play as an address to teenagers through the medium of live performance and in their own social/cultural spaces. Under the production of the Royal Court Theatre Upstairs a touring production of the play, directed by Antonia Bird, was taken to a series of youth clubs and community centers in Birmingham and the Greater London area (including a number of stops in East London, where National Front support was particularly strong) between 12 May and 5 June 1981. *Oi* opened to the general public at the Royal Court on 9 June; separate productions of the play subsequently toured in Nottinghamshire and South Yorkshire.[43] By presenting the play in non-Fringe community venues, Griffiths sought a more localized cultural intervention in the lives of working-class youth audiences (as part of this concern, he adapted the play's local references to reflect the different places of performance). Performances of the play took place as part of other community center activities, and postperformance discussions were conducted to allow the audience to deepen their engagement with the play's issues.

Accounts of the original touring production suggest both the problems and opportunities involved in transporting a play like *Oi for England* from its traditional theatrical audience into the environment of those neither socialized into conventional (or avant-garde) play watching nor automatically won over to its political viewpoint. Kids at times seemed unaware that they were watching a play, responding to the actors as real-life skinheads; they talked during the performance and often seem puzzled by the play's politics. During some performances audience comments even had a disturbingly racist edge. Early in the run few stayed around to participate in the discussion, and even when more did (at a subsequent production) they "had to be pressed into connecting the play with issues like unemployment or racism and were much happier simply talking about how it confirmed their own experience of skinheads as 'nutters' full stop."[44] Griffiths, who had already made a number of changes in the script (dropping the guitar-smashing finale and adding two additional musical numbers, making it more like a musical production), made further changes in response to the play's early reception—taking some of the rhetorical force out of the Man's racist speech, for instance—and the company restructured the discussion format. By the end of the London tour one journalist wrote:

> the performances are tighter and the whole evening more closely structured to fit the expectations of the audience. These changes are reflected in the quality of the discussion that follows. There is a lot of talk about how the play captures the frustrations of being young in 1982 and about how unemployment and skinhead violence go hand in hand. One black youth goes right to the heart of Griffiths's concerns when he expresses an affinity with the problems faced by the skins in the play. A number of whites in the audience are visibly shocked.[45]

To an extent even beyond Griffiths's other texts, then, *Oi for England* is less a "work" than a shifting series of interventions, exploring the politics of culture in both its performance and its represented world. In its willingness to take its concern with racism and aggression into the actual world of working-class youths and to engage the politics of culture at those sites where its stakes were highest, the touring production of *Oi for England* represented an opening within Griffiths's dramatic practice to a new, potentially powerful form of cultural engagement. Like Rock against Racism, which staged a number of concerts between 1976 and 1981 to combat the growing influence of the far Right in Britain, the *Oi for England* project was a challenge to the cultural appropriation attempted by the Man and his real-life surrogates. And, like the Theatre in Education movement (which Griffiths had long been interested in), the touring project was an attempt to take theater into the environments where the young come to know themselves as social and political subjects. In this respect *Oi for England* is very much a counterpoint to *Country*, with its public school world of discipline and class training. Although Griffiths would not return to the specific form of cultural intervention represented by the *Oi for England* project, the political struggle over Britain's youth, and the specific form of *nation* that they were asked to join, would remain very much in his mind. If *Oi for England* carries *Comedians* to its next incarnation by returning to the politics of working-class youth aggression, *Thatcher's Children* (Griffiths's 1993 play) will employ workshop techniques to tell the story of disempowerment through youth's own voices.

National Fictions: *Judgment over the Dead* / *The Last Place on Earth*

The seeds of Griffiths's most ambitious critique of the British national myth were laid in December 1980, when producer Robert Buckler and Roland Joffe (who had directed *Bill Brand*) approached him with the idea of writing a television screenplay based on Roland Huntford's book *Scott and Amundsen*. Huntford's book, published in 1979, was a revisionist account of the 1911–12 race to the South Pole between expeditions headed by the British naval Captain Robert Falcon Scott and the Norwegian Roald Amundsen. The race, as every Briton knows, ended with the Norwegians arriving at the Pole first and the bitterly disappointed Scott perishing with the other members of his polar party on the return journey, just eleven miles from one of their supply depots. History, in this case, had its recompenses: when news of this tragedy reached Britain, the expedition was hailed as an example of heroic failure, a triumph of the British spirit in the face of insurmountable obstacles, while the Amundsen triumph was denigrated as crass professionalism. Scott became the embodiment of national courage for a Britain suffering from postimperial malaise, and his expedition was offered as evidence that the British "race" had not lost its manhood. The value of the expedition, the *Times* argued, was

> spiritual, and therefore in the truest sense national. It is proof that in an age of depressing materialism men can still be found to face known hardship, heavy risk and even death, in pursuit of an idea. . . . That is the temper of men who build empires, and while it lives among us we shall be capable of maintaining an Empire that our fathers builded.[46]

With that distinctly British logic by which failure is rewritten as heroism (the "Dunkirk syndrome"), Scott became a symbol of gallant magnificence in the face of defeat. One prominent dramatization of the Scott myth, the 1948 Ealing Studios film *Scott of the Antarctic*, closes with the memorial cross erected in McMurdo Sound for the Scott expedition; its Tennysonian inscription reads: "To strive, to seek, to find, and not to yield."[47] History books recirculated this account; some schoolchildren were actually taught that it was Scott who discovered the South Pole.[48]

As Huntford demonstrated, this heroic account originated with Scott himself, whose self-mythologizing journal entries through the expedition's final days reveals an acute awareness of history's gaze, and with those (including Scott's wife Kathleen) whose vested interests in the Scott myth led them to excise passages from this journal before authorizing its publication. Revisiting the historical events underlying this myth, Huntford challenges the official verdict on all counts. Whereas Amundsen's polar journey was a triumph of skill, forethought, and organization, Huntford argues, the Scott expedition revealed an appalling level of ineptitude in all aspects of its planning and execution.

Although Griffiths was impressed by Huntford's book, he initially declined the project, feeling suspicious of the male adventure story aspects of the narrative and wondering if he could find "a politics within this piece that could be inserted into a contemporary discourse and the present struggle." When he was reapproached ten months later, Griffiths's sense of the contemporary climate was shifting: "We were a year closer to Falklands . . . and maybe one could feel the build up to the

Falklands in advance or something, some recrudescence of imperialist ideology. . . feeling . . . silliness."[49] Griffiths agreed to take on the project and began writing a six-part television script entitled *Judgment over the Dead* (the phrase is taken from the *Hávamál*, an ancient Norse poem). Three directors after Joffe dropped out of the project (it was eventually directed by Ferdinand Fairfax) and production began on what was now a seven-episode series entitled *The Last Place on Earth*. In February 1984 the Antarctic scenes were filmed on location at Frobisher Bay, close to the Canadian Arctic Circle, under what turned out to be exceptionally difficult working conditions: the temperature hit −57 degrees Celsius (colder than the temperatures Scott and Amundsen were exposed to), and Fairfax was permanently marked by frostbite. But the scenic effects achieved in this way were certainly breathtaking, and *The Last Place on Earth*, produced at an estimated cost of seven million pounds, was broadcast by Central TV between 18 February and 27 March 1985.[50]

"The spirit of Scott is with us today," Griffiths commented. "Palpable, breathing in the way we perceive the world, the way we seek to change it or retain it."[51] Recognizing in Huntford's book a powerful deconstruction of official history, he conceived of his own screenplay as a similar act of counterhistory, an attempt (as we have seen throughout his writing) to "retrieve real histories and make them usable in the present in ways that are not so supportive of the dominant ideology."[52] Given that Scott and his failed expedition had become another in a line of national fictions, Griffiths's project was to challenge the selective amnesia by which history is transformed into myth and to renarrate the race to the South Pole in terms of documentary and other evidence. Griffiths was concerned to contextualize the Scott expedition in terms of broader social and historical forces: labor unrest; the different manifestations of nationalism in Britain and Norway; technological change; militarism and the looming shadow of the Great War. One of the techniques by which Griffiths sought to "write" this backdrop into his screenplay was through the intercutting of montage sequences that challenge and contextualize the narrative of expedition (many of these sequences ended up being cut from the final television version): a scene of Scott being welcomed by the burghers of Manchester, with Union Jacks waving everywhere, is counterpointed by a shot of militant trade unionists demonstrating outside, their own banners refusing the façade of nationalist unity: "Jobs not Glory," "Send an expedition to Manchester and discover Poverty."[53]

Taking his lead from Huntford, Griffiths underscored the ideological importance of Scott's "gallant sacrifice" to Britain's military mobilization two years later. In the closing moments of the play's final episode Griffiths juxtaposes a montage of World War I carnage with the words of a contemporary writer:

> If nothing else, Scott showed his countrymen the way to die. We have so many heroes among us now, so many Scotts, holding sacrifice above gain . . . and we begin to understand what a splendour arises from the bloody fields of Flanders and Gallipoli. (305)

The outbreak of the Falklands War in the spring of 1992, when he was halfway through writing his script, allowed Griffiths to deepen the dialogue between past and present and thereby sharpen his critique of postimperial mythography and the rhetoric of national identity and pride. In its militaristic Britishness Thatcher's evocations of the "spirit of the South Atlantic" in the war's aftermath recalled the *Times'* commemoration of that earlier naval expedition to the Southern hemisphere seventy years earlier. Against those who feared "that Britain was no longer the nation that had built an Empire and ruled a quarter of the world" she exulted: "Britain found herself in the South Atlantic and will not look back from the victory she has won."[54] Speaking to the Royal Society of Literature, C. M. Woodhouse drew the historical connection more explicitly:

> Ladies and Gentlemen, we meet on the morrow of a national triumph in the South Atlantic. It recalls a former member of this society, Sir Arthur Quiller-Couch, on another memorable episode in the same area of the world, exactly seventy years ago. Let us keep our language noble for we still have heroes to celebrate.[55]

To drive home the historical parallels and continuities Griffiths titled his final episode "Rejoice!" So deliberately was contemporary history being refashioned as myth, so perfect the analogies, he almost didn't need to.

"Poles apart": as the title of the series' opening episode makes clear, Griffiths sees the rival expeditions and their leaders as embodiments of radically different operational procedures and worldviews. In Scott, Griffiths portrays "an imperial class in action,"[56] bound by institutional and class protocols, outmoded procedures, and a self-consciously British outlook that embraces civilized values, "sporting" amateurism, and a willingness to muddle through that borders on recklessness and masochism. In Lukácsian fashion his character "gathers at an important point of confluence all the contradictory social forces of a particular soci-

ety in a particular period."[57] The results of these contradictions are mis-
guided and ultimately catastrophic decisions. While the Norwegians
rely on dogs and skis, Scott (against all advice and evidence) includes
horses and motor sleds in his polar expedition. The latter fall through
the ice and break down, and, when the former show signs of labor and
exhaustion on a crucial supply run, Scott's refusal to have them shot
forces the party to lay down its supply depot crucially short of its
intended latitude (a fatal choice, it turns out).

Behind Scott is his wife, Kathleen, who drives him in his mission to
conquer the South Pole with a ferocity reminiscent of Lady Macbeth.[58]
Kathleen is one of the series' least sympathetic characters—a scene
showing her having an affair with the older Norwegian explorer
Nansen is juxtaposed with Scott's disappointed arrival at the Pole—and
this links her in uncomfortable ways with betrayer women in Griffiths's
earlier plays. But the curious self-unsexing that links her both with Lady
Macbeth and with the representatives of Strindberg's "third sex"—she
desires a world in which "there would be no women, just beautiful hus-
bands and darling sons" (114)—is itself symptomatic of a social order
that creates the dream of glory but allows only men the opportunity to
pursue it.

Griffiths highlights the differences between the two expeditions
through specific scenic contrasts. The opening scenes of *The Last Place on
Earth* show Amundsen sitting with Eskimos in a Canadian igloo, learning their craft and way of life, while Scott is shown being reprimanded
by an admiral at a naval club for his inefficiency while commanding a
ship. The admiral is playing snooker—"easily aware of his class" (John
Tulloch observes in his discussion of these scenes), "constructing out of
this meeting a potent combination of gamesmanship, adventurism,
amateurism, and hierarchy that is emblematic of the British imperial
dream."[59] Later scenes expand and underscore the contrast. While the
Norwegians' expeditionary base is a model of efficiency and egalitari-
anism, the British hut is a microcosm of British society, with barriers
separating officers from the "lower orders" and with the unnecessary
luxuries of privilege. While the Norwegians dress in Eskimo animal
skins, the British brave the elements in inappropriate traditional gear.
Montage segments reinforce the contrast between the polar parties during their final push to the pole and their return: the Norwegians ski
gracefully over the terrain, their dogs accompanying them, while the
British must labor through brutally inefficient man haulage. In one of
the script's most powerful visual ironies, when the members of the Scott

party finally reach the Pole and stare dejectedly at the Norwegian flag, their gaze includes dog droppings and paw prints.

At the heart of the differences marking the two parties lie fundamental questions of leadership and social organization, and Griffiths explores these subjects with an intensity that recalls *Occupations, The Party, Absolute Beginners,* and other plays of the early 1970s. Scott, a product of naval hierarchy and procedures, exercises an autocratic command over his party and permits no disagreement; as he tells one of his men who questions his orders concerning the ponies: "it must be clearly understood between us that it is not my practice or indeed the Navy's to have one's orders questioned" (72). Oates, one of the members of the party, raises in private one of the series' central questions: "Is loyalty to the leader the *highest* virtue? Does plain *reason* not occasionally override it?" (122). Whatever the initial miscalculations concerning the expedition, it is clear that Scott's unwillingness to subject his decisions to debate is what ultimately costs him his life; in this sense he is as much a victim of the British hierarchy as its figurehead.

In the character of Amundsen, Griffiths considers the issue of alternative forms of leadership. Amundsen, whose personality combines personal asceticism with a deep respect for nature and the primitive cultures most adapted to it, practices a style of leadership that seeks to combine discipline and collective participation. He asks his men to sign a statement promising to "obey the leader of the expedition in everything at any time" (81), but on an earlier expedition he posted the words "On this ship we are all captains, we are all crew" (82). Whereas Scott comments in his journal on the importance of officers not waiting on themselves in the Antarctic base camp, Amundsen works with his men and respects the abilities for which he selected them. He is, in Griffiths's words, "primus inter pares," and in his mixture of authority and shared cooperation he represents the development of "a more socialist approach to leadership" (this contrast between leadership styles and the ideologies that they evoke are reflected in forms of address: Scott's men refer to him as the "Owner," British naval slang for the captain of a warship, while Amundsen's men call him the "Chief").[60] The members of Amundsen's polar party contrive to have him arrive at the Pole first, but when it comes time to plant the flag Amundsen insists that this be a communal act: "Come, comrades. This must be done by all of us" (232).

"Comradeship" here is the model through which Griffiths seeks to reconcile the contradictory imperatives that polarized his earlier plays of revolutionary leadership. There are touches of the idyllic in Griffiths's portrait; certainly, the isolated microcosms of ship, polar hut, and sledding party and the romance of primitive practices and social structure feel remote from the revolutionary historical stages of Griffiths's earlier work. At the same time, Amundsen's experiment in leadership does not always manage to negotiate the potential contradictions of authority and comradeship. In the aftermath of a failed expedition Amundsen is openly confronted by the veteran explorer Johanssen. Amundsen reestablishes his leadership with a naked assertion of authority, and, though this is, under the circumstances, demonstrably necessary, the rupture it causes shadows—and to some extent challenges—the utopian portrait of comradely leadership.

When Amundsen learns the news concerning Scott's party, he acknowledges that the British adventurer managed to win after all: "It's quite a coup. (*Pause*) He wins at the last." His bitter words on the career of Frederick Cook, an earlier explorer now jailed in the United States for fraud, are prophetic of his own erasure in the mythologizing that will follow Scott's death: "Thirty years on the ice, never lost a single comrade's life . . . and already the world's forgotten him. Never learnt the British habit of dying, the glory of self-sacrifice, the blessing of failure, that's where he went wrong" (296). In taking on the Scott expedition, Griffiths was as concerned to show the process by which history is recycled as myth as he was to correct the historical verdict on the expedition itself. *Judgment over the Dead*, like Griffiths's earlier television plays, is filled with references to the myriad ways in which history is recorded: letters, journals, news conferences, journalistic interviews, radio broadcasts, photographs, filming sessions in Antarctica.[61] Like Huntford, Griffiths sees in Scott a figure who worked to shape the public perception of his expedition, who in a sense created the mythologized account by which his actions would be judged. Griffiths's Scott writes in his journal with an intensity that only deepens as the expedition progresses further into disaster, transforming death into myth, as if the glory of narrative were the unconscious goal all along. In order to measure the discrepancy between myth and reality Griffiths juxtaposes voice-over passages from Scott's diary with the incidents they describe, and he decenters the univocal textuality of Scott's account by including the private dissenting voice of other expedition members.

But the management of myth is by no means restricted to Scott and his personal ambitions. In the aftermath of Scott's tragedy Griffiths demonstrates the concerted effort by those with vested interests in the expedition to shape its public reception. As Huntford's book discloses, Scott's journal was heavily edited (under the insistence of Kathleen Scott and others) to remove passages damaging to the explorer and the expedition's reputation. An official reconstruction of the final scene in the tent was commissioned by, of all people, the playwright and fantasist J. M. Barrie.[62] Going even further than Huntford, Griffiths directs attention to this official suppression of information. As early as the moment when the frozen bodies have been discovered, Atkinson (the expedition's surgeon) seeks to suppress reports that the dead showed evidence of scurvy (and hence of mismanaged diet). Subsequent scenes show a committee organized by Kathleen Scott and Sir Clements Markham, Scott's patron, circumventing public inquiry into the causes of death ("as a way of countering any criticism that may have arisen as to the organization and leadership displayed" [299]) and cutting potentially incriminating passages from the journal in preparation for its publication. In this, as with all aspects of the project, Griffiths's target is as much the present as the past: "At a time when news management has reached such appalling levels as in the reporting of the Falklands, the Korean Airlines disaster and the invasion of Grenada, it seems important to look at how a myth of glorious and heroic failure was constructed in that way."[63]

As it turned out, the battle over Scott's reputation—what Tulloch calls "the *circulation* of its meanings as history"[64]—extended to the production and broadcast of *The Last Place on Earth*. The Scott estate had already taken legal action against Huntford's book, and a group including Peter Scott (the explorer's son), Lord Kennet (Kathleen Scott's son by a subsequent marriage), and Robert Hemming (director of the Royal Geographic Society) sought to block production of the television series. Although they failed in this attempt, they were allowed a private screening before the series was aired, over the objections of Griffiths, the director, and others involved in the process. Having seen the episodes, the Scott establishment was in a position, in Griffiths's words, to "frame the public response" surrounding the series.[65] Kennet made a request to the Independent Broadcasting Authority to have the series labeled "fictional drama," and, when this was turned down (Central TV acquiesced somewhat by labeling it "Fiction based on Fact"), Kennet circulated the letter detailing his objections to a press eager for controversy. The Scott establishment attacked the series in the press over questions of accuracy, prompting an angry letter from Griffiths to the *Observer* in response to an article of Kennet's. Arguing that playwrights have always "used the terrains of the past to construct, together with audiences, contemporary social, political and moral meanings," he confronts his attacker on the latter's chosen terrain, historical honesty:

> If Lord Kennet does indeed have such passionate regard for "history" and "truth," perhaps he could explain why it took 55 years to make his non-relative's last journals available in full to the public and the community of historians; and why his mother's diaries remain unpublished in full until this day.
>
> All the evidence I've seen—and it's a lot—persuades me that the Scott I wrote . . . is inestimably closer to the "real" Scott than anything offered us by the Official Mythography.[66]

As a direct result of this carefully orchestrated opposition to the series, *The Last Place on Earth* was criticized, like Huntford's book, for what was seen as its one-sided demythologizing.[67] Eight years after the series was broadcast, journalists and letter writers were still attacking Griffiths's portrayal.[68] Such, clearly, is the strength of public investment in the heroic account of Scott's expedition. But, despite the harshness of Cook's verdict within the script itself ("Scott killed *himself*, it's what the British do best, they have such contempt for the work it's just as well they do" [303]), Griffiths himself disclaimed any intention to denigrate Scott personally. "I think the case against Scott is devastating," he argued, "but at the end of the series I don't think you see him as a black-guard."[69] While the play's "poles apart" strategy for conducting its act of historical correction may occasionally risk an unproblematic moral and political dichotomizing, Griffiths's historical understanding and dialectical sensibility once again provide the check. Character is finally assessed not only in terms of personality but also in terms of the social and ideological contradictions it throws into relief. Speaking of the final scene in the Antarctic tent, Griffiths rejected the accusation that his characters were two-dimensional: "When you follow the British from base camp to the Pole and half-way back again, you live their dying, moment by moment in what I believe to be a wholly proper way. And you see their contradictions and you see them seeing their contradictions, like Oates, like Wilson."[70] In contrast to the traditionally romanticized portrayal of these deaths (like that of the 1948 film), Griffiths's deployment of emotion in this scene is classically Brechtian: feeling and "caring" are allowed their play but only within a field of response sensitive to contradiction, multiple awareness. The cutting of montage and background scenes during production may have undermined Griffiths's broader historicizing efforts in the television series, but the spectacle of individuals living and dying the contradictions of their society is the center of both versions.

Huntford's "judgment over the dead" may, in the end, have rested on Scott himself; for Griffiths it is in the imperial class, its traditions, and its myths of nation that the real tragedy arose.

7

Screen/Plays

The 1980s

With the exception of the years 1981–82, which saw a striking concentration of produced work on Griffiths's part, the 1980s have sometimes been treated as a kind of missing decade in the playwright's career. No doubt, this attitude reflects Griffiths's relative lack of interest in the theater during these years, the medium by which academics and critics tend to gauge literary productivity (*Real Dreams* was his only stage play between 1982 and 1990), and the fact that some of his most extensive projects during this time were never produced. As with Edward Bond, Caryl Churchill, and Howard Brenton, however, whose work in the 1980s has also tended to receive less attention, such neglect may reflect a broader uncertainty over how to talk about British political theater at a point when its heyday was in the past. As the postscript to Catherine Itzin's 1980 *Stages in the Revolution* makes clear, there was an awareness at decade's end on the part of writers and observers alike that the flowering of political culture in the 1960s and 1970s was over.[1] In 1979 Griffiths noted: "Anybody knows the different feel around now from four or five years ago. . . . There could be changes inside the theater that will make it extremely difficult for us to get work."[2]

And yet, despite the sense of contacting cultural opportunities and a changed political climate, the 1980s were an enormously busy decade for Griffiths; with as many as four or five projects going on at once, he was easily one of the most active dramatists writing at this time. Griffiths's search for projects that would allow him "impacts and detonations and reverberations"[3] embraced an impressive range of subjects: the Scott-Amundsen race to the South Pole, William Wharton's novel about World War II, South African activists, the life of Tom Paine. The central feature of this decade, of course, is Griffiths's deepening involvement with the medium of film: during the 1980s he had two screenplays produced (*Reds* and *Fatherland*), and he wrote a number that remain unproduced. That Griffiths devoted so much attention to film reflects both his long-standing interest in the medium and the changing and diminished opportunities for "strategic penetration" in the 1980s: "the doors were being closed and slammed almost daily to the kind of roots for ideas you had: the BBC, ITV, British movies and, crucially, British stage, British theater."[4] This work with film was essential to Griffiths's development as a writer during this decade. Not only did screenwriting introduce Griffiths to a new (and challenging) cultural institution; it exposed him to a medium with strikingly different representational possibilities. As a result of this exposure, Griffiths's plays (for theater and television alike) underwent their most radical transformation. After *Country* and *Oi for England* Griffiths relinquished dialectical realism for a more imagistically grounded dramatic style: his plays display a more intricate, plastic treatment of history and temporality, and his work as a whole reveals an increasing willingness to cross the boundaries of form and medium. In his own words he began to write "screenplays for the stage." *Real Dreams* is a pivotal text in this regard; in it one can see the emergence in Griffiths's work of a representational field in which the cinematic and the theatrical occupy their own form of dialectical relationship. For a dramatist who learned his craft in television and the theater it is film, ironically, that provides this dramaturgical opening.

Hollywood Collaboration: *Reds*

As Griffiths's initial foray into the Hollywood film industry, *Reds* (cowritten with Warren Beatty) occupies an important place in the playwright's career. At the same time, because of the project's vexed history, the film is also the most difficult of Griffiths's works to assess; indeed, it is hard to call the finished film "Griffiths's" without radical qualifications. The film is Beatty's, and yet Griffiths's hand is everywhere in evidence.

Griffiths has called the two and a half years he spent working on the *Reds* project "among the most intense, passionate and conflicted years I've spent as a writer."[5] He met Beatty when he flew to New York in early 1976 (his first trip to the United States) to discuss the planned Broadway production of *Comedians*. A couple of weeks later Griffiths received a call from the actor asking him if he might be interested in working on a film project on the life of John Reed, the American socialist and journalist whose book *Ten Days That Shook the World* was an influential account of the Russian Revolution (Lenin, who read it "with the greatest interest and with never-slackening attention," wrote an introduction for the book).[6] Beatty had been interested in John Reed since he himself was asked by Russian producers in the late 1960s to play the radical journalist in a Soviet film on his life. He turned down the Soviet offer, but he began to read extensively on Reed's life for a film project of his own; by 1971 he had produced a step outline for such a film and begun filming people who had known Reed and his lover/colleague, Louise Bryant, earlier in the century. Before asking Griffiths to take on the screenplay, Beatty considered Lillian Hellman, Arthur Miller, and Paddy Chayefsky.

Griffiths was intrigued by the idea of a Hollywood project on such a radical subject and spent the next six months considering Beatty's offer and thinking over the potential "yield" in terms of his own cultural politics. In January 1977 he and Beatty agreed on a tentative contract, and Griffiths began work on the project.[7] Griffiths's initial title for his screenplay was *John Reed*, but he later changed this to the more politically resonant title *Comrades*. He finished his first draft in spring 1978 and sent it to Beatty. When Beatty and Griffiths met in September, Beatty presented a number of critiques of the screenplay. The two agreed to work together on a second draft and spent ten to twelve weeks together reworking the script. By this point fundamental differences in how each conceived the project had emerged, and by the time they finished working on it the script was structured along more conventionally romantic Hollywood outlines, and its political dimension had receded. The two met again that December in England for an additional several days' work, and Griffiths's unhappiness over the direction the script was taking deepened: "It was more like a marketing ideas session in advertising: ideas were not rooted in moral value or a sense of history or character any longer."[8] Griffiths resigned from the project, while Beatty continued with *Reds* and began filming in August 1979.

Griffiths reestablished contact with Beatty in the middle of 1981, when the film was in the late stages of editing. He saw a preliminary edit of the film, still mostly in black and white, and was surprised by his response. "I imagined that I was going to see something which whilst I might admire it technically I would find repugnant politically, but it was much more difficult to weigh its positive and negative yields." He felt that there was "much to admire"—that, despite its capitulation to Hollywood, it had succeeded in recovering an impressive amount that had been marginalized or suppressed entirely in accounts of early-twentieth-century American history.[9] Beatty and Griffiths agreed to share screenplay credit for the film; the two are listed together, with Beatty (who also directed the film) listed first. Paramount released the film in the United States in December 1981 and in Britain two months later.

Because of this history, critical readings of *Reds* must negotiate unusually difficult critical terrain. The fact that nearly six years elapsed between Beatty's initial approach to Griffiths and the release of *Reds*—a time lag resulting, in large part, from the film industry's financing and production procedures—makes the project, we will see, hard to "place" in Griffiths's overall career. And the difficult collaboration between Beatty and Griffiths leaves the question of authorship murky, at times even undecidable. In what is the most extensive and judicious examination of this problem, based on a careful reading of both the *Comrades* typescript in the British Film Institute National Library and the finished *Reds* film text, Poole and Wyver conclude that the film follows the structure of Griffiths's manuscript fairly closely. The script underwent numerous changes before and during production: in addition to the changes that Beatty contributed during his revision sessions with Griffiths, at least two additional writers contributed to the script, and actors were often asked to improvise dialogue. Poole and Wyver, however, argue that "the architecture and overall scope of the narrative *are* Griffiths's" and that the most striking differences are often those "of inflection and emphasis, of the varying weight and interpretation given to the material handled within it." Griffiths's original intentions were certainly compromised, but to blame this entirely on Beatty is to neglect the role of the Hollywood production process in the film's eventual shape.[10]

Inevitably, then, discussion of *Reds* must take into account its complicated and elusive status as text: multiply authored, marked as much by its absences as by what it contains, the finished film dramatizes the struggle—institutional and personal—over what the John Reed–Louise Bryant story will be allowed to mean. Reading the *Comrades* typescript allows us to see *Reds* in terms of the influences that realize and deflect Griffiths's textual intentions. Rather than approach it as a site of stable meanings, such a text invites us to consider the process by which meaning is translated and displaced, subjected to a range of pressures and constraints.

The potential yield that Griffiths discerned in the John Reed project was threefold: the chance to recover a particularly vital segment of the American radical tradition that had been largely suppressed in the light of official anticommunism; to explore further (through the relationship of Reed and Bryant) the intersection of the personal and the political; and to discover what openings were available to a radical cultural project in Hollywood, "the hardest factory in the world in which to get serious work done seriously."[11] Griffiths organized his screenplay in four carefully balanced parts: the United States before 1917, revolutionary Russia in fall 1917, the United States during the Red Scare, and the Soviet Union after 1917 (during the Civil War). By counterpointing the sections in Russia and the United States, Griffiths clearly intended a set of mirrorings and contrasts: that the United States in the years surrounding World War I had its own revolutionaries and that both countries played out the confrontation between revolution and reaction that characterized Europe and the United States during this particular historical juncture. *Comrades* hinges on this four-part structure and the ideological, political, and cultural forces that the centerpiece year 1917 brought to crisis.

Beatty, by contrast, was interested primarily in the Reed-Bryant relationship, and during the rewrites and the production process that followed Griffiths's resignation from the project this aspect of the screenplay came to dominate the film. Griffiths had approached the relationship in terms of the politics of intimacy. Can the conflicting demands of freedom and commitment be reconciled? How can love and sexuality both fulfill and transcend themselves through wider political participation? Is comradeship achievable in affairs of the heart? For such an investigation history is not mere backdrop; it establishes the conditions of constraint and possibility. In the film *Reds*, however, the relationship has become the defining focus of the play, in a way that undermines the personal-political dialectic that Griffiths intended. By the end of the second rewrite this shift had already occurred: the Reed-Bryant relationship was foregrounded, the political life of the characters was pushed into the "middle distance," and the central action of the script had become "human love and need as conventionalized romantically."[12] The struggle over commitment (in all its personal and political ramifications) that characterized the Reed-Bryant relationship in Griffiths's script is sentimentalized with all the force of Hollywood convention in the film. A childlike song written by Bryant on a whim at Provincetown becomes a refrain throughout the film, and a poem written for her by Reed on the back of an Industrial Workers of the World (IWW) handbill reappears with equal poignancy at moments of loneliness and loss. For calculated cuteness a Christmas gift dog is matched only by the puppy dog gazes of Beatty and Diane Keaton (the former winningly boyish, the latter pouty). This change of emphasis is starkly evident toward the film's end, when Reed and Bryant are reunited at a Russian train station shortly before Reed's death; as Reed clasps Bryant, dressed in peasant smock and scarf, the moment is classic Hollywood: "Don't leave me," he murmurs, as the music rises. "Please don't leave me."[13]

There are other ways in which the film, by de-emphasizing political context, changes the issues that Griffiths's screenplay originally addressed. By cutting speeches by Lenin and Trotsky, the film relegates these figures to the background during the revolutionary sequences. The former comes across as almost inhumanly hard; in one of the few references to him Reed calls him "colorless, humorless, uncompromising" (this greatly misrepresents the portrait of Lenin in *Ten Days That Shook the World*). Reed's own developing attitude toward the Revolution is skewed differently as a result of Beatty's screenwriting choices. Part of the interest in Reed's character is the process by which this journalist, described by Upton Sinclair as "the Playboy of the Revolution,"[14] becomes radicalized to the point that he comes to assent to the Revolution's harshest measures. In one of the film's central exchanges he answers Emma Goldman's declaration that the Bolsheviks are destroying "any hope of real communism in Russia" by assuming the voice of one of Griffiths's "hards": "It's a war . . . and we have got to fight it like we fight a war, with discipline, with terror, with firing squads, or we just give it up." Idealism and the promise of new beginnings is followed by moral contradiction and the hard questions involved in carrying through the revolutionary process. But the emphasis on Reed's (mis)handling of his relationship with Louise in the film's second half (and the trimming of scenes devoted to party organization) casts Reed's deepening radicalism as obsession, linked in psychological terms to his failures with his wife. In Griffiths's summary, "These are the dangers of ideals and obsessions, here is a monomaniac going crazy, here is a man driven to a point where he cannot observe how badly he is behaving in his primary relationships."[15]

It is Bryant who suffers the most in the sentimentalization of Griffiths's script. The film opens with Bryant scandalizing her husband and the other members of Portland society with photographs that include nudes of herself. Her sexual unconventionality is clear as she seduces Reed and leaves her marriage to join him in the bohemian and politically radical world of Greenwich Village. From the moment when she asks him, "What as?" (he has just invited her to come to New York), she demands to be taken seriously as a writer in her own right. But, despite the strength she demonstrates throughout the film, an undercurrent of neediness and bourgeois domesticity tends to undermine her independence. This is particularly pronounced in the film's second half, in which she grows increasingly troubled by Reed's political involvement in the American Socialist Party and his role in the infighting that will lead to the emergence of rival American Communist Parties. She pouts and glowers and acquires the accusing attitude of a disappointed wife. One of the concerns of Griffiths's script is the process by which Bryant (like Reed) takes possession of herself politically and arrives at the point where, in the story's closing moments, she can affirm her relationship with Reed as one of "comrades." This does comes through in the film: in a moment of gender equality and mutuality all too rare in Griffiths's work, a montage of scenes in the early stages of the October Revolution is narrated through a voice-over interweaving both Reed's and Bryant's written accounts. Double voiced, the sequence challenges the historical emphasis on Reed as chronicler of the Revolution and returns Bryant to her collaborative place alongside him. But, on the whole, the film seems very conflicted about her: although Reed accuses her early on of not taking herself and her work seriously, the film itself seems at odd moments to trivialize her. It's hard to take seriously a figure whose theme music is a song entitled "I Don't Wanna Play in Your Yard." And, despite the overall accomplishment of Keaton's portrayal, her character's stature is not helped by a certain Annie Hall self-deprecation.

One of the most striking features of *Reds* is the intercutting of its narrative with the filmed testimony of historical witnesses. From early on in his conception of the project Beatty had intended to use actual testimony in the film, and he and Griffiths discussed what they called "the old folk." Since these filmed interviews were not completed when Griffiths started writing his script—Beatty's 16 mm shots were never used; the interviews that appear in the film were shot against dark backdrops by Vittorio Storaro—Griffiths wrote fictionalized testimonies by Old Wobblies, Old Bolsheviks, and the like. It was only after Griffiths had left the project that the historical figures assumed their final form as "witnesses," offering their recollections about Reed, Bryant, and the climate and events of the time. The intention, presumably, was to establish a certain grounding in historical accuracy, a legitimizing link between past and present. But the effect of these witnesses in the actual film is far more problematic. Their names are listed at the beginning of the film (Henry Miller, Rebecca West, Oleg Kerensky, etc.), but the speaking figures themselves are never identified. This omission undermines the kind of historical links that might have authorized their individual testimonies, and it leaves the witnesses oddly disengaged from the events they describe. Indeed, it is hard to know why some were included at all, since their testimony is often imprecise and contradictory; some barely remember Reed ("I've forgotten all about 'em. Were they socialist?"). Edward Buscombe defends these witnesses as an essentially modernist device for denying a fixed point of truth and offering us (instead) "a multi-layered discourse in which each view is presented only to be countered by another." Poole and Wyver take a harsher view, arguing that these figures offer oral history at its most hopelessly relativistic: "The overall impression . . . is of a discourse bordering on senility and madness, a Babel of competing memories most of which have long since become unhinged from the events they are meant to be living traces of."[16] That audiences often responded to them as comic, sometimes wacky, figures within the film suggests how uneasy their "legitimizing" presence is.

Final assessment of *Reds*, then, must negotiate the same ambivalence that Griffiths experienced when he saw the final product of a process he had abandoned in protest. Responding to Hollywood's treatment of its political subject, some reviewers accused the film of being a fatuous historical romance, a "period piece" love story that just happened to have a revolution as its backdrop. But such a judgment may, in the end, be too easy. Watching *Reds* after reading *Comrades,* one is impressed not only with the massive changes that ended up being made in Griffiths's text but also with how much made it into the completed film. Although much of Griffiths's historical detail was eliminated from the final screenplay, the film succeeds in recreating currents largely absent from America's official historical memory: its radical heritage, its bohemianism, and the political repression and puritanism that opposed both. Oddly, it is on points of history and cultural climate that the witnesses make their most decisive contribution to the film's attempt to recover the past: they speak in vivid and affectionate detail about the worlds of Greenwich Village and Provincetown, and they offer a level of information and historical contextualization often hard to achieve in a strictly realistic form (one of the witnesses points out that the United States participated in military actions against the young Bolshevik state, a historical origin of the Cold War unknown to most Americans).

Similarly, despite the cutting of scenes, speeches, and dialogues, an impressive amount of Griffiths's political debate remains. Scenes that very well could have been cut—the internal battles in the American Communist Party, for instance, or the Reed-Goldman debate—remain, and these assert an authority independent of the Hollywood romance on which the film is centered. Of these none is more powerful than the scene between Reed and Grigori Zinoviev, head of COMINTERM, on a train in Soviet Asia. Reed confronts Zinoviev with having changed his speech while translating it into Russian, and the two have an angry exchange that widens to address truth and propaganda, art and revolution, the nature of individuality and its contradictions. Confronting an authoritarianism that will find its flower in Stalinism, Reed insists to Zinoviev: "When you purge dissent, you kill the Revolution! Revolution *is* dissent." As he shouts, a shell fired as part of a counterrevolutionary ambush blows open the wall behind him, counterpointing his democratic humanism with the realities of a Revolution under threat. *Reds* may finally be a Hollywood film, but Griffiths's dialectical touch, never surer, is reproduced here with absolute clarity. As he himself has noted, for a Hollywood film even to *show* Lenin is revolutionary in its own right.

It is possible, then, to view *Reds* as a considerable achievement in terms of challenging the genre conventions of Hollywood and the ideological outlines that support these. Even scenes marked by compromise resist, in the end, easy dismissal. The central revolutionary sequence is one such segment. Griffiths had insisted on "a massive filmic event at the heart of the piece" to convey a sense of the Revolution's "power and resonance in our lives."[17] The sequence that made its way into *Reds* was filmed with all the stylistic devices of cinematic extravaganza. The scene opens with Reed addressing a workers' meeting, as Louise watches in admiration; cheered by the workers as a hero, he joins the proletariat on the march across Petrograd. The Internationale plays stirringly in the background, and the workers sing against a backlighting drawn straight from a musical; the effect is not unlike that of the West End / Broadway hit *Les Misérables*, which would also portray revolution in terms of the passions of love and heroism. But the sequence somehow manages to be more than stirring, and the intercut scenes of Bryant and Reed writing their stories, walking through the Winter Palace after it was stormed, and making love establish important cross-meanings. It is possible to see the sequence as Hollywood's trivializing of the Revolution, but it can also be seen as stretching both the Reed/Bryant relationship and Hollywood itself to encompass an event that transcends them all. That such an event is recounted in part within the limits of Hollywood's cinematic vocabulary may suggest the boundaries of possibility within which such a radical gesture must operate; even Griffiths acknowledged that Beatty's changes in the second draft made the screenplay more "capitalizable."[18] The fact that so much made it through the processes or rewriting and production—and that a two hundred–minute film about the Russian Revolution was made at all (at a cost of thirty-four million dollars)—should be recognized, despite all reservation, as the accomplishment it was.

In the end *Reds* hovers between influences and historical moments in Griffiths's career. Griffiths took on this project about the Russian Revolution less than two years after *Absolute Beginners* was broadcast and less than a year after Gethin Price took the stage in the symbols of Manchester United's "Red Army." Although the militancy of the early 1970s had given way to the malaise of the Callaghan years, the vision of people taking their lives and the shape of their society into their own hands was still not completely extinguished. The Portuguese Revolution, which began in April 1974 with a military coup that ended almost fifty years of right-wing dictatorship, was still playing itself out. Griffiths, having followed the revolution's progress (which raised echoes of the "classic" revolutions in France and Russia) traveled to Lisbon in the summer of 1975, and he later called that moment one of the two happiest of his life. Griffiths's only experience of actual revolution—"in a crowd of over a million, breathing the revolution they'd made"—translated directly into his account of Russia's exuberant, world-shaking ten days.[19]

But a text *about* history also exists *in* history, and the world that *Reds* entered in late 1981 was dramatically different than that of 1975–76. What some historians have called "the second Cold War" was well under way, with its rhetoric of "evil empire" and its escalating military spending. The intensified anticommunism of the late 1970s and early 1980s presented additional obstacles to the *Reds* project, and one wonders if the changed ideological climate may have influenced some of the textual changes to Griffiths's original script (the decisions concerning Lenin's representation, for instance). The odd "fit" of a play titled *Reds* with the political and ideological landscape of Reagan America has led some to accuse the film of ahistoricism and nostalgia. In *Born to Be Wild: Hollywood and the Sixties Generation* Seth Cagin and Philip Dray call *Reds* "remote, its politics displaced," and they wonder how the film might have been received in 1970 when its politics were more current.[20] For Poole and Wyver the early 1980s were the wrong time to present a project about the Russian Revolution; they see Griffiths's participation as an odd return on the playwright's part to political and dramaturgical concerns that he had started to move beyond in *Comedians*.[21]

Like the film itself, such assertions are difficult to judge. A certain nostalgia does make itself felt in both the *Comrades* typescript and *Reds:* for the moment when events in Russia seemed to herald a world being reborn, for the triumph of human will in the swell of collective solidarity. There is a nostalgia of the Left, Robert Hewison notes, and the memories of community and class solidarity with which the Left confronts contemporary setbacks often serve the function of myth.[22] Griffiths's earlier work, we have seen, is not free of such myths. As the political possibilities of the 1980s diverge from those of earlier historical moments, however, the question of nostalgia—its functions and liabilities—will become more urgently at issue, both in terms of Griffiths's work and in terms of the wider politics of the Left.

Clearly, *Reds* would have entered a different ideological climate ten years earlier. But it is also possible to contest the accusation of ahistoricism and nostalgia or at least to complicate such a judgment. The emphasis of both *Comrades* and *Reds* is less on the Revolution itself (which occupies only a fourth of the film) than on its subsequent development; more centrally still, much of the film is about the United States and its reactionary campaign against the Soviet state and America's own "Reds"—socialists, labor activists, and communists. A number of Griffiths's scenes detailing such repression—the 1918 Chicago mass trial of IWW members, vigilante attacks on Socialist Party headquarters, and others—were cut from the film version, but enough remains to establish, in powerful shorthand, the brutality of America's first Red Scare. From this perspective *Reds* has profound resonances for the early 1980s, and the screenplay that Griffiths contributed to the project can be seen as a precursor to *Country, Oi for England,* and other later works that address the New Right's political and cultural ascendancy.[23]

Finally, to the extent that *Reds* is "about" the Russian Revolution itself, represents this historical watershed at a number of removes. The actual events of the Revolution are presented through the perspectives of Reed and Bryant—"inspired sightseers," Griffiths calls them[24]—and attention is continually directed to the process by which the Revolution is "written" for a public unable to experience its events (in this sense the two are the film's principal "witnesses"). Despite the completed film's sentimentalizing, its multiple acts of historical observation—watching the Reeds watching the Revolution, watching their elderly contemporaries watching their memories—contributes an odd sadness to the film. Even as the Revolution is taking place, its promise (and its idealism) are already slipping away. With over half the film yet to follow, this sense of loss deepens. Reed returns in the film's second half to a Russia that has already changed, and the Revolution's betrayal by the Stalinism that will follow is already evident. "Jack, I think we have to face it," Emma tells him, "the dream that we had is ending in Russia." Rather than dismissing this sense of loss as "nostalgic," it might be more useful to consider the *Reds* project as, in part, Griffiths's beginning the work that has occupied him to the present: coming to terms with the twilight of the utopian possibilities that burst open in 1917 (indeed, earlier, in the American and French Revolutions), mourning what's lost, and trying to understand what can be reconstructed out of the "real dreams" that remain.

Postscript: Showing up the Reds
Leftist counternarrative and Hollywood romance—in the end we are left with the contradiction and paradoxes that characterize this internally conflicted film as cultural intervention. Perhaps no moment more strikingly illustrates the range of receptions that *Reds* could be accorded than one that occurred around the time of its American release. In what he called "Saturday afternoon at the movies" Ronald Reagan hosted a private showing of the film to about thirty guests at the White House in early December 1981. Among those in attendance were Cary Grant, Douglas Fairbanks Jr., Beatty ("casual in a herringbone jacket"), and Keaton ("in a brown derby and tapered leather pants"). Afterward Reagan thanked Beatty and Keaton for an enjoyable afternoon's entertainment but expressed one disappointment: "I was hoping for a happy ending."

When one guest raised the apparent inconsistency of a film about the Russian Revolution being shown at the White House, Reagan responded, somewhat cryptically: "I look at it as showing up the Reds."[25]

Film for the Stage: *Real Dreams*

Griffiths was by no means done with the United States. In 1981 an American writer named Jeremy Pikser wrote a story entitled "Revolution in Cleveland." This story, which was to form part of a novel entitled *Five Nights in Unamerica*, is set in a Students for a Democratic Society (SDS) collective in Cleveland in the summer of 1969. Told from the point of view of Geoff Sandler, one of the collective's members, "Revolution in Cleveland" centers on the efforts of the largely former student revolutionaries to form roots in the working-class community. In an unexpected response to their overtures the members of the collective are commanded by a radical Puerto Rican group (through Ramon, an intermediary) to burn down the local A&P grocery store. Afraid of losing all credibility with those they want most to reach, the group's leader, Jack, agrees to the ill-planned venture. The expedition ends in failure, as several of the youthful revolutionaries are spotted trying to siphon gasoline from a parked car. When the would-be arsonists return and discover an unexplained fire burning in a car across the street and the fire department there in force, their Hispanic "comrades" accuse them over the phone of betraying the mission. Ordered to hand over one of their women members for interrogation or be killed, the group spends the night armed, guarding the house against attack. Although they are taunted by bird and animal calls from unseen figures outside, nothing happens, and the incident is never mentioned or explained by the Puerto Ricans. The group fails to recruit a single working-class youth, and Sandler eventually leaves the collective and drops out of the movement.

Pikser, who had known Griffiths since he stayed with him and his family as a teenager on a trip to Europe in the 1960s, sent the playwright a copy of his story. Griffiths, enthusiastic, asked Pikser if he would allow him to write a play based on it. Pikser agreed, and the two spent several weeks together talking about the story and about the period in question. In the spring of 1984 Griffiths wrote *Real Dreams*, his final retrospective on 1960s radicalism and a play that signals many of the political and aesthetic preoccupations of the playwright's most recent work. Griffiths dedicated the play to "those many Americans who continue to struggle for justice and equality against all the odds in a land, long mad, whose Dream has by now become, almost literally, the rest of the world's nightmare; and if to one in particular, to the friend, comrade and writer of promise who gave me his story."[26] Fittingly for this, the only one of Griffiths's stage plays to be set in the United States, *Real Dreams* received its premiere at the Williamstown Theater Festival (in Massachusetts) on 8 August 1984, in a production directed by Griffiths himself (and featuring Kevin Spacey in the role of Jack). The play was subsequently produced in London by the Royal Shakespeare Company at the Barbican Pit; directed by Ron Daniels, this production opened on 30 April 1986, nearly four years after *Oi for England*, Griffiths's previous stage play, and more than four years before *Piano*, his next one.

By revisiting the historical territory of *Dropping Out* and *The Party*, Griffiths was concerned both "to recover the Sixties from the trashing that the Seventies and Eighties have given them"[27] and to explore the revolutionary vision animating this period from the vantage point of the present. The result is a work that plays with its own distance on the events it portrays. Despite the decade's importance to his political development, a certain detachment has always formed part of Griffiths's dramatic interest in late 1960s activism: "In 1968 I was 33; I wasn't 18. I was somehow rooted in a struggle and a practice [in which], even if I didn't understand it finally, I had my bearings. And so '68 in France, and then what happened in Europe and Britain and America— it seemed necessary, it seemed right, but I didn't feel that it was all or nothing there."[28] A decade and a half later, when revolutionary idealism felt (to many) as dated as sideburns and Nehru jackets, the sense of historical remove was even deeper. Rather than ignore this distance, Griffiths writes it into the play's mise-en-scène. Throughout the action of *Real Dreams* a video monitor provides running footage of late-1960s political struggles, intercut with a chronicle of the Vietnam War. The intent, as with Griffiths's use of such projected or televisual material in *The Party*, is to suggest the broader historical register of the "revolutionary summer" of 1969 (Griffiths works additional historicizing references into the play's dialogue). But the effect of this video material is also, paradoxically, to emphasize the remoteness of a period increasingly consigned to history, to evoke memory in order to underscore it as such. Griffiths subjects the play's onstage action to a similar telescoping. Sandler speaks at moments throughout *Real Dreams* as a kind of narrator figure, casting the stage events in the completed realm of retrospect: "Summer of '69. Kids off the campuses. Fanning out across the country. Bringing the war home. Building the Revolution. We're in Cleveland." A touch of irony or cynicism makes itself felt here: the phrases and slogans feel quoted, remembered. This, like other scenes (particularly near the play's opening), is illuminated with "unreal light," as if the play's action were taking place in memory or dream (7). The difference from Griffiths's earlier dramaturgical practice is subtle but marked: the dialectical field is shifting from dramatic interaction to historical memory itself.

Real Dreams sticks closely to the details and characters of "Revolution in Cleveland" but extends and amplifies these in light of Griffiths's own concerns. Central to these is the playwright's fascination with moments of missed revolutionary opportunity, that sense of a dream deferred or derailed that gives all his plays and films an aura of loss. "America at the end of the sixties is a very dark period," Griffiths said in a 1986 interview, "but it's also full of a beauty—glimpsed but not achieved."[29] Like the story it's based on, *Real Dreams* shows the reasons why the revolution *didn't* happen in Cleveland. The story of the botched arson attempt and the panicked siege that follows it enabled Griffiths to approach his characters with an honest awareness of their limitations and well-meaning ineptness. For all their earnestness the student revolutionaries gathered together in their collective are caught up in personal issues and are irretrievably separated by class and education from the working classes they seek to radicalize. They refer to the People's War but eat hot dogs on china plates and sit on a Louis Seize sofa. One woman calls her aunt after the expeditionary band has left the house because she's nervous, and another agrees to participate in "the action" because "I've got to get into heavy shit some time. I'm 27, I've never even bin fuckin' busted" (26). They participate in criticism sessions (like the characters in *The Party*, they talk all the time), observe the rules of revolutionary communal living, and have such facility with the discourse of Marxist analysis that they can even play with it ("The correct line on dinner is definitely dogs, salads and stuff" [14]). But their inexperience and the limitations of their background show themselves at every turn: given the recalcitrant realities of working-class life and the strength of the power structures they seek to overthrow, their revolutionary efforts continually skirt the naive and the comic. Firebomb the A&P? Even as he announces that the group will go along with Ramon's order, Jack is aware of the action's absurdity: "Pure fuckin' farce" (26). As the ill-planned venture unfolds—they don't bring gasoline, a drunken Ramon screams curses at the driver who spotted them siphoning it from a parked car, they abandon the expedition in confusion—it's hard not to agree.

Their overall mission in Cleveland is to forge links with the working class, to establish the coalitions that will "bring home the War" to the streets of America, but they end up barricaded in their house, armed against the very people they had tried to enlist. Here, too, Jack perceives the ironies: "This is fuckin' *Wagon Train*. . . . We're protecting our god-dam womenfolk. From the savages. Only what we're sup*posed* to be doin' is *joinin'* the savages. It wasn't supposed to turn out like this" (52–53). Although the motives and actions of the largely invisible Puerto Ricans remain unexplained, the subtitle of Griffiths's opening scene suggests that the A&P mission, the fire across the street, and the night of terror are all a "set-up"—designed either to toy with the student revo-lutionaries or to illustrate a point. One of the characters defending the house speculates: "Maybe this is the people's first lesson for us: respect grows from the barrel of a gun" (48). Even with this lesson in hand, however, the West-of-the-flats Cleveland Collective fails to recruit a single working-class kid for the National Action planned in Chicago.

Despite their ineffectuality and frequent absurdity, Griffiths never allows his ironic presentation of these student revolutionaries to descend into parody; his irony and the dialectical recognitions it negoti-ates are precisely calibrated. As one of the play's London reviewers put it, "Griffiths's achievement is to have marshalled all the negative evi-dence against his characters . . . and still reactivated their cause as a 'real dream' of more than nostalgic power."[30] For all the ways in which the play's characters fall short of their beliefs, for all the times that convic-tion plays itself out as farce, these revolutionaries are nonetheless ani-mated by a commitment that transcends the mundane. "Revolutionaries must dream," Lenin wrote in *What Is to Be Done?*[31] Sandler, a borderline defeatist who spends much of the play dealing with the pain of being dropped by his girlfriend, Pauline, addresses the relationship between their actions and the larger struggle: "Maybe this, after all, is what rev-olution, war, history is like: unlikely people doing things they're afraid to do and maybe don't want to do in the first place. We wade in gaso-line, who knows which match will send it up?" (31). That night, while the two stand guard in the darkened house, Jack confides his doubts about the course of action they've followed: "We're supposed to know what we're doing." Sandler responds: "Who in hell *ever* knew what was goin' on and what the fuck to do about it? Lenin?" (53). Whatever they do,

> there *is* a revolution goin' on out there, and there's not a part of the world can't feel it. We didn't start it, we're not gonna finish it, and we're not

gonna have a lot to say about what happens in between. But we know what it's for and what it's against. And we know who's gonna win. All we can do is push. In whatever direction looks like the right one. Hard, and as long as we can.

They may make mistakes, but "no one's gonna tell me there's anything better to *be* in this pig world than what we're trying to become. After we're all dead, maybe someone will know if any of us were worth anything" (54).

Real Dreams, then, locates itself in the space between commitment and evidence, idea and experience. Sandler himself will soon abandon the struggle, leaving the collective, he tells us, for the escape of drugs and eighty-three straight hours of television watching. Optimism of the will, perhaps, is no longer sustainable in light of the intellect's pessimism. Sandler's story reflects the broader retreat from vision and activism that will characterize the intervening years. Even as he delivers this coda, however, he acknowledges that the claims of revolutionary vision remain: "But these are dreams that will not go away. These are real dreams" (55). At this point he is joined by the other cast members, dressed in white judo suits with red scarves. One of the actors waves a Sandinista flag, and the actors—standing both in and outside the characters they have played, "nuclear, unified," illuminated by a "dreamlike" white light—recite Ho Chi Minh's "Prison Poem" ("High in the trees, amongst / the brilliant leaves / all the birds sing at once. / Men and animals rise up reborn" [56]). The light fades down to the flag, and the monitor reflects images of the 1979 Sandinista victory.

Unabashedly utopian, the play's conclusion seeks to transcend the awkwardness and disappointment of everyday struggle through a poetry of harmonized movement (as he did in *Oi for England*, Griffiths finds in the martial arts a physical language of disciplined synchronicity). As always with utopias, such recourse is not without its problems. To the extent that the play seeks to resolve itself in this image of harmony, it risks the charge of escapism, abandoning its capacious but unsentimental ironies for an uncomplicated faith. To the extent that it finds its transcendent symbols in the Vietnamese and Sandinista Revolutions, it risks romanticizing third-world struggles and naively seeing them as antidotes to the failure of Western revolutionary activism. As the nostalgic Irishness of *Oi for England* and the primitive Eskimo scenes of *The Last Place on Earth* illustrate, Griffiths was not free from this temptation during the Thatcher/Reagan 1980s; for a while during this decade, he actually entertained the idea of moving to Africa. But to overstress these dangers is to miss the self-consciousness that frames Griffiths's staging of utopia here. By 1984 (and 1986, when the play was staged in Britain) the Vietnamese and Nicaraguan Revolutions were entangled in the world of action and consequence. The balletic unity of the play's closing sequence, on the other hand, and the vision of social harmony that it attempts to give form to, exist as dreams, imperatives, imagined possibilities, counterfactual spaces. Contrary to the popular sense of utopia as something insubstantial, Griffiths suggests, the dreams of social justice are real, a demand of the human spirit. From this point of view the end of *Real Dreams* represents a desire on Griffiths's part, in the deepening failure of the Western socialist project, to understand the indestructible imperatives that lie at its heart and to insist on its "real" claims.[32] This search for experiential foundations—of hope, refusal, and action—will become central to Griffiths's plays of the late 1980s and 1990s.

Real Dreams is an important play in Griffiths's career for formal reasons as well. As its title suggests, the play is a meditation not only on the nature of revolutionary experience but also on the nature of realism as an aesthetic for representing this experience. If the dream of revolutionary change—rooted, as it is, in the imagined and the unseen—is allowed to challenge the empirical as a field of truth and evidence, then the Real itself is disclosed as something multiple, destabilized, incomplete. It is possible to see this shift as a response to the profound, disillusioning changes that characterized the political landscape of the 1980s: as the evidence of contemporary history increasingly challenged Marxism's prediction of a historically inevitable socialist revolution, a turn from the empirically real to the spheres of memory and aspiration became increasingly attractive. But it is equally possible to see the formal innovations of *Real Dreams* as an extension of Griffiths's long-standing interests in the status of the Real as both a political and aesthetic category. As early as 1975, Griffiths was arguing that "our social imagination [has been] hammered by naturalism until we rejected the surreal or the expressionistic. . . . The real world has been defined as the world you can touch, to the exclusion of all other worlds, counter-worlds, meta-worlds."[33] As we have seen, Gethin Price's expressionistic clown performance was one of a number of formal innovations by which Griffiths's earlier drama explored the boundary regions of its realist self-positioning. Before *Real Dreams* these innovations consisted largely of theatrically reflexive moments, in which the illusion of the dramatically real was disrupted by the real of performance: Sam One's stand-up comic performance, Groucho's opening in *The Party*, the play with real time in *Comedians*. Such moments are still present in *Real Dreams:* in addition to the monitor that serves to frame the play's action as history, Sandler serves an intermittently narratorial function (in addition to providing a kind of historical retrospect on the play's events, he announces the subtitles of the play's first two scenes). But Griffiths's formal experimentation goes much further than this. Always interested in the stage's technical possibilities, the playwright makes even more dramatic use of the stage as technologized space: as noted earlier, he deploys lighting to locate certain scenes at different pitches of "unreality," and during several monologues he uses a radio microphone to denaturalize the actor's voice (specifying, in one instance, that it is to be "relayed, flexibly acoustic . . . remote" [30]).

The effect of such changes is cinematic, and we can see in *Real Dreams* the impact on Griffiths's stage practice of his experience with film (in the *Reds* screenplay and in the filming of *Country*). Griffiths would later refer to the play as "my first film for the stage."[34] Scenes follow one another like shots in a screenplay, displaying less a theatrical sequencing than a kind of "editing." This is particularly pronounced in the play's opening, in which the filmic effect is underscored by nonnaturalistic lighting; in the play's second act it is also evident in the way Griffiths cross-cuts among groups of characters guarding different parts of the house. Finally, the play's closing scene is illuminated in "bright unreal light"—like Ingmar Bergman's film 1955 *Dreams* (*Journey into Autumn*), Griffiths's direction notes (53). Framed by memory—individual, cultural—*Real Dreams* is intensely imagistic, and its use of the stage is characterized by a uniquely cinematic visuality ("Real Dreams," in this case, are also "Reel Dreams").

The play retains its grounding, of course, in real social and historical circumstances; as with all of Griffiths's work, its characters are conceived in the material specificity of their time and place. But the terms by which the Real is understood are changing, and, as a category in Griffiths's work, it is assuming an increasingly complex relationship to the empirical. Realism, the aesthetic of the visible, is being forced to make room for the "other worlds, counter-worlds, meta-worlds"—the realm of memory, dream, fantasy, technologized modes of spatiality, cross-media sleight-of-hand. *Real Dreams* reflects an intensification of Griffiths's investigation of the Real, but it also marks the point at which his work begins to enter a postrealist phase. By opening the realism that has underpinned his career to nonrealistic modes of stylistic apprehension, Griffiths has pointed his dramatic practice toward the narrative and dramaturgical landscapes of *The Gulf between Us, Hope in the Year Two,* and his other plays and films of the 1990s.

Border Crossings: *Fatherland*

Shortly after he had finished *The Last Place on Earth,* Griffiths began work on another text of international ambitions. In collaboration with filmmaker Ken Loach, Griffiths conceived the idea of writing a screenplay loosely inspired by Milan Kundera's novel *The Book of Laughter and Forgetting.* Kundera's novel was a natural work for Griffiths to be drawn to. Its analysis of the politics and metaphysics of laughter made it one of the few works of contemporary literature to explore the same terrain as *Comedians,* and its doubled investigation of the political and the erotic would appeal to Griffiths's interest. But what *The Book of Laughter and Forgetting* opened up most fully for Griffiths was Europe itself, its ideological mappings, and the particular political and cultural formations that characterized what would turn out to be the twilight of the Cold War. To the extent that the publication of Kundera's novel was a cultural event in its own right—published in French in 1979 and translated into English the following year, it was quickly picked up by Penguin as part of its "Writers from the Other Europe" series—*The Book of Laughter and Forgetting* also raised issues concerning the marketing of dissidence, a commercial interest that (particularly since the late 1970s) had formed part of the West's stance toward the East. Griffiths's interest in dissidence had deepened after meeting exiled playwright Thomas Braesch at the 1982 Toronto Film Festival (Braesch had been expelled from East Germany in the 1970s for dissident activities). In Toronto and in Zurich (where Griffiths visited him the following spring) Braesch talked to Griffiths about his experiences, some of which made their way into Griffiths's text.

Griffiths completed the screenplay for *Fatherland* in May 1984, and Loach shot the film in fall 1985. In keeping with the film's European subject, it was jointly produced for Film Four International by Kestrel II (a London company), Clasart Film (Munich), and MK2 Productions (Paris). The film was first shown in September 1986 at the Venice Film Festival (where it won the UNICEF A Award), ran at the London Film Festival that November, and over the next two years was shown at Toronto, Dublin, and fourteen other festivals around the world.[35] In

March 1987 it opened for a brief public run at the Institute of Contemporary Arts (ICA) in London, and it had limited screenings in the United States in early 1988 under the title *Singing the Blues in Red*. As part of the arrangement by which Film Four supports such productions, *Fatherland* was broadcast on Channel 4 on 20 April 1989, two weeks before Hungarian troops began removing barbed wire along the border with Austria.

The film's principal character is another of Griffiths's artists, or cultural workers. Klaus Drittemann, an East German *Liedermacher* (or protest singer), is allowed after years of dissident activity to leave East for West Berlin in what is a kind of expulsion (the character of Klaus Drittemann was played by Gerulf Pannach, an East German *Liedermacher* who was imprisoned and later expelled from East Germany because of the political content of his songs).[36] After observing the life of sponsorship and commodification offered him by record company representatives and others in West Berlin, Drittemann leaves with Emma De Baen, a Dutch woman journalist, in search of his father, a socialist hero who emigrated from East Germany in 1953 and who subsequently vanished in the West. *Fatherland*, then, falls into two relatively distinct sections, which take place over three geographical locales: East Berlin, West Berlin, and Britain, where Jacob Drittemann, now an old man, is found. Presiding over both screenplay and film is the Berlin Wall, graffiti-covered icon of post–World War II ideological division. The Wall serves a central symbolic function in *Fatherland*, reflecting the fascination with borders that has increasingly come to characterize Griffiths's work: borders of ideology, political system, nationality, and language (with both German and English spoken, *Fatherland* is the first of Griffiths's multilingual texts); interpersonal divides; and the often precarious psychological borders separating idealism and despair, resistance and capitulation, innocence and guilt. The Wall marks the border, too, between realism and something far more expressionistic, a landscape at the psyche's deepest reaches, where the political issues of Cold War Europe find phantasmagoric form. In keeping with Griffiths's other departures from realism in the mid-1980s, this landscape—covered with what Griffiths calls "the unfinished business of the psyche"— appears in a series of "Wall Dreams," surreal vignettes in which Drittemann dreams his own, and Europe's, conflicted socialist history.[37]

In *Fatherland* Griffiths is concerned with clarifying the nature of the social divide that separates East and West and to free this polarity from the moralistic categories with which the capitalist world has invested it.

Erected to keep the residents of East Berlin from leaving, the Wall
stands as an image of repression in the Stalinist East German state: its
intolerance of dissent and the network of controls through which it
attempts to monitor the actions and expression of its citizens. Drittemann is shown in prison, his back tellingly against a brick wall, and
even when he is released his life and that of his friends is a network of
strategies for eluding surveillance. But *Fatherland* challenges the rhetoric
of heroic individualism with which the "Free World" has traditionally
appropriated Eastern dissidence as ideological symbol. Although Drittemann opposes the Stalinism under which he lives, he remains a committed socialist. In an argument with his mother (a hard-line communist
who fought in Spain as a young woman) Drittemann defends the commitment to socialism at the heart of his dissent: "I want socialism. My
wanting it is a part of the socialism I want. I claim importance not for
myself but for what I do."[38] He and his friends may be legally and politically unfree, but they have realized a degree of socialism in their daily
lives that allows them, in Griffiths's view, expansiveness of mind, seriousness of purpose, and a freedom from exploitation in their relationships with one another. At Drittemann's farewell party, friends engage
in a discussion of the Polish question: "it's serious, wide-ranging, well-
informed [. . .] the thrust and tenor of argument are socialist rather than
'dissident,' anti-party not anti-DDR" (7). With the support of her second
husband, who recognizes the importance of such intimacy, Klaus and
his former wife, Marita, leave to spend the night together; as Griffiths
specifies, their lovemaking is "direct, honest, unsentimental," marked
by "custom and trust" (8). The East German state may have betrayed its
ideals, but the vision it stands for is very much alive in the "actually
existing socialism" of people's lives (4). The distinction is important;
when Drittemann's stepfather tells him good-bye, he waves his hand at
the country around him: "Don't forget us, eh?" (11).

    "Stalinism is not socialism," reads one of Griffiths's scene captions.
"Capitalism is not freedom" (44). Unlike the East, which is characterized
by a certain plainness and austerity, West Berlin is a "hyperactive terrain" of peep shows, neon signs, consumer goods, styles, speed, and
human variety: GI's, prostitutes, punks, street clowns, Turkish guest
workers (19). Griffiths underscores the contrast by specifying that the
scenes in East Berlin are to be filmed in black and white and that the film
should move into full color as Drittemann crosses into West Berlin.[39]
The intense visuality and frenetic individualism of the capitalist West

reflect a decadence in which people are reduced to commodities and their relationships are caught up in exploitation and inauthenticity. Drittemann's sister works in a plastic surgery clinic, giving the rich "New faces. New dreams. New possibilities. Costed by the millimeter" (27). When Klaus attends a party at the house of Rainer Schiff, another émigré musician, the scene—cocaine snorting, bored sexual pickups—is contrasted with Klaus' farewell party. The differences are underscored when Drittemann goes to bed with Lucy Bernstein, the woman assigned to him by the record company trying to sign him up: their sex is bruising, "trustless" (39).

By allowing *Fatherland* to cross the ideological border at its center, Griffiths is able to intensify his exploration of the politics of culture—in specific, the intersections of popular and media culture (*Fatherland*, in this respect, continues the work of *Comedians* and *Oi for England*). In an apartment that Taube Records (recently purchased by an American multinational) has procured for him in West Berlin, Klaus finds mock-ups of record covers, all featuring his image. One of these covers shows him arriving at a mythic border control, guitar on his back, under the title "Grossefreiheitstrasse" (Great Freedom Street); another, playing off one of his signature songs "In Praise of Nicaragua," displays him in a Sandinistan combat uniform. Drittemann encounters a capitalist machine intent on marketing anti-Stalinist dissidence and thereby containing it within its own cultural practice. In a disarming moment Schiff acknowledges the dynamics of commodification and its cost: "The only reason the West needs fewer instruments of repression is because it has learnt to calibrate seduceability. We are still unfree" (24). Central to this containment, as the record jackets make clear, is image commodification, and the West Berlin scenes of *Fatherland* are filled with photographs and other forms of media representation: newspaper photos (one of which re-presents the scene of Drittemann crossing into West Berlin), rock videos, snapshots, a wall-length photo of Drittemann that serves as backdrop to his press conference.

At this conference Drittemann is greeted by the West German Culture Senator, a former fascist, and welcomed to the "free" West. Drittemann refuses the terms of this welcome:

> I thank the Culture Senator for his words of greeting, but would remind
> him that citizens of the DDR do not require lessons on freedom and its
> uses from those who stand in the direct line of German Fascism. My quar-
> rel with the government of my country is my business and will be settled

between us. Under no circumstances will I allow it to be collapsed into a
reactionary capitalist critique of post-capitalist society. And I would
remind the Culture Senator that oppression comes in many guises: tolerance is one of them; the whole apparatus of secret surveillance and
Berufsverbot is another. 'Peace and freedom' courtesy of the CIA and the
Verfassungsschutz—both of whom are almost certainly represented at this
gathering here today—may satisfy the Culture Senator and his kind but
they should never be confused with real peace and real freedom, especially in 1986.

As Drittemann himself recognizes, however, even anticapitalist critique
can be appropriated by a system that transforms political gestures into
images. In the words of the Culture Senator himself, "The louder you
shout, the larger your subsidy, very often" (42–43).

In keeping with Griffiths's practice of writing with and against the
received narratives of social, economic, and political life, *Fatherland*
evokes a number of genres in tracing the political and ideological map
of contemporary Europe. Chief among these is the genre of espionage
fiction and film. Crossing the border at Checkpoint Charlie; working out
elaborate ruses to spot and elude surveillance; reading incidents, individuals, and objects to discern the covert agenda to which they are subordinated—Griffiths draws upon the classic devices of Cold War spy
narrative. Ironically, this aspect of *Fatherland* only intensifies when Drittemann leaves Berlin, the traditional seat of Cold War espionage, with
Emma De Baen in search of his father. Drawing upon information that
Emma has collected in her research and the items in an oilskin package
that once belonged to the elder Drittemann, the two track him down in
England, where he lives outside Cambridge under an assumed name.
The geographical shift allows Griffiths some additional observations on
Thatcher's Britain. Klaus and Emma encounter a group of drunken
British soldiers on the ship to England, one of whom recalls the Falklands and slurs antiforeigner insults at Klaus; when they disembark,
they encounter a line of black families confronting "the joyless and
unwelcome face of official Britain on its borders" (46). True to its place
in the Cold War international alliance, the Britain of *Fatherland* is now
also a place of American bases, cruise missiles, and Western intelligence
organizations, with Ronald Reagan's face on the television set.

As Klaus and Emma close in on Jacob Drittemann, the implications
of their search in terms of the broader agendas of Cold War pursuit and
surveillance loom with increasing ambiguity. Part of Griffiths's strategy
in deploying the devices of Cold War espionage narrative is to implicate

the West in the technologies of social control.⁴⁰ But Griffiths is also interested in espionage as a figure for governmental and corporate operations in the postwar world. Who wants Jacob Drittemann (alias James
Dryden) and why? Their phone calls in Cambridge are monitored by
British intelligence agents, and it turns out that Klaus's Berlin record
contacts are aware of his location and mission in England. As the truth
about Jacob Drittemann emerges—that this socialist hero was recruited
by the Fascists during the Spanish Civil War, worked for the Nazis in
Holland in World War II, and was recruited by the Americans for an
operation in postwar Berlin—it becomes clear that "his masters" (as he
calls them) have been behind the effort to track him down and ultimately (it turns out) have him killed.

The devices of espionage narrative, in short, allow Griffiths to
explore questions of readability and agency, innocence and guilt. Lucy
and Taube Records turn out to be players in a high-stakes Western intelligence operation; Emma turns out to be working for a Dutch organization that tracks down former Nazis. Every move Drittemann makes is
ambiguous, potentially scripted according to invisible agendas; his
search for his father, motivated by personal reasons, is what leads his
father's pursuers to their prey. Nothing, it seems, is innocent in terms of
the broader workings of power and interest. Klaus's journey forces him
to face this truth. The musician who earlier boasted that "the son of
Jacob Drittemann cannot sing on his knees" discovers that his father, a
decrepit old man, now photographs women antinuclear protestors and
paints them in grotesque close-up (14). The life of this socialist hero, it
turns out, is one of betrayal. When Klaus finally confronts him (anony-
mously), the elder Drittemann describes how his own life diverged from
that of his idealistic wife: "I was a child, too, nineteen, twenty, seeking
the ancient battleground between right and wrong, but I glimpsed what
she would never see: the hand of the puppet-master, controlling the
dance" (66). Referring to the cruel paintings in front of him, he defends
his position:

> I've seen these faces all my life: in Hitler's Germany, in Stalin's Spain, in
> Roosevelt's America, in Ulbricht's Democratic Republic; it's the face of
> innocence, it's the face of the drinkers of blood. There *is* only power. Those
> who have it know it. Those who don't must learn it. [. . .] It's the first law
> of humankind. The innocent think there is a choice. And stop at nothing to
> prove it. Do you choose to be here now? You serve your masters. Did I
> choose to return to my country after the war as an agent of American intel-
> ligence? We have both learned the second law of humankind: any life is

better than no life. Later still, you learn the third law: it's all one, life is nothing. (67)

Like the narrator of *The Book of Laughter and Forgetting*, Jacob Drittemann has looked in the faces of zealous innocence—dancing in the circle of visionary unity—and seen the seeds of totalitarianism. To borrow one of the central metaphors of Kundera's novel, he has refused the laughter of Angels and crossed the border into nihilism, the Devil's laughter: "It takes so little," Kundera writes, "so infinitely little, for a person to cross the border beyond which everything loses meaning: love, convictions, faith, history."[41]

The words *guilt* and *innocence* recur throughout *Fatherland* as markers of the ethical boundaries of human being-in-the-world. Like Waters in *Comedians*, Jacob Drittemann has stared at the exterminating ovens of history and realized his own implication in political and social violence; unlike Waters, he responds to this disillusionment by denying agency and ethical choice. As the term *Fatherland* suggests, the Holocaust and German fascism form an essential backdrop to the film's investigation of guilt and responsibility in postwar Europe, a guilt that Griffiths felt Europe had not yet faced up to.[42] But the title has another reference point, of course. When Emma admits to Klaus that she was aware of the details of Jacob's life, she defends her silence: "I knew he was your father. And that fathers are men's necessary fictions." Like William Waite in *All Good Men* (a similar "father play" structured in terms of pursuit and exposure), Klaus must come to terms with the spectacle of betrayal as it affects his father's authoring presence in his own political beliefs and commitments. "I had imagined," he admits, "we were comrades. Somehow" (70). The actual death of his father is of far less consequence than this death of his father as an emblem of uncontaminated values. It is the death of history, to the extent that history represents a source of external inspiration and authority, a field of precursors.

"He's old. Mad. Rotted away," Klaus tells Emma, when she declares her intent to bring his father to justice. "So's Europe," she responds. "We have to begin somewhere" (70). For Klaus the question of how and where to resume his cultural practice is a lonely one, since he must operate outside the ideological frameworks of East and West (in so doing, he functions as a figure of Griffiths himself, who in the mid-1980s was increasingly experiencing his own sense of exile as a writer).[43] But creative spaces remain within "the orchestrated mendacities of the East and the West."[44] Drittemann's name, after all, means

"Third Man," and, as he finds, there exist margins, spaces, within which he can continue his subversive cultural work. When Klaus returns to the Continent, he does so in order to perform not at a pop concert in Munich (the record company's preference) but at a gig for young people in Zurich. In the film's closing sequence he sings the song "Fatherland." It is, Griffiths specifies, "complex, hard, affirmative: a celebration of necessary innocence," and in its progression it suggests Drittemann's response to Emma's challenge:

> The first half of the song is a modern history of white Europe and its horrors, in the pure German Liedermacher style of early Konstantin Wecker. The song breaks in the middle [. . .] as the second half affirms the necessity of innocence in rock. Fireworks lay out the peace symbols across the sky. Long white candles light in ones and dozens and hundreds all round the stadium. Faces gleam at the future from the darkness. (76–77)

The moment has utopian resonances, but its affirmations are complicated by the journey that has preceded them. The German word for innocence—*Unschuld*—translates as "nonguilt," but even innocence has been shown to be implicated in Europe's nightmare (the opening of the Stasi's files on agents and informers after the fall of the East German regime would reveal that the categories of guilt and innocence are problematic indeed). At the end of a century that produced Auschwitz and the horrors of Stalinism, "necessary innocence" suggests something different, more strategic: the embracing of idealism and resistance as a necessary beginning point, the choice of innocence despite the evidence of experience. Innocence, for Griffiths, is the real "necessary fiction": it may never be free from guilt, but—embodied in the women of the British antinuclear movement, in youth and its forms of culture, and in Klaus's decision to embrace the socialist vision despite his father's failure—it represents Europe's, and the world's, best and only hope. It represents a step beyond the "terminal" laughter of Kundera's devil, and its affirmation is "complex, hard," an act of political will.

Postscript: Production

Although its subject matter and the circumstances of its production were very different from those of *Reds* and *The Last Place on Earth*, the *Fatherland* project was beset by some of the problems that faced these earlier productions. With a defensiveness that mirrored the Conservative establishment's reaction to the Scott project, figures on the Left sought to protect their own political myths; the film's French distributor, for instance, objected to the portrayal of Jacob Drittemann on the grounds that there was no evidence that any comrade had been turned by the Gestapo during the Spanish Civil War.[45] Additional pressures were applied for different reasons: Jack Lang, French minister of culture, required that Emma become a French character and be played by a French actress. But more significant for the final shape of *Fatherland* were differences that emerged between Griffiths's conception of the film script and Loach's. A practitioner of a certain kind of documentary filmmaking, Loach believed that form and textual truth emerged from his actors' unrehearsed spontaneity. As a result of this commitment to naturalistic verisimilitude, he approached individual scenes with a willingness to reshape and even abandon the details of Griffiths's text. John Tulloch characterizes the difference in this way: "Where . . . Ken Loach was interested in 'being,' Trevor Griffiths was concerned with fiction, construction, reflexivity, and genre."[46] Although the final film has its strengths, the collaboration—like the earlier one with Beatty—was at times a difficult one, and the film departs in a number of ways from Griffiths's textual specifications. Feeling that too many of his textual meanings were lost in the translation, Griffiths remains ambivalent about the final product.[47]

Out-takes: Unproduced Screenplays

In spite of the difficulties he experienced with both *Reds* and *Fatherland* Griffiths continued to be drawn to film as a medium in which to pursue his interventionist cultural work. Speaking of television and theater in the 1980s, he later observed: "Every time I took a look at these two terrains of struggle, I knew that I was not going to be able to place work there with any confidence or certainty that it was going to be produced. . . . I felt that I had to do work as unremittingly *me* as the previous decade or whatever, and the only space I would comfortably find for that would be the alternative and marginalized space of independent cinema or small-scale theater."[48] In the midst of a decade that he characterized as increasingly "wintry and bleak . . . where everybody's running for cover," Griffiths produced a number of "possible and important" projects in film.[49] That so many of these projects were never produced reflects the precariousness of the financing/production process, the continuing resistance to radical work within the film industry, and Griffiths's established unwillingness to compromise what he writes in response to outside pressures. The quality of this work is quite high, however, and these unproduced projects are an important part of this critical juncture in Griffiths's career.

The first of these was a screenplay adaptation of *A Midnight Clear,* William Wharton's 1982 World War II novel about a group of American soldiers who establish a brief rapport with a band of German soldiers in the Ardennes. Griffiths was contacted about the project by Andy Meyer of A&M Films, and he produced a screenplay (entitled *Midnight Clear*) in December 1983. Griffiths saw the project as a chance to write about individuals who "step out from under the sheltering skies of their states and their roles and their uniforms" and make a "private peace."[50] He wrote a second draft in September 1984, but he argued with Meyer over such matters as who would direct the film, and after Meyer left A&M Griffiths ran into even more difficulties with his replacement. When this new producer wrote Griffiths suggesting substantive changes, Griffiths broke off from the project.[51]

Even as this project was going on, Griffiths had begun discussions concerning another screenplay with Paula Weinstein of Warner Brothers. Weinstein approached Griffiths to do a screenplay about white antiapartheid activists in South Africa. Griffiths was initially dubious about a film concerning two white people "out to save South Africa," but he agreed to take on the project.[52] He made a research trip to South Africa in early 1985 (returning in time for the broadcast of the first episode of *The Last Place on Earth*), and he completed a first draft of *Acts of Love* that August. Disagreements with Weinstein over the text began immediately and were heated (Griffiths flew to Los Angeles several times). Because of his contractual obligations, Griffiths completed a second draft in April 1986, but his heart was no longer in the project, and, when Weinstein herself presumed to revise Griffiths's script, its death knell had sounded. Despite these problems, *Acts of Love* remains an interesting project. In its attempt to relate antiapartheid activism with sexuality as "acts of love," it represents a continuation of Griffiths's concern to bridge the political and the relational. Griffiths's understanding of this correlation is complicated by his awareness of racial difference and the lack of symmetries in apartheid South Africa. As one of the play's lovers tells the other: "It's the blacks write the history now. We walk the margins."[53] The concept of margins was a resonant one for Griffiths at this point in his career. Increasingly sensing his own marginalization within Thatcherite Britain, he found himself drawn to tropes of exile; this preoccupation, of course, is at the center of *Fatherland,* which Griffiths completed the year before he wrote *Acts of Love.* As England in the mid-

1980s continued to "harden and darken into dystopia,"[54] Griffiths spoke increasingly of the attraction of the Third World as a margin from which to understand and critique the First World. Certainly, the experience of visiting South Africa introduced Griffiths to a political culture that had largely vanished in Britain: "The opportunities to experience colleague-ship, comradeship . . . I think are diminishing in Europe. . . . I see more comradeship in South Africa than I see here."[55]

Griffiths's next unproduced project in the mid-1980s was for televi-sion, not film. The idea for a project on the 1984–85 Miners' Strike, the most extensive and acrimonious industrial dispute in Britain since 1926, originated with a BBC producer named Chris Curling. Through Curl-ing, Griffiths met some of the key figures involved in the organization of the strike in South Wales and many of the miners themselves. The proj-ect was originally conceived as four one-hour episodes, and as part of his research Griffiths made a number of trips to Wales in 1986–87 (between March and May 1987 he and Gill Cliff rented a cottage in South Wales). Griffiths completed the first episode of *Heartlands* that August but ended up withdrawing it because one of the people involved felt "used" in ways he found unacceptable. Griffiths then reconceived the project, renamed it *The Truth and Other Fictions*, and completed an entirely different first episode in May 1988. By this time the main people supporting the project at the BBC had moved on to other jobs, and those who replaced them were not prepared to take on a screenplay based on such a politically sensitive subject. "I was writing [this piece] for a door that was that far open," Griffiths later recalled, "and I could already see the light fading as the door was closing."[56]

Some of Griffiths's experience researching and writing this project would find its way into *Food for Ravens*, his 1997 film for television about Nye Bevan, the Labour leader who began his life in the mining country of South Wales. In the interim Griffiths's interest in industrial activism resulted in another, ambitious project that both paralleled the Miners' Strike screenplays and surpassed them in terms of experimentation. In September 1985 Griffiths had begun discussions with Stewart McKin-non, a socialist friend who was then running a small production com-pany named Trade Films. After securing interest from the commission-ing editor at Channel 4, McKinnon asked Griffiths to write a screenplay that would approach working-class activism in a broader context: specifically, he wanted the film to open during the 1920s, on the eve of the Great Depression, and move forward to the mid-1980s. Griffiths signed a contract on the project in April 1986 and completed a first draft of *March Time* in February 1987. In the meanwhile, in a repeat of one of the patterns that characterized these projects, the Channel 4 commissioning editor was fired. McKinnon shopped the *March Time* screenplay around but found no takers. In the early 1990s there were glimmers of interest from the BBC, and Griffiths proposed reworking the conclusion, but nothing has yet come of this.

Although it has not been produced, *March Time* is a pivotal work in Griffiths's artistic development. Griffiths's story follows a group of miners from Easley, a pit village near Durham, who, under the leadership of Jack Dunn, embark on a march to London as part of a nationwide protest. Recalling the famous Jarrow March of 1936, in which unemployed workers walked from the northeast of England to London to present their grievances to the government, *March Time* traces the journey of Dunn and his companions across England (their group is soon joined by Ellen Pearson, the widow of a miner who committed suicide). What makes *March Time* formally so significant is its doubled time frame. As the characters advance toward London, the play's historical setting advances through the decades; they leave Easley in March 1927 and arrive in London in the mid-1980s. The screenplay thus represents an extension of Griffiths's manipulations of time and a decisive break with the naturalist representation of history and temporal sequence. In Griffiths's proposal for reworking the screenplay's ending the march's final stages are presented in a "story/dream/vision," and this further subverts the notions of temporal linearity and objectivity.[57]

Griffiths has underscored the centrality of *March Time* to the transformation that his work underwent in the 1980s: "*March Time* is where the dream play is born for me. . . . I'm not talking about the style of the film particularly, but how the form of the thing is itself a response to the cul-de-sac in which the present political project of the Left finds itself."[58] As it relinquishes the control of historical linearity, Griffiths's text opens to "regenerative circularities"[59] and to the possibilities—utopian and actual—that lie on the edges of narrative and political certainties. Ellen describes the march to her mother, a socialist teacher: "This . . . action, this march . . . defines me anew, every mile we cover . . . gives me comrades. . . . Takes me to the edge of something . . . a new politics, a new practice, a new . . . person."[60] The sense of being on the edge of things looks ahead to *The Gulf between Us, Who Shall Be Happy . . . ?* and *Food for Ravens* (which this text particularly anticipates). *March Time* emerges from the concerns of the 1980s, but, formally and politically, it is the first of Griffiths's texts of the 1990s.[61]

Finally, the most ambitious of Griffiths's projects during this time is surely his screenplay on the life of Tom Paine, which occupied the playwright during much of 1988–89. Griffiths was first approached with the idea by director Sir Richard Attenborough, who phoned the writer in early 1987 while the latter was in South Wales working on the Miners' Strike project. Griffiths spent 1988 researching and writing the script, eventually completing a first draft of a screenplay titled *These Are the Times* in January 1989. After a number of meetings with Attenborough, Griffiths completed a second draft that June and a revised version of this draft in December. Attenborough has continued to try to line up financing, and though it has appeared at several points on the verge of being launched, the project is still ongoing. Griffiths completed a third draft in January 1995 and remains hopeful concerning a text that he considers a favorite of his.

These Are the Times is an epic script, equal in scale and ambition to *Comrades / Reds*. Indeed, Griffiths's Paine screenplay recalls the earlier film in a number of ways, most notably in its parallel narratives of revolution and revolutionary activism: part 1 deals with Paine's arrival in the American colonies and his participation in the American Revolution, while part 2 focuses on Paine's experience during the French Revolution (Griffiths researched both halves extensively, consulting such sources as street maps of Philadelphia; his research on part 2 took him to France, where, among other things, he researched guillotines). Following *Reds* and *Real Dreams*, *These Are the Times* can be seen as the continuation of Griffiths's interest in the radical tradition central to American national identity. It also represents a deconstruction, on Griffiths's part, of the largely Anglo-Saxon idea of America that would serve such repressive functions in the nation's subsequent history. Griffiths's portrait of colonial America is a richly multicultural one, a polyphony of different languages and people, including blacks and Iroquois Indians (Paine makes a point of insisting that Indians, too, are Americans). And, consistent with his practice throughout his career, Griffiths challenges the prevailing myths of the American Revolution and the "Founding Fathers" by portraying them in terms of conflicting visions and class interests. As *These Are the Times* suggests, the Revolution began writing itself as myth from the very start (Griffiths's Washington is particularly given to self-iconicizing).

Against the backdrop of both revolutions Paine stands as a truth seeker, even when this activity conflicts with official versions of reality. Griffiths acknowledges that his portrait of Paine draws very much on his sense of himself as a writer in the late 1980s: "I think a lot of how I was feeling in the '80s . . . goes into that piece."[62] The connections are particularly evident in the second half as Paine, whose life has been spent negotiating the borders of cultures and worlds (England, America, France), now finds himself out of place in all three countries, insisting on ideals and imperatives in worlds in which they no longer seem to belong. Romantically unattached for most of the years covered by Griffiths's text, he is an increasingly lonely figure as *These Are the Times* progresses, overtaken by age and increasingly an anachronism. Perhaps the most poignant moment comes when Paine, released from his French prison, returns to the United States. He meets his friend Jefferson in the White House banquet room only to discover that, on the wall of portraits commemorating the heroes of the Revolution, his portrait is missing—"erased from the record," as Griffiths's direction states.[63]

In the conclusion to his March 1983 speech to the National Association of Evangelicals (the famous occasion on which he branded the Soviet Union an "evil empire") Ronald Reagan quoted Paine: "We have it within our power to begin the world over again."[64] *These Are the Times* is Griffiths's effort to reclaim this vision of rebirth and transformation from the social and political conservatism that has historically appropriated it—to defamiliarize the language of American democracy and reveal the radically liberationist discourse at its heart. In his last official action in France Paine addresses the National Assembly as it debates the proposed French Constitution. Paine dismisses the document as "contemptible" and recalls the vision of Jefferson's Declaration of Independence: "One phrase above all others lit a beacon that burns now in men's hearts everywhere: All men are created equal. All men. Not all gentlemen, not all men of wealth and property and education, not all men of power, privilege, connexion. All."[65] At the dawn of a modernity that the United States will eventually preside over (Griffiths's closing camera shot tilts from the site of Paine's New Rochelle grave to reveal a modern highway) the vision that these words embody represents the country's founding dream of human justice and equality.

8

Politics over the Gulf

1989: Redescriptions

In a January 1992 interview with Douglas Kennedy of the *Sunday Telegraph* Griffiths lamented the current state of British political theater: "The social function of theater is dead—someone should call the priest to say last rites over British theater."[1] During the late 1980s and early 1990s he was not alone in his anger and concern. In a May 1988 symposium on the state of the theater in Thatcher's Britain, John McGrath observed, "The number of new plays being done now is a third of what it was ten years ago. There's a real chance that within the next five years they will disappear completely."[2] This symposium was followed (in December 1988) by a conference of British theater professionals and academics entitled "Theatre in Crisis."[3]

The 1980s were clearly a decade of attrition for the British theater, particularly on the Left, and the 1990s have offered little change in the underlying policies and trends that brought about this attrition. Yet, despite McGrath's dark prediction, the early years of the 1990s saw a remarkable, if limited, resurgence in the field of British political theater. This resurgence, ironically enough, was precipitated by the historic changes of 1989, the year that saw the dismantling of the Berlin Wall and the symbolic end of the Cold War. In his poem "1989" Howard Barker wrote: "Whilst dates are only hooks to swing catastrophes upon / this was a year to carve along the spines of sentimentalists / and determinists both."[4] The theatrical impact of this year was most clearly and immediately evident in the flurry of plays written by political playwrights who first emerged on the public stage in the 1970s: David Edgar (*The Shape of the Table* [1990] and *Pentecost* [1994]), Caryl Churchill (*Mad Forest* [1990]), and Howard Brenton (*Moscow Gold* [1990, with Tariq Ali] and *Berlin Bertie* [1992]). In the hands of other dramatists additional plays on Eastern Europe have appeared, reflecting a fascination with events on the Continent unmatched since the 1950s and 1960s. To quote Barker again, "The roar of falling monuments is our culture's music."[5]

At the same time, the renaissance of political theater that followed the fall of the Berlin Wall has involved a return neither to former models of political theater nor to the ideological certainties upon which these models often relied. If the end of the Cold War was initially greeted with guarded euphoria, it has also confronted political dramatists—as it has the British Left as a whole, in considerable disarray after over a decade of Thatcherite government—with the profound, often unsettling challenges of a world no longer "readable" in terms of traditional political paradigms, a world in which capitalists stand at the vanguard of liberation movements; in which globalization, finance capitalism, and technological advance have challenged traditional notions of class, labor, and nationhood; and in which Cold War polarities of East and West have given way under resurgent nationalism and socialism's ideological retreat. As Ali and Brenton said of their collaboration on *Moscow Gold:* "Uncertainty has replaced the tried and tested formulas of both Right and Left. The nettle we had to grasp, as socialist writers, was that there are no longer easy ideological solutions."[6] The crisis of the international Left has forced such dramatists to rethink the ideological and dramaturgical foundations of political theater. The best of their work is characterized by the search for new paradigms, new forms of audience address, new strategies for mapping the contemporary.

Griffiths has been at the forefront of those seeking to rethink dramatic practice in light of recent political and ideological changes. His work in the 1990s has been visible in a way that much of his work in the 1980s was not, and it embraces all of the media within which he has chosen to work: theater, television, and film. *Piano*, a Chekhovian play based on the Russian film *Unfinished Piece for Mechanical Piano*, was produced in August 1990; *The Gulf between Us, or, The Truth and Other Fictions*, Griffiths's impassioned response to the Gulf War, opened in January 1992, on the anniversary of the war's outbreak; and *Thatcher's Children*, a portrait of the generation that came to age during the 1980s, was produced in May 1993. *Hope in the Year Two*, Griffiths's television play on Danton's final hours, was broadcast in May 1994; a theatrical adaptation entitled *Who Shall Be Happy . . . ?* was produced in November 1995; and his "film for television" *Food for Ravens* was broadcast in November 1997. In spring 1996 Griffiths completed a screenplay on Maud Gonne and William Butler Yeats.

Griffiths, to be sure, has differed from Edgar, Churchill, and Brenton in his response to the events in eastern and central Europe. In 1990 he cowrote a screenplay entitled *Dead Drop* with Bob Rafelson (director of *Easy Rider* and *Five Easy Pieces*) that dealt with the continuing activities of Western intelligence agents after the fall of the Berlin Wall—a kind of New World Order spy story set in a fictional East European country named Tirania—but for the most part he has distinguished himself from his contemporaries in his relative lack of attention to the historical drama of the revolutions themselves.[7] As someone who has always been critical of state socialism in the communist bloc, Griffiths says of the events of 1989, "I didn't feel too much had happened. . . . It was clear that that system could not be sustained."[8] In his plays of the 1990s Griffiths has focused his dramatic attention less on change in the East than on hegemonic continuity in the West, less on the death throes of the Communist system than on the ideological and economic consolidations by which capitalism has eclipsed the socialist project, at home and abroad. To Griffiths Thatcherism and Reaganism (and their ideological reinforcement under Major and Bush) reflected the dominant term of a wider and deepening political imbalance, one that manifests itself in the fragmentation of collective action and the dispersal of radical social thought. The flight of progressive, socialist culture on the domestic and international fronts is, for Griffiths, all of a piece, and the political vertigo of the former Eastern bloc is mirrored by political disablement at home. Griffiths describes the crisis of the British Left in these terms:

> A serious job of disempowerment has gone on, not just culturally but politically and socially. . . . It has left us with our political culture in tatters. . . . All the old moorings and harbors have been blasted away. There are bits of bloody driftwood with people hanging on, wondering which way the currents are going.[9]

The rollback of socialism in Eastern Europe, the Gulf War, and the lives of British youth at century's end are intricately related: all are symptoms of a late-century capitalist order that has asserted its economic, technological, and military hegemony in multiple, interrelated areas.[10] The elections of Clinton and Blair have, for Griffiths, done little to reverse these trends.

In view of the profound changes in the political and ideological terrain since the 1970s, and faced with a certain eclipsing of the very notion of the political itself, it is not surprising that Griffiths's plays of the 1990s have entailed a different mode of political drama from that of plays like *Occupations* and *The Party*. Not surprisingly, these plays have proved controversial for theater critics, who have approached them with expectations derived from *Comedians* and other plays of the 1970s. But, as Griffiths himself points out, "I don't think you can construct a political play in the Nineties in the same way as in the Seventies. It's very difficult to make political art, to make art out of politics, at a time when people aren't making politics out of politics."[11] The representational principles governing his recent plays must be seen as a way of rethinking theater and politics in a late-twentieth-century world whose economic, political, and epistemological parameters have radically changed.

After Thatcher, Griffiths suggests, "we have to learn to describe the world again."[12] At a historical moment when the Left's traditional "moorings and harbors" have been called into question, these plays represent an attempt to devise new forms of political theater and, through these theatrical forms, to achieve new modes of what Fredric Jameson calls "cognitive mapping," the aesthetic working out of a radically altered social and cultural space and a reimagining of the possibilities for political action.[13] This shift in direction is apparent in *These Are the Times*, which explores the American and French Revolutions as radical remappings of human society, acts of political re-vision that draw upon the broader revolution of Enlightenment modernity and its modes of seeing. Paine is fascinated with globes—post-Copernican models of the world—and with his friend Rittenhouse's perfectly arranged planetarium; for his part Rittenhouse compares *Common Sense* to Newton's *Optics*.

Such mapping participates, for Griffiths, in a broader task of reinvention, the urgency of which has not diminished in the contemporary world despite its deepening crisis of realization. As he argued in a 1993 interview, "We've got to reinvent new structures for democratic struggle, for community safety and security, for a modicum of joy, for pleasuring and self-pleasuring, all of that—all of this has got to be reinvented from the ground."[14] Redescribing the world, reinventing the structures by which it can be humanized: these tasks are obviously related. They entail a search for origins, or beginnings, in aesthetic as well as political terms, and they add a new urgency to the writer's cultural role. There is anger, and a certain anguish, in Griffiths's plays of the early 1990s, but there are also intimations, in what he sees as the rampant nightmare of capitalist postmodernity, of certain seeds, or roots, from which the vision of a just world might reconstitute itself. In a scene from the *Dead Drop* screenplay that points ahead to the edgy, occasionally surreal world of the late plays and films, Zero, a sinister contact person with partially deformed hands, fishes for misshapen, diseased fish in a polluted lake. He describes the setting:

> They call it Death Valley. Waste from the nuclear plant, acid rain, lead deposits, sulphur from the brown coal plants coursing down the rivers. On the edge of the future, we know less than ever. [. . .] Back to Zero. The perfect nothing. The point from which all measurement begins [. . .] I fish innocently, hoping for just one creature that has grown up whole.[15]

In a world in which political culture lies "in tatters," wholeness is more than an individual need. The isolation of political subjects constitutes the deepest, most intractable manifestation of the "gulf between us" in Griffiths's recent work, and the search for ways of bridging this isolation is a guiding drive behind the playwright's cognitive and political remapping. Starting with Tom Paine's project for a single-span bridge— "big enough to cover the Schuykill, the Hudson, the Thames, even"— references to bridges recur throughout Griffiths's recent work.[16] The possibility for such bridging, however, often lies outside the more public narratives of history and political behavior, in the fissures of representation. Occupying a different register than the play of language and ideas for which Griffiths has earned his dramatic reputation, the search for possibility is often elusive, momentary, fragile. But, as Emma says in *Fatherland*, "We have to begin somewhere."

Perhaps more than those of any other dramatist of the British Left, Griffiths's plays and films of the 1990s demonstrate the aesthetic opportunities that await a political theater willing to rethink its assumptions and foundations. Extending the stylistic experimentation of *Real Dreams* and Griffiths's work with film, these works revisit the scene of realism in order to reposition it within a wider field of postrealist possibilities. *Piano*, which marked Griffiths's official return to the stage after a six-year absence (and his first production at the National Theatre since the 1970s), may have suggested reassuring continuities with the dramatist's earlier work. But even here, as we shall see, Griffiths's realism is under

stress, challenged by cinematic effects and by the play's textual reflexivity. In *The Gulf between Us* and *Thatcher's Children* realism forms part
of a wider field of stylistic possibilities, and in its experiential grounding and its claims to representational completeness it must contend
with rival modes of narrative and visuality. Although Griffiths is
ambivalent about the term *postmodernist*, his plays and films of the
1990s draw upon postmodern devices, setting realism and the postmodern in a relationship of mutual interrogation. In *Hope in the Year
Two / Who Shall Be Happy . . . ? Food for Ravens*, and the recently completed *Willie and Maud*, Griffiths returns to history, but the field of
vision has changed. Deeply textualized, history is now multiply
refracted, playing out its narrative both on the stage of public record
and in the haunted space of memory. Realism shimmers between the
mirrors of retrospect and anticipation, and in the play of images time
itself becomes destabilized: as the present looks to the past, it finds its
own future gazing back. Emerging from the artistic crisis that Griffiths
faced at the beginning of the decade, these most recent pieces are
among his most powerful, nuanced, and haunting works to date. With
Churchill's *Mad Forest* and Edgar's *Pentecost* they stand as defining
works of British political theater in that liminal, structureless decade
between the fall of the Wall and century's end.

When We Dead Awaken: *Piano*

Griffiths returned to Chekhov for his first play of the 1990s, though he
did so at a series of removes. *Piano*, which opened on 8 August 1990 at
the National's Cottesloe Theatre in a production directed by Howard
Davies, is based on the 1977 Soviet film *Unfinished Piece for Mechanical
Piano*, which was itself based on Chekhov's earliest preserved play,
Platonov. Chekhov wrote his untitled four-act drama at the age of eighteen, and, though he continued to tinker with it, the play proved too
unwieldy for production. It was discovered only after his death and
published in 1923 (it was subsequently titled *Platonov* after its central
character). In greatly edited form—the uncut text is more than twice as
long as any of the dramatist's other plays—Chekhov's portrait of a decadent aristocratic and nouveau-riche culture has received other productions and adaptations, most recently in Michael Frayn's 1984 play *Wild
Honey*. In the mid-1970s Alexander Abadashian and Nikita Mikhalkov
(one of the then younger generation of Soviet directors) drew upon
Platonov and several of Chekhov's short stories for a film that explored

both the neurosis of prerevolutionary cultured Russia and, indirectly, the stagnancy of the ruling circles in Brezhnev's Soviet Union.[17] Abadashian and Mikhalkov gave shape to the extravagant plot of Chekhov's text and muted its melodrama: instead of being murdered by a former mistress, for example, Platonov now survives a farcical attempt at suicide. In keeping with the dramaturgical principle that character-izes Chekhov's later, more mature writing, *Unfinished Piece for Mechanical Piano* eschews the sensational for an anticlimactic representation of social inertia.

In his preface to the text of *Piano* Griffiths calls his play a "theatrical mediation" of *Unfinished Piece*, and he thanks the Soviet filmmakers for allowing him "to plunder their own piece in order to find my own."[18] Like its principal "ur-works" [v], *Piano* takes place on the Russian estate of Anna, a general's widow, and it brings together a group of aristocrats and nouvelle bourgeoisie who represent the changing social structure of late nineteenth-century Russia. Among these are Anna's son, Sergei, an idealist who (with his recent wife, Sophia) champions local philan-thropy; Porfiry and Shcherbuk, neighboring landowners; Triletski, a doctor who refuses to interrupt his time at the party to visit a local woman who is ill; and Petrin, the son of a serf who has risen to become a local man of wealth. Mired in inertia, these people sit around and talk, engage in tired intrigues and infatuations, and seek to ward off the crises of anger and disappointment that occasionally threaten their rou-tines. The play's central prop—a player piano that is hauled to their estate and sits incongruously on the garden veranda—reflects their con-dition: mechanical, lifeless, robbed of the spontaneous, the creative, the individual. When it plays, it does so with an eerie lack of animation, a ghost machine performing among ghosts.

Into this world arrives Platonov, a former landowner who has been forced to find work as a village teacher. Married to the timid Sashenka, he was once Sophia's lover and has since carried on a somewhat bored affair with Anna. A figure of promise at one point in his life, he has now settled into the ranks of Chekhov's useless, and though his force of char-acter makes him a valued member of the others' company—"He's the only one of us who dares live to the hilt" (17)—his bitter self-contempt manifests itself in brittle cynicism and caustic irony. Platonov and Sophia, it turns out, were idealists when they were young and in love, but when she left both lives retreated into compromise and disillusion-ment. Platonov's participation in the life around him is an uneasy one, and in his acute awareness of self-betrayal he serves as a potential reproach to those he comes in contact with. "I'm looking in a mirror," he tells Triletski in the play's second act: "I'm just like the rest of you. A nothing" (53).

Piano, as one reviewer characterized it, "captures that eerie, humid moment which precedes the storm of disintegration and defeat."[19] As with his adaptation of *The Cherry Orchard*, however, Griffiths is concerned with locating counterprinciples to aristocratic decadence and lament. Griffiths has noted the relative absence of peasants from Chekhov's plays, and he attributes this to the threat of censorship under which they were written and produced.[20] To counteract this absence Griffiths expanded additional material and characters from Chekhov's short stories into the characters of Radish and Zakhar. *Piano* opens with the two peasants hauling a large, heavy object—the piano, it turns out—across a narrow plank bridge. The work is laborious, bruisingly slow. Against the picture of leisured indolence their presence (like that of other servants in the play) renders visible the labor that sustains the house and its extravagant forms of consumption (the piano, after all, is being hauled across the Russian countryside for the sake of whimsy). In Radish's story of a house painter who was sent to Siberia for insubordination, the opening scene also calls attention to the repressive class and state apparatus that undergirds the aristocratic rural life. "Sometimes [. . .] I think the Lord does not like the peasant," Zakhar tells him when the story is over (3). But Radish also represents *Piano's* firmest grounding in the material world and its most direct statement of the possibility of change. When asked if he believes in anything, he answers: "There are things I know. [. . .] Grass dies. Iron rusts. Lies eat the soul. Everything's possible" (4).[21]

The inclusion of peasants in the play's portrait of aristocratic ennui allows Griffiths to sharpen the class dimension within his Chekhovian source material. An awareness of the realities of violence and political repression give added edge, for instance, both to Sophia's well-meaning but impractical proposal to bottle-feed the village babies whose mothers work in the fields and to Petrin's Lopakhin-like reminder that Anna's wealth derives from him, the son of serfs. In order to amplify the issue of class antagonism Griffiths has Petrin read aloud the news of a workers' strike in Moscow; in order to link this antagonism with contemporary racialist and class-directed discourse, he also makes Shcherbuk into a protofascist who offers a Darwinian justification of aristocracy as the repository of civilization and defends "the race" against "this rising scum" (39) of the lower classes.

The peasants in *Piano,* therefore, extend the play's social realism through a fuller register of class positions and historicize the characters' social relations in terms of a specific moment of class instability and its historically specific conditions (the poverty and dislocation brought on by Emancipation, the repressive apparatus of the czarist state). But the peasants also reinforce a counterprinciple to the play's ruling realism. When Zakhar asks Radish to read his story of the Moscow house painter (for the hundredth time) and assures him, "It's a fine tale," Radish responds: "It's not a tale. It's my life" (2). His remark suggests the intensely personal register of the social violence he goes on to describe: this account is not fictional; it's real. At the same time, since both Radish and the tale he tells come from Chekhov's 1897 story "My Life," his disclaimer entails a reflexive bit of play on Griffiths's part. Versions of this reflexivity characterize Radish's presence throughout the opening scene. During his story, for instance, the focus of Radish's narration is as much on his telling as on the experience he recounts. A born performer—he tells a joke then "bows ironically" to Zakhar's applause (4)—his storytelling skills recall Griffiths's earlier comics and anticipate the mercurial O'Toole, narrator figure of *The Gulf between Us.* But the metafictional and metatheatrical principle that begins to emerge in the character of Radish is also consistent with *Piano's* broader stylistic reflexivity. Radish reads the story of "my life" out of a grubby notebook, and Griffiths directs attention to the quotation marks that frame his performance as textual citation. Countering the sociohistorical and psychological realism of its Chekhovian sources is the play's dramaturgical awareness of its own intertextual foundations. In the play's closing moments Petrin quotes, as if reading from one of his newspapers, a journalistic account of Chekhov's death; Griffiths set the play in 1904 in part to enable this metafictional gesture.

Given the nature of *Piano's* network of citations—it is a play, after all, based on a film, a play, and stories, and the film it mediates draws upon further works of drama and fiction—the textuality it foregrounds is a particularly complex one.[22] If *Piano* marks the terrain of Griffiths's later work of the 1990s with its touches of narrative and textual self-consciousness, it does so as well through its attention to the borderlines of medium and the self-consciousness with which it negotiates the theatrical, the cinematic, and the literary. Like *Real Dreams, Piano* makes use of techniques that reflect the playwright's deepening interest in the representational possibilities of film. Its opening scene is lit by "shadowy unreal light" (1), as if to suggest the vague unreality of a peasant world glimpsed only in the periphery of aristocratic vision. The cinematic becomes more pronounced in the play's second half, when Griffiths uses lighting to fragment and distort the unbroken visuality of the realist mise-en-scène. With the cross-cut logic of filmic editing, lighting shifts the scene through the use of darkness, fade up, and directed spot lights.

In *Piano*, then, Griffiths establishes a core of realism in order to destabilize it throughout excursions into the reflexive and cinematic. At the end of the second act, in an effect that (anticipating *The Gulf between Us*) is both theatrical and cinematic, the stage is illuminated by flashes of fireworks—"a series of brilliant flare-like explosions," Griffiths's directions read, that "convuls[es] their settled world order" as it does the stability of the realist stage (45). In a discussion from *Modern Tragedy* that Griffiths cites in his preface to *Piano* Raymond Williams calls Chekhov "the realist of breakdown, on a significantly total scale,"[23] and the effect of this sequence is of impasse, individual as well as social. Stumbling in the darkness, Platonov is stricken with remorse at the "nothing" he has become: "One thing I now know: only once betray, only once deny what you love and believe in, and the web of pretending and lying you spin will hold you fast for ever." He comes upon Sophia, who thanks him for bringing her "back from the dead": "We'll start a new life, fresh as spring water, bright as the sun. We'll work till we drop and eat only the bread we earn, we'll find our joy in work and each other. Our lives will be a festival of truth and justice and honesty" (51). The moment is richly allusive, not only to Chekhov but to Ibsen's late plays as well. But rebirth in Griffiths's *When We Dead Awaken*, fitful at best, turns out to be as much a phantasm as the characters themselves. Platonov refuses her offer—"To see you day on day on day, to hear your silly voice and despise you almost as much as myself, and know nothing's possible" (53)—and he attempts a mock-serious suicide. He survives, of course, and, as the characters gather onstage to watch the sun rise, life begins to return to normal. Anna, a specter among specters, delivers this play's Judgment over the Dead: "Nothing changes. Everything will be as it was" (55).

As the sun's radiance spreads upward, it illuminates the figures of Radish, Zakhar, and Shcherbuk's child Petya, holding hands on the plank bridge. Looking down on the figures below them, Radish repeats his credo: "Grass dies. Iron rusts. Lies eat at the soul. [. . .] Everything's possible" (55). Griffiths clearly intended Radish's closing words as a counterstatement to the stasis that precedes them. The brightening dawn, too, suggests the beginning of something new, even if it seems to offer Anna and her guests little hope for transcendence or transformation. But *Piano* is a different play than Griffiths's version of *The Cherry Orchard*. Griffiths may have set the play on the eve of the short-lived 1905 revolution, but there is no Trofimov to connect the world of stasis and breakdown with a viable revolutionary program. Sergei speaks of "the common folk" as "rain clouds hovering over the field of humanity, in which the seeds of our future are already sown and waiting" (7), and Radish seems to bear this out with his affirmation of possibility. But such affirmations are qualified by the play's own historical position in the aftermath of the Russian Revolution's decline and collapse. To the extent that *Piano*'s conclusion asserts the possibility of a better world, this assertion stands—like the gazing faces at the end of *Fatherland*—in utopian relation to the spectacle of social breakdown. There is eloquence in Radish's simple affirmation, but the problem—to draw upon the play's opening and closing image—is one of *bridging* the gulfs it opens up: between faith and nihilism, breakdown and transformation, the individual and history.

These opposites remain in dialectical tension with each other in Griffiths's *Cherry Orchard*. But *Piano* is a far darker play than the playwright's earlier Chekhovian intervention.[24] The thunder and flashes of light that rock the stage in the play's second act are less the signals of a new future than the reverberations of an apocalyptic unknown. In contrast to Trofimov's visionary rhetoric, the illumination they suggest is intermittent, incoherent. The sunlight that bathes the stage in the play's concluding moments may come as a relief, but it cannot dispel the vision of impasse that came before. There is a quality of insistence to the closing image of Radish and his companions, as if Griffiths were trying, by imposing this affirmation, to resist the implications of the political and spiritual condition his play opens up. But there is also a determination, on Griffiths's part, to confront this condition. One of the characters in Chekhov's *Platonov* characterizes the play's protagonist as "an admirable representative of our modern uncertainty."[25] Griffiths was obviously drawn to this awkward apprentice work for a reason. "Should *Piano* prove to be about anything at all," he writes, "I suspect it may prove, like its illustrious forebears, to be about just this felt sense of breakdown and deadlock; and thus perhaps, in a nicely perverse irony, about what it's like to be living in our own post-capitalist, post-socialist, post-realist, post-modern times" [vi].

Arabian Nights, Narrative Crossroads:
The Gulf between Us

If Griffiths's work of the 1990s dramatizes the struggle of an aesthetic
formed in the aftermath of 1968 to come to terms with a radically altered
political and theatrical landscape, then *The Gulf between Us, or, The Truth
and Other Fictions* displays the changes in Griffiths's political dramaturgy with particular force. Set outside a desert shrine during a war,
the play abandons the dialectical realism that Griffiths deployed earlier
in his dramatic career for a looser, more dreamlike and imagistic style,
in which incidents move with the fluidity of fable. The play's stylistic
pastiche—its peculiar mixture of realism and what Griffiths calls "third-
world magic realism"[26]—reflects its genesis and development. *The Gulf
between Us* originated as a project with Paul Slack and Dave Hill that
involved the building of a wall—"in real time, on stage, every night."[27]
When the Gulf War erupted in January 1991, Griffiths was in southern
California working on the *Dead Drop* screenplay. As he watched the
progress of the war, "drowning in rage and pity and an awful sense of
impotency" (v), he decided to shift the locale of this activity to the
Middle East, and he proceeded to research a play that he originally entitled *Building Baghdad*. Griffiths describes the play's evolution: "I imagined it in strongly realistic terms. . . . But I found myself reading more
and more Arabic literature and looking at that 10,000 year history."[28]
Griffiths read widely in classical Arab texts: the Koran, *The Epic of Gil-
gamesh*, and the *Tales of a Thousand and One Nights*. He was particularly
drawn to the *Thousand and One Nights* because of its popular, vernacular
origins: "It's the first literature in Arabic that challenges the rule of the
priests and the law-makers and the kings, basing itself in the lives and
the language of the people" (vi).

The resulting play—which centers on two men from the British
isles who are stranded in an unnamed country at the outbreak of war
and who rebuild the wall of a bombed shrine under the supervision of a
young Arab guard—draws upon these texts and others: stories of the
fall of Jerusalem in the First Crusade, the nativity story from the New
Testament. Under the influence of these narrative sources, and in keeping with Griffiths's attempt to establish "a formal discourse between
realist and post-realist modes,"[29] the action of *The Gulf between Us*
acquires the aura of one of Scheherazade's tales: "Wherein it came to
pass, on the twenty-first night was told the Tale of the Builder, the
Gilder, the Minder and the Gulf between them" (3). Griffiths deploys

stage devices, technical as well as conventionally theatrical, to heighten the play's nonnaturalistic effects: a "voice-coil" tape of Arabic words interwoven with their English derivations, taped narration, cockpit videos of missiles honing in on their targets, sudden shifts of lighting and sound effects. Throughout *The Gulf* hooded Arab workers, or "Ancients," move soundlessly over the stage as a kind of mute Chorus, while the stage itself—with its vivid sky and its surreal bombed-out desert landscape—feels both cinematic and theatricalized. Griffiths himself has referred to *The Gulf between Us* as "a kind of dreamplay" (viii); elsewhere he has referred to it as one of his "film[s] for the stage."[30]

Style in *The Gulf between Us* is more than dressing for the play's content; as in Griffiths's other recent work, it is an attempt to fashion a way of seeing, to activate and negotiate modes of perception in relation to a world that no longer lends itself to the critical realism and dialectic argumentation of the playwright's earlier work. Style also negotiates the multiple gulfs between the present and its historical and textual referents. Although the play's setting evokes the war in Iraq with visceral immediacy, Griffiths's choice to leave its locale unspecified positions the military conflict between West and East in a broader historical and literary landscape. Grounded in a recognizable present and in the topical allusions to a specific historical event while also evoking the realms of history and fable, the play acquires a complex referentiality: to the specific war still fresh in its audience's minds and passions (preview performances of *The Gulf between Us* opened on the one-year anniversary of the war's outbreak, and the West Yorkshire Playhouse was the site of demonstrations by veterans' groups)[31] and to a more generalized legacy of war and cultural collision. When the doctor Aziz discovers that the shrine contains the bodies of children who died in the bombing, her cries of grief evoke the specific horrors of the Baghdad suburb air-raid shelter bombing and an almost mythical legacy of such atrocities and laments. The real, the surreal, and the hyperreal interact against the backdrop of a war that was presented to the West with a mixture of real and make-believe and its own, often fabulous, modes of visuality.

As a corollary to this referential layering, the word *Gulf* in the play's title denotes both a complex historical, geopolitical event and a cultural and political condition of fragmentation and mutual estrangement. The two are related, of course, and the meeting and collision of cultures is a central feature of the play's political, military, and interpersonal fields. Set "at the crossroads of the East and the West" (vi), *The*

Gulf between Us is a strategically multicultural play, and this emphasis was underscored by Griffiths's decision to cast the play with Palestinian actors in the roles of the Arab characters (believing that it was important to have performers with a "lived experience" of being Arab, Griffiths flew to Israel and the West Bank to recruit these actors).[32] The Third World, we have seen, has occupied a growing place in Griffiths's political sensibility, and the inclusion of multiracial vantage points in his work since *Oi for England* represents a striking expansion of the political and cultural field from the more narrowly Caucasian/European political and cultural arena of the earlier plays. By setting *The Gulf* in the Middle East, Griffiths decenters the Western point of view on the Gulf War and the Middle East in general, making the British characters the play's foreigners and intensifying the play's focus on cultural difference. Parts of the play are spoken in Arabic, while the background tapes explore both the phonic differences and etymological relationships between Arabic and English. Ryder, an English brickie who is coerced into repairing the damaged wall, mutters racist comments about the Arabs, the Irishman O'Toole, and the Asian Chatterjee and thereby demonstrates the cultural insularity by which the West has disowned its relationship with the East and constituted the Arab (like members of other groups) as cultural Other. But, as the background sound loops indicate, the relationship between West and East is a complex one, grounded in common origin. Emerging from the bombed shrine with a charred body in her arms, Aziz shouts at the sky and its invisible bombers: "You destroy your past with these acts. Your future too" (49).

Dancing between cultures and presiding over *The Gulf between Us* is Rafael Finbar O'Toole, "the Wandering Gilder" who operates both as an anarchic character within the play's action and as a storyteller who stands outside the events he recounts. Indeed, he seems to exist inside and outside time itself. When the young guard Ismael (the "Minder" of the play's narrative trio) seems to remember having seen him before, O'Toole observes: "Spent a lot of time here. I was in this place before you were born, son" (12). Apparently killed in an explosion, he nonetheless rises to move on at the play's end. Griffiths describes O'Toole's presence in the play in terms of the Gukha (also called Goha or Joha) in Arab folklore:

> At the heart of the piece I put a character who is both in the present tense of the play, trapped in the war zone, yet at the same time is above the action—a kind of trans-historical narrator. . . . He's called The Gukha in

Arabic. He is doomed to live forever and keeps coming back. He's like the flea under the king's nightshirt. He's anarchic, anti-authoritarian, devious, cynical and compassionate. . . . And he's the storyteller—he shows you where to look for the next part of the story."[33]

O'Toole repeatedly steps outside the play's events to present them as narrative. He calls attention throughout to "the story," narrates events and lines of dialogue before they happen ("Exit the guards"; "Builder says"), and describes even himself in a discourse imbued with the legendary and the fabulous ("It is written"). His storyteller's detachment in relation to these events is heightened through the golden spot of light—the "Gilder's Lamp"—that isolates him in a kind of metanarrational space.

At the same time, O'Toole is a fallible narrator, given to narrative ellipses and memory breakdowns. Griffiths continues: "The only trouble is that in our play, in his 9,000th recurrence on earth, he's come up with a body that is quite fragile—his eyes are going and his brainpan's a bit burnt out. He can't remember the story that's unfolding and that he's supposed to negotiate!"[34] Even as he prepares to carry out his escape plan, he must contend with the forces of dissolution: "Our Wandering Gilder, his plans deep laid and all but ready to spring, struggles to recall the details of his tale from the wearying darkness that engulfs him" (15). At the decisive moment when Aziz appears surreptitiously to prove or disprove the government's assurances that the shrine was not inhabited by children, O'Toole undergoes one such breakdown, as if the story has suddenly escaped its narrative frame: "A faint glow strikes up at his face from the pool, turning it ghastly. The glow comes and goes, like his fragmenting narrative." O'Toole stumbles to regain narrative control:

> (*Blank*) Gilder Builder Minder Soldier Major
>   Caliph Wall War Play Lamp Crown
> Prisoner Doctor
>   (*Tries again.*)
> Doctor . . . (46)

By refusing her scripted role, Aziz violates precedence and expectation: "This is not written," O'Toole marvels, as he watches his cognitive mastery over events rupture: "Too late for new pages" (45).

Such moments of slippage and fragmentation reveal much about the dramatic and epistemological world of Griffiths's recent work, an arena that opens up in the failure of the great nineteenth- and twentieth-century narratives. Characterized by shifts and improvisations in the face of both the obsolete and the uncharted, it is an increasingly post-modern territory, operating out of and within the fissures of politics and representation. Informing—indeed, invading—this territory is the world of New World Orders, video-guided precision bombs, and the official narratives of the West with its "collateral damage" and the Arab government with its secrets and cover-ups. By the final scene of *Thatcher's Children* this cultural and technological landscape will be one of virtual reality machines, with their final conflation of the truth with other fictions. But in Griffiths's view this contemporary world is not without agency or the opportunity for political stance, even if the sense of revolutionary possibility and its guiding visions have diminished since his plays of the 1970s. The rupture in O'Toole's narrative is pre-cipitated, after all, by an act of resistance in the search for truth: "Because I cannot know the truth," Aziz says, "unless I see for myself" (45). As O'Toole tells Billy Rider (the Builder): "It's in the voice, man, this is a woman in the act of drawing a line, she won't be deflected this side of paradise" (46).

Later, O'Toole speaks of "the bits we never remember. The bits we edit . . . out" (48). In her resistance to both the West's language of "col-lateral damage" and her own government's cynical use of a nursery/shrine for military purposes, Aziz challenges the official narratives of political reality and succeeds in finding a space for action within the pockets and gaps that these narratives seek to render invisible. Resis-tance, it turns out, is not foreclosed; new pages remain to be written. In claiming the space of resistance, she is joined by O'Toole, the Gukha as gadfly, who participates in the subversion of the narrative he recounts. Both characters reflect a deepening emphasis in Griffiths's work on the individual as a site of political activity. They reflect, too, a return to the foreground of the anarchistic tendencies that have always characterized Griffiths's political instincts. Griffiths speaks of political action in the absence of the earlier revolutionary ideologies: "I suspect you have to start simply with the urge to undermine and to criticize. It's no longer attached to a political credo or anything like that—the nearest you could get might be anarchism (not anarchy)."[35] Such a politics is decidedly not individualistic: Griffiths is concerned with distinguishing his dra-maturgy of the political subject from the capitalist individualism that forms the cornerstone of Thatcherite (and post-Thatcherite) Britain. Anarchism, in this sense, represents a stand independent of overarching political frameworks, whether these derive from the Left or the Right, and it manifests itself in an intrinsic resistance—"that spark that stays inside the human process, human struggle, that will not surrender, that will not give in."[36] Griffiths's own stance as a writer, driven by the urge to undermine and critique, is an attempt to exploit, Gukha-like, this anarchistic space—to embrace not only its opportunities but also its contradictions. As O'Toole observes, looking at the bombed-out site and, beyond that, the world as a whole: "The new world order. We're the joke" (14).

The individual, of course, has always been the ethical and political center of Griffiths's plays and films, the site of conflicting imperatives (political, economic, psychological, sexual), the origin of revolutionary hope. As the possibilities for larger revolutionary transformation have receded in the subsequent years, the individual in contact with his or her life (and world) has deepened in dramatic importance for Griffiths. In the face of a "political culture in tatters" and a late-capitalist devaluing of the Real, this emphasis reflects the search, on Griffiths's part, for the experiential foundations of shared life and aspiration. Hence the importance, in *The Gulf between Us*, of its original conception as a work play. In his introduction to the play Griffiths is careful to emphasize this dimension: "This is not a play about presidents and secretary-generals and prime ministers, it's a play about people much closer to the earth— building workers, British building workers and the Arab workers of one kind or another" (vi). Countering the play's self-reflexive narrativity, its recourse to fable, and its increasingly technologized conception of theatrical space is its grounding in the experience of life and work.[37] The play is filled with the shorthand references to working-class culture now familiar in Griffiths's plays: drawing upon the lingua franca of popular culture, O'Toole and Ismael banter about English soccer, and the Irishman gives his young guard his Manchester United shirt. But it is work itself—the process of shared productivity, self-motivated, self-rewarding—that provides the image of the individual grounded in communal life.

The most emblematic instance of this common life—and the bridgings it makes possible—occurs in act 1 of *The Gulf between Us*, as Ryder and O'Toole work at laying the bricks, gradually establishing a "rhythm and work pattern" (23), while their guard, Ismael, lies on his back and talks to his girlfriend on the phone. Like the clock on the wall in *Comedians*, which registers the actual time of performance, the building of the wall occurs not only within the fictional time of the play's narrative but in real time—the theater's time, the world's time.[38] By making a wall the play's central image, Griffiths reappropriates a symbol from the late twentieth century's political iconography—the pivotal prop of the Cold War narratives of West and East—and redefines it within the productive activities of work and leisure. What once divided now joins. Recalling Marx's vision of nonalienated labor, the moment is self-generating; in dramatic terms it draws upon the theater's immediacy to assert a suspension of preexisting narrative orders. As O'Toole later recalls:

> The dance was real. It happened. Yet it was not written; rather the dance wrote itself. Rose up from the sand, already inside these unrecorded peasants, and brought the foreigners gently to their senses, stilled time itself, wrought place anew, shared out joy and ease in common purpose. (32)

The music dies, of course, and the war "resume[s its] customary clamor" (32). But the moment lingers, an oasis in the play's narrative and political desert. If it is idyllic, it is deliberately so, meeting the challenge of what Jameson calls the "Utopian problem" in Marxist thought—"the task of trying to imagine how a society without hierarchy, a society of free people . . . can possibly cohere"[39]—by reclaiming that which is most ordinary. Within the context of Griffiths's cognitive remapping the scene stands as a powerful, if fleeting, emblem of a political foundation that survives the collapse of systems and the onslaught of others, a collective creativity affirmed in common acts of living. In 1969 Herbert Marcuse wrote: "No economic and political changes will bring this historical continuum [of domination and servitude] to a stop unless they are carried through by men who are physiologically and psychologically able to experience things, and each other, outside the context of violence and exploitation."[40] Such glimpses of a shared life, bridging the gulfs of culture and nationality, constitute the play's sharpest denunciation of the war in Iraq and its violation of the human; as Aziz holds the charred remains, she says accusingly: "Not quite . . . one of you. Arab. Yes. But when the mouth takes the nipple, the womb shivers just the same" (49–50). Like the play's more overt acts of resistance, such glimpses happen in the breaks and margins of more public narrative orders. Ironically, it is in moments *outside* the "written" that the fabric of political culture begins to be repaired.

The present and future "currently on offer" may be resistant to intersubjective bridgings,[41] but such moments are no less central to Griffiths's dramatic and political redescription. Their importance will continue to make itself felt in Griffiths's work, even as the public space for action and resistance continues to narrow.

Identity Politics: *Thatcher's Children*

Thatcher's Children, Griffiths's next play, represented a departure from the playwright's compositional practice. In 1991 Griffiths had been commissioned to write a play for fourteen- to seventeen-year-olds as part of the BBC Schools General Certificate of Secondary Education (GCSE) English course. When he presented them with a play called *God's Armchair*, the BBC turned it down, objecting to the play's strong language and to scenes like that of a drug user shown injecting drugs. In early 1992, however, the project was resurrected in different form when the Bristol Old Vic received a grant under the Arts Council's *Be Bold* scheme to work with Griffiths on a new play. *Be Bold*, a Thatcherite enterprise initiative, was launched in 1992 to encourage new writing and innovative forms of theater, particularly on the part of regional building–based theater companies. Griffiths proposed developing a play that addressed the major issues facing Britain from the 1970s and to the early 1990s, and he expressed his interest in working with a culturally diverse group of artists. "Warmly" applauding the Bristol Old Vic's ambition "to bring such a distinguished writer back to the main stage of a regional theater with new work," the Arts Council awarded the company the maximum grant of twenty-five thousand pounds, which funded not only the commissioning of the play but also a series of workshops, during which the script was developed.[42]

These workshops were, for Griffiths, an essential part of the play's conception. For *God's Armchair* he had made the effort to meet with young people in different circumstances and ask them questions.[43] But workshops would allow him a more intense encounter with the lived experience of the youth who came of age during the Thatcher 1980s: "I could get people together who were like vessels of the '80s, carrying cargo with them, and pull it out of them that way."[44] Griffiths and the project's participants (including director Andrew Hay and the play's seven young actors) spent two weeks in a workshop in November 1992. During these sessions the actors (three men and four women) "workshopped their lives,"[45] and Griffiths received twenty-seven hours' worth of videotaped material. He went home to write his play and returned to his actors with "a play in which they see themselves, but only part of themselves."[46]

Thatcher's Children, which premiered on 19 May 1993, was described in one of its publicity fliers as "a hard comic stare at the thatchering of Britain." Panoramic in its historical scope, the play carries its characters from childhood in the early 1970s through young adulthood at the eve of the coming millennium. Like Robert Patrick's play *Kennedy's Children,* which enjoyed considerable popularity on the Fringe and West End in the mid-1970s, *Thatcher's Children* is an attempt to distill the ethos of an age. The production of Griffiths's play coincided with the twenty-five-year anniversary of the events of May 1968, but the generation it sought to examine was one that came of age in a dramatically different political and social climate. *Thatcher's Children* is a searing indictment of the 1980s (and 1990s), and it directs its anger at the failure of Thatcher's Britain to address the spiritual and material needs of its youth.[47] The young have always represented, for Griffiths, society's true absolute beginners, the embodiment of its energy and its aspirations. To thwart these aspirations is to betray not only an important segment of Britain's population but also the country's hope for a humanized future.[48]

As if to underscore this sense of possibility, Griffiths opens *Thatcher's Children* with a group of children preparing to present a school nativity pageant. The play's characters reflect the multiracial and multiethnic face of late twentieth-century Britain: white, black, Sikh, Jewish, Irish, northern, southern. This opening scene is both touching and comic: when the ten-year-old actors finally take the stage, one of the wise men, misunderstanding his lines, announces that he will follow the star "as far as Leeds, me" and the innkeeper is so flustered that he offers Mary and Joseph a room.[49] There are scrapes and hurts, but throughout this metatheatrical opening the emphasis is on solidarity and play: "All friends, all friends" (47).

The rest of the play traces these characters as they negotiate the field of possibilities permitted them in Thatcherite (and post-Thatcherite) Britain. Mona, the daughter of Jamaican immigrants, ends up working in a massage parlor, earning a living in the shadow of the Nationality Law that makes her right to be in the country increasingly tenuous. Her sister Hester embarks upon the fast-track of Thatcher's enterprise culture, becoming (in Mona's words) "a real little Tory, a real little black Brit" (91), but, despite her attempt at assimilation, she comes to realize that, under the antigay Clause 28, as a lesbian she is once again an outsider. Daisy, the daughter and granddaughter of Jewish peace activists, does investigative journalism, but, when her documentary on the homeless is blocked by higher-ups as too political, she ends up working for Sky News, covering events while endorsing hair products. Tom, of upper-class Irish descent, works in the British government in the Middle East and is driven mad after flying a fighter plane during the "turkey shoot" on the highway to Basra. Sandra becomes a Goth; after her abusive marriage to Wayne leads to the death of her child, she drops out of society entirely to join a motorcycle group. For his part Wayne, a Welshman, joins the police force, participates in the violence against demonstrators at the Orgreave coking plant during the Miners' Strike, and is fired for lying after his superiors arrange a cover-up.

By the end of the 1980s, Griffiths suggests, each of the characters has hit his or her own "brick wall."[50] Of all the paths into capitulation none is more complex than that traveled by Gurvinder, the play's Sikh character. In the opening scene Gurvinder cuts off his Sikh braids, refusing this sign of his heritage because he is ashamed at being called "Girlie." But Gurvinder is also the play's earliest dreamer, transfixed with the thought of Gotscam Chairs, or God's Armchair, a nearby mountain peak that he visits with his father (this peak reminds his father of a legendary mountain he himself used to visit as a child in India, and he passes the legends on to his son). While Gurvinder will never forget the image of this magical place, his experience over the course of the play will take him far from its innocence. Arrested after the Chapeltown riots, Gurvinder is put in jail and immediately attacked by members of the National Front. There he is taught by Barbados "brothers" to take advantage of a divided British society: "they gave me a map of the world and a path through it, ours and theirs, us and them" (104). When he emerges from prison he turns himself into a perfect reflection of the Thatcherite ethos, with its ideology of exploitation and self-interest: he works the investment and trading game on the surface and runs a drug racket behind the scenes. He makes a fortune but at the cost of a deeper wholeness and connectedness: "What am I? I'm a businessman. What do I do? I fuck the world" (103).

Wholeness and connectedness—these are the challenges that the play's opening scene, with its spontaneous expressions of individuality and the communal, pose to the rest of the play and the late-twentieth-century world it portrays. As elsewhere in Griffiths's work, political life finds its strength in a natural intersubjectivity that seeks to bridge the separation between fragmented subjects that Griffiths sees as the principal form of political disempowerment. Like the characters of *The Gulf between Us* and like Danton in Griffiths's subsequent play *Hope in the*

Year Two, the characters of *Thatcher's Children* are faced with the challenge of discovering the origins of ethical/political life in the creative intersection of self and others. Engaging with the question of representation at its most fundamental level, Hester confronts the issues of identity and intersubjectivity in terms of language:

> In Jamaica, no matter how many sentences you start with an "I" you always fetch up with a "We." Maybe it was the same here once, I don't know. But I try. I try to keep to I. I am. I do. I will. I want, I have. I own, I hope. (*Jamaican again.*) But you know, it's a poor tongue you teach we. And a poor tongue pauperizes its people. (64)

In the play's closing scenes there are movements toward reclaiming the self's grounding in its own experience and its connection with others—movements from the space of an alienated "I" toward the space of "we." Mona and Hester share the process of going through their late mother's belongings, finding a connection there with her life in all its difficulty and love. Daisy, too, reestablishes contact with her family roots by visiting her Jewish grandmother's coffin and honoring her memory. The space of "we" is also made apparent when the play's seven characters, friends since childhood, gather under Gurvinder's leadership at the base of Gotscam Chair to await the sunrise. Twenty years after the play's first scene they still enjoy one another's company. Griffiths stages their interweaving moments of dialogue in separate pools of half-light that blend the individual and the communal. Even Sandra, far removed in her own damaged life, makes a brief appearance to commemorate the bond.

But this idyllic space—another of the oases in Griffiths's recent work—is temporary, and the cathartic sunrise that Gurvinder has sought throughout the play is never shown (the friends mistakenly take tranquilizers and sleep through it). As the play hastens toward the millennium, it also "bleakens" (Griffiths's word),[51] and the image of shared affection fragments into images of isolation and loss. *Thatcher's Children* ends with Gurvinder strapped into a virtual reality machine, watching images of Gotscam Chair and the nativity play. As an emblem of the individual divorced from his or her life, he offers a scathing judgment on the world in which he has lost himself:

> I don't know if you know. Or if you care. But this place is turning. Into shit. I don't know if you know. Or if you care. But you fucked up. We. You're going to have to start again. We. Start again. (114)

Reaching into a bag, he pulls out his Sikh braids: "For a start. How do I
get this back on?" But even this question remains unanswered. As the
images around him disappear, he is left calling out "I don't hear you. I
don't hear you."

Thatcher's Children was an important project both in terms of the
issues it raised (the state of Britain in the aftermath of Thatcherism and
on the eve of the twentieth century) and in terms of Griffiths's career as
a whole. In its micropolitical analysis of late twentieth-century Britain
the play reflects the shift in political and cultural discourse from a traditional class-based politics to the politics of identity. Stuart Hall has
described the material and cultural climate of the contemporary West in
terms of the "multiplication of social worlds and social 'logics.'" "The
'self,'" he writes, "is conceptualized as more fragmented and incomplete, composed of multiple 'selves' or identities in relation to the different social worlds we inhabit, something with a history, 'produced,' in
process." Hall calls this post-Fordist era "New Times," and he sees the
challenge for the Left as finding a politics that recognizes this proliferation of differences.[52] In part because of his own background, of course,
class has never lost its privileged role as a sociopolitical category in Griffiths's thinking (the escalation of economic inequality that characterizes
Britain in the 1980s and 1990s certainly support its continued centrality).
But class in *Thatcher's Children* forms part of a broader field of vari-
ables—including gender, race, ethnicity, sexual orientation, region—by
which the political subject is positioned. In a play that contains (among
other characters) an economically mobile black lesbian, difference tra-
verses the social world in multiple directions, disclosing the contradictions and multiple locatedness at the heart of identity.

Thatcher's Children is significant in terms of Griffiths's career in
other ways as well. For a dramatist whose experience of collaboration
has often been fraught, the workshop format for generating material
represented an unprecedented foray into collective authorship. "The
whole of my process is transforming itself into another process," Griffiths observed during the rehearsals: "another set of practices where I
find the play more and more in the act of writing it rather than the act of
planning it."[53] One of the results of this authorial decentering is that the
play more openly embraces a range of voices and subject positions. In
no other play of Griffiths's, for instance, are the claims of female experience foregrounded with such complexity. As a corollary to this, Griffiths allows himself unprecedented space to challenge the hardness and

aggression that has marked the predominantly male-defined world of his earlier work. "Someat, someat makes men so angry," Sandra wonders, "I don't know what it is, is it me, is it the world?" (77). To the extent that Griffiths tends to write himself into his work this current of self-questioning reflects the playwright's increasing concern with what he calls "the politics of the feelings": "I've stopped using myself as a bald fist and started to listen to and hear a lot more that is tender, caring—alive."[54]

Finally, *Thatcher's Children* represents a culmination of Griffiths's exploitation of the stage's technological possibilities. From the projected historical images, taped music, and onstage video screens of *Occupations* and *The Party* through the spectacular visual and sounds effects of *The Gulf between Us*, Griffith has always tended to conceive the stage in terms of multiple channels of address—as a space in which the corporeal and the electronic, the live and the mediated, exist in a relationship of mutual commentary. *Thatcher's Children* carries this multimedia experimentation to new levels. Scenes of live action are intercut with visual and auditory montages of events from the years in question, and these montages cite an array of media information outlets: pop radio headlines, BBC radio news, breakfast TV, Sky TV. Music and other visual and sound effects interact with the dramatic action, establishing points of dialogue between the experience portrayed and its cultural and subcultural expression: neon lights, club dance music, the Talking Heads' song "We're on the Road to Nowhere." To reinforce the play's political critique, official rhetoric is set against the realities of individual lives. At one point, after a taped segment of Margaret Thatcher's voice is heard announcing, "Where there is despair, may we bring hope" (58), an image of Thatcher is projected on the stage. This image presides over the action that follows, only to burst into flames as the sounds of inner-city rioting come up. Later, as the play descends toward dystopia, John Majors's image and voice call for Britain to approach "the millennium with head and spirits high" (109). In keeping with Griffiths's other plays of the past fifteen years, this intercutting of scenes and media is cinematic in effect. At the same time, it gives the play a televisual feel, approximating in its rapid editing and shifts of attention something like Raymond Williams's concept of "flow."

But experimentation is not the only criterion for a work's effectiveness. Both despite and because of its innovations, as it turned out, *Thatcher's Children* was widely criticized by its reviewers. In part, of course, the play's critical reception represents the tendency of critics, since the 1970s, to judge Griffiths for what Jonathan Bignell terms his "failure to live up to the meanings of his own signature" (in other words, his unwillingness to keep on writing *Occupations* and *Comedians*).[55] The British theater press has never shown itself particularly generous when it comes to change and experimentation. But this tendency does not obscure the fact that there are dramatic and political problems with *Thatcher's Children* and that the result of Griffiths's experimentation is, in many ways, an unsatisfactory play. Some of these problems derive from the project's very ambitiousness; others from the new emphases that Griffiths here embraces. Many result from Griffiths's attempt to negotiate the gap between the play's narratives of individual lived experience and its overarching historical framework. The initial difficulty is a logistical one. Faced with the challenges of covering a thirty-year period, *Thatcher's Children* resorts to what is essentially a headline presentation of contemporary British history, with predictable moments of crisis following one another in rapid succession. History in this kind of politicized shorthand can work comfortably in less naturalistic theatrical frameworks, but it sits less easily in a play so deeply grounded in individual lives. Griffiths has insisted that he intended to write not "a searing agitprop critique of the Thatcher years, but a story that is internal to the characters."[56] Yet the need to make these lives register a changing age's issues and events tends to pressure the play's characters toward the representative and the schematic. The problem is one of conflicting strategies; despite Griffiths's disclaimer, an agitprop imperative often distorts the play's experiential realism.

There are problems, too, both theoretical and dramaturgical, in the play's reliance on individual experience and the "politics of feeling." In the absence of the hard-soft dialectic that characterized Griffiths's plays of the 1970s (Kabak countering Gramsci) feeling edges dangerously toward sentimentality. The humor of *Thatcher's Children*, of course, helps keep this tendency in check. But the focus on experience has other risks. In the second act Daisy recalls a message passed down to her from her grandmother and mother: "Your life is the only truth you have. And the only truth you need" (78). Earlier in the play a teacher has written on the blackboard: "FOR ME, THE HEART OF POLITICS IS NOT POLITICAL THEORY, IT IS PEOPLE AND HOW THEY WANT TO LIVE THEIR LIVES" (52). The subjectivism and retreat from theory in statements such as these have disquieting implications for shared political action, and Griffiths's faith in an intrinsic intersubjectivity goes only part of the way toward addressing these doubts. To the extent that the play advocates reclaiming selfhood, it suggests paths that are themselves problematic. For Mona, Hester, Gurvinder, Daisy, and Tom (who ends the play dreaming of "Ireland, my mum's country" [110]) wholeness is caught up in the rediscovery of racial and ethnic identity, a rootedness in one's people and their heritage. As in *Oi for England*, which also uses ethnicity to underwrite wholeness and emotional sensitivity, this particular solution hinges on a nostalgic, potentially regressive notion of identity, and it counters the more hybridized, internally divergent model of identity that the play otherwise advances.

Finally, there are problems with the play's strategy for analyzing and identifying responsibility for the condition it protests. *Thatcher's Children* targets specific Thatcherite initiatives in its political critique, and it offers a general condemnation of an enterprise culture that defines human relationship in terms of exploitation. But the play's "relentless misericordia" of contemporary history also includes a much wider chronicle of disaster both actual and imminent (72): homelessness, famine in Africa, urban decay, unemployment, recession, AIDS, the degenerating ozone layer. Thatcherite and post-Thatcherite policies may be implicated in these calamities, but it is analytically reductive to isolate Thatcher and her policies as the source of contemporary evils. "Thatcher" in Griffiths's play functions as a sign covering complex global and historical changes—changes of which Thatcherism as a historical political formation is more symptom than cause. Ironically, whereas Griffiths's portrayal of the younger generation engages more complex notions of identity positioning, his portrayals of power and social dislocation are monolithic and personalized.

Looking back over the 1980s and early 1990s, Griffiths was justly angry at the Thatcherite legacy for contemporary Britain and its youth, and Majors's unexpected victory in the April 1992 general election faced him with added despair at the seeming endlessness of Conservative ascendancy. But the play's political demonizing reflects (and, in a way, obscures) a broader fear of postmodernity and the changing cultural and social landscape of late-twentieth-century capitalism. Interestingly, when Griffiths discusses the plight of contemporary youth, he describes a condition that implicates Thatcherism only indirectly:

> There were kids growing up in the '80s who spent more time with computers than with their peer group . . . and that has to shape the mind and the imagination, and what's thinkable and what's not thinkable. I suspect that the more we displace primary experience, that's to say subjective

experience, an experience based on the subject relating to an object—an Other, the Otherness, the non-"Me"ness of the world—the more we displace that by apparent interactions which are in fact only extensions of the self, the subject, as for example, playing games on the screen, or entering virtual reality, then the more reality itself will feel virtual rather than actual. So actually sorting out what's real and what isn't is going to be increasingly difficult.[57]

This is Baudrillardian territory, in which the Real is displaced by the play of simulacra. What concerns Griffiths most about Gurvinder's retreat into the virtual reality machine at the close of *Thatcher's Children* is less the continuation of Conservative rule under Major's successor (*"Minor, perhaps"* [111]) than the prospect that the Real itself is being lost as a field of political agency and creative interaction. This concern gives an added edge to Griffiths's deployment of stage and other forms of technology. If technology has allowed Griffiths throughout his career to extend the stage's representational capabilities by multiplying its channels of address, in his plays of the early 1990s it is also used to explore an increasingly mediated (and mediatized) individual and social experience. The question of "the truth and other fictions" is urgently at issue: as the opening of *The Gulf between Us* (a military photographic sequence of a precision missile honing in on its target) suggests, the technologized stage space of Griffiths's recent plays seems to address both the politics of postmodern representation and the postmodern mediatizing of the political.

While *Thatcher's Children* may be an unsatisfactory play, then, its very problems make it interesting and revealing. In its conflicting strategies and unrealized aims it reflects the difficulties of imagining the political self in a social field now understood in micropolitical, identity-based terms, and it suggests the challenges involved in confronting a changing political, cultural, and epistemological landscape. What theatrical power it has may reside less in the political critique its title promises than in its evocation of an apocalyptic energy and apprehension. "Such a bloody waste. Everywhere ye look," says Mona (103). "Riots, famine, disaster" (72)—the imagery is eschatological, and, as the play pushes toward the millennium, it realizes what Griffiths sees as the dystopic implications of the contemporary political and social world. Like *Hope in the Year Two*, which was written shortly after it, *Thatcher's Children* was intended as "a raid on the past, an address to the present and a rejection of the future currently on offer" [vii]. For Griffiths apocalypse becomes a way of drawing out the "future on offer" and imagining the world it would provide. If, as Ruth Levitas suggests, the essence of Utopia is desire, then Dystopia is rooted in aversion and refusal.[58] In *Thatcher's Children* Griffiths evokes the language of endings and beginnings intrinsic to millenarian discourse so that the seeming drift of history can be confronted and, where possible, resisted. "This play sees people who have been atomized, broken up into fragments of their own potential," Griffiths has insisted: "and that's all I'm saying—does it have to be like this? When can we resume the human project and stop this silly nonsense?"[59]

9

Specters of History

If it—learning to live—remains to be done, it can happen only
between life and death. . . . The time of the "learning to live,"
a time without tutelary present, would amount to this . . . to
learn to live *with* ghosts, in the upkeep, the conversation, the
company, or the companionship, in the commerce without
commerce of ghosts. . . . And this being-with specters would
also be, not only but also, a *politics* of memory, of inheritance,
and of generations.
                                        —Jacques Derrida, *Specters of Marx*

Living with Ghosts

Griffiths was not done with the political and dramaturgical issues he
addressed in *The Gulf between Us* and *Thatcher's Children*; in fact, one of
his next projects was a hybridized offshoot of the two. Although the
production of *The Gulf between Us* that Griffiths hoped to have mounted
in the Middle East never came off, the playwright remained in touch
with the Palestinian actors who had worked with him on the project. As
a result of these contacts, Griffiths conceived a project that was in many
ways a third-world mirror to *Thatcher's Children*. Provisionally titled
Arafat's Children, the project involved "using the model of *Thatcher's
Children* to uncover an essential political history through the lived experience of those who've taken that journey."[1] The moment seemed right:
under the limited autonomy granted by the Israeli-Palestinian peace
accord, the Palestinian community in the West Bank, Gaza, and elsewhere appeared poised at a historic threshold. Griffiths conducted
workshops in East Jerusalem and Nazareth over several weeks in the
summer of 1995 and began writing a play that he hoped to bring back to
the new Theatre of the Arab on the West Bank. As Griffiths worked on
the play (now titled *Filastinuna*, which is Arabic for "Our Palestine"), he
decided to organize the text around a Palestinian wedding.[2] But the

project proved difficult for Griffiths—he found the writing agonizingly slow—and by early 1997 the project was on hold. Griffiths had embarked on other projects, and the changing political and military situation in Israel and the Palestinian homeland meant that the circumstances in which the project had been conceived (the fragile "peace" period) were radically altered.[3]

But it may also be that *Filastinuna* proved difficult to write because Griffiths's dramatic energies in the mid-1990s were increasingly directed elsewhere—into new, more intimate theatrical and filmic territory. With *Hope in the Year Two / Who Shall Be Happy . . . ?* (written in early 1993 while Griffiths was involved in the *Thatcher's Children* project) and continuing with *Food for Ravens* and *Willie and Maud* (written in 1996 and 1997, respectively), Griffiths returned to the mode of historical retrospect that had governed so much of his earlier work. But the landscape of this retrospect had changed: it was now deeper, more interiorized. Having directed his anger outward in his plays of the early 1990s, having confronted the collapse of institutional socialism in the spectacle of late-capitalist postmodernity, Griffiths turned to include himself in the field of vision. The result is a profound rethinking of history in the space of late-twentieth-century memory. History, in these plays and films, is no longer an objectivized field in which past, present, and future stand in reassuring continuity. Relocated in a much more multilayered space, history is now a site of traces, fragments, ghosts, a deeply textualized space in which the material and the objective are caught up in the play of reflexivity, refracted through the lenses of memory and dream.

There are autobiographical motivations, of course, for this dramaturgical shift. In 1995 Griffiths turned sixty, and, while this is by no means elderly, an awareness of age and personal mortality began increasingly to inform the playwright's response to the late twentieth century's more public endings. The body beginning to fail, growing strange and unfamiliar to itself, makes itself noticed throughout these works, and for the central figures in these plays (even Danton, executed in his 1930s) there is a melancholy sense of being cut off from the vigor—political, erotic—of earlier life. But the personal plays a broader role in the dramaturgical contours of Griffiths's most recent work. On a number of occasions Griffiths has spoken about finding himself, in his sixties, "on the edge of things—of life . . . of hope . . . of meaning."[4] Griffiths's recent protagonists—revolutionaries all, in their different ways—occupy this epistemological/cognitive border zone. Drawn not at the flush of personal, political, and creative achievement but at a point where political and other causes have yielded to failure and disillusionment, Griffiths's Danton, Bevan, Gonne, and Yeats are figures who must confront what lies beyond the horizons of conviction and certainty. As in other ways, Tom Paine is their precursor: shown struggling to extract meaning from nonmeaning at a number of points in the first half of *These Are the Times*, he comments to a friend after the American Revolutionary War: "Feels like the end of something. I need to think, know more. I feel I've reached the edge of what I understand just now."[5]

It is this juncture that allows Griffiths's plays of retrospect to resonate with the broader struggles of memory and anticipation that characterize the present historical moment, marked as it is by the eclipse of Marxism's emancipatory narrative. In *Specters of Marx* Derrida writes of Marxism as a "specter" that has long haunted Europe and a world that has sought to disown it. In the aftermath of communism's fall, this specter has continued to haunt the present with the challenge of its inheritance and its uncanny status between the real and the unrealized. To come to terms with such specters (and in the case of Marxism, Derrida argues, there are more than one) is part of a broader ethical imperative that includes the ghosts of past and future:

> It is necessary to speak *of the* ghost, indeed, *to the* ghost and *with* it, from the moment that no ethics, no politics, whether revolutionary or not, seems possible and thinkable and *just* that does not recognize in its principle the respect for those others who are no longer or for those others who are not yet *there*, presently living, whether they are already dead or not yet born.[6]

History, for Derrida, is a spectral field, and the field of specters is likewise intrinsically historical. A being-with-specters, Derrida writes, "would also be, not only but also, a *politics* of memory, of inheritance, and of generations."[7] The specter, for Derrida, is that which survives its own death (and precedes its own birth), and it unsettles a present that seeks to constitute itself through the specter's disappearance. Against the widespread repudiation of state socialism the West has attempted to commemorate such a disappearance. But, despite the rush with which neoliberalism and late-century capitalism hurry to celebrate the demise of Marxism, the specter of Marx continues to haunt the present ideological regime's claim to self-sufficiency: "Haunting belongs to the structure of every hegemony."[8]

Derrida's figure of the specter is a useful one to bring to Griffiths's

staging of history in these innovative recent works. It suggests the limi-
nality of a socialist past—never fully realized in itself, always on the
threshold of becoming—that has always haunted the political field of
Griffiths's work. To the extent that Griffiths's recent plays and films
explore the terms of this haunting and the questions of legacy and
responsibility, the figure of the specter also illuminates the stylistic and
representational complexities that mark Griffiths's current writing. For
the specter is that which challenges the sharp distinction between "the
real and the unreal, the actual and the inactual, the living and the non-
living, being and non-being" as well as the category of objectivity. The
specter, in short, is that which "disjoins the living present" and "secretly
unhinges it."[9] The present, whether of now or then, continues to assert
itself as a field of material circumstances and relations in Griffiths's
work; the historical subject remains shaped by its conditions, grounded
within the social possibilities they open up. But, with a complexity that
surpasses even his earlier experimentation with a postrealist aesthetic,
Griffiths's recent plays and films decenter realism's "living present"
through a dramaturgy of shifting, mutually interfering ontological
realms. Dream, memory, vision, spectral visitation, increasingly displace the realist field and challenge its claims to political and representational adequacy. Driving Griffiths's recent work is a dramaturgy of
thresholds, edges, landscapes; at the heart of this dramaturgy is a growing conviction that history's meanings—its legacies, outlines, and
imperatives—manifest themselves, specterlike, across the boundaries of
time, space, and the Real. Griffiths's latest work, we might say, decon-
structs history in order further to disclose its voices, its challenges, and
its intersecting gazes. In formal terms Griffiths extends the exploration
he initially embarked on in *Real Dreams*, opening the category of the
Real itself to the dreamed, the remembered, the dead, the not-yet—in
short, what Derrida calls "the virtual space of spectrality."[10]

When the Berlin Wall was opened and the East German government resigned in November 1989, playwright Heiner Müller—whose
plays of the 1970s and 1980s had already begun to stage the specters of
Marxism—wrote a three-part poem in which he reflected on the stunning historic events. In the final part, entitled "SELFCRITIQUE," he wrote:
"On the tube I see my compatriots / With hands and feet vote against
the truth / That forty years ago was my own / What grave will protect
me from my youth?"[11] Griffiths's attitude toward the fall of communism was, of course, less personally fraught than Müller's. But the
movement toward self-examination that Müller's poem exemplifies is

similar in direction and tone to the reflexive/reflective movement in Griffiths's most recent work. Like "SELFCRITIQUE," these plays and films are reconsiderations of a life—Danton, Bevan, Gonne, Yeats, Griffiths— forced to survive the repudiation of its youth. In the space of its "presumable death" (Danton is discovered in his prison cell lying "as if embalmed") the self must confront the meaning of its existence in history, must rediscover, in the rubble of old certainties, the origins of hope and belief. The question, again, is one of ghosts. What claims does the past exert on the present? What is the nature of its inheritance? What claims does the future exert on both past and present?

Hatching the Future: *Hope in the Year Two* / *Who Shall Be Happy . . . ?*

Griffiths, we have seen, chose not to write about the 1989 revolutions in Europe, preferring instead to address the social, political, and technological developments of late-twentieth-century capitalism as these played themselves out at home and abroad. Yet, even as he wrote *The Gulf between Us* and *Thatcher's Children*, Griffiths was attempting to understand the historic events in Europe and their implications for the tradition of leftist politics. Griffiths noted in a 1992 interview:

> I'm starting to think now about what the destruction of the Soviet empire actually means. What it actually means is that the full agenda of the French Revolution has now resurfaced. The Russian Revolution was meant to transcend it, which it singularly failed to do. And now those three elements [liberty, equality, and fraternity] are back at the forefront. How to solve the relationship between political freedom and economic freedom remains the key problem; it was Tom Paine's agenda, it was Robespierre's agenda, it was Danton's agenda. So I've been thinking for about a year now about a play called *Danton's Life*—I want to take a look at that agenda through a historical figure.[12]

If Brenton, Churchill, and Edgar responded to the rollback of organized socialism by commemorating the ideologically problematic spectacle of social transformation in Eastern Europe, Griffiths elected to trace the newly eclipsed socialist project back to its germinating moment: what Sloman (in *The Party*) called "the Revolution in France[,] that . . . implosive moment not yet complete, not yet in the past" (67).

    Even before the events of 1989 confirmed the eclipse of European communism, Griffiths had already revisited the French Revolution in the second half of *These Are the Times.* In early 1993 he completed a tele-vision play on Danton's final hours. Under the title *Hope in the Year Two* (and in a production directed by Elijah Moshinsky) the play was broad-cast by the BBC on 11 May 1994 to mark the two hundred–year anniver-sary of Danton's death (on 6 April 1794). Griffiths subsequently adapted the play for the stage and gave it his original screenplay title. *Who Shall Be Happy . . . ?* opened at the Old Museum Arts Centre in Belfast on 8 November 1995, in a production mounted by Mad Cow Productions and directed by Griffiths himself. Not since *Comedians* had a play of Griffiths received such critical acclaim, and this acclaim followed the production through touring performances at the West Yorkshire Play-house and the Aarhus in Denmark and into its London opening at the Bush Theatre on 4 June 1996. In this case critical reception proved itself equal to Griffiths's dramatic accomplishment; "it has actually restored my faith in theater," one critic exclaimed.[13] Remarkable both for its con-tinuities with and departures from Griffiths's earlier works, *Hope in the Year Two* offers a complex, stylistically innovative exploration of the revolutionary past and of the search—in history—for personal and col-lective meanings. In addition, it represents Griffiths's most searching investigation of the nature of historical representation, a self-reflexive meditation on the dialogue between present and past.

Griffiths had been interested in writing a play about Danton for some time, and the Frenchman features prominently in the Paine screenplay. But the true outlines of what became *Hope in the Year Two* are buried in a different, abandoned project. In the early 1980s Griffiths spoke about returning to Antonio Gramsci and writing a play about the Italian revolutionary in prison. By 1984, with Reaganism and Thatch-erism firmly entrenched, "this whole idea of the revolution in chains, the revolution in prison," became more compelling.[14] The shift in Grif-fiths's interest from the Gramsci of 1920, theorizing the direction of pro-letarian revolt, to Gramsci in prison—dying but nonetheless fiercely active, producing the *Prison Notebooks* and a range of other writings—reflects the dramatic shift in his sense of revolutionary possibility. As Stuart Hall suggests, the late Gramsci had to confront "the turning back, the failure" of the "proletarian moment" of the early 1920s, and he had to confront "the capacity of the right—specifically, of European fas-cism—to hegemonize that defeat."[15] Borrowing the term that the Italian Communist Party applied to the period of Gramsci's imprisonment, Griffiths planned to call this play *Days of Iron and Fire.* Griffiths even intended a scene (echoing *Marat/Sade*) in which Gramsci and his fellow

prisoners rehearse a play they have been writing about the world outside. By the early 1990s what would have been Griffiths's second Gramsci play became a play about Danton, imprisoned and facing his death
during an earlier revolution in crisis. The seeds of this transformation
may have been sown in Griffiths's extensive research on Gramsci for
Occupations: Alessandro Pertini, the future president of the Italian
Republic who was imprisoned with Gramsci for more than a year in the
early 1930s, recalled the Sardinian as having "the weak body of a pygmy
and, on this body, the head of a Danton."[16]

Hope in the Year Two is set in the Luxembourg Palace, where Danton
is imprisoned in a large cage, during the evening and morning preceding his execution on 16 Germinal in Year Two of the Free Republic. With
the exception of several flashbacks to past events, the play's action consists of Danton's solitary reminiscences, his exchanges with his sans-
culotte guard Henry, and his urgent efforts to remember a question put
to him by a beggar at the coronation of Louis XVI: "Who shall be happy,
if not everyone?"[17] Written, like *Thatcher's Children,* in the year after the
1992 British general election, the play is easily Griffiths's darkest work,
charged with disillusionment and agonized self-questioning. Griffiths
has described the play's composition as "a terminally bleak experience.
I went to a space inside me I shan't return to in a hurry. I might not come
out next time."[18] In its spareness and often brooding retrospect, its
stretches of monologue taped and spoken, Griffiths's portrayal of Danton's final hours has, at moments, an almost Beckettian feel. Its protagonist has more in common with Shakespeare's imprisoned Richard II—
"peopl[ing] this little world" with his thoughts[19]—than with the
world-weary but public hero of Georg Büchner's *Danton's Death,* who
remains surrounded by friends even as he awaits his execution. In 1993
Griffiths stated: "I've been wanting to have an argument with Büchner
. . . ever since I read that play. It's a great play, and it's deeply wrong. It's
deeply wrong because it's hugely romantic."[20] Crude yet eloquent, Griffiths's Danton is a more complicated figure: defender of the Revolution's noblest ideals as well as a venal pursuer of his own self-interest,
lover of the earth and a devotee of sensuality as well as an early sup-
porter of the Terror to which he is now being sacrificed. Both hero and
antihero, he offers an extended reflection on the agenda of the Revolution and its betrayal, and he does so from the perspective of someone
who has lived and exploited its moral contradictions. Thinking back on
the massacres at Nantes and Lyons, Danton reflects: "When I said. One
year ago. When we were young. 'Let *government* take terrible measures,

so that the *people* may not have to take them themselves' . . . Is this what I had in mind?" (31).

History, for Griffiths, has always been the site of the present's formation, a repository of the culturally disowned, the voices of who we were and are. *Hope in the Year Two* is dedicated to the late Edward Thompson, one of the foremost figures of the New Left historiography (we have seen) that was so influential in Griffiths's developing conception of history as a revisionist dramatic field. At the same time, as Griffiths is aware, history in the 1990s finds itself in crisis, its "end" proclaimed from a range of ideological standpoints. Spearheading a conservative intellectual response to recent international events, Francis Fukuyama's 1989 article "The End of History?" hailed the fall of communism as "the end point of mankind's ideological evolution and the universalization of Western liberal democracy as the final form of human government."[21] Certain theorists of postmodernism have likewise challenged the notion of history—most radically, Jean Baudrillard, whose writings of the 1980s increasingly argued for history's disappearance in "a hyperspace where it loses all meaning."[22] Even those currents of postmodernism that assume a less apocalyptic stance toward modernity and its master narratives often fragment history, recasting it in the form of pastiche and problematizing the notion of the past in ways that Terry Eagleton and others have called a form of historical "forgetting."[23]

Griffiths, it goes without saying, rejects the proclamations of history's end—his Danton alludes sardonically to "the meticulously staged death of history" (33)—and the dehistoricizing of the present that such claims reinforce. Like *Thatcher's Children* (with which it was published), *Hope in the Year Two* represents "a raid on the past, an address to the present and a rejection of the future currently on offer." The play thus extends Griffiths's concern with the often complex forms of dialogue between different historical moments; indeed, it foregrounds this dialogue with a self-consciousness unusual even for Griffiths. Since Year Two of the Free Republic is year five of the Revolution itself, Danton's reflections are themselves acts of historical memory, directed toward an upheaval that had already transformed itself through a number of stages. Danton reads his past, and the past of the Revolution, with a historian's questioning mind, seeking to understand the significance of the events of which he was a central participant. As he insists: "It's not life I ask. / It's meaning" (17). Danton also looks forward, envisioning a future that represents the outcome of the events he has witnessed and lived: "Still there? Aye, I see ye. Little white faces in the dark. The future we are hatching here" (1). Danton's introspective monologue is conducted as a form of address to this invisible audience, a technique underscored by the character's frequent direct stare at the camera lens ("Still there?"). Historical subject confronts the future's historical regard in an exchange of gazes, and history becomes the site of doubled interpretive scrutiny. The audience of Danton's monologue is both an imagined entity and—in an inclusion that shatters historical illusionism—the actual spectators of the late twentieth century. Danton challenges these spectators with the poverty of their own present and future: "Looking back's all that's left ye, *you* spent what was left of the future long since, you have nowhere else to look save back, do ye, poor sods . . . (*Looks at lens, smiles*)" (33).

The reciprocal gazes of past on present and present on past reflect a set of ontological and epistemological questions that distinguish *Hope in the Year Two* from Griffiths's earlier historical plays and films. Griffiths, to be sure, has always been interested in the past as construction, official and otherwise. Here, however, the ontological status of the past and the problematic nature of historical understanding have emerged as central issues within the dramatization of history. This shift in interest is evident in the interaction between camera lens and protagonist. At several points in the play, after a flashback or after tracking shots through the prisoner's surroundings, the camera lens (in Griffiths's frequent textual direction) "finds" Danton, squatting beneath a table, sitting in an armchair, leaning against a door. By characterizing the lens of history as searching, exploratory, Griffiths calls attention to the pursuit of the past inherent in the acts of historical retrospection and reconstruction.

With Griffiths's subject, such a focus was perhaps inevitable. Few periods raise questions of historical knowledge and interpretation more forcefully than that of the French Revolution, which from its opening moments became the subject of its own mythmaking and that of later publicists and historians. The second half of 1989, which saw the fall of the Berlin Wall, also witnessed the Bicentennial of the storming of the Bastille, a television event saturated with revolutionary iconography. This backdrop of myth is felt throughout *Hope in the Year Two*. Griffiths counterpoints his scene of the massacre at Lyons conducted by the turbanned members of the Marat Company, for example, with a shot of Jacques-Louis David's painting *The Assassination of Marat* propped on an easel by a riverbank and with Danton's discussion of the "Empire of Images" by which the Revolution sought to transform nature.

Similarly, few participants in the Revolution have proven more historically elusive, open to interpretation, or layered with myth than Danton. As Norman Hampson, one of his biographers, points out, Danton
was notoriously reluctant to put anything on paper, and what he did
write has been lost or destroyed. One is left with the conflicting Dantons
of legend and historical account and the possibility, based on what evidence there is, that the historical figure, who surfaces in the historical
record with a mixture of forcefulness and unreadability, could have
been "either a generous and open-hearted *bon viveur* or a cynical
crook."[24] To Alphonse de Lamartine, Danton was an unprincipled revolutionary, a figure of heroic intellect and equally heroic vices; to
Auguste Comte he was a proto-positivist; to François-Alphonse Aulard,
the most modern statesman of the Revolution. In the words of Daniel
Guérin, a Marxist historian of the French Revolution, "Danton obscures
and confuses everything he touches."[25]

Rather than select a single Danton from the divergent historical
accounts, Griffiths makes this undecidability the cornerstone of his dramatic representation. Coherence and consistency, after all, are the
domain of Robespierre, "a system on legs" (in Danton's words) who
"has outlawed doubt. Doubleness. / All blur, haze and hover" (12–13).[26]
With Danton, Griffiths marshals the results of his own research to main-
tain a multiple, contradictory characterization: "The whole piece is
about the nature of identity," he notes. "What I found was that there
were as many as six Dantons."[27] This multiplicity forms the impetus for
Danton's own monologic memory journey through history, personal
and public. "Did Danton do this?" he asks, remembering Lyons: "Did
any of us? For what?" (32). Danton returns obsessively to the events of
his life—trying to reconcile outcomes with intentions, seeking to understand the intentions themselves, confronting the painful contradictions
between "a Titan, Hero of the Republic" (4) and the opportunist who cut
deals in Belgium, "fucking / Everything in skirts / That moved" (38),
while his first wife lay dying in childbirth. Like the play's setting—a
broken armchair, rubble, lumber, a shattered chandelier, "scraps of earlier meanings" (15)—identity in Griffiths's play is fragmentary, disjointed, "chained to the present" of its own noncoincidence (33). This
fragmentation is underscored in the Moshinsky television production,
in which Danton's face is filmed (on two occasions) reflected within a
cracked mirror.

In *Hope in the Year Two* Griffiths carries his focus on identity and
historical recuperation into the play's narrative itself. One of the play's

central narrative and dramatic threads concerns the existence of a Danton impersonator, a madman disguised as Danton and housed in the Conciergerie to confuse any rescue plot (no one outside the Committee of Public Safety is told which prisoner is the real Danton). Griffiths has suggested that the audience itself remains uncertain "whether it's the real Danton or not."[28] Indeed, although his protagonist establishes his identity in the play's opening minutes ("I would not lie to the future. I *am* Danton" [2]), one would not fault the audience for allowing its certainty to waver in the face of the prisoner's histrionic performance. The historical Danton, after all, *was* imprisoned in the Conciergerie the night before his execution, and Griffiths's directions identify his protagonist only as "the Prisoner." The question "Who is Danton?" is thus foregrounded within the play itself. Danton, attempting to bribe the guard Henry to smuggle a coded message to his wife and friends, pretends that he is the madman, imprisoned as a surrogate for "the Man," who is confined elsewhere. When Henry grows suspicious (he has seen a messenger impersonating the real Danton and recognizes his prisoner in this performance), Danton claims to have learned the mannerisms of "the Man-in-Question, the Hero of the Republic" in order to play him in the heroic propaganda play *Danton Saves France* (27). Danton proceeds to reenact a segment of this "role" for the suspicious Henry, adopting a self-consciously histrionic performance style.

Danton playing an actor playing Danton as conceived in a piece of revolutionary agitprop—the moment is remarkable in its Chinese box of performative levels and in its Pirandellian intertwining of role-playing and madness ("It is not possible to be Georges-Jacques Danton and not mad. [. . .] Henry . . . Why do you imagine the Committee had *me* put here this night?" [27]). At the same time, the effect of this metadramatic episode (and the intrigue of actors and doubles of which it forms part) is as much Brechtian as Pirandellian: it serves not only to theatricalize identity ("Our lives are much like the theatre, Henry" [8]) but to reconfigure history itself as an essentially presentational space of gestures and language invested with public recognizability and meaning. The Brechtian, or gestic, style of this theatricalization is reinforced when Danton, alone in his cell, impersonates Marat and Robespierre, assuming the characteristic bearing and mannerisms of each and redelivering passages from their public speeches in a kind of ironic quotation.

The preoccupation with acting and role-playing, in other words, discloses "Danton" as, in part, a construct or performance, synthesized out of the myriad details of biography and public action. The metahistorical implications of this theatricality are clear. If a collection of events as public as the French Revolution is intrinsically histrionic, the act of historical reconstruction by which these events and their participants are represented is no less caught up in forms of staging. *Hope in the Year Two* displays the fictionality of historical interpretation through a metadramatic awareness of its own act of historical narration. Griffiths's dramatic text opens with the shot of a theater curtain, which parts to reveal a safety curtain; this second curtain has a large guillotine blade painted on it, and it "creak[s] slowly up" to reveal the Luxembourg room (1). When Danton has left this room on the way to his execution at the play's end, this safety curtain guillotine "slices down" with emblematic finality (39).[29]

Commenting on his recent drama as a whole, Griffiths observes, "I'm now interested in writing plays that know they're plays. I've always looked for a reflexive moment within the naturalist/realist play."[30] With the painted safety curtain and the layers of performativity, reflexive awareness becomes a guiding representational principle. The effect of this metadramatic intensification is to underscore the status of history itself as a retrospective construction, always to some extent a dramatization, as much staged as recovered. *Hope in the Year Two* displays an extensive amount of research into the biography of Danton and the history of the Revolution, and its details establish an impressive texture of historical accuracy. But the play also acknowledges the fictionalization that necessarily accompanies historical recuperation in the absence of historical record (even the famous sayings attributed to Danton during his imprisonment and execution are largely apocryphal, a matter of story—as Henry implicitly suggests when he invites his prisoner to join him in playing the game of "Famous Last Words").[31] Danton's anti-illusionistic address to the future skews the notion of historical verisimilitude, and his references to later centuries join other textual features that underscore his own createdness as a dramatic character. Not surprisingly, given the strategic provisionality of its historical dramatization, *Hope in the Year Two* is characterized by a powerful intertextual awareness—not only of the anecdotal lore of Danton's life and death and the contradictory tradition of historical assessment but also of other dramatizations: Büchner's play, Peter Weiss's *Marat/Sade*, Andrej Wajda's 1983 film *Danton* (starring Gerard Depardieu), heroic revolutionary stagings like the *Danton Saves France* mentioned within Griffiths's play. In tandem with the play's other literary and theatrical allusions, references such as these establish Griffiths's Danton play as a

version among versions, linked to the other literary and historical inter-
pretations across a network of intertextual quotation.

Hope in the Year Two, then, represents a movement in Trevor Griffiths's career toward a metahistorical heightening of the fictionality
inherent in historical reconstruction. In this respect his most recent
approach to history evokes the work of such contemporary theorists of
historiography as Hayden White, who has argued that historical narratives are "verbal fictions, the contents of which are as much invented as
found."[32] At the same time, Griffiths resists a more radically postmodern textualizing of history, in which (to quote Fredric Jameson's characterization of late-capitalist society) "the past as 'referent' finds itself
gradually bracketed, and then effaced altogether, leaving us with nothing but texts."[33] To Griffiths *Hope in the Year Two* is grounded in the
actual, "the real world of . . . a guy waiting to die in a historic mansion
that is still there."[34] History may be knowable only through its traces,
but the historical field in Griffiths's play retains its integrity, its ability to
testify to the life of the human project in time. Historical truth is multiple in origin, and its meanings are referentially complex. The past of
revolutionary France—illuminated and constructed by the present's retrospective gaze yet pressuring this present with an otherness always
outside the present's self-reflection—becomes both measuring point
and mirror, a vehicle through which the present can gauge the distance
and direction it has traveled and see, reflected back, the face of its current predicament.

As Griffiths's Danton and his descendants contemplate one another
with the scrutiny of shared preoccupations, the truth they uncover has a
strange circularity, as if present and past are ghosting each other in their
pronounced (if imperfect) resemblance: "Place de la Révolution. Where
all this . . . history began. Alpha and Omega" (36). Danton refers to the
French Revolution as the birthplace of modern history—indeed, of the
very conditions of modernity itself. The future "hatched" by this revolution carries an ambiguous, paradoxical inheritance:

> Everything we have thought, everything we have tried or imagined,
> everything dreamt and whispered, designed, done . . . you will develop
> and perfect. Such a dish of worms we've served ye and ye'll eat 'em, every
> one. The free dance of capital, the human imperative. The sovereign
> people, the all-seeing all-saying State. Owner, worker. Nation and war,
> people and peace. The power of the machine, the machinery of power. Me,
> all. The impossible and the necessary dream. The road to freedom, mined
> every step of the way. (33)

In the darkness of the Terror in Year Two of the Free Republic (and in what Griffiths sees as an equivalent bleakness of the twentieth century's final decade) the legacy of the Revolution appears most glaringly in the late-twentieth-century state, with its "vocabulary for a new world order" (30), its Empire of Images, and its mechanisms of repression. "You have filled me with such fear for the future," Danton says. "How will I tell you, as I scan your tiny faces in the gloom, you are yourselves already dead, immured inside the dungeon walls of cant and lies and language this revolution has all the while and under our noses been a-building?" (6–7). Ostensibly directed to his revolutionary contemporaries, the lines are spoken to the camera and, through this, to the "faces" of the late-twentieth-century audience. At moments like this, as Griffiths's play skirts a nihilism unprecedented in the playwright's earlier work, the Revolution seems to have bequeathed to later generations only its cynicism and its failure. "The future," Danton murmurs, "lies in an alley, its throat slit" (15).

Yet, as Danton's catalogue of the future's inheritance makes clear, the Revolution is equally the birthplace of "the impossible and necessary dream," a crucible out of which the vision of a better future, based on peace and social justice, is placed on the world's agenda. "I play this game for hope," Danton states; "without it, what are we if not already dead?" (10). Even the speeches of Marat and Robespierre, parodied as part of Danton's impersonations of his fellow revolutionary leaders, bear eloquent witness to the Revolution's originating ideals. *Hope in the Year Two* can be understood not only as a brooding meditation on the failure of revolutionary promise but as a search for the grounds of hope and affirmation, an effort to rediscover the roots of the Revolution's transformative project. Over the course of the play the human grounds for the reclamation of this project become clearly, if fleetingly, apparent behind the scenes of history's more public stages: the love and natural sensuality between Danton and his second wife (evoked in flashback); the interactions between Danton and Henry and their guarded, failed search for trust; the recollection of life's ordinary pleasures ("Kissing a son on the mouth. Knowing my mother eats. Horse sweat. [. . .] Men's laughter" [15]). These grounds are equally evident, of course, in the profound self-questioning by which a man of vision, "still seeking to extend the range of human possibilities" (13–14), affirms his life's (and the Revolution's) central commitment: "Who shall be happy, if not everyone?"

Hope and a question—they may not seem much against the failure of revolutions then and now. But in the apparent rollback of the socialist project in Year Two (and on the eve of the year 2000), they stand, for Griffiths, as seeds in time, the opportunity for new beginnings that history—across the space of mutual scrutiny—offers the present. At one point in *Hope in the Year Two* Danton plays with the name of the month in which he has been imprisoned under the new revolutionary calendar: "Germ. Germinate. Germinal. April. Growing weather" (8). Images of seeding and birth recur throughout the play as symbols of latency and the possibility of rebirth. They point us again to what is irreducible in Griffiths's moral and political universe: the spark of resistance, the imperative of social justice, and a resilience of aspiration. As Danton elaborates:

> In these few years, in this unlikely place, these people have lived and fought and died to claim hope for the human project, to make hope the inalienable right of the living. They have decreed it: to hope is to be human; to hope is to define ourselves as human. Nobody can change that now; it will be so, part of the condition. Like me tonight, you too cannot live but in hope. Liberty may wither, Fraternity evaporate, Equality rot on the vine, Hope's a survivor; and will not die. (10)

In the midst of this dark night of the revolutionary soul, at the heart of history and its Grand Guignol, hope asserts itself, for Griffiths, as both a presence and a promise, the Revolution's better face.

To note the existence of this rhetoric of rebirth and indestructibility is not to minimize the obstacles that confront the play's politics of hope—the mines on the road to freedom—or the anger and despair that accompany it. According to one account of his final days (written by a fellow prisoner), the historical Danton "talked constantly about trees, the country and nature."[35] He also swore a lot.

Postscript: Mad Cow

When Griffiths adapted *Hope in the Year Two* for the stage and presented Mad Cow Productions with the play (renamed *Who Shall Be Happy . . . ?*) for the 1995 Belfast Festival, he achieved more than a simple change of medium. Indeed, *Who Shall Be Happy . . . ?* may be the only one of Griffiths's plays to turn out more successful in its adaptation than in the original. Not surprisingly, given its intrinsic theatricality, the play achieved a vitality onstage that was noticeably lacking from the television production, which was (on the whole) remote, somewhat muted. In the hands of Hayden Griffin (Griffiths's set designer) the play made powerful use of its physical environment: the floor in and around Danton's cage was scattered with straw, giving the French revolutionary the look of a caged animal, and the interior of the Belfast Old Museum Arts Centre was "trashed" (and its windows boarded up) to create an environment of disintegration and collapse.[36] Stanley Townsend played Danton with a fierce energy, and Kulvinder Ghir (who played Chatterjee in *The Gulf between Us* and Gurvinder in *Thatcher's Children*) brought "intelligence and stealth" to the role of Henry.[37] The fact that *Who Shall Be Happy . . . ?* was acted by Irish and Asian-Yorkshire performers—and that it was first performed in Belfast—allowed Griffiths's play to operate over and through contemporary racial, ethnic, and geopolitical fault lines.

In keeping with Griffiths's conception of the two plays as "a stage play for the screen and a screenplay for the stage,"[38] *Who Shall Be Happy . . . ?* deployed cinematic devices to underscore its play with history and representation. Throughout the play the back wall served as a screen for the projection of a modern cityscape, Danton's dreamscape, and a reflected audience—the "tiny faces" that Danton addresses. When Danton has been led off to his execution and Henry has trudged off stage, the back wall was illuminated with these faces one last time, and the audience was left facing its spectral double.

Death and Entrances: *Food for Ravens*

Griffiths's interest in the "ghosting" of history deepened in his next project. In early summer 1996 Griffiths finished the screenplay for a "film for television" on the life of Aneurin ("Nye") Bevan, the socialist Labour politician who, born and raised in a Welsh mining community, rose to become a leading member of the Attlee Government of 1945–51 (as minister of health, he was the architect of the National Health Service [NHS]) and one of the century's most influential and uncompromising voices for parliamentary socialism. It had a number of different working titles: *Short Days, Health, Better Days, Man and Boy.* Under its final title, *Food for Ravens*, the film was produced the following summer by BBC Wales, with Griffiths as director (for the first time) of one of his films. Although much of the film was shot in England (including the actual house outside London where Bevan lived and died), Griffiths was based in Cardiff during the film's production. *Food for Ravens* was broadcast in Wales on 18 November 1997 and (after controversy over scheduling) in England the following night.[39]

Like others of Griffiths's plays and films, *Food for Ravens* is positioned within an interlocking set of watershed moments and anniversaries. The idea for the Bevan project came to Griffiths from Dai Smith, an academic whom Griffiths had worked with on the Miners' Strike project and who was now head of English Language Programming for BBC Wales, to commemorate the hundred-year anniversary of Bevan's birth and (a year later) the fifty-year anniversary of the founding of the NHS. 1995 had been the fifty-year anniversary of the historic Labour election of 1945, and this anniversary was itself commemorated in a number of ways.[40] With Bevan, Griffiths would write about the figure who, more than any other, represented the socialist aspirations that swept the Attlee government to power. Throughout the war it was Bevan who presented the conflict as an opportunity for social revolution and who argued most passionately that the choice at its end would be a choice of futures: "Out of the war, whatever else comes, will come an opportunity for the working class of the world to do something effective to save themselves from fresh tragedies and suffering."[41] Bevan represented the promise of 1945, and when, in subsequent years, that promise showed itself to have been squandered it was Bevan who spoke most passionately for the continued urgency of its vision and values.

The 1995 anniversary of Labour's postwar victory was a decidedly muted affair, and the events that marked it were characterized by a mixture of nostalgia and melancholy. True socialism, it turned out, was never in the cards; sixteen years after the Thatcherite reaction, even the Welfare State had grown to feel like a vestige of a time now gone. Bevan's career points to this failure and its immediate political consequence: his bitter split with Hugh Gaitskell in the early 1950s marked the division between Left and Right that would polarize Labour politics for the next four decades. By 1995 Tony Blair was well into the process of "revitalizing" the Labour Party, and when Griffiths wrote *Food for Ravens* the following year it was clear to most observers that the next election was Labour's to win. But, if Labourism was back on the agenda, it was there in large part because New Labour had, in the main, distanced itself from its Bevanite inheritance.[42] If the life of Nye Bevan presented Griffiths with the chance to explore the generative moments of postwar Labourism (with a nod to *Bill Brand* and his earlier plays about British Labour politics), it also enabled him to resurrect the visions and imperatives that animate its past—ghosts, again, that a post-Thatcher, post-Marxist world has tried to conjure away. When Griffiths's Bevan is shown addressing the Brighton Labour Conference of 1957, the scene is

filled with banners for CND, Socialist Doctors, Peace News—"vivid sig-
nifiers," Griffiths notes in his preproduction screenplay, "of an active
politics all but erased in the flattened landscape of current practice."[43]
Since this was the moment of Griffiths's own political awakening, this
filmic resurrection is an act of personal memory as well.

In the end it is the *way* that Griffiths handles his biographical material that makes *Food for Ravens* such a complex, innovative, and nuanced
work. Abandoning the linear structures that governed his earlier dramatic and filmic biographies (*Such Impossibilities, Reds, These Are the
Times*), Griffiths crafts the life of Nye Bevan into a self-reflexive meditation on time in all its interior forms of dialogue, memory, and projection.
This texturing of time and space is reflected in the completed film,
which is marked by an attention to form and visual composition more
generally associated with Continental films. Underscoring the film's
reflexivity and its conception of realism as something plastic, self-trans-
forming, Griffiths told his production crew that what he wanted in *Food
for Ravens* was a painting, not a photograph.[44]

Griffiths's film is set in the closing weeks of Bevan's life in 1960, as
the sixty-two-year-old politician battles what he thinks is an ulcer but is
in reality abdominal cancer. His wife, Jennie, and his doctor have not
disclosed his actual condition to him, and Bevan continues to anticipate
his return to political activity and the possibility that he could lead the
country in a future Labour government. He grants an interview to the
Manchester Guardian and entertains his old friend Nehru for a brief but
warm reunion. But his condition has also left him with intimations of
impending death: he is shown reading Dylan Thomas's *Death and
Entrances,* and the scenes in and around his Buckinghamshire home are
imbued with a sense of loss and mortality. Not since *Through the Night*
has the body's physical disability been presented with such directness:
Bevan's body is racked with pain; it moves slowly and must be relieved
with morphine and other medication. Though his relationship with Jen
displays an affection born in intimacy and the meeting of intellect—
"Finest comrade a man ever had," he says, using Griffiths's highest term
of respect—he envies in others the sexual vitality he has lost.[45] Not surprisingly, these scenes have a quality of urgent personal retrospect. His
study is full of the mementos of his life and career, and in one of his last
scenes he is shown consulting a cuttings book in which additional articles and photographs are kept. Like Edward Waite in *All Good Men,* in
many ways his political antithesis, Griffiths's Bevan finds himself
already slightly outside a life that has entered history. The interview

scene, during which Bevan speaks to the reporter while a photographer prowls the room looking for the right shot, echoes Griffiths's earlier play about an aging Labour leader; both explore the recording of life as history, the registering of legacy on film.

But the past makes incursions into the present—and vice versa—in more radically transgressive ways. In sleep, under the influence of morphine, and in moments of deep reflection, Bevan journeys into the past, recalling scenes from his childhood in Tredegar, Wales; his earlier adult life; and his political career: speaking in Parliament against the Means Test in the 1930s, for example, and to the Labour Conference of 1957. Although these memory sequences are often filmed with historicizing stylization—the childhood scenes are shot in monochrome, and a scene featuring Nye and Jen as young lovers is filmed in late 1930s color—the boundary between past and present remains fluid. As Nye lies in a hospital ward recovering from an operation, his closing eyes return him to "his quarrel with the world." As Griffiths specifies, the sounds of that quarrel begin to "surround the dreaming face" (11). The dreamed/recollected scene is established—Bevan's infamous 1948 Manchester speech, in which he referred to the Tories as "lower than vermin"—but, before it can become more than an echo, a nurse's flashlight picks out the older Bevan's face on the pillow. Later, as Nye walks painfully in the outdoors near his home, the landscape "bends and straightens in the shimmering haze, the image imperceptibly transposing to dreamscape" (50). Language, too, works to "presence" the past, and its evocations of earlier moments draw history into the present with the weight of lived meanings: "Once I was youngest union deputy in all Wales. Nineteen. Youngest councillor. Youngest MP. Cabinet Minister. And I am gone sixty. And that may have to be enough" (47). Time in *Food for Ravens* is a field of displacement; like the sun on the Buckinghamshire countryside in this, the most imagistic of Griffiths's works, memory and dream "shimmer" the present, "endlessly redrawing the space" (42). It is a field, too, of openings, channels: using a metaphor from contemporary physics, Griffiths has spoken of the presence of "wormholes of time" in this and other recent works.[46] When Bevan delivers a speech in a barn on his estate (Griffiths crafted his argument out of a number of Bevan's historical major speeches) his rhetorical performance refigures the moment with the voices—spectral, echoic, yet still powerful—of times long gone.

Temporal displacement organizes the film's very structure. The film opens in the Rhymney Valley, 1911, with a shot of the fourteen-year-old Nye carrying a stool across a mountain in order to read a poem he has written for a girl who, it turns out, never arrives (the poem ends: "O come to me my lovely / And no delays / The road ahead awaits us / And better days" [9]). The elder Bevan's voice narrates the incident and recounts the poem. When the scene shifts to the hospital room in the present (monochrome bleeding up to full color), the bedridden Nye awakens to discover the Boy staring at him from across the room. As the play progresses, the Boy reappears, unseen by anyone else, and the two engage in increasingly intimate conversation. The Boy is an uncanny apparition, both the child that Bevan never had and his own earlier self. He confides to his doctor:

> I'd have liked a son. Aye. When the nights get long, I think it's him I'm talking to, I dunno, I dunno. Little bugger sits there bright as a pin starin' me down. Funny thing is. He's all me. . . . And. He wants something. Searching something. An' I don't know what it is. (37)

With a parent's (or a teacher's) patience, the elder Nye answers the Boy's questions about his life and his accomplishments, unselfconsciously encouraging him upon the path to the future self he has become. But the Boy also provides Nye with a connection to his beginnings, in childhood and the Wales from which he came. The monochrome scenes show Nye's mother making him a pair of moleskin trousers as he prepares to start work in the mines, and the Boy speaks of his father and his grandfather Tadcu. At one point Nye calls the Boy "an old soul": "One who carries the past of the tribe in his being. Like a. Revelation. Like an. Illumination. Arabs use it of their hakawati, storytellers, poets of the people . . . Old souls" (46). As the elder Bevan embarks on the journey of memory, it leads him—across the gulf of time, space, class, and experience—to the self's early formation, to the birth of spirit, and the mystery of place. On the threshold of death the past assumes virtual life, and memory confronts itself in an impossible space both inside and outside of time. When the elder Nye gazes at a pond, the reflection of his youthful face looks back.

But the reflection is not exactly a mirroring, for the younger Nye is a visitor from a world that has gone, a world with its own material relations and its own thresholds of the possible. When the Boy accuses the elder Nye of being a "toff" because he lives in a big house, drives a car, and has a wife who gets her hair done, the latter acknowledges, "That's your truth. I can't say you're wrong" (44). Bevan offers a passionate claim that such things as "good clothes and good health" are a human birthright, but the act of debate itself is perhaps what is most significant here. It reveals Griffiths's understanding of experience as something marked and bounded, its truths shaped by the enabling yet constraining forces of history, material conditions, and culture. The self is subject to these thresholds and divergences, and in the exercise of memory the subject encounters a principle of difference at the heart of identity. In *Food for Ravens* it is language that offers the tool for bridging such gulfs and articulating a shared world. One of the ironies of Nye Bevan's career is that this most passionate of orators, who argued for social justice with a Welsh sensitivity to language and its possibilities, had a severe stuttering problem as a child. When the Boy timidly raises this problem, the elder Nye urges upon him the importance and power of language: "Reason and science show us reality in all its material unshiftability. Language alone lets us grasp it not simply as something material to be endured but as something living to be worked. [. . .] Between the stammer and *le mot juste*, boy, we learn to word the future" (50). By figuring the Real and the subject's relationship within it, language creates the world as something manipulable; in the struggles for articulation, on the edges of meaning, the threshold of the future is brought into being. As if in response to Nye's impassioned argument, the scene is followed by a monochrome scene of the younger Nye practicing his delivery.

"As if in response": the dramaturgy of thresholds makes the Boy's presence in *Food for Ravens* uncannier still. Griffiths provides cues to suggest that the Boy and the Tredegar scenes with which he is associated are visual objectifications of the elder Bevan's memory: Nye's eyes close and reopen before the Boy's appearances, and the monochrome Tredegar scenes are identified as a "dreamscape." But there are counterindications that the Boy's world may be the actual one and the "present" of 1960 a future (actual? imagined?) into which his world opens. The play opens and closes with the Boy, and in both sequences the elder Nye's narrating voice causes the young figure to look up, as if startled by an unexpected visitation. At one point, talking to the Boy, the elder Nye remembers:

> Once. Your age. In dreams. I'd set out on these long. Walks. On my own. And find myself . . . in some future world not yet my own. Watching, weighing. Talking. With strangers I felt I somehow knew. Searching something, never sure what. (49)

To the extent that these indications establish a contradictory set of temporal groundings, the play's framing devices and its hierarchy of ontological levels are radically destabilized. With the oscillations of a Gestalt experiment, figure and ground alternate in undecidable ambiguity: the child Nye exists as figure from the past as externalized in the elder Nye's memory; the elder Nye exists as figure in a landscape of future imaginings. Caught in the ambiguity of reality levels (actual, dreamed, imagined) and in the shifting lines between past and future, the present is displaced as a centering term of individual and narrative experience. Instead of grounding his film in a self-sufficient moment, Griffiths locates it within a self-reflexive double narration, in which past, present, and future exist—in and for one another—as competing horizons of meaning. "S'like History, isn't it," to quote the younger Nye when he looks at Bevan's clippings book (65).

It is hard not to evoke Derrida one last time or to see in *Food for Ravens* (like *Hope in the Year Two*) a realization of the French theorist's deconstructive meditation on time and history: "Without this *noncontemporaneity with itself of the living present*, without that which secretly unhinges it, without this responsibility and this respect for justice concerning those who *are not there*, of those who are no longer or who are not yet *present and living*, what sense would there be to ask the question 'where?' 'where tomorrow?' 'whither?' "[47] At no point in *Food for Ravens* is the present's deconstructive slippage more directly and powerfully conveyed than in the film's concluding sequence. After Nye awakens from a coma to ask Jen to "Take me home," the film embarks on its coda. The Boy is shown running, in an inverted March Time, "on down the years to Wales and home" (76). In a sequence intercut with scenes of Bevan's memorial procession, he passes the scenes of history: the photographing of a 1936 antifascist brigade on its way to Spain, a Miner's Band and demonstrators proclaiming the 1926 Lockout. While Nye's voice delivers segments of his political speeches, the Boy stands "rooted, watching, apart and part of, sniffing a future, some distance from the marchers" (78). Back in Tredegar, the young Nye is awakened by his mother, and with the monochrome replaced by full color, it is the future that now seems the dream. Walking with his father and brother for his first day's work at the mines, he sees the funeral procession across the valley. In alternating voice-over and (now monochrome) "live" shots Jen delivers an outdoor public eulogy on her husband ("if it is true he was born a man, it is also true that he died a boy" [54]), and a voice sings a passage from *The Gododdin*, written by the seventh-century

Welsh poet Aneirin: "A man in courage but a boy in years / Brave in the din of battle" (79). The elder Nye's ashes are scattered to the wind against a "big monochrome sky," while the young Boy, preparing to descend into the mine, "turns to face the shot, eyes wide with expectation" (82). Nye's voice completes the passage from the *Gododdin*— "Before we could bury him / He was food for ravens" (83)—and the film ends with an image of the memorial stone superimposed with the printed text of Aneirin's lines.

Having pressed history to a variety of services throughout his career, Griffiths has found, in *Food for Ravens*, a dramaturgy capable of registering its inner landscapes in all its self-referential displacements and complexities. But the innerness of this register is by no means a retreat from the public. For Nye Bevan's was a life lived in history, and the moments of time that constitute this life are animated by his aspirations for that world. On the edge of life, his body's failure mirroring the disappointment of his socialist hopes, Bevan's eyes are still alive with will, with the conviction that the people will look again to Labour and "we will lead our people to the future they deserve" (30). And, while the journey home may bespeak a longing for rest, the past that gazes back does so with the same will and the same questioning sense of urgency. When Nye, shortly before his death, comes upon the Boy reading aloud in the kitchen, the two talk with deepening intensity, "searching meanings, on the edge of things" (77). They talk about Tadcu, who, on his deathbed, said, "they won't go on doing this to us forever, you know. Because we'll stop them." As his wife and friend try to bring him back to bed, he calls to the vanished Boy: "You have to remember it *all*, bach, not just the easy bits. Not just the cause but the cure" (75).

The answer never comes, or, if it does, it isn't spoken. But, like the question that haunted Griffiths's Danton play, Nye's question represents an imperative that persists through the eddies of memory and time, a refusal that, more than anything else, constitutes the political self in history. As the Boy begins his run through time, Nye speaks in voice-over about social injustice and the dream of better days: "There is no such things as forever, boy. It'll last as long as there are folk left with the faith to fight for it" (76).[48]

Afterword: *Willie and Maud*

Griffiths's most recent completed project (as of the end of 1998) is a screenplay about the relationship between Maud Gonne and William

Butler Yeats. Actress Anjelica Huston, who had been marketing the idea of a film about Gonne for a number of years, approached Griffiths in 1995 to see if he was interested in taking on the project. Griffiths had a number of reservations, including his concerns about working with Hollywood again; he was reluctant to invest his time in a screenplay that might end up not being made or made in a way "that counterproduces all the meanings you set out to make."[49] But he eventually agreed to do so and completed a first draft of *Willie and Maud* in May 1997, shortly before beginning production on *Food for Ravens*.

The proximity of the two projects underscores their mutual preoccupations. Like the Bevan film, *Willie and Maud* displays Griffiths's deepening interest in the Celtic fringe. A concern with Ireland is not new: in addition to the references to Ireland and Northern Ireland in such plays as *Don't Make Waves* and *Oi for England*, Griffiths directed a Field Day Theatre Company production of *Saint Oscar*, Terry Eagleton's anti-imperialist play about Oscar Wilde, in March 1990.[50] And Griffiths's work with the Miners' Strike in the mid-1980s reflects his attraction to Wales as still another political vantage point outside England. But the interest in "those other, more marginalized Celtic areas" that emerges full-blown in Griffiths's most recent works signals more autobiographical considerations as well.[51] The playwright's "long look at Welshness" in *Food for Ravens* was motivated in part because Bevan's early life lay so close to Griffiths's family past: his paternal grandfather, who used to tell Griffiths stories when the playwright was a boy, also was a member of a Welsh mining family.[52] And Ireland was home to his mother's family, including the grandmother who taught him to read as a child. Griffiths's interest in the intersections of this personal, dynastic history with more public history is evident in a project he contemplated in 1992–93. Working with the title *Rags to Rags*, Griffiths envisioned a series of ten one-hour television episodes, each one set in a different decade of the twentieth century; it would open in Ireland and draw heavily upon material from Griffiths's family past.

The Ireland of *Willie and Maud*, of course, is an Ireland oriented in terms of political and literary renaissance. In keeping with his rejection of the conventional bio-pic, Griffiths explores the pivotal moments of Irish national self-articulation through devices of retrospect. The "present" of *Willie and Maud* is a house on Dublin Bay during the summer of 1938, where Maud visits her old friend a year before his death. The two are living national symbols: Willie, Ireland's greatest living poet, and Maud, an icon of the Republican cause—"Woman of the Sidhe. Queen

Maeve. Cathleen naHoulihan. Madame Republic" (10).[53] Maud has visited Willie to solicit his endorsement of the first volume of her autobiography *A Servant of the Queen,* and the film's action is framed by the
presence of this public account of Gonne's life. That Gonne used this
account as part of her own mythmaking is essential to Griffiths's screenplay: "I was writing against the myth of Maud Gonne, I suppose: that
she was effortlessly heroic . . . above life, implacable, never self-doubt-
ing. . . . It's an argument between what we ourselves as actors, as agents,
in history write about our agency and what other people know to be
true and untrue about it. So it's text on text, you know."[54] Yeats's own
textualizing of his experience is also in evidence, as Griffiths's screenplay interposes the scene of history with Willie's poetic, sublimated versions of it. With characters named Sweeney, Finnegan, and (Crazy) Jane
blurring the line between this imagined present/past and the literary
landscape of Anglo-Irish modernism, a heightened textuality is evident
throughout Griffiths's script.

Like *Food for Ravens, Willie and Maud* focuses its dramaturgical
unsettling on the categories of time and reality. The notion of the Real is
challenged in the screenplay's opening moments, when the voice of
Maud composing a letter to Willie is counterpointed by the caption
"none of this happened" (1). The caption is a teasing one, as Griffiths
plays with the terms that were deployed against him so resolutely
around the Scott project. The words are not so much disavowal as challenge, and they point to a space between the factual and the counterfactual. This play with the status of the Real extends to Willie's occultism—
he is surrounded by the paraphernalia of psychic experimentation, and
he summons Maud to him by projecting his voice and presence to her. It
extends, too, to the play's central narrative device. Willie has invited
Maud to visit him, it turns out, because he wants her to participate with
him on a journey into the past. Their journey takes place through a
series of visions, drug-induced trances, and dreams that the two share
and participate in. Conjured in this fashion, the film's formal "Visions"
(a Yeatsian term) emerge from a sequence of frozen, abstract memory
screens. Willingly, apprehensively, Willie and Maud revisit the scenes
of the past, exploring the progress of their intense relationships and the
intersecting narratives that rendered it both personally and publicly turbulent: Maud's affair with Lucien Millevoye and her child by him, her
marriage to John MacBride, and the difficult history of Irish nationalism
and independence.

In its superimpositions of history, memory, and vision *Willie and*

Maud is, like its companion plays and films, dream play and ghost sonata in one. Looking out the window at two lovers sparring with each other, the two septuagenarians are drawn to a scene from their past. "Ghosts, is it?" Willie asks Maud (6). In a temporal slippage the two lovers shortly reappear in nineteenth-century dress as the younger Willie and Maud. Later in the screenplay, as Maud looks out the window of the prison where she has been confined, she watches, in the courtyard below her, the execution years earlier of those convicted in the Easter Uprising. Throughout the script faces replace faces: characters are absent when present, already vanished from the scenes they inhabit, and present in their absence, through auras, projection, memory.

But the journey is not only into the past and its ghosts not only those of recollection. Like Danton and Nye Bevan, Griffiths's Yeats is driven in this journey by a need to find something that's been lost, something that inhabits that spectral Derridean space between presence and absence: "Even now," he tells Maud, "at the end, bags packed, work done, set to go, your knuckle on the door, your hand on the latch, and suddenly I fill with doubt, glimpse something else I must know, something there and not there, blowing through my head and heart and shaking to its root the peace I felt I'd found . . . I can not die like this" (19). But, though their shared journey passes through "wormholes of time" into the past, its final destination is a vision within a vision, the Room of the Future in the Castle of the Heroes that the two had dreamed of together when young. Yeats finally sees what Maud glimpsed in that room: a montage of the horrors that await the twentieth century, a jeremiad in images. Like the conclusion of *Thatcher's Children,* the vision is deeply dystopic, though it is complicated by the fact that, as the screenplay's imagined audience watches this filmic nightmare, it observes a future that is simultaneously its own past and present.

Through the same temporal sleight-of-hand that ends *Food for Ravens* the seascape that Maud sees through her window as she rides the train back to Dublin suddenly contains the Irish frigate bringing Yeats's body back from France the following year. What remains, for Maud and the film, are his voice and the poetry with which he has rendered mythic both her presence and his longing: "But O that I were young again / And held her in my arms" (121). As present and future slide past each other in transparent superimposition, the lines float free of the scene that contains them. The words are those of a ghost, and the memory they celebrate is a haunting one.

Notes

Introduction

1. Trevor Griffiths, introduction to *Sons and Lovers: Trevor Griffiths' Screenplay of the Novel by D. H. Lawrence* (Nottingham: Spokesman, 1982), 7.

2. Trevor Griffiths, "Trevor and Bill: On Putting Politics before News at Ten," interview by Nigel Thomas, *Leveller* (Nov. 1976): 12.

3. Trevor Griffiths, interview by Nicole Boireau, *Coup de Théâtre* 6 (Dec. 1986): 1.

4. Trevor Griffiths, "Current Concerns," interview by Peter Ansorge, *Plays and Players* 21 (July 1974): 20.

5. Catherine Itzin, *Stages in the Revolution: Political Theatre in Britain since 1968* (London: Eyre Methuen, 1980), 5.

6. Mike Poole and John Wyver, *Powerplays: Trevor Griffiths in Television* (London: BFI, 1984), 10. *Powerplays* was published to coincide with a season devoted to Griffiths's work for film and television at the National Film Theatre, 5–31 Mar. 1984.

7. Trevor Griffiths, letter, *Plays and Players* 22 (Oct. 1974): 6.

8. Trevor Griffiths, "Countering Consent," interview by John Wyver, *Ah! Mischief: The Writer and Television*, ed. Frank Pile (London: Faber and Faber, 1982), 36.

9. The only book-length study to devote equal time to Griffiths's work in different mediums is Hans-Peter Müller-Hartwigsen, *Trevor Griffiths: Politik im Drama—Drama als Politik(um)* (Essen: Verlag Die Blaue Eule, 1989). Müller-Hartwigsen's study originated as a dissertation at the University of Marburg.

10. Benedict Nightingale, rev. of *Real Dreams, New Statesman,* 23 May 1986, 30.

11. Griffiths, interview by Boireau, 7. Griffiths's plays and films have provided vehicles for some of the most prominent actors in Britain and the United States: Patrick Stewart, Ben Kingsley, Sir Laurence Olivier, Jonathan Pryce, Jack

Shepherd, Milo O'Shea, Leo McKern, James Fox, Wendy Hiller, Warren Beatty, Diane Keaton, Jack Nicholson, Kevin Spacey, Stephen Rea, Sinead Cusack.

12. Tom Stoppard, quoted in Steve Grant, "Preview: Piano," *Time Out* (8–15 Aug. 1990): 27.

13. Trevor Griffiths, *Bill Brand*, episode 1, rehearsal script, Trevor Griffiths Special Collection, British Film Institute National Library, 24.

14. Griffiths, interview by Thomas, 12.

15. Trevor Griffiths, interview by Melvyn Bragg, "South Bank Show," London Weekend Television, 26 Feb. 1984.

16. Albert Hunt, "A Theatre of Ideas," *New Society*, 16 Jan. 1975, 138.

17. Griffiths, interview by Bragg; quoted in John Tulloch, *Television Drama: Agency, Audience and Myth* (London: Routledge, 1990), 89.

18. Trevor Griffiths, "In Defence of *Occupations*," *Occupations*, rev. ed. (London: Faber and Faber, 1980), 8.

19. Griffiths, interview by Thomas, 12.

20. Trevor Griffiths, quoted in Janelle Reinelt, *After Brecht: British Epic Theater* (Ann Arbor: University of Michigan Press, 1994), 145.

21. Griffiths, interview by Wyver, 39.

22. Griffiths, introduction to *Sons and Lovers*, 10.

23. Trevor Griffiths, *These Are the Times*, screenplay, typescript (rev. second draft, 1 Dec. 1989), in Griffiths's possession, 7.

24. Trevor Griffiths, "Trevor Griffiths: Politics and Populist Culture," interview by Alison Summers, *Canadian Theatre Review* 27 (summer 1980): 25.

25. Robert Hewison, *The Heritage Industry: Britain in a Climate of Decline* (London: Methuen, 1987), 47.

26. Irving Wardle, rev. of *Occupations*, *Times*, 14 Oct. 1971.

27. Jacques Derrida, *Specters of Marx: The State of the Debt, the Work of Mourning, and the New International*, trans. Peggy Kamuf (1993; trans., New York: Routledge, 1994), 54.

28. Raymond Williams, *The Year 2000* (New York: Pantheon, 1983), 268.

29. See Andy Lavender, "Drama and Mid-Life Crisis," *New Statesman and Society*, 22 May 1992, 34; and Gregory Motton, "At the Stage of Hollow Moralising," *Guardian*, 16 Apr. 1992.

30. John Bull, *New British Political Dramatists* (London: Macmillan, 1984), 133–34.

31. Trevor Griffiths, "Caught in the Crossfire," interview by Sarah Hemming, *Independent*, 8 Jan. 1992.

32. Trevor Griffiths, "Transforming the Husk of Capitalism," interview by Catherine Itzin and Simon Trussler, *Theatre Quarterly* 6 (summer 1976): 46.

33. Trevor Griffiths, *All Good Men*, *Collected Plays for Television* (London: Faber and Faber, 1988), 63.

34. Derrida, *Specters of Marx*, 91.

35. Trevor Griffiths, *Hope in the Year Two and Thatcher's Children* (London: Faber and Faber, 1994), 39.

36. Derrida, *Specters of Marx*, 54.

37. Trevor Griffiths, *Food for Ravens* (London: Oberon Books, 1997), 75.

Chapter 1

1. Griffiths, interview by Boireau, 1.
2. Griffiths, introduction to *Sons and Lovers,* 9.
3. Griffiths, *Bill Brand,* episode 1, rehearsal script, 54–55. In quotations taken from Griffiths's plays and films unbracketed ellipses are Griffiths's, bracketed ellipses are mine.
4. Griffiths, interview by Boireau, 1.
5. Griffiths, interview by Itzin and Trussler, 28.
6. Trevor Griffiths, "A Failed Student: But a Highly Successful Television Playwright," interview by Guy Rubin, *Mancunion,* 24 Feb. 1981. Griffiths had been entered in an open competition for a scholarship to Cambridge, but his father had been unwilling to pay the ten-pound examination fee (this was the equivalent of a week's wages).
7. Griffiths, interview by Boireau, 4.
8. Griffiths, interview by Itzin and Trussler, 29.
9. Trevor Griffiths, interview by the author, 6 July 1995.
10. Griffiths, interview by Itzin and Trussler, 30.
11. On the history of the New Left, see E. P. Thompson, "The New Left," *New Reasoner* 9 (summer 1959): 1–17; Peter Sedgwick, "The Two New Lefts," in David Widgery, *The Left in Britain 1956–68* (Middlesex: Penguin, 1976): 131–53; and Lin Chun, *The British New Left* (Edinburgh: Edinburgh University Press, 1993). On the history of British cultural studies, see Graeme Turner, *British Cultural Studies: An Introduction,* 2d ed. (London: Routledge, 1996); and Dennis Dworkin, *Cultural Materialism in Postwar Britain: History, the New Left, and the Origins of Cultural Studies* (Durham: Duke University Press, 1997).
12. Editorial, *Universities and Left Review* 1 (spring 1957): ii.
13. Editorial, *New Left Review* 1 (Jan.–Feb. 1960): 2.
14. Griffiths, interview by the author, 6 July 1995.
15. E. P. Thompson, "Socialist Humanism," *New Reasoner* 1 (summer 1957): 109.
16. Ibid., 143.
17. Trevor Griffiths, "The Correspondent Questionnaire," compiled by Rosanna Greenstreet, *Sunday Correspondent,* 7 Oct. 1990, 54. Griffiths dedicated the 1994 published edition of *Thatcher's Children* and *Hope in the Year Two* to Thompson after Thompson's death.
18. Ibid.
19. Poole and Wyver, *Powerplays,* 16.
20. Griffiths, interview by the author, 6 July 1995.
21. Griffiths, interview by Boireau, 6.
22. Trevor Griffiths, "Short Toccata and Lasting Fugue," *King* (Mar. 1966): 89–91; "Not Even. Perhaps. To Him," *North* 4 (summer 1966): 2–6.
23. Trevor Griffiths, interview by John Wyver, summer 1981; quoted in Poole and Wyver, *Powerplays,* 15.
24. Griffiths, interview by Boireau, 20.
25. Ibid., 6.

26. Griffiths, interview by Itzin and Trussler, 32.

27. Griffiths, interview by Rubin.

28. Sydney Newman, "TV's Dramaturge," interview by John Wyver, *Time Out* (6–12 Apr. 1979); quoted in Poole and Wyver, *Powerplays*, 16. Information at the start of this paragraph is drawn from Poole and Wyver's study.

29. As part of his effort to get *The Daft 'Un* produced, Griffiths revised the play and retitled it *Friday Night Is Friday Night;* a subsequent revision was titled *Friday Night*. Until recently *The Mob at the Door, The Bastard Childe,* and *The Daft 'Un* were presumed lost; typescripts of all three plays (and the revised versions of *The Daft 'Un*) are in Griffiths's possession. A two-page play entitled *Histoire de Jeremy,* about a dominatrix and a man brought in as a potential submissive (he turns out to be homosexual), was probably also written around this time (manuscript also in Griffiths's possession).

30. Trevor Griffiths, "Enabling Perception to Occur," interview by Ken Swallow, *Liberal Education* 45 (spring 1982): 14.

31. Williams comments on the importance of adult education to the figures of the New Left: "this was the social and cultural form in which they saw the possibility of reuniting what had been in their personal histories disrupting: the value of higher education and the persistent educational deprivation of the majority of their own originary or affiliated class" ("The Uses of Cultural Theory," *NLR* 158 [July–Aug. 1986]: 25). Education would remain one of Britain's leading social and cultural battlefields: in the early 1970s Margaret Thatcher served as Edward Heath's secretary of state for education.

32. Trevor Griffiths, *The Love Maniac,* undated typescript (with unnumbered pages), Trevor Griffiths Special Collection. A shortened, revised version of the play, also available in the Trevor Griffiths Special Collection, is dated 30 May 1968.

33. Trevor Griffiths, letter to the author, 13 Nov. 1995.

34. Trevor Griffiths, *Dropping Out,* MS, Trevor Griffiths Special Collection, 24.

35. Colin Ward, *Anarchy in Action,* 2d ed. (London: Freedom Press, 1982), 16. David Stafford discusses anarchism's influence on the early New Left in "Anarchists in Britain Today," *Anarchism Today,* ed. David E. Apter and James Joll (London: Macmillan, 1971), 84–104.

36. Marc Rohan, *Paris '68: Graffiti, Posters, Newspapers and Poems of the Events of May 1968* (London: Impact Books, 1988), 76, 80.

37. D. Keith Peacock discusses the conflict between anarchism and Marxism as it informed British historical drama of the 1970s; see *Radical Stages: Alternative History in Modern British Drama* (New York: Greenwood, 1991), esp. 59–77.

38. Griffiths, interview by Boireau, 8.

39. Griffiths, *The Wages of Thin,* typescript in Griffiths's possession.

40. Griffiths, interview with Poole and Wyver, 15 Mar. 1983; quoted in *Powerplays*, 21.

41. Griffiths, interview by Itzin and Trussler, 35.

42. Irving Wardle, rev. of *The Wages of Thin, Times,* 15 Dec. 1970.

43. Griffiths's account of this incident can be found in "Love and Flannel," interview by Merete Bates, *Guardian,* 6 Nov. 1970.

44. Griffiths later adapted *The Big House* for the stage; a production of this version opened on 15 Jan. 1975 at the University Theatre, Newcastle-upon-Tyne.

45. Trevor Griffiths, *Occupations and The Big House* (London: Calder and Boyars, 1972), 93, 102.

46. Poole and Wyver, *Powerplays*, 19.

47. For an exploration of this interest, see Stuart Laing, *Representations of Working-Class Life 1957–1964* (Houndmills: Macmillan, 1986).

48. Trevor Griffiths, "A Play Postscript," interview by Nigel Andrews, *Plays and Players* 19 (Apr. 1972): 82.

49. Chas Critcher, "Sociology, Cultural Studies and the Post-War Working Class," in *Working-Class Culture: Studies in History and Theory*, ed. John Clarke, Chas Critcher, and Richard Johnson (1979; rpt., New York: St. Martin's, 1980), 16–17.

50. Richard Hoggart, *The Uses of Literacy* (London: Chatto and Windus, 1957), 239.

51. Griffiths, interview by Boireau, 3.

52. Griffiths, interview by Ansorge, 20.

53. Trevor Griffiths, *Sam, Sam*, Plays and Players 19 (Apr. 1972): 65.

54. Richard Allen Cave describes the effect of this and other framed scenes in act 1: "Each scene is played straight and sustained just long enough to engage our imaginative sympathies, then Sam comes leaping out of it to tackle our satisfaction" (*New British Drama in Performance on the London Stage: 1970 to 1985* [Gerrard's Cross: Colin Smyth, 1987], 215).

55. William J. Free, "Class Values and Theatrical Space in Trevor Griffiths' *Sam, Sam*," in *Within the Dramatic Spectrum*, ed. Karelisa V. Hartigan (Lanham, MD: University Press of America, 1986), 50. Of Griffiths's stagecraft Free writes: "Performance space has become a way of experiencing the nuances of class structure" (52).

56. Griffiths, interview by Itzin and Trussler, 36.

57. Ibid., 35.

58. Ibid., 30.

59. Trevor Griffiths, "Send in the Clowns," interview by Jack Kroll, *Newsweek* (13 Dec. 1976): 98.

60. Trevor Griffiths, "Trevor Griffiths—Attacking from the Inside," interview by Ronald Hayman, *Times*, 15 Dec. 1973.

61. Griffiths, interview by Itzin and Trussler, 35.

Chapter 2

1. Itzin, *Stages of the Revolution*, 1.

2. Editorial, *New Left Review* 52 (Nov.–Dec. 1968): 1. See also Tariq Ali, *1968 and After: Inside the Revolution* (London: Blond and Briggs, 1978); and Ronald Fraser, *1968: A Student Generation in Revolt* (London: Chatto and Windus, 1988).

3. Trevor Griffiths, "Playwright Unexpectedly Charming," interview by Bruce Blackadar, *Toronto Star*, 30 May 1979.

4. Trevor Griffiths, "Griffiths—One of Life's Fathers," interview by Myron Galloway, *Montreal Star*, 26 May 1979. When Griffiths returned to the late 1960s in *The Party* and *Real Dreams*, he did so at removes of five and sixteen years, respectively, and with additional distancing devices.

5. See Reinelt, *After Brecht*, 143–47. Reinelt subtitles her chapter on Griffiths "Counterpoint to a Brechtian Aesthetic."

6. Bertolt Brecht, "A Short Organum for the Theater," *Brecht on Theater: The Development of an Aesthetic*, ed. and trans. John Willett (New York: Hill and Wang, 1964), 190.

7. Griffiths, interview by Hayman.

8. Eric Hobsbawm, "The Historians' Group of the Communist Party," in *Rebels and Their Causes: Essays in Honor of A. L. Morton*, ed. Maurice Cornforth (London: Lawrence and Wishart, 1978), 21.

9. Bill Schwarz, "'The People' in History: The Communist Party Historians' Group, 1946–56," in *Making Histories: Studies in History-Writing and Politics*, ed. Richard Johnson, Gregor McLennan, Bill Schwarz, and David Sutton (London: Hutchinson, 1982), 54. See also Harvey J. Kaye, *The British Marxist Historians: An Introductory Analysis* (Cambridge: Polity Press, 1984).

10. John Saville and E. P. Thompson, Editorial, *New Reasoner* 1 (summer 1957): 2.

11. Schwarz, "'People' in History," 95.

12. Trevor Griffiths, interview by Summers, 26.

13. Ibid.

14. Perry Anderson, "Introduction to Gramsci 1919–20," *New Left Review* 51 (Sept.–Oct. 1968): 23. For further information on the factory occupations, see John M. Cammett, *Antonio Gramsci and the Origins of Italian Communism* (Stanford: Stanford University Press, 1967), 96–122; Paolo Spriano, *The Occupations of the Factories: Italy 1920*, trans. Gwyn A. Williams (London: Pluto, 1975); and Gwyn A. Williams, *Proletarian Order: Antonio Gramsci, Factory Councils, and the Origins of Italian Communism* (London: Pluto, 1975).

15. Anderson, "Introduction to Gramsci," 24.

16. D. A. N. Jones, "Socialist from Sardinia," rev. of Giuseppe Fiori, *Antonio Gramsci: Life of a Revolutionary*, *New Society* (17 Dec. 1970). By 1978 Anderson could write: "Today, no Marxist thinker after the classical epoch is so universally respected in the West as Antonio Gramsci" ("The Antinomies of Antonio Gramsci," *New Left Review* 100 [Nov. 1976–Jan. 1977]: 5.

17. See Ali, *1968 and After*, 143–44. Poole and Wyver discuss the social and political contexts of *Occupations* in *Powerplays*, 31–32.

18. Research notes for *Occupations*, in Griffiths's possession.

19. Trevor Griffiths, *Occupations*, rev. ed. (London: Faber and Faber, 1980), 17.

20. Giuseppe Fiori, *Antonio Gramsci: Life of a Revolutionary*, trans. Tom Nairn (London: NLB, 1970), 192.

21. Cave, *New British Drama in Performance*, 222.

22. Griffiths, "In Defense of *Occupations*," 7 *Days*, 8 Dec. 1971, 22; rptd. in *Occupations*, 8.

23. Hunt, "Theatre of Ideas," 139.

24. Thompson, "Socialist Humanism," 116.

25. Griffiths, "In Defense of *Occupations*," 9.

26. Trevor Griffiths, interview by Mike Poole and John Wyver, 15 July 1983; quoted in *Powerplays*, 35.

27. The original ending of *Occupations* featured an extensive monologue by Angelica, reaching back to her prerevolutionary life. Griffiths cut most of this speech when revising the play for a 1980 Dutch production. The original ending is printed as an appendix to the Faber and Faber edition of *Occupations*. For further discussion of Griffiths's use of Angelica in this play, see chapter 3.

28. Kenn Stitt, rev. of *Occupations*, *Tribune*, 13 Nov. 1970.

29. Brief surveys of the critical response to Griffiths's principal plays for theater can be found in Stanton B. Garner Jr., "Trevor Griffiths," in *British Playwrights, 1956–1995: A Research and Production Sourcebook*, ed. William W. Demastes (Westport, CN: Greenwood, 1996), 183–94.

30. Graham Stackpool, rev. of television production of *Occupations*, *Workers Press*, 7 Sept. 1974.

31. Tom Nairn, "Mucking about with Love and Revolution: Gramsci on Stage at the Place," *7 Days*, 10 Nov. 1971, 18–19.

32. Griffiths, "In Defense of *Occupations*," 8. Subsequent references to this essay will be indicated parenthetically within the text.

33. Nairn, "Mucking about with Love and Revolution," 19.

34. Trevor Griffiths, "Brand of the Recent Future," interview by Graham Taylor and Nigel Grey, *Street Life* (20 Mar.–2 Apr. 1976): 22.

35. Griffiths, interview by Hayman.

36. Trevor Griffiths, "Party Piece," interview by Kathleen Tynan, *Sunday Times Magazine*, 9 Dec. 1973, 85.

37. Stuart Burge, interview with Mike Poole and John Wyver, 29 June 1983; quoted in *Powerplays*, 52.

38. Griffiths, interview by Itzin and Trussler, 39.

39. Edward Braun, introduction to Griffiths, *Collected Plays for Television*, 11.

40. Griffiths, interview by Edward Braun, 8 May 1979; quoted in ibid. For a fuller discussion of the genesis of *Absolute Beginners*, see Edward Braun, "Trevor Griffiths," in *British Television Drama*, ed. George W. Brandt (Cambridge: Cambridge University Press, 1981), 63–64.

41. Trevor Griffiths, *Absolute Beginners*, *Collected Plays for Television*, 89–90.

42. Peter Weiss, *The Persecution and Assassination of Jean-Paul Marat as Performed by the Inmates of the Asylum of Charenton under the Direction of the Marquis de Sade*, English version by Geoffrey Skelton, verse adaptation by Adrian Mitchell (New York: Atheneum, 1984), 16. For a discussion of the politics of the revolutionary body, see Stanton B. Garner Jr., *Bodied Spaces: Phenomenology and Performance in Contemporary Drama* (Ithaca: Cornell University Press, 1994), 166–76.

Chapter 3

1. Griffiths, interview by Andrews, 82.

2. Howard Brenton, "Petrol Bombs through the Proscenium Arch," inter-

view by Catherine Itzin and Simon Trussler, *Theatre Quarterly* 5 (Mar.–May 1975): 16.

3. "When we wrote *Lay By*, it was like a Rugby outing. Whoever could yell loudest got their line in. Trevor yelled louder than anybody" (David Hare, qtd. in Tynan, "Party Piece," 82–85).

4. *Lay By* was published by Calder and Boyars (London, 1972).

5. Trevor Griffiths, résumé, Peters Fraser and Dunlop.

6. Elizabeth MacLennon, McGrath's wife and a member of 7:84, writes: "When he is feeling extraordinarily generous McGrath has been known to say that he only wrote *Trees* to provide something to precede Trevor's play[s?]" (*The Moon Belongs to Everyone: Making Theatre with 7:84* [London: Methuen, 1990], 120).

7. Nicholas de Jongh, rev. of *Apricots, Guardian*, 31 Aug. 1971.

8. Trevor Griffiths, *Apricots and Thermidor* (London: Pluto, 1978), 1.

9. "I've read as much Pinter as the next man," the Labor Exchange Clerk tells Sam One in *Sam, Sam* (66).

10. This use of the past as field of contest bears uncanny resemblance to the memory struggles in Pinter's *Old Times* (which opened in London four weeks before *Apricots*); Pinter's Kate, after all, uses the words "I remember you" to silence that play's Anna in the play's closing scene.

11. Griffiths, interview by Summers, 29.

12. Griffiths, interview by Karin Gartzke; quoted in Itzin, *Stages in the Revolution*, 172.

13. Griffiths, interview by Blackadar.

14. Griffiths, *Apricots and Thermidor*, 12.

15. Catherine Itzin, introduction to Griffiths, *Apricots and Thermidor*, [vi].

16. *Poems* opened on 29 March 1971 and played two weeks; typescripts of this and *Gun* are in Griffiths's possession. In addition to the plays mentioned in chapter 1, note 29, and chapter 4, note 21, and a number of dramatic sketches and fragments, typescripts of the following unproduced plays from early in his career are also in Griffiths's possession: *The Dream Life of Balso Snell*, a radio adaptation of Nathaniel West's short story, probably written in the mid- to late 1960s; and *Stud*, a television play; *Beano*, a play for theater; *Mopping Up*, a television adaptation of an unpublished short story; and *Cop Shop*, a television play, all written in the early 1970s.

17. Griffiths, interview by Boireau, 10.

18. An interesting glimpse into the behind-the-scenes negotiations concerning *The Party* can be found in Kenneth Tynan, *Letters*, ed. Kathleen Tynan (London: Weidenfeld and Nicolson, 1994), 537, 545–46.

19. Griffiths, interview by Boireau, 11. The use of the British Museum as a backdrop for the Lenin/Martov meeting in *Absolute Beginners* is an example of such appropriation.

20. See Loren Kruger's discussion of national theater and theatrical nationhood in *The National Stage: Theatre and Cultural Legitimation in England, France, and America* (Chicago: University of Chicago Press, 1992), 83–131.

21. Peter Hall, "Towards the Mountain Top," interview by Robert Cushman, *Plays and Players* 21 (Aug. 1974): 19.

22. Trevor Griffiths, letter, *Plays and Players*, 6.

23. Griffiths, interview by Boireau, 11.

24. Herbert Marcuse, "Repressive Tolerance," in *A Critique of Pure Tolerance*, by Robert Paul Wolff, Barrington Moore Jr., and Herbert Marcuse (Boston: Beacon Press, 1965), 81–117.

25. Trevor Griffiths, *The Party* (London: Faber and Faber, 1974), 12.

26. Cave describes this effect: "A disturbing sense of unreality prevails as the walls of the room dissolve (undermining one's conventional response to a naturalistic box-setting) to be replaced by the different dimension of film which reduces the actors to frozen silhouettes against the brightness of the screens" (*New British Drama in Performance*, 226).

27. Benedict Nightingale, rev. of *The Party*, *New Statesman*, 4 Jan. 1974, 25. For a different perspective on the play's mediated presentation of the events in Paris, see chapter 7, note 28.

28. Fraser, *1968: A Student Generation in Revolt*, 244.

29. Hugo Young, "Politics outside the System," in *The Decade of Disillusion: British Politics in the Sixties*, ed. David McKie and Chris Cook (London: Macmillan, 1972), 220.

30. Fraser, *1968*, 245. The parallel between this conservative reaction and Britain's response to earlier French revolutions was not lost on Griffiths.

31. Griffiths, interview by Itzin and Trussler, 40.

32. Sir Laurence Olivier, quoted in Peter Lewis, *The National: A Dream Made Concrete* (London: Methuen, 1990), 75. Griffiths parodies the actor's rhetorical bravura. In the play's prologue Groucho introduces "*an Olivier*" who performs a speech from *Timon of Athens*; when he's finished and disappears from the stage, Groucho remarks: "There's nobody speaking like that anymore, believe me" (11). Additional awareness of Olivier as a legend of the Shakespearean stage is suggested when Sloman exits the room quoting from *King Lear* at the end of act 1: "Go thou! I'll fetch some flax and whites of eggs, to apply to his bleeding face" (43).

33. Nightingale, rev. of *The Party*, 25; Harold Hobson, rev. of *The Party*, *Sunday Times*, 23 Dec. 1973; Robert Cushman, rev. of *The Party*, *Observer*, 30 Dec. 1973.

34. Michael Billington, rev. of *The Party*, *Guardian*, 5 Jan. 1974.

35. Griffiths, interview by Itzin and Trussler, 42.

36. Billington, rev. of *The Party*. Griffiths acknowledged a number of problems in the original production and in the play itself; he addressed many of these latter problems when revising *The Party* for its touring production.

37. John Elsom, rev. of *The Party*, *Listener*, 3 Jan. 1974, 30.

38. For an example of the leftist arguments against *The Party*'s cultural strategy, see Janet Wolff, Steve Ryan, Jim McGuigan, and Derek McKiernan, "Problems of Radical Drama: The Plays and Productions of Trevor Griffiths," in *Literature, Society and the Sociology of Literature*, ed. Francis Barker, John Coombs, Peter Hulme, David Musselwhite, Richard Osborne (Colchester: University of Essex, 1977), 133–53. Using *The Party* among his examples, John McGrath addressed the problems involved in challenging the bourgeois ideology from within established theater institutions. On the one hand, McGrath suggests,

such plays are in danger of being appropriated by the very ideology they seek to oppose (as when Olivier turned his role into a star vehicle). On the other hand, "this challenge to the dominance of bourgeois ideology on its own ground is important; it creates allies for the movement and is a weapon to use, and we are not in a position to throw any weapons away" ("The Theory and Practice of Political Theatre," *Theatre Quarterly* 9 [fall 1979]: 46).

39. Griffiths, interview by the author, 15–17 Nov. 1997.

40. Excerpts from Clive Morrison's log were published in "Building the Party," *Plays and Players* 364 (Jan. 1984): 11–14; and 365 (Feb. 1984): 18–20.

41. Griffiths, interview by Itzin and Trussler, 35.

42. Griffiths, interview by Summers, 24.

43. For a fuller discussion of this somewhat bizarre project, see Kathleen Tynan, *The Life of Kenneth Tynan* (London: Weidenfeld and Nicolson, 1987), 330–32. The typescript of *Come,* and Griffiths's extensive notes on it, are in the playwright's possession. After Tynan's death, in 1980, Griffiths assessed the critic's career in "Lost Leader," review of Kenneth Tynan, *Show People—Profiles in Entertainment, Quarto* (Dec. 1980): 19.

44. Colin Chambers and Mike Prior, *Playwright's Progress: Patterns of Postwar British Drama* (Oxford: Amber Lane, 1987), 114.

45. Ibid.

46. Ibid., 108.

47. At moments these encounters acquire an almost erotic quality: when Lenin and Martov greet each other in *Absolute Beginners,* they do so with "a love kiss of sorts" (88).

48. Michelene Wandor, *Look Back in Gender: Sexuality and the Family in Post-War British Drama* (London: Methuen, 1987), 107.

49. Ibid., 106.

50. Griffiths, interview by the author, 15–17 Nov. 1997. Griffiths describes the conflict underlying his experience of sexuality at that time: "I had a sort of libertarian take on sexuality because that was the air you breathed in the sixties. But I was coming out of a period and class space in which sexuality was nothing like that—it was very much repressed and suppressed and extraordinarily difficult to discourse—and where there was almost no help around in terms of literature, in terms of people" (ibid.).

51. Ibid.

52. Trevor Griffiths, *March Time,* unproduced screenplay, typescript (in folder dated Feb. 1987) in Griffiths's possession, 10.

53. Griffiths, interview by the author, 15–17 Nov. 1997.

Chapter 4

1. Griffiths, interview by Boireau, 16.

2. Griffiths, interview by Andrews, 83.

3. Arthur Marwick, *British Society since 1945* (Middlesex: Penguin, 1982), 121.

4. Griffiths, interview by Thomas, 12.

5. Griffiths, interview by Wyver, "Countering Consent," 36.

6. Raymond Williams, *The Long Revolution* (London: Chatto and Windus; New York: Columbia University Press, 1961), 38. See also *Communications*, rev. ed. (London: Chatto and Windus, 1966); and *Television: Technology and Cultural Form* (London: Fontana, 1974).

7. For a discussion of *Adam Smith*, see Poole and Wyver, *Powerplays*, 21–29. Although they were credited to other writers, additional episodes in the show's second series appear to be closely based on Griffiths's scripts (190). An incomplete collection of Griffiths's scripts for the series can be found in the British Film Institute's Trevor Griffiths Special Collection. By the time many of the episodes he had written were aired, Griffiths had quit his job with the BBC.

8. Griffiths, interview by Wyver, "Countering Consent," 32.

9. Trevor Griffiths, preface to *Through the Night, Collected Plays for Television*, 126.

10. Griffiths, preface to *Through the Night*, 128. See Hans Magnus Enzensberger, *Raids and Reconstructions: Essays on Politics, Crime, and Culture* (London: Pluto, 1976). In a paradox relevant to Griffiths's own sense of himself as a writer, one of the central contradictions of the consciousness industry, according to Enzensberger, is its dependence on intellectuals and other potentially radical voices: "This is an industry which has to rely, as its primary source, on the very minorities with whose elimination it is entrusted: those whose aim it is to invent and produce *alternatives*" (18).

11. Griffiths, interview by Summers, 23.

12. Trevor Griffiths, letter to Margaret Hare, 23 July 1971, Trevor Griffiths Special Collection.

13. Griffiths, preface to *Such Impossibilities, Collected Plays for Television*, 181.

14. Poole and Wyver, *Powerplays*, 48.

15. Colin McArthur, *Television and History* (London: BFI, 1980), 40; quoted in Poole and Wyver, *Powerplays*, 48.

16. Griffiths, preface to *Such Impossibilities*, 181.

17. Griffiths, *Such Impossibilities*, 206.

18. McArthur, *Television and History*, [ii], 29.

19. "Film footage of the police violence taken by a Pathé news cameraman was privately shown to a few of the strike's leaders, but the authorities warned that the pictures were not to be shown in public—'or else'" (Joseph White, *Tom Mann* [Manchester: Manchester University Press, 1991], 176).

20. Griffiths, preface to *Such Impossibilities*, 181. See Poole and Wyver, *Powerplays*, 49.

21. Griffiths's script for *The Silver Mask*, along with notes on the project, can be found in the Trevor Griffiths Special Collection. In 1973 Griffiths was commissioned to write a second play for London Weekend Television. Another of Griffiths's plays about the alienation attendant upon class translation, *There*, is the story of two brothers (a shirt cutter and a television producer) who meet to spend a day together in Manchester. This play, a typescript of which is in Griffiths's possession, was never produced. Information on other unproduced plays for television can be found in chapter 1, note 29, and chapter 3, note 16.

22. Trevor Griffiths, *All Good Men, Collected Plays for Television*, 39.

23. Poole and Wyver, *Powerplays,* 64.

24. Like others of Griffiths's plays, *All Good Men* succeeded in both overtaking and being overtaken by its own historical moment. In November 1973 the National Union of Mineworkers had declared a ban on weekend and overtime working in response to the Heath government's wage controls (this would be supported by railwaymen and electrical supply workers). By the date of the play's broadcast the country was in a declared state of emergency; in less than two weeks the miners would go on strike, and Heath had declared an election for the end of the month. The General Strike of 1926, also precipitated by a miners' strike, was very much on people's minds; a documentary by Robert Vas entitled *Nine Days in '26: The General Strike* was broadcast on BBC2 (opposite *Absolute Beginners,* it turned out) in April. Because of the 10:30 P.M. television curfew mandated by the state of emergency, the production text of *All Good Men* had to be cut from seventy-five to sixty-three minutes (see Poole and Wyver, *Powerplays,* 63).

25. Waite's memories, here and elsewhere, also include the voice of his estranged wife, who taunts him with a class condescension reminiscent of that heard in *Sam, Sam* and *Apricots.*

26. Stuart Hall, "Television and Culture," *Sight and Sound* 45 (fall 1976): 250.

27. McArthur, *Television and History,* 7.

28. Braun, introduction to Griffiths, *Collected Plays for Television,* 8.

29. Characterizing *All Good Men* as a bearbaiting, Patricia Beer writes: "The confrontation of the Labour leader about to turn peer . . . and his much-farther-to-the-Left son William . . . aroused sympathy not only for the bear but for the dogs, partly because the bear declared himself to be indestructible, which is what we always like to hear" (rev. of *All Good Men, Listener,* 7 Feb. 1974, 187).

30. A stage adaptation of *All Good Men* opened in a National Theatre lunchtime production at the Young Vic Studio on 13 May 1975.

31. Hall, "Television and Culture," 252.

32. See Garner, *Bodied Spaces,* esp. 32–34.

33. Griffiths, *Through the Night, Collected Plays for Television,* 159.

34. Revised (like other parts of the text) in response to solicited medical opinion, the scene between Christine and Pearce "bears all the torsions of organized BBC advice" (Griffiths, interview by Edward Braun, 8 May 1979; qtd. in "Trevor Griffiths," 71). Elsewhere Griffiths has commented on his concern with the play's potential message: "The fear was that the play would so frighten women at risk that, when a lump appeared in their body, they would not refer it . . . It was extremely important not to dissuade people from acting intelligently in their own lives" (interview by Taylor and Grey, 23).

35. Trevor Griffiths, *Bill Brand,* episode 11, rehearsal script, 56.

36. Griffiths, *All Good Men,* 41.

37. *BBC Audience Research Bulletin,* 1094 (6–12 Dec. 1975).

38. Marie Proops, "The Fear That Grows from a Tiny Lump," *Sunday Mirror,* 21 Dec. 1975; Eileen Price, "Screen Test for Fitness," *Somerset County Gazette,* 12 Dec. 1975.

39. Michael Rose, "End of an Illusion," *World Medicine,* 14 Jan. 1976, 7. Rose also writes: "At its worst [medicine] is practiced much as Trevor Griffiths' play

showed. The people work in a framework which mitigates against anything human. The institutionalization of health care has produced a ghastly caricature, to the extent that I question whether anyone who starts off human can remain human and still work in a hospital" (9).

40. Letters in Griffiths's possession.

41. Ibid.

42. Raymond Williams, *Culture and Society, 1780–1950* (New York: Columbia University Press, 1958), 303.

43. Griffiths, interview by Thomas, 12. For a fuller discussion of the genesis of *Bill Brand* and illuminating discussions of the series itself, see Poole and Wyver, 71–100; and Braun, "Trevor Griffiths," 72–79.

44. Braun, "Trevor Griffiths," 72.

45. Griffiths, interview by Taylor and Gray, 23.

46. Ibid.

47. Griffiths, *Bill Brand*, episode 7, 34. In the absence of a complete set of camera scripts, quotations from *Bill Brand* throughout this book are taken from the rehearsal scripts in the Trevor Griffiths Special Collection; episode and page numbers are indicated parenthetically. These scripts often differ from the broadcast episodes.

48. Griffiths, interview by Thomas, 12.

49. Ibid.

50. In an echo of Griffiths's aborted collaboration with Tynan, the group's touring show is entitled *Come*. Brand's friend (Jamie Finn) was played by Jonathan Pryce, who had recently electrified theater audiences in *Comedians*. Poole and Wyver discuss this avant-garde performance piece in the context of the series' ruling naturalism (*Powerplays*, 99–100).

51. In "Ten Years of Political Theater, 1968–78" (*Theater Quarterly* 8 [winter 1979]: 25–33) David Edgar used *Bill Brand* to question the strategy of appropriating mass-populist forms like television for radical ends. After suggesting that television addresses its audience in the "atomized, a-collective arena of the family living room, the place where people are at their least critical, their most conservative and reactionary" (30), he proposed that the majority of the spectators of Griffiths's series took an individual-psychological view of its lead character's actions and that they identified with Brand's socialism only for the duration of the play.

Chapter 5

1. Griffiths, *Bill Brand*, episode 8, rehearsal script, 31–32.

2. Translations of *Comedians* have also been published in Italian and Hungarian.

3. Trevor Griffiths, "Anything for a Laugh?" interview by Heather Neill, *Times Education Supplement*, 25 June 1993.

4. Griffiths, interview by Itzin and Trussler, 43–44.

5. Tise Vahimagi, *British Television: An Illustrated Guide* (Oxford: Oxford University Press, 1994), 195.

6. Griffiths, "From Home to House" interview by Jonathan Croall, *Times Education Supplement*, 25 June 1976. Elsewhere Griffiths remarks: "For a long time I'd done a double-take on my immediate response to gags and stand-up comics. Some of the things you find funniest you also find most reactionary, most supportive of prejudice. You get absolutely trapped inside a sort of dialectic: what the man is telling you is that it's right to despise Pakistani immigrants. Yet he makes you laugh *with* the proposition, not *at* it. So what has he liberated in me and what has he trapped in me?" ("Joking Apart," interview by Stephen Dixon, *Guardian*, 19 Feb. 1975). For a discussion of *Comedians* as a "meta-comedy," see Susan Carlson, "Comic Collisions: Convention, Rage, and Order," *New Theatre Quarterly* 12 (1987): 303–16.

7. Colin Mercer, "Complicit Pleasures," in *Popular Culture and Social Relations*, ed. Tony Bennett, Colin Mercer, and Janet Woollacott (Milton Keynes: Open University Press, 1986): 51. See also David Harris, *From Class Struggle to the Politics of Pleasure: The Effects of Gramscianism on Cultural Studies* (London: Routledge, 1992).

8. Mercer, "Complicit Pleasures," 54.

9. Trevor Griffiths, *Comedians* (London: Faber and Faber, 1976), 7.

10. Griffiths's handling of a dramatic time now identified with the time of performance has another, equally metatheatrical effect worth noting. When Waters arrives, he announces that the public performances that will constitute act 2 are set for 9:00 and that they need to be done with their preliminary business (the material of act 1) by 8:25. At the end of the act, he mentions, in reference to their postmortem back in the classroom (act 3), that they need to have the room vacated by 10:00. Since these times coincide with the play's own time, their specification directs attention to Griffiths's actors as performers working within segments and deadlines. Act 1 needs to be completed in no more than sixty minutes, and the play as a whole now must conclude by 10:00. If one of the conditions of realism is that the actor's histrionic performativity be submerged within the presentation of fictional character, then Griffiths's reflexive temporality calls attention to the actors as skilled performers in their own right, creating the play within their own performance constraints.

11. The absence of this live interaction is one of the reasons why Griffiths's television adaptation of *Comedians* was less successful than the stage version. For a discussion of this version, see Poole and Wyver, *Powerplays*, 101–14.

12. Griffiths, interview by Dixon.

13. Griffiths, interview by Croall.

14. This horrific image originated a couple of years before the play was written when Griffiths was bitten by a rat on a street in Rome. As he watched, "a blossom of blood" appeared through his trouser leg (Griffiths, interview by Neill).

15. Albert Wertheim, "Trevor Griffiths: Playwriting and Politics," in *Essays on Contemporary British Drama*, ed. Hedvig Bock and Albert Wertheim (Munich: Huber, 1981), 278. Wertheim compares Price to Vindice in Cyril Tourneur's *The Revenger's Tragedy*. Another engaging discussion of Price's routine can be found in Cave, *New British Drama in Performance*, 242–45.

16. For a discussion of *Comedians* in relation to Grock's clown theater, see Joel Schechter, *Durov's Pig: Clowns, Politics and Theatre* (New York: Theatre Communications Group, 1985), 134–41.

17. Benedict Nightingale, "Trevor Griffiths Isn't Kidding in 'Comedians,'" *New York Times*, 21 Nov. 1976. Pryce's performance in the play's original British and American productions (his role was taken over by Kenneth Cranham for the West End production only) was singled out by critics for its unnerving power; Harold Hobson wrote: "There is something of the charnel house about Mr. Pryce's long emaciated body and chalk-white face" (rev. of *Comedians, Sunday Times*, 5 Oct. 1977).

18. Eric Dunning, Patrick Murphy, and John Williams, *The Roots of Football Hooliganism: An Historical and Sociological Study* (London: Routledge and Kegan Paul, 1988), 173–77. Before a spring 1972 match between United and London's Arsenal club, a thousand red-scarved Manchester fans marched from King's Cross Station to Arsenal's North London stadium, breaking windows, smashing cars, throwing rocks, swearing at passersby, and virtually taking over part of London's North End (David Robins and Philip Cohen, *Knuckle Sandwich: Growing Up in the Working-Class City* [Middlesex: Penguin, 1978], 151). After the Red Army stormed the field during a match with Manchester City at the end of the 1973–74 season, a fence was erected to separate them from the field and from other fans; inspired by this cagelike segregation (and by the labeling of hooligans as "animals" in the British press), the "Stretford Enders" (as they were also called) adopted the chant, "We hate humans" (Dunning et al., *The Roots of Football Hooliganism*, 175).

19. Cave, *New British Drama in Performance*, 245.

20. Griffiths, interview by Summers, 28.

21. Griffiths, interview by Jack Kroll.

22. Griffiths, interview by Neill.

23. Griffiths, interview by Silburn, 33.

24. Oscar Lee Brownstein, "The Structure of Dramatic Language and of Dramatic Form," *Assaph* 2 (1985): 14.

25. Griffiths, interview by Boireau, 13.

26. Trevor Griffiths, "Closed Circuit," interview by W. Stephen Gilbert, *Guardian*, 17 Oct. 1981.

27. Ibid.

28. Raymond Williams, quoted in Griffiths, preface to *Through the Night*, 128.

29. Chambers and Prior, *Playwright's Progress*, 53.

30. Richard Eyre, interview by Stuart Young, 6 June 1985; quoted in David Allen, "'The Cherry Orchard': A New English Version by Trevor Griffiths," in *Chekhov on the British Stage*, ed. Patrick Miles (Cambridge: Cambridge University Press, 1993), 156–57.

31. Vera Gottlieb, "'The Dwindling Scale': The Politics of British Chekhov," in *Chekhov on the British Stage*, 149.

32. Trevor Griffiths, preface to *The Cherry Orchard: An English Version by Trevor Griffiths from a Translation by Helen Rappaport* (1978; rpt., London: Faber and Faber, 1989), [v].

33. Anton Chekhov, letters to Olga Knipper, 15 Sept. 1903 and 21 Sept. 1903; Konstantin Stanislavsky, letter to Chekhov, 20 Oct. 1903 (qtd. in Laurence Senelick, *Anton Chekhov* [Houndmills: Macmillan, 1985], 119).

34. Raymond Williams, *Modern Tragedy* (Stanford: Stanford University Press, 1966), 145.

35. Trevor Griffiths, interviews by David Allen, 19 Feb. 1987 and 1 Apr. 1987; quoted in Allen "'The Cherry Orchard,'" 166. I am indebted to Allen's essay for excerpts from these interviews.

36. Ibid., 163.

37. Ibid., 162.

38. Ibid.

39. "Why do you say in your telegram that my play is full of tears? Where are they? Only Varya, Varya alone, by her very nature, is a crybaby, and her tears must not promote a sense of sadness in the audience. You can often find in my plays the stage-direction 'through tears' but this points to the condition of the character and not the tears" (Chekhov, letter to Nemirovich-Danchenko, 21 Oct. 1903; qtd. in Senelick, *Anton Chekhov,* 119).

40. Griffiths, interviews by Allen, 157.

41. Ibid., 159.

42. Anton Chekhov, *The Cherry Orchard,* in *The Oxford Chekhov,* ed. and trans. Ronald Hingley (London: Oxford University Press, 1964), 3:170.

43. Benedict Nightingale, rev. of *The Cherry Orchard, New Statesman,* 18 Mar. 1977, 372. A television adaptation of Griffiths's *The Cherry Orchard,* also directed by Eyre, was broadcast by the BBC on 13 Oct. 1981.

44. For a fuller account of these problems and negotiations, see Poole and Wyver, *Powerplays,* 140–41.

45. Trevor Griffiths, "The Party Revisited," interview by Paul Allen, *Marxism Today* (May 1985): 39.

46. Trevor Griffiths, "Sons and Lovers," interview by John Charlton, *Socialist Worker,* 23 Jan. 1981, 13.

47. Trevor Griffiths, "Labours of Love," interview by Michael Hickling, *Yorkshire Post,* 16 Jan. 1981.

48. Griffiths, introduction to *Sons and Lovers,* 11. A shorter version of this essay was published as "A Novel Lawrence," *Radio Times* (10–16 Jan. 1981): 84–86.

49. Griffiths, interview by Charlton, 13.

50. Poole and Wyver, *Powerplays,* 147.

51. Trevor Griffiths, "The Classic Gets Some Class," interview by Mike Poole, *Time Out* (30 Jan.–5 Feb. 1981): 16.

52. Ibid.

53. Griffiths, interview by Swallow, 13–14.

54. Poole and Wyver provide an extensive and useful discussion of the production and design issues involved in the filming of *Sons and Lovers* (*Powerplays,* 141–46).

Chapter 6

1. *Deeds* was published in *Plays and Players* 25 (May 1978): 41–50 [act 1]; and 25 (June 1978): 43–50 [act 2].

2. Peter Jenkins, quoted in Alan Sked and Chris Cook, *Postwar Britain: A Political History*, 3d ed. (London: Penguin, 1990), 327. For examples of the writings on the "decline of Britain," see Stuart Hall, Chas Critcher, Tony Jefferson, John Clarke, and Brian Roberts, *Policing the Crisis: Mugging, the State, and Law and Order* (London: Macmillan, 1978); and Isaac Kramnick, ed., *Is Britain Dying? Perspectives on the Current Crisis* (Ithaca: Cornell University Press, 1979).

3. Tom Nairn, *The Break-Up of Britain: Crisis and Neo-Nationalism* (London: NLB, 1977), 51.

4. Stuart Hall, *The Hard Road to Renewal: Thatcherism and the Crisis of the Left* (London: Verso, 1988), 2.

5. Benedict Anderson, *Imagined Communities: Reflections on the Origin and Spread of Nationalism*, rev. ed. (London: Verso, 1991).

6. Raphael Samuel, "Continuous National History," in *Patriotism: The Making and Unmaking of British National Identity*, ed. Raphael Samuel (London: Routledge, 1989), 1:16.

7. Ibid., 9.

8. John Brecher, "Britain's Days of Rage," *Newsweek*, 20 July 1981, 34–36.

9. Margaret Thatcher, quoted in Anthony Barnett, *Iron Britannia* (London: Allison and Busby, 1982), 64.

10. Margaret Thatcher, speech at Cheltenham Race Course, 3 July 1982; reprinted in Barnett, *Iron Britannia*, 152, 150.

11. Barnett, *Iron Britannia*; Stuart Hall and Martin Jaques, eds., *The Politics of Thatcherism* (London: Lawrence and Wishart, 1983); Hall, *Hard Road to Renewal*; Geoff Hurd, ed., *National Fictions: World War Two in British Films and Television* (London: BFI, 1984); Paul Gilroy, *"There Ain't No Black in the Union Jack": The Cultural Politics of Race and Nation* (Chicago: University of Chicago Press, 1987). For an example of the immediate response to the Falklands War in the Marxist press, see Robert Gray, "Left Holding the Flag," *Marxism Today* 26 (Nov. 1982): 22–27.

12. Trevor Griffiths and Snoo Wilson, *Don't Make Waves*, typescript (rehearsal script?), Trevor Griffiths Special Collection, 28. Griffiths has referred to *Don't Make Waves* as "a sort of state of England play" (interview by Wyver, "Countering Consent," 38).

13. Griffiths, interview by Boireau, 19.

14. Trevor Griffiths, *Country: "A Tory Story," Collected Plays for Television*, 298.

15. Nairn, *Break-Up of Britain*, 273.

16. Angus Calder, *The People's War: Britain, 1939–1945* (New York: Random House, 1969). See also Richard Johnstone, "Television Drama and the People's War: David Hare's *Licking Hitler*, Ian McEwan's *The Imitation Game*, and Trevor Griffiths's *Country*," *Modern Drama* 28 (June 1985): 189–97.

17. Robert Hewison, *The Heritage Industry: Britain in a Climate of Decline* (London: Methuen, 1987), 10.

18. In addition to Hewison, see Patrick Wright, *On Living in an Old Country: The National Past in Contemporary Britain* (London: Verso, 1985); Corner and Harvey, eds., *Enterprise and Culture*; and Raphael Samuel, *Theatres of Memory*, vol. 1: *Past and Present in Contemporary Culture* (London: Verso, 1994).

19. Gilbert, "Closed Circuit." See also Mike Poole, rev. of *Country*, *New Statesman*, 30 Oct. 1981, 33. As Poole and Wyver note, *Country* is also indebted to Dodie Smith's *Dear Octopus*, a 1938 West End play that also deals with a family reunion at a rural mansion (*Powerplays* 161–62). In words that have special relevance to Griffiths's project, one of Smith's characters toasts the family, which is "like nearly every British institution, adaptable. It bends, it stretches—but it never breaks" (qtd. in ibid., 162).

20. Griffiths, "A View of the Country," interview by Jim Crace, *Radio Times* (17–22 Oct. 1981).

21. Griffiths, interview by Boireau, 19.

22. Braun, introduction to Griffiths, *Collected Plays for Television*, 24. Braun's discussion of *Country* is particularly insightful concerning the stylistic shift from Griffiths's earlier plays for television (22–27).

23. Dynastic in origins, the Carling Brewing and Malting Company was founded in Ontario in 1840 by Thomas Carling, who passed the business on to his son Sir John (Michael Jackson, ed., *The World Guide to Beer* [Englewood Cliffs, NJ: Prentice-Hall, 1977], 200–201).

24. Poole, rev. of *Country*, 34. Griffiths: "The key metaphor is that they're brewers, and that's the interface between that class and my class" (interview by Bragg).

25. Trevor Griffiths, interview by Mike Poole, "Mistaken Identities," *City Lights* (16–22 Apr. 1982): 38.

26. "I've always been interested in street behavior and street people," Griffiths commented in his 1984 *South Bank Show* interview, "because I was one as a kid growing up and because my own son, to some extent, replicates this in his own life" (interview by Bragg).

27. Dave Laing, *One Chord Wonders: Power and Meaning in Punk Rock* (Milton Keynes: Open University Press, 1985): 112.

28. The skinheads, Clarke writes, "were the 'dispossessed inheritors'; they received a tradition which had been deprived of its real social bases. The theme and imagery still persisted, but the reality was in a state of decline and disappearance" (John Clarke, "The Skinheads and the Magical Recovery of Community," in *Resistance through Rituals: Youth Subcultures in Post-War Britain* [London: Hutchinson, 1976], 100). See also the brief but suggestive discussion of skinhead subculture in Dick Hebdige, *Subculture: The Meaning of Style* (London: Methuen, 1979), 54–59.

29. Michael Billig, *Fascists: A Social Psychological View of the National Front* (London: Academic Press, 1978), 293.

30. Margaret Thatcher, television interview, 30 Jan. 1978; quoted in Billig, *Fascists*, 348; Stuart Hall, "The Great Moving Right Show," in Hall and Jaques, eds., *Politics of Thatcherism*, 22.

31. Hall, *Hard Road to Renewal*, 77.

32. Eddie Morrison, in *Spearhead* (Mar. 1981); quoted in Gilroy, *"There Ain't No Black in the Union Jack,"* 124.

33. See Lucy Hodges, "Racists Recruit Youth through Rock Music," *Times*, 3 Aug. 1981; and "Bands Deny Right-Wing Allegiance," *Times*, 4 Aug. 1981. John Jacobs, drummer for the 4-Skins, said about the National Front: "We don't need it; it's no good for us" (qtd. in James LeMoyne and Ann Jennings, "Oi—Music to Riot By," *Newsweek*, 31 Aug. 1981, 35).

34. Griffiths, interview by Poole, "Mistaken Identities," 38.

35. Hall and others offered a similar challenge in *Policing the Crisis*, their influential study of the social discourse surrounding mugging. A recent book on gay skinheads demonstrates how radically even skinhead subculture can be appropriated to ends different from those of many of its participants; see Murray Healy, *Gay Skins: Class, Masculinity and Queer Appropriation* (London: Cassell, 1996).

36. Trevor Griffiths, *Oi for England, Collected Plays for Television*, 303.

37. Griffiths, interview by Paul Allen, 39.

38. Gilroy, *"There Ain't No Black in the Union Jack,"* 52.

39. Poole, "Mistaken Identities," 39.

40. Griffiths, quoted in ibid., 39.

41. Poole and Wyver, *Powerplays*, 175; Stuart Cosgrove, "Refusing Consent: The 'Oi for England' Project," *Screen* 24 (Jan.–Feb. 1983): 93.

42. Alan Sinfield, "Culture and Contest: *Oi for England* by Trevor Griffiths and the End of Consensus Politics," *Thema* 3 (1986): 425.

43. A German version of *Oi for England*, with the title *Skins*, was produced in Tübingen in May 1987.

44. Mike Poole, "Trying to Get under the Skins," *Guardian*, 7 June 1982; reprinted in Poole and Wyver, *Powerplays*, 177.

45. Ibid, 178. The play's South Yorkshire tour ran into controversy. Local councillors objected to the play's language, and one left-wing councillor refused to fund the project out of concern that it might promote racism and that audiences wouldn't stay for the post-performance discussion. See Robin Thornber, *"Oi* Hits a Cultural Brick Wall," *Guardian*, 8 Oct. 1982.

46. Quoted in Roland Huntford, *Scott and Amundsen* (1979; rpt., New York: G. P. Putnam's Sons, 1980), 560.

47. Charles Friend, dir., *Scott of the Antarctic*, Ealing Studios, London, 1948. As a figure of heroic failure, Scott retains his cultural currency. When British tennis hopeful Greg Rusedski lost his 1995 fourth-round Wimbledon match to defending champion Pete Sampras, the model of American tennis efficiency, Martin Wainwright of the *Guardian* characterized his loss as "in the best British Captain Scott tradition" ("Home Town of Hero's Mother Tries for Net Gain," *Guardian*, 4 July 1995).

48. Huntford, 574. Amundsen, understandably, was bitter over this.

49. Trevor Griffiths, "Truth Is Otherwise," interview by Misha Glenny, in *Judgment over the Dead: The Screenplay of* The Last Place on Earth (London: Verso, 1986), ix, x.

50. For further information on the genesis and production of *The Last*

Place on Earth, see Minty Clinch, "Scott on the Rocks," *Sunday Times,* 10 Feb. 1985; John Wyver, "Hero Caught in the Blast," *Times,* 11 Feb. 1985; and Mike Poole, "Follow the Leader," *Listener,* 14 Feb. 1985, 27–28. American playwright Ted Talley also dramatized the Scott expedition in his 1977 play *Terra Nova.*

51. Griffiths, interview by Glenny, xxiv.

52. Trevor Griffiths, "Hope and Glory," interview by Geoff Dyer, *City Limits* (15–21 Feb. 1985): 15.

53. Griffiths, *Judgment over the Dead,* 67–68. Unless otherwise indicated, references to the series will refer to Griffiths's published script, which does not reflect the extensive cuts and changes made during production.

54. Thatcher, speech at Cheltenham Race Course, 150, 153.

55. C. M. Woodhouse, quoted by Griffiths, interview by Glenny, xxxv.

56. Griffiths, interview by Glenny, xix.

57. Trevor Griffiths, interview by John Tulloch, Nov. 1985; quoted in Tulloch, *Television Drama: Agency, Audience and Myth* (London: Routledge, 1990), 143.

58. This comparison is noted in Poole, "Follow the Leader," 28.

59. Tulloch, *Television Drama,* 101.

60. Griffiths, quoted in Poole, "Follow the Leader," 27; Griffiths, interview by Dyer, 15.

61. Poole, "Follow the Leader," 27.

62. Huntford, *Scott and Amundsen,* 564.

63. Griffiths, quoted in Wyver, "Hero Caught in Icy Blast."

64. Tulloch, *Television Drama,* 142. Tulloch provides the fullest account of the controversy surrounding *The Last Place on Earth;* see esp. 142–51.

65. Griffiths, interview by Glenny, xxvii. Examples of this framing include Lord Kennet's *Times* letter, 18 Feb. 1995, printed the day the first episode was to air, and his letter to the *Observer,* 24 Feb. 1985. D. J. Drewry, director of the Scott Polar Research Institute, attacked the series in a letter to the *Times,* 16 Feb. 1985, while Peter Scott expressed outrage at the treatment of his parents (see Lynda Lee-Potter, "The Love Lies about My Mother," *Daily Mail,* 12 Feb. 1985). For a discussion of press response to the series, see Tulloch, 142–49. As the previously cited articles by Wyver, Poole, and Dyer attest, *The Last Place on Earth* did receive sympathetic coverage by journalists on the Left.

66. Griffiths, letter, *Observer,* 10 Mar. 1985.

67. A *TLS* reviewer wrote: "What seems particularly unfair . . . is that, in many ways, Scott's mentality strikingly resembles Griffiths's own: both are dourly doctrinaire; locked into an ideological way of viewing things, they have virtually no awareness of individual complexity, and see life in crude oppositions" (Peter Kemp, rev. of *The Last Place on Earth, TLS,* 5 Apr. 1985).

68. See, for example, Bernard Levin, "What Made Scott Brave," *Times,* 9 Mar. 1993; and Ann Shirley, letter, *Times,* 23 Mar. 1993.

69. Griffiths, quoted in Wyver, "Hero Caught in Icy Blast."

70. Griffiths, interview by Glenny, xxxviii.

Chapter 7

1. Catherine Itzin, "Postscript: 1970 and the Future," *Stages in the Revolution,* 337–39.

2. Trevor Griffiths, interview by Catherine Itzin, 1979; quoted in ibid., 174–75.

3. Griffiths, interview by the author, 15–17 Nov. 1997.

4. Ibid.

5. Griffiths, interview by Boireau, 21.

6. Nikolai Lenin, introduction to John Reed, *Ten Days that Shook the World* (London: Penguin, 1966), [7].

7. For those interested in Griffiths's work on the *Reds* screenplay, a folder in the Trevor Griffiths Special Collection marked "John Reed a.k.a. Comrades a.k.a. Reds" includes preliminary notes, research materials, and scattered jottings that show Griffiths visualizing scenes, shaping lines and passages. The folder also contains drafts of *John Reed* and *Comrades.*

8. Trevor Griffiths, "History to Hollywood," interview by Mike Eaton, *Screen* 23 (July–Aug. 1982): 64. For my account of the *Reds* project I am indebted to this interview, to Poole and Wyver, *Powerplays,* 122–39, and to Griffiths himself. After dissociating himself from the *Reds* project, Griffiths published the final scenes of *Comrades* (Reed's death in a Moscow hospital) in *Write thru the Year,* ed. Nigel Gray (Northampton: Northampton Press, 1980), 13–16.

9. Griffiths, interview by Eaton, 65.

10. Poole and Wyver, *Powerplays,* 123, 127.

11. Griffiths, interview by Boireau, 21.

12. Griffiths, interview by Eaton, 63–64.

13. Warren Beatty, dir., *Reds,* film, Paramount, 1981. Subsequent references to *Reds* are taken directly from the film.

14. Upton Sinclair, quoted in Poole and Wyver, *Powerplays,* 124.

15. Griffiths, interview by Eaton, 64.

16. Edward Buscombe, "Making Love and Revolution," *Screen* 23 (July–Aug. 1982): 73; Poole and Wyver, *Powerplays,* 129.

17. Griffiths, interview by Eaton, 65.

18. Ibid., 63.

19. Griffiths, "Correspondent Questionnaire," 54.

20. Seth Cagin and Philip Dray, *Born to Be Wild: Hollywood and the Sixties Generation,* 2d ed. (Boca Raton, FL: Coyote, 1994).

21. Poole and Wyver, *Powerplays,* 138–39.

22. Hewison, *Heritage Industry,* 47.

23. *Reds* also spurred a round of publishing ventures: paperback reissues of Reed's *Ten Days That Shook the World* (Penguin) and Bryant's *Six Red Months in Russia* (Journeyman) and the publication of historical polemical texts, some for the first time. Griffiths contributed a preface to the published text of Dora Russell's 1921 pamphlet *The Soul of Russia and the Body of America* (London: Open Head Press, 1982), 3.

24. Griffiths, interview by Eaton, 65.

25. This account is taken from "Washington Talk," *New York Times*, 8 Dec. 1981.

26. Griffiths, *Real Dreams* (London: Faber and Faber, 1987), 3. Jeremy Pikser's "Revolution in Cleveland" is also published in this edition. *Five Nights in Unamerica* has never been published. Pikser, who helped Griffiths research *Reds* and worked on the film after Griffiths left the project, later collaborated with Warren Beatty on the screenplay for the 1998 film *Bulworth*.

27. Trevor Griffiths, "Back to the Barricades," interview by Desmond Christy, *Guardian*, 28 Apr. 1986.

28. Griffiths, interview by the author, 6 July 1995. Griffiths elaborates: "I've always tried to see '68 in relation to the '50s rather than as a cataclysmic moment . . . When I come to look at '68 in *The Party*—and the passion is there, in the film and whatever else I used to try and give the sense of action—it's also quite cool, in the play's center. It's both momentous and contained; it doesn't sweep people away. It's something to be looked at and judged, evaluated. One's identity [is] not massively challenged. That's how I felt in '68. I didn't know what to make of France. I was hugely excited by it, but I sensed that it could structurally go nowhere."

29. Trevor Griffiths, "Back to the Stage," interview by Lynn Truss, *Times Higher Education Supplement*, 9 May 1986.

30. Irving Wardle, rev. of *Real Dreams*, *Times*, 17 May 1986.

31. Lenin, *What Is to Be Done?* quoted in Georg Lukács, *The Meaning of Contemporary Realism*, trans. John and Necke Mandes (London: Merlin, 1963), 126.

32. In this respect *Real Dreams* bears interesting resemblance to David Edgar's 1983 play *Maydays*, which also offers a retrospective analysis of postwar Marxism. At the end of a play in which organized socialism reveals its flaws and former radicals embrace versions of 1980s reaction, one of the characters affirms "something in the nature of our species which resents, rejects and ultimately will resist a world that is demonstrably and in this case dramatically wrong and mad and unjust and unfair" ([London: Methuen, 1983], 146). In the program to the London production of *Real Dreams* Griffiths acknowledged a debt to Edgar's play.

33. Griffiths, interview by Dixon.

34. Griffiths, interview by Hemming.

35. See John Page, *Film on Four: 1982–1991* (London: BFI, 1992), 145.

36. Pannach and his partner, Christian Kunert, with whom he was expelled, wrote the music for *Fatherland*. The character of Drittemann also clearly owes a debt to Wolf Biermann, a dissident East German poet and singer who had been popular in both Germanies during the 1970s. In November 1976 Biermann was allowed to accept an invitation to play two public concerts in West Germany, but after the first concert his visa was revoked, and he found himself unable to return. Though Biermann's songs were critical of the East German government, he remained a committed Marxist, defended the existence of the first German socialist state, and expressed his dislike for the West German state on a number of occasions. In the wake of his forced emigration he was offered lucrative television and recording contracts. For an example of the widespread media cov-

erage of Biermann's forced exile, see Dan van der Vat, "Marxist Songster as Out of Place in West Germany as in East," *Times*, 19 Nov. 1976.

37. On the Wall dreams in *Fatherland* Griffiths has observed: "They attest the pressure under which people like Drittemann operate—the unfinished business of the psyche, of the materials of the inner life that get so flattened and bleached out in social living in the DDR. . . . A lot of people that I talked to in both East and West Berlin have Wall dreams" (interview by John Tulloch, Nov. 1985; qtd. in Tulloch, *Television Drama*, 157).

38. Trevor Griffiths, *Fatherland* (London: Faber and Faber, 1987), 13.

39. These directions were not followed in Loach's film.

40. This is a long-standing interest: in the fall of 1977 Griffiths was named to an international tribunal set up by the Bertrand Russell Peace Foundation to look into allegations that human rights in West Germany were being threatened by anti-terrorist measures ("'Tribunal' to Hear Charges against Bonn," *Times*, 29 Oct. 1977).

41. Milan Kundera, *The Book of Laughter and Forgetting*, trans. Michael Henry Heim (Middlesex: Penguin, 1981), 206. The figure of Kurtz from Conrad's *Heart of Darkness* also stands as backdrop here.

42. "Europeans tend to have an unexamined sense of their own history, imagining that we have a morally defensible or even proud record, when the truth is it stinks. *Fatherland* begins a deconstruction of that false history" (Trevor Griffiths, "Drittemann, Poor Man," interview by Simon Banner, *Guardian*, 26 Mar. 1987).

43. "This film is about someone coming from East to West but in a deeper biographical sense it's also about where I am now and where writers like me are *now*. . . . Where do we live?" (Trevor Griffiths, "No Place like Home," interview by Steve Grant, *Time Out* [25 Mar.–1 Apr. 1987]: 24).

44. Griffiths, interview by the author, 15–17 Nov. 1997.

45. Tulloch, *Television Drama*, 156.

46. John Tulloch, *Television Drama*, 161. I am indebted to Tulloch's discussion of the *Fatherland* project for information in this paragraph (see 155–65).

47. Among other changes the two sex scenes were cut from the final film, and the closing concert scene was replaced with a scene of Klaus in rehearsal. For a critique of the film, see John Hill, "Finding a Form: Politics and Aesthetics in *Fatherland, Hidden Agenda*, and *Riff-Raff*," in *Agent of Challenge and Defiance: The Films of Ken Loach*, ed. George McKnight (Westport, CN: Greenwood, 1997). Loach himself acknowledges: "*Fatherland* was a big disappointment. I directed in a way that was not appropriate to the script and so it was a lost opportunity" (interview by John Hill, Nov. 1994, *Agent of Challenge and Defiance*, 163).

48. Griffiths, interview by the author, 15–17 Nov. 1997.

49. Ibid.

50. Ibid.

51. A different adaptation of *A Midnight Clear*, written and directed by Keith Gordon, was produced in 1991 by Beacon Communications and A&M Films.

52. Griffiths, interview by the author, 15–17 Nov. 1997.

53. Trevor Griffiths, *Acts of Love*, 52, typescript (revised first draft, dated Apr. 1986) in Griffiths's possession.

54. Griffiths, interview by the author, 15–17 Nov. 1997.

55. Griffiths, interview by Tulloch, 111.

56. Griffiths, interview by the author, 15–17 Nov. 1997. I am indebted to Gill Griffiths for information on the Miners' Strike project and, indeed, for information concerning all the projects in this section.

57. Trevor Griffiths, "*March Time:* Notes for Reworking the Last Section of the Play," in Griffiths's possession.

58. Griffiths, interview by the author, 15–17 Nov. 1997.

59. Ibid.

60. Griffiths, *March Time*, 87.

61. For additional discussion of the *March Time* screenplay, see Müller-Hartwigsen, *Trevor Griffiths*, 231–39.

62. Griffiths, interview by the author, 15–17 Nov. 1997.

63. Griffiths, *These Are the Times*, 220. For Griffiths there are personal echoes to this. In the fall of 1986 the BBC celebrated its fiftieth anniversary with events and retrospectives. When it came to drama, Griffiths recalls, the leftist dramatists who had been such an important presence in the 1960s and 1970s were almost completely absent, "filleted out" (interview by the author, 15–17 Nov. 1997).

64. Ronald Reagan, speech to the Annual Convention of the National Association of Evangelicals, Orlando, 8 Mar. 1983, in *Speaking My Mind: Selected Speeches* (New York: Simon and Schuster, 1989), 180.

65. Griffiths, *These Are the Times*, 215.

Chapter 8

1. Trevor Griffiths, "Still Thinking about the Revolution," interview by Douglas Kennedy, *Sunday Telegraph*, 12 Jan. 1992.

2. John McGrath, quoted in "Theater in Thatcher's Britain: Organizing the Opposition," *New Theatre Quarterly* 18 (May 1989): 121.

3. A report on this conference can be found in Andy Lavender, "Theater in Crisis: Conference Report, December 1988," *New Theatre Quarterly* 19 (Aug. 1989): 210–16.

4. Howard Barker, "1989," *The Ascent of Monte Grappa* (London: Calder; New York: Riverrun, 1991), 56.

5. Ibid.

6. Tariq Ali and Howard Brenton, explanatory note to *Moscow Gold* (London: Nick Hern, 1990), [viii].

7. Rafelson, who had a three-picture deal with Carelco, approached Griffiths with the idea in November 1989. Griffiths completed a first draft in November 1990 and a second draft the following March. The screenplay was not produced.

8. Trevor Griffiths, interview by the author, 29 July 1993. With *Fatherland*, which preceded the initial wave of British post–Cold War plays by four years,

Griffiths had already written his State of Europe text; indeed, its portrayal of globalizing capitalism anticipates the forces that will bring the Wall down with remarkable prescience.

9. Trevor Griffiths, "New World Order," interview by Quintin Bradley, *Northern Star* (9–16 Jan. 1992).

10. In 1992 Griffiths commented on *The Gulf between Us:* "This play is partly about the anger within me about the Gulf War, but it's tied in with a great many other things around the world: the collapse of the post-Stalinist bureaucracies, the assertion of political and economic hegemony over this society by Reagan, Bush, and their cohorts" (ibid).

11. Trevor Griffiths, interview by Hemming.

12. Trevor Griffiths, "The Politics of Coping," interview by A. C. H. Smith, *Guardian*, 17 May 1993.

13. Fredric Jameson, "Cognitive Mapping," in *Marxism and the Interpretation of Culture*, ed. Cary Nelson and Lawrence Grossberg (Urbana: University of Illinois Press, 1988), 347–57.

14. Griffiths, interview by the author, 29 July 1993.

15. Trevor Griffiths and Bob Rafelson, *Dead Drop*, 42, typescript (first draft, 29 Nov. 1990) in Griffiths's possession.

16. Griffiths, *These Are the Times*, 113. Referring to Paine's voyage back to Europe and the French Revolution, one character states, "He had a bridge to build and Europe seemed the place" (120).

17. Anna Lawton, *Kinoglasnost: Soviet Cinema in Our Time* (Cambridge: Cambridge University Press, 1992), 27. For more information on *Unfinished Piece for Mechanical Piano*, see Margarita Kvasnetskaya, "A Matter of Conscience," *Soviet Film* 77, no. 5 (1977): 13–15.

18. Trevor Griffiths, author's preface, *Piano* (London: Faber and Faber, 1990), [v].

19. John Peter, rev. of *Piano, Sunday Times*, 12 Aug. 1990.

20. Trevor Griffiths, quoted in Peter Sherwood, "Playing with a Play's Peasants," *TLS*, 17 Aug. 1990. Chekhov's fiction, of course, was not immune to this interference: both "My Life," a story of a young man's rejection of upper-class for working-class life, and "Peasants," a harrowing account of the poverty and hardship of peasant life in Russia, were heavily censored before publication; these deletions were restored when the stories were subsequently published in book form. See Simon Karlinski, ed., *Anton Chekhov's Life and Thought: Selected Letters and Commentary*, trans. Michael Henry Heim, in collaboration with Simon Karlinski (Berkeley: University of California Press, 1975), 290–92.

21. For Chekhov's original version of these lines, see "My Life," in *The Oxford Chekhov*, ed. and trans. Ronald Hingley (London: Oxford University Press), 8:134–35.

22. The cross-citing of media is more complicated still, since *Unfinished Piece* had been a stage play before Abadashian and Mikhalkov made it into a film.

23. Williams, *Modern Tragedy*, 139; cited in Griffiths, author's preface, *Piano*, [v].

24. "I think the tone in *Piano* is more Gorky than Chekhov. It's harsher, blacker" (Trevor Griffiths, "And Now the Play of the Film of the Play," inter-

view by Lynn Truss, *Independent on Sunday*, 5 Aug. 1990). Griffiths faults the National Theatre production for abandoning the play's dangerous qualities in favor of something "classic, safe . . . very well defended" (interview by the author, 15–17 Nov. 1997). *Piano* was subsequently produced, twice, in Tokyo.

25. Anton Chekhov, *Platonov*, trans. David Magarshack (New York: Hill and Wang, 1964), 26.

26. Griffiths, interview by the author, 29 July 1993.

27. Trevor Griffiths, introduction, *The Gulf between Us or The Truth and Other Fictions* (London and Boston: Faber and Faber, 1992), v.

28. Griffiths, interview by Hemming.

29. Griffiths, interview by the author, 29 July 1993.

30. Griffiths, interview by Hemming.

31. See Caroline Lees and John Furbisher, "Gulf War Play Angers Veterans," *Sunday Times*, 12 Jan. 1992.

32. Trevor Griffiths, "The Plot Thickens," interview by Anne Creyke, *Yorkshire Evening Post*, 27 Dec. 1991.

33. Griffiths, interview by Hemming. Georgia Makhlouf describes the traditional Gukha/Goha as a marginal, ambiguous character who participates in different social worlds but does not belong to either and who is "an anarchist in spontaneous revolt against the prevailing social order which imposes its own vision of reality" ("Goha the Simple or the Wisdom of Folly," *UNESCO Courier* 35 [June 1982]: 27). One of the most recognizable Western descendants of the Gukha/Goha is the character Azdak in Brecht's play *The Caucasian Chalk Circle*.

34. Griffiths, interview by Hemming.

35. Ibid. "I'm probably more anarchist now than I've ever been" (Griffiths, interview by the author, 29 July 1993).

36. Ibid.

37. Michael Billington, one of the few reviewers who appreciated the play's stylistic innovations, characterized *The Gulf between Us* as "a strange, dreamlike mix of Arabian Nights fable and Storey-esque work-play" (rev. of *The Gulf between Us*, *Guardian*, 23 Jan. 1992).

38. Since actors are not bricklayers, the wall collapsed on stage "with depressing regularity" (Trevor Griffiths, "Play It Again, Trevor," interview by Eric Roberts, *Yorkshire Post*, 4 May 1996).

39. Jameson, "Cognitive Mapping," 355.

40. Herbert Marcuse, *An Essay on Liberation* (Boston: Beacon, 1969), 25. "The practice of shared life," Griffiths has suggested, "is buried alive in your muscular memory" ("Theatre of Hope," interview by Max Farrar, *Red Pepper* 25 [June 1996]: 22).

41. Griffiths, introductory note and dedication, *Hope in the Year Two and Thatcher's Children* (London: Faber and Faber, 1994), [vii].

42. Arts Council Drama director Ian Brown, letter, 13 May 1992; quoted in the theater program for *Thatcher's Children*.

43. For the central character Gyp, Griffiths also drew upon the experience of his son Joss. Both Griffiths and his son contributed song lyrics to *God's Armchair*.

44. Griffiths, quoted in the theater program for *Thatcher's Children*.

45. Griffiths, introductory note and dedication, *Hope in the Year Two and Thatcher's Children*, [vii].

46. Griffiths, interview by Smith.

47. *Thatcher's Children* is also, Griffiths suggests, the story of his own children; when the play opened, both of his daughters had left the country in search of work, and his son was unemployed (interview by Smith).

48. Griffiths has always been drawn to the young: in 1972, when he was establishing himself as a writer, he published a children's story entitled *Tip's Lot* (London: Macmillan, 1972) for a progressive Macmillan series about working and middle-class kids (it sold quite well), and over his career he has accepted numerous invitations to visit schools.

49. Griffiths, *Hope in the Year Two and Thatcher's Children*, 51.

50. Trevor Griffiths, "Never Time for Sleeping with the Enemy," interview by Andrew Billen, *Observer*, 16 May 1993.

51. Trevor Griffiths, "Lines of Greatest Resistance," interview by Andy Lavender, *Times*, 18 May 1993.

52. Stuart Hall, "The Meaning of New Times," in *New Times: The Changing Face of Politics in the 1990s*, ed. Stuart Hall and Martin Jaques (London: Verso, 1990), 129, 120.

53. Griffiths, quoted in the program for *Thatcher's Children*. In its development the *Thatcher's Children* project recalls the collaborative work of Joint Stock and other theater collectives of the 1970s.

54. Ibid.; Trevor Griffiths, "Trevor's Thatcher," interview by Kate Withers, *Venue*, 27 May 1993, 46.

55. Jonathan Bignell, "Trevor Griffiths's Political Theatre: From *Oi for England* to *The Gulf between Us*," *New Theatre Quarterly* 37 (Feb. 1994): 56.

56. Griffiths, interview by Smith.

57. Griffiths, quoted in the program for *Thatcher's Children*.

58. Ruth Levitas, *The Concept of Utopia* (Hemel Hempstead: Philip Allan, 1990), 181.

59. Trevor Griffiths, interview by Withers.

Chapter 9

1. Trevor Griffiths, letter to the author, 7 Feb. 1995.

2. The title and narrative design of this project were also influenced by Eduardo de Filippo's comedy *Filumena: A Marriage Italian Style*.

3. Griffiths resumed work on *Filastinuna* in summer 1998.

4. Trevor Griffiths, author's note, program for *Who Shall Be Happy . . . ?*

5. Griffiths, *These Are the Times*, 109–10.

6. Derrida, *Specters of Marx*, xix.

7. Ibid.

8. Ibid., 37.

9. Ibid., 11, xix.

10. Ibid., 11.

11. Heiner Müller, from "SELFCRITIQUE" (pt. 3 of "Television"), in *The Battle:*

Plays, Prose, Poems, ed. and trans. Carl Weber (New York: PAJ Publications, 1989), 176.

12. Trevor Griffiths, interview by Hemming.

13. Linda Henderson said this on "Night Waves," BBC Radio 3, 7 Nov. 1995. Michael Billington called it "political theater at its most intelligent and Griffiths's best play in years" (*Guardian,* 8 June 1996).

14. Griffiths, interview by Boireau.

15. Stuart Hall, "Gramsci and Us," *Hard Road to Renewal,* 162. This relevance may also animate what Tony Bennett calls "the turn to Gramsci" in contemporary political and cultural theory ("Introduction: Popular Culture and 'the Turn to Gramsci,'" in *Popular Culture and Social Relations,* xi–xix).

16. Alessandro Pertini, quoted in Frank Rosengarten, introduction to Antonio Gramsci, *Letters from Prison,* ed. Frank Rosengarten, trans. Raymond Rosenthal (New York: Columbia University Press, 1994), 1:7.

17. Griffiths, *Hope in the Year Two and Thatcher's Children,* 39. Because Griffiths's television version was the first to be produced and published, and because the two plays are very close, the following discussion will focus on *Hope in the Year Two.*

18. Trevor Griffiths, interview by Smith.

19. William Shakespeare, *Richard II,* 5.5.9, in *The Riverside Shakespeare,* textual editor G. Blakemore Evans (Boston: Houghton Mifflin, 1974), 835.

20. Griffiths, interview by the author, 29 July 1993.

21. Francis Fukuyama, "The End of History?" *National Interest* 16 (summer 1989): 4.

22. Jean Baudrillard, "The Year 2000 Has Already Happened," in *Body Invaders: Panic Sex in America,* ed. Arthur and Marilouise Kroker (New York: St. Martin's, 1987), 36. Baudrillard discusses the Berlin Wall as an example of this postmodern disappearance of history in "The Anorexic Ruins," in *Looking Back on the End of the World,* ed. Dietmar Kamper and Christoph Wulf (New York: Semiotext[e], 1989), 35–36.

23. "Postmodernism must at all costs efface [history], or spatialize [it] to a range of possible styles, if it is to persuade us to forget that we have ever known or could know any alternative to itself" (Terry Eagleton, "Capitalism, Modernism and Postmodernism," *New Left Review* 152 [July–Aug. 1985]: 68). For a different view of postmodernism's attitude toward history, see Linda Hutcheon, *A Poetics of Postmodernism: History, Theory, Fiction* (New York and London: Routledge, 1988), esp. 15–16, 87–101.

24. Norman Hampson, *Danton* (London: Duckworth, 1978), vii–viii. Hampson provides a useful survey of historians' changing portraits of Danton (1–17).

25. Daniel Guérin, *La Lutte de classes sous la Première République, 1793–1797,* rev. ed. (Paris: Gallimard, 1968); quoted in Hampson, *Danton,* 17.

26. For a brief time in the late 1980s, it was Robespierre who most interested Griffiths as a potential dramatic subject: "The more I read about Robespierre the more he reminds me of Thatcher. . . . I mean, the essence of bourgeois thinking" (Griffiths, interview by Hans-Peter Müller-Hartwigsen, 1988; qtd. in *Trevor Griffiths,* 241).

27. Trevor Griffiths, "French Resolution," interview by Steve Grant, *Time Out* (11–18 May 1994).

28. Ibid.

29. This framing device was omitted from the television production.

30. Griffiths, interview by the author, 29 July 1993.

31. The most complete historical discussion of the lore surrounding Danton's final days can be found in François-Alphonse Aulard's "Derniers moments et exécution de Danton," *La Révolution Française* 75 (1922): 5–25.

32. Hayden White, "The Historical Text as Literary Artifact," in *The Writing of History: Literary Form and Historical Understanding*, ed. Robert H. Canary and Henry Kozicki (Madison: University of Wisconsin Press, 1978), 42.

33. Fredric Jameson, *Postmodernism; or, The Cultural Logic of Late Capitalism* (Durham: Duke University Press, 1991), 18.

34. Griffiths, interview by the author, 29 July 1993.

35. Honoré Riouffe, "Mémoires d'un détenu," in *Mémoires sur les prisons* (1823); quoted in *Voices of the French Revolution*, ed. Richard Cobb (Topsfield, MA: Salem House, 1988), 218.

36. Jane Coyle, "Kaleidoscope," BBC Radio 4, 9 Nov. 1995.

37. Lorcan Roche, rev. of *Who Shall Be Happy . . . ? Irish Independent*, 30 Nov. 1995.

38. Trevor Griffiths, "Long Live the Drama of the Margins," interview by W. Stephen Gilbert, *Independent*, 5 June 1996. *Who Shall Be Happy . . . ?* was published in *Plays International* 11 (Jan. 1996): 36–46. Mad Cow was subsequently renamed Prime Cut Productions.

39. When the BBC announced that it was considering not broadcasting *Food for Ravens*, widespread outcry and coverage in the press led them to schedule it (bury it, many felt) at 11:15 P.M. on Sunday night. For a discussion of this controversy, see Rob Brown, "Fury as BBC Restricts Screening of Bevan Film," *Independent*, 24 Oct. 1997; and Aleks Sierz, "Is the BBC Burying a Play about Nye Bevan?" interview with Trevor Griffiths, *New Statesman*, 14 Nov. 1997, 48–49. In March 1998 *Food for Ravens* earned BBC Wales the Royal Television Society Award for Best Regional Program.

40. The National Theatre, for instance, mounted *Absolute Hell*, a revival of Rodney Ackland's 1952 play *The Pink Room*, set in postwar London with the election as backdrop; on the anniversary of the day the election results were announced, it scheduled a retrospective platform that included former Labour MP Barbara Castle.

41. Aneurin Bevan and Stafford Cripps, article in *Tribune*, 8 Sept. 1939; quoted in John Campbell, *Nye Bevan and the Mirage of British Socialism* (London: Weidenfeld and Nicolson, 1987), 87.

42. In his foreword to a recent collection of essays and reminiscences on Bevan, Tony Blair focuses as much on the former minister's managerial skill as on his radical calls for social justice (*The State of the Nation: The Political Legacy of Aneurin Bevan*, ed. Geoffrey Goodman [London: Victor Gollancz, 1997], 11–13).

43. Trevor Griffiths, *Better Days*, unpublished screenplay of *Food for Ravens*, typescript (revised version, 18 June 1997) in Griffiths's possession, 13.

44. Griffiths, interview by Sierz, 49.

45. Griffiths, *Food for Ravens,* 37.

46. Griffiths, interview by the author, 15–17 Nov. 1997.

47. Derrida, *Specters of Marx,* xix.

48. The implications for the present are clear; as Griffiths commented in an interview on *Food for Ravens,* "Until New Labour becomes as brave as [Bevan] was, most of the population won't notice that the government's changed" (interview by Sierz, 49).

49. Griffiths, interview by the author, 15–17 Nov. 1997.

50. Griffiths's production of *Saint Oscar* played at the Hampstead Theatre, London. In November 1980 Griffiths spoke at a seminar at Goldsmith's College devoted to the media and Northern Ireland.

51. Griffiths, interview by the author, 15–17 Nov. 1997.

52. Griffiths, interview by Sierz, 48.

53. Trevor Griffiths, *Willie and Maud,* screenplay, typescript (first draft, 30 May 1997) in Griffiths's possession, 10.

54. Griffiths, interview by the author, 15–17 Nov. 1997.

Index